WOMEN IN ITALY, 1350–

Manchester University Press

WOMEN IN ITALY, 1350–1650
IDEALS AND REALITIES

A sourcebook

selected, translated and introduced by
Mary Rogers and Paola Tinagli

Manchester University Press

Manchester and New York

distributed exclusively in the USA by Palgrave

Published by Manchester University Press
Oxford Road, Manchester M13 9NR, UK

and Room 400, 175 Fifth Avenue, New York, NY 10010, USA
www.manchesteruniversitypress.co.uk

Distributed exclusively in the USA by
Palgrave, 175 Fifth Avenue, New York,
NY 10010, USA

Distributed exclusively in Canada by
UBC Press, University of British Columbia, 2029 West Mall,
Vancouver, BC, Canada V6T 1Z2

British Library Cataloguing-in-Publication Data
A catalogue record for this book is available from the British Library

Library of Congress Cataloging-in-Publication Data applied for
ISBN   0 7190 7208 5   *hardback*
EAN   978 0 7190 7208 6
ISBN   0 7190 7209 3   *paperback*
EAN   978 0 7190 7209 3

First published 2005
14 13 12 11 10 09 08 07 06 05   10 9 8 7 6 5 4 3 2 1

Typeset by Carnegie Publishing, Lancaster
Printed in Great Britain
by Biddles Ltd, King's Lynn

Contents

Part II **Life cycles**

Part III **Roles**

List of plates

Acknowledgements

This book could not have been written without the work and inspiration of many scholars too numerous to list in full, some of whom are also friends. However, we would single out Patricia Allerston and Joanna Woods-Marsden, who read the manuscript at an early stage; Michael Bury, Catherine King, Gabrielle Langdon and Paola Splendore; and Peggy Osborn and Susan Steer, who provided a reference each. It could not have been written without the facilities and the assistance of the staff of the Biblioteca Nazionale in Florence, the Bibliotheca Herziana and the Biblioteca Nazionale in Rome, the Biblioteca Civica Correr and Biblioteca Nazionale Marciana in Venice, and in the UK, the National Library of Scotland, Edinburgh, the University Libraries of Edinburgh and Bristol, and the British Library and the Warburg and Wellcome Institutes in London. Financial assistance was given by the Dr M. Aylwin Cotton Foundation, the University of Bristol Faculty of Arts Research Fund and the Wellcome Foundation. Lastly, but most importantly of all, John Dunstan and Stuart Wallace have given constant and invaluable moral support during the years this project was in train.

Frequently cited sources

PRIMARY SOURCES

Alberti, Leon Battista, *I libri della famiglia*, ed. G. Mancini (Florence, 1908); ed.
C. Grayson, in *Opere volgari*, vol. 1 (Bari, 1960); *The Family in Renaissance
Florence*, ed. and trans. R. Neu Watkins (Columbia, SC, 1969)

Aretino, Pietro, *Lettere*, ed. P. Procaccioli, 2 vols (Milan, 1991)

Bernardino da Siena, S., *Le prediche volgari*, ed. C. Cannarozzi, 2 vols (Pistoia,
1934); *Prediche volgari sul Campo di Siena 1427*, ed. C. Delcorno, 2 vols (Milan,
1989)

Betussi, Giuseppe, *Libro de M. Giovanni Boccaccio delle donne illustri* ... (Venice,
1547; Florence, 1596) [Betussi/Boccaccio]

Castiglione, Baldesar [Baldassarre], *Il Libro del Cortigiano*, ed. B. Maier (Turin,
1955, repr. 1981); ed. N. Longo (Milan, 1981); *The Book of the Courtier*, ed.
V. Cox (London, 1994)

Dolce, Lodovico, *Dialogo della institution delle donne* (Venice, 1545, repr. 1547,
1553, 1558); *De li ammaestramenti pregiatissimi* ... (Venice, 1662)

Fonte, Moderata, *Il merito delle donne* (Venice, 1600); ed. A. Chemello (Venice,
1988); *The Worth of Women*, ed. and trans. V. Cox (Chicago, 1997)

Garzoni, Tommaso, *La piazza universale di tutte le professioni del mondo* (Venice,
1586, repr. 1599)

Garzoni, Tommaso, *Le vite delle donne illustri della scrittura sacra* (Venice, 1588)

Lando, Ortensio, *Lettere di molto valorose donne* (Venice, 1548)

Macinghi Strozzi, Alessandra, *Tempo di affetti e di mercanti: lettere ai figli esuli*
(Milan, 1987); *Selected letters of Alessandra Strozzi*, trans. and introd.
H. Gregory (Berkeley and Los Angeles, 1997)

Marinella, Lucrezia, *Le nobiltà, et eccellenze delle donne: et i difetti, e mancamenti de
gli huomini* (Venice, 1601); *The Nobility and Excellence of Women and the Defects
and Vices of Men*, ed. and trans. A. Dunhill, introd. L. Panizza (Chicago, 1999)

Morigia, Paolo, *La nobiltà di Milano* (Milan, 1595)

Sabadino degli Arienti, Giovanni, *Gynevera de le clare donne*, ed. C. Ricci and
A. Bacchi della Lega (Bologna, 1888)

Vasari, Giorgio, *Le Opere di Giorgio Vasari*, ed. G. Milanesi, 8 vols (Florence,
1906, repr. 1981); *Le vite de' piu eccellenti pittori scultori e architettori*, ed.
R. Bettarini and P. Barocchi, 6 vols (Florence, 1984)

Vecellio, Cesare, *De li habiti antichi, et moderni di diverse parti del mondo* (Venice,
1590); *Habiti antichi et moderni di tutto il mondo* (Venice, 1598)

Vespasiano da Bisticci, *Libro delle Lodi delle donne,* ed. G. Lombardi (Rome, 1999);
Le vite, ed. A. Greco, 2 vols (Florence, 1970–76)

Vives, Juan Luis, *De l'istitutione de la foemina christiana, vergine, maritata o vedova,*
trans. P. Lauro (Venice, 1546)

SECONDARY SOURCES

Bornstein, D. and R. Rusconi, *Women and Religion in Medieval Italy,* trans.
M. J. Schneider (Chicago, 1996)

Chojnacki, S., *Women and Men in Renaissance Venice: Twelve Essays on Patrician
Society* (Baltimore, 2000)

Dean, T. and K. J. P. Lowe, eds, *Marriage in Italy, 1300–1650* (Cambridge, 1998)

Johnson, G. and S. Matthews Grieco, eds, *Picturing Women in Renaissance and
Baroque Italy* (New York, 1997)

Klapisch-Zuber, C., *Women, Family and Ritual in Renaissance Italy,* trans.
L. Cochrane (Chicago, 1985, repr. 1987)

Labalme, P. H., ed., *Beyond Their Sex: Learned Women of the European Past* (New
York, 1980)

Matter, E. A. and J. Coakley, eds, *Creative Women in Early Modern Italy: A
Religious and Artistic Renaissance* (Philadelphia, 1994)

Panizza, L., ed., *Women in Italian Renaissance Culture and Society* (Oxford, 2000)

Reiss, S. E. and D. G. Wilkins, eds, *Beyond Isabella: Secular Women Patrons of Art in
Renaissance Italy* (Kirksville, Miss., 2001)

Tinagli, P., *Women in Italian Renaissance Art: Gender, Representation, Identity*
(Manchester, 1997)

Trexler, R. C., *Power and Dependence in Renaissance Florence,* 3 vols (Binghamton,
NY, 1993): vol. 1, *The Children of Renaissance Florence;* vol. 2, *The Women of
Renaissance Florence*

Wisch, B. and D. Cole Ahl, eds, *Confraternities and the Visual Arts in Renaissance
Italy* (Cambridge, 2000)

Introduction

This book has been written to fill what seems to be a gap in the still burgeoning literature on all aspects of the lives and roles of women in many periods, not least the centuries between 1300 and 1700. Though an enormous amount has been published on women as subjects and as agents elsewhere in Europe at that time, the country that must be central in discussing major cultural innovations, whether in humanism and literature, or in the visual and musical arts, is, of course, Italy. This is also true for the study of women. Between *c.*1350 and *c.*1650, Italian urban societies saw much debate on women's natures, women's roles, women's education or behaviour within the family or at court. We have explicit records of this in sermons, treatises, dialogues and poetry, some by famous Renaissance names, such as Ariosto or Castiglione. More obliquely or fragmentarily, letters, diaries or legal documents may carry the traces of current attitudes to women and their roles. More may have been written by men than by women, given the exclusive male occupation of official roles as notaries or secretaries, the greater prevalence of male literacy and perhaps the greater tendency for men to travel for mercantile or diplomatic reasons. Certainly more male letters or diaries have been preserved, given the greater importance attached to men's words and deeds. However, women too – though overwhelmingly upper-ranking ones – wrote some letters, poetry, prose and polemical works that have survived. Especially from the 1990s onwards, scholarship has done much to uncover, make available and translate such material: the University of Chicago Press 'Other Voice' series has been of particular importance in introducing the translated work of Italian women writers. At the same time, social historians on both sides of the Atlantic have given imaginative attention to a huge range of topics, from charitable institutions to marriage and the family, from sexuality to sanctity, to name just a few, where women's involvement was certainly crucial and where women's agency, within limitations, was possible. While there might be no consensus on whether the status of women actually rose or fell during the Renaissance as compared with the Middle Ages, and if it changed, in which respects, for which women, and in which parts of Italy,[1] it cannot be doubted that the subject of women generated lively debate both during the Renaissance and now.

As we know from our experience as teachers, students from many backgrounds – art and social history, or literary, social, religious and women's studies – have responded with as much enthusiasm to this cross-fertilisation of ideas as have scholars in a range of humanistic disciplines. However, many have been hampered in their efforts to carry their enthusiasm forward by a lack of knowledge of the Italian language, preventing their direct engagement with the words of the men and women of the period. While some major works substantially concerned with women, such as Alberti's *On the Family* or Castiglione's *Book of the Courtier*, have not lacked translations, there is a surprising paucity of English versions of other writings either influential in their own day or representative of common Renaissance attitudes. Historical and biographical work, and conduct literature, have been patchily treated, and diaries and letters, with few exceptions, have fared little better. Legal documents, inventories and wills – from which much can be gleaned about women's relationships and women's property and the significance they attached to these – have made their way into collections of sources for historians of particular geographical areas in, or aspects of, Renaissance Italy. No such collection, however, brings all these sources together and focuses exclusively on the lives and roles of Italian women during the Renaissance.

In presenting a wide selection of many types of text dealing with women from the Italy of *c*.1350 to *c*.1650, this book aims to remedy this situation. Rather than attempting to present new archival findings, we have selected and translated a very broad range of material from all over the peninsula, although the geographical weighting has been affected by the realities that more material is available from Florence, which provides an abundance of family records, letters and early humanist writings, and from Venice, the seat of much the largest publishing industry of the sixteenth century. Our overriding aim has been to provide a selection that illuminates the civic and courtly culture of Renaissance Italy as it affected women. This has meant that

---

1 Debate intensified following Joan Kelly's 1977 essay, 'Did Women Have a Renaissance?', reprinted in L. Hutson, ed., *Feminism and Renaissance Studies* (Oxford, 1999), pp. 21–47. A good summary of ensuing work is in Samuel F. Cohn, *Women in the Streets: Essays on Sex and Power in Renaissance Italy* (Baltimore, 1996), pp. 1–15, who stated that, of the cities he examined, 'Florence was the worst place to have been born a woman' (p. 55).

both the countryside with its peasant inhabitants and the lower classes in the cities have been relatively neglected. While much interesting recent work has been done on lower-class groups such as artisans and servants,[2] extracting suitable sources may still present problems. References in parish records or censuses might be overly brief; trials might involve highly complicated events and relationships,[3] fictional characters might be based on stereotypical preconceptions rather than actualities.

This book would have been easier to write at twice its present length. Constraints of space have forced us to present many short extracts, rather than fewer longer ones, in order to achieve the range we desired. This risks wrenching a few sentences from their contexts, whether an edifice of wider arguments, a lengthy narrative or a poetic sequence. Similarly, introductions have had to be brief, and we are well aware that most excerpts deserve both more contextualisation and more nuanced critical commentary than space allows. We hope that a combination of the introductions and bibliographies in modern editions of the texts we cite (where these exist) and in secondary liter-ature mentioned in footnotes (again, both very abbreviated and confined to works in English) will further illuminate both historical contexts and controversies in interpretation that have had to be glossed over. We have attempted to be discreet in advocating our own arguments, or in pushing self-consciously novel 'approaches' that may all too quickly come to seem dated. Similarly, we have tried to avoid modern jargon which is either alienating to the reader or imposes anachronistic concepts or categories on the past.

Writing as art historians, we naturally also wished to include a number of images to demonstrate the relevance of sources like those we present for the understanding of art, and to help the reader visu-alise the appearance or environments of women of the time. We have striven for variety in date and in place of production, trying to avoid very familiar paintings by 'great masters' (although it would be fruitful to consider major artists' *oeuvres* in connection with women as subjects or patrons). We looked primarily for works which connect with themes treated in each chapter, many of them in more than one.

---

2 Outstanding are the works by D. Romano, *Patricians and Popolani: The Social Foundation of the Venetian Renaissance State* (Baltimore, 1987) and *Housecraft and Statecraft: Domestic Service in Renaissance Venice 1400–1600* (Baltimore, 1996).

3 Two of several using such trials are G. Ruggiero, *The Boundaries of Eros: Sex, Crime and Sexuality in Renaissance Venice* (Oxford, 1985); T. V. and E. S. Cohen, *Words and Deeds in Renaissance Rome: Trials before the Papal Magistrates* (Toronto, 1993).

In both the historical and contemporary personages who are figured and in their iconographic and visual interpretations, male ideals of women are dominant. Only one image is physically made by a woman, and only a few were probably patronised by women, acting alone or together with others. Several, however, would have been made for the spaces inhabited or visited by women, whether family chapels, convents, female institutions or the chambers or reception rooms of private dwellings. It is important to bear in mind both how contexts and functions might have varied from image to image, and also how these might be multiple for any one work, shifting over time and for different viewers. Some might seem relatively easy to define: traditional forms like altarpieces were meant to edify, to uplift and to channel devotion, and 'famous women' cycles meant to inspire through virtuous exemplars. There was certainly awareness at the time that visual means could be especially powerful in achieving these goals. Others, such as the portraits by Andrea del Sarto and by Lavinia Fontana, belong to distinct genres, but their full meanings cannot be discerned if we are uncertain of the identity of the sitters or the circumstances of their lives at the time of the commission. Yet others, such as the Palma, come from an artistic culture where traditional genres had become fluid, so that we cannot confidently say whether this is a portrait of a courtesan or a purely imaginary ideal. Even images that may seem straightforwardly documentary, both portraits and book illustrations being examples, may have been attempts to mould rather than reflect reality, to promote an ideal image of a writer or a midwife as much as to describe observed actualities. So though understanding of social structures and cultural contexts enriches our understanding of art, images can only with caution be used as evidence about historical reality.

This leads on to our title and structure, which implies our core theme: the interaction of ideals and realities in the lives of Italian women and in the notions of them held and communicated by their contemporaries. We did not wish simply to record women's material circumstances and doings, although we hope we have done that, chiefly in Part II, dealing with life cycles from birth to death punctuated by betrothal, marriage and widowhood: physical processes which may seem ahistorical and rites of passage which may be common if not universal, but which were often attended by customs and rituals specific to early modern Italy, and capable of shaping emotional experience. In this and in Part III, on women's roles in the convent, court and workplace and in cultural life, the reader will probably become aware of the enormous gulf separating Renaissance attitudes from modern ones, dominated by ideals of freedom and autonomy. A bridge may be found through the great interest that was shown in the minutiae of physical appearance, movement and dress, apparent when a future mother-in-law assesses her son's potential brides, a brother describes his sister entering a convent or an ambassador reports on the demeanour of a duchess. Letters, diaries, biographies and histories are characteristic Renaissance genres which convey this lively scrutiny of appearances and communicate to later centuries the texture of the times. These are, in a sense, symptoms of a Burckhardtian 'rediscovery of the world', as is much visual art. Yet all too often their verisimilitude wrongly convinces even sophisticated readers or spectators that, for example, biographies simply present what actually happened, portraits simply present what was actually there. Rather, Renaissance writers or artists sought to use concrete personalities and situations to reinforce and make credible ideals that could inspire a present and future audience. Biographers may, or may not, actually invent episodes that never took place, but they are more likely than modern writers committed to 'warts and all' approaches to suppress or gloss over the more negative aspects of their subjects. Writers would certainly shape their selection of material, both in events, in physical details and in interpretation of personality and behaviour, according to the conventions of their literary genre, which might be hagiography, 'famous men' biography, encomiastic rhetoric, or indeed seemingly more artless, but also conventional, forms such as the family record or the will. Portraitists, too, would usually strive after a convincing likeness, but also suggest ideals of beauty, power, wealth, virtue or correct behaviour through the deportment and the embellishment of the body. Read and regarded over time, both biographies and portraits might come to exert their own power to shape the memory and the sense of its worth and significance of a family, a dynasty, a religious order, an institution – including the feminine members of these.

These examples pinpoint the need to investigate what some of these ethical or aesthetic ideals, influencing the selection and the manipulation of observed actualities, might be in relation to women. This is done in Part I, starting with the necessary parameters, the perceived limitations to women's potential dictated by current notions of female biology and divine purpose. Other chapters explore virtues which, either in general or as manifested in concrete exemplars, were held to be especially relevant to women, virtues which need to be kept in mind as the reader scans many of the sources later in the book, or indeed other Renaissance writings or works of visual art. This is facilitated by writers often referring to the ideal exemplars when confronting concrete situations. A beautiful actress will be likened to a Muse, a grieving widow related to Judith or Artemisia, however much the author knew that actuality did not really accord with example. Modern readers might at times feel that conventional ideals of virtue or beauty delimit much Renaissance writing and art, or obscure reality rather than ennoble it, but perhaps the material we present will enable them to approach such passages with a more sympathetic under-standing, even in examples remote from, even repellent to, modern sensibilities.

The period we have covered in this book could be dubbed 'the long Renaissance', spanning approximately three centuries from about 1350 to 1650. What changes may the reader notice over this period in society's attitude to ideals and realities relating to women? A brief generalisation in relation to fundamental ideals might be that orthodox thinking on theology, biology and social ethics, as they pertained to women, did not change much, and that, as Margaret King has put it, 'very little changed, or changed for the better, in their [women's] social condition'.[4] This seems true of Italian women's legal position and participation in political life, areas on which we have provided little coverage, except in relation to aristocratic females.[5] Against King's claim, though, several social historians, of whom Stanley Chojnacki is perhaps the best known, have argued for the increased social influence within their families of at least some affluent women, showing how their considerable dowry money enabled them to fund a variety of projects, and also to the increasing respect and affection shown towards their wives by male testators in the course of the fifteenth and sixteenth centuries.[6] Others have demonstrated considerable variety of conditions within early modern Italy, and women's creativity in manipulating situations that would seem unbearably oppressive by modern standards, so that, rather than a

---

4 M. L. King, *Women of the Renaissance* (Chicago and London, 1991), p. 238.

5 For legal issues, see T. Kuehn, *Law, Family and Women: Towards a Legal Anthropology of Renaissance Italy* (Chicago, 1991).

6 'Patrician Women in Early Modern Venice' and 'The Power of Love: Wives and Husbands', in Chojnacki, pp. 115–31 and 153–68.

landscape of entrenched misogyny and female misery, there was 'neither autonomy nor subjection'.[7]

King, however, also stressed 'Something changed during the Renaissance in women's sense of themselves'. For her, this was manifested firstly in women's impact on Christian practice, something well in train before c.1350, leading some historians of late medieval religion to speak of a 'feminisation' of religion. This continued during the period covered in this book: women founded new groupings and organisations as confraternity members, and even more importantly as tertiaries or nuns, who came to outnumber male religious for the first time during our period (a situation continuing in our own day), and whose distinctive culture spawned both charismatic individuals and remarkable writing and music. Perhaps this was short-lived, to the extent that the more rigorous late sixteenth-century discipline associated with the phrase 'Counter-Reformation' controlled and repressed much activity for nuns, as for other women. Yet major Catholic reformers and reform movements also harnessed the spirituality of and gave a sense of purpose to certain types of women, such as poor girls or pious widows, creating charitable and educational institutions which proved serviceable until quite recent times.

If religious involvement could validate some women's activities and voices, less committed women were also encouraged from early in our period to be literate, to read devotional literature and impart its benefits to their families. Such literacy could have unintended consequences, such as the other change mentioned by King, women's involvement in creative and polemical writing, to which medium we would add the visual arts and, perhaps even more, musical and theatrical performance. Moreover, notions of creative involvement need broadening to include phenomena other than the recorded authorship by a woman of a treatise, a painting or a piece of music. Such works, in early modern times, were embedded in networks of relationships between the author (in the inclusive sense) and patron, dedicatee, performer or audience members: women, and their tastes and concerns, could often have been prominent if not dominant in all of these, crucially affecting the character of the work. An increased awareness of women as members of the audiences which males addressed in different media and contexts has given us new

---

7 E. G. Rosenthal, 'The Position of Women in Renaissance Florence: Neither Autonomy nor Subjection', in P. Denley and C. Elam, eds, *Florence and Italy: Renaissance Studies in Honour of Nicolai Rubinstein* (London, 1988).

perspectives on striking fifteenth-century phenomena such as the popular preaching of S. Bernardino da Siena, often directed at women, or the visual arts in the home, viewed by females who would have spent much time in their living quarters.

How might the need to take account of a female audience have affected literary genres much more closely connected with 'the Renaissance' in its more traditional senses of the revival of antiquity or the emergence of self-conscious creative individuals? Two such genres that figure prominently in this book are humanist conduct writings and 'famous women' biographies. Although the former genre was heavily dependent on Aristotle, criticised then as now for his opinions on women, and initially was addressed to males, by the sixteenth century more treatises were dedicated to and aimed at a female audience, which had become very much larger with the advent of printing. Some such books not only assume women's literacy and leisure, but register their pleasures, complaints and ambitions, notably those around 1600 by the female polemicists Moderata Fonte and Lucrezia Marinella. Another genre aimed at women since its inception, that of 'famous women' biography, tended to reinforce old exemplars and an old morality whereby virtue for a woman must mean primarily chastity, yet by the sixteenth century it could be flexible enough to include some of the new ideal women of the age, the courtly beauties and the female intellectuals and writers. In these areas ideals, then, were modified in the course of the Renaissance.

Traditionally, the striving for a civilised grace in actions, appearances and surroundings as well as in art have been seen as the distinguishing feature of the Italian Renaissance and connected with the presence or influence of women at court. This has been extended by more recent historians who, grounded less in literary than in economic studies, have singled out the greater abundance and diffusion of artefacts in urban Italy as distinctively new, a material phenomenon fostering more discriminating judgements and more evolved language.[8] The nature and significance of women's contribution in shaping these domestic environments is only now being fully explored by historians of material culture.[9] Women's dress, in particular, can be seen as an area in which women, even those far down the social scale,

8 Primarily R. Goldthwaite, *Wealth and the Demand for Art in Italy, 1300–1600* (Baltimore, 1993).

9 D. Thornton and L. Syson, *Objects of Virtue: Art in Renaissance Italy* (London, 2001) and P. Fortini Brown, *Private Lives in Renaissance Venice* (New Haven and London, 2004) are two recent examples.

asserted and expressed themselves, with some serious female writers delighting in the fact while others chided their sex for their frivolity.

We hope, therefore, that readers will discover from the texts assembled here that our period saw no single 'Italian Renaissance', because Italy was socially and legally diverse and the three centuries encompassed several different phases. Equally, we hope they will find that there was no single 'Renaissance woman', that the realities of women's experiences were various and not just an unending succession of imposed limitations and restrictions, and that their voices, with those of their menfolk, speak of diverse possibilities for emotionally rich and socially useful lives.

Lastly, some words are needed on translations, which are our own unless indicated to the contrary. For modern readers, Renaissance writing can be both verbose and overly complicated in its structure. Consequently, in the interest of readability we have simplified syntax and punctuation and cut out repetition and over-abundant illustrative examples. At the same time, we have tried to retain the sense of the difference in tone between, say, informal letters and literary treatises, elegant sonnets and legalese.

Mary Rogers, London
Paola Tinagli, Florence

Part I
Ideals

1 Woman's nature and characteristics

A tradition of misogynist vituperation, partly deriving from ancient Roman literature, often of a satirical kind, and partly from early Christian ascetic suspicion of woman, was very much alive during the Renaissance.[1] However, other voices in the fifteenth and, especially, sixteenth centuries, building on the legacy of the late Middle Ages, emphasised woman's value. This was often the case in the new Renaissance genre of treatises on women's character and conduct,[2] which debated women's nature, and their inferiority, equality or superiority to men. Their arguments were based on a variety of grounds, but almost all saw differences between the sexes which were fundamental and innate, following God's design and the workings of nature. This chapter aims to illuminate the theological and biological ideas cited in support, and to suggest how their alleged consequences were held to justify limitations in women's social roles. Though the writings underpinning woman's inferiority – chiefly Genesis, St Paul and Aristotelian works – were canonical, their implications were contested, and some held that, as well as her flaws, they could suggest woman's positive attributes: these could form the basis of a range of virtues thought particularly fitting for women. Later chapters will look at women cited as concrete examples of such virtues, or vices, connected with alternative poetic, historical and hagiographical traditions.

THE CASE AGAINST WOMEN

1.1 Men are the nobler sex

In 1526 the Milanese Galeazzo Flavio Capra (Capella, 1487–1557), though generally defending women, states the case for the prosecution.

---

1 The classical and medieval background is sketched in K. M. Rogers, *The Troublesome Helpmate: A History of Misogyny in Literature* (Seattle, 1966), in I. MacLean, *The Renaissance Notion of Woman* (Cambridge, 1980) and in N. Tuana, *The Less Noble Sex: Scientific, Religious and Philosophical Conceptions of Woman's Nature* (Bloomington, Ind., 1993).

2 Discussed in R. Kelso, *Doctrine for the Lady of the Renaissance* (Urbana, Ill., 1956), C. Jordan, *Renaissance Feminism: Literary Texts and Political Models* (Ithaca, NY, 1990), P. Benson, *The Invention of the Renaissance Woman* (University Park, Pa., 1992), pp. 9–90, and V. Cox, in Fonte (1997), pp. 12–17.

Galeazzo Flavio Capra, *Della eccellenza et dignità delle donne,* ed. M. L. Doglio (Rome, 1988), pp. 65–6.

That men are nobler is also clearly shown by the fact that civic and divine offices are forbidden to women, and that the laws prohibit them from practising law and many other professions solely reserved for men ...

Apart from this, man was created in God's image. The ranks of Heaven would have been filled had they not been emptied by the pride of Lucifer and his followers, and had it not been woman who dared to eat the forbidden fruit, with such disobedience and temerity. From this sin followed the universal damnation of all people, so that the son of God needed to offer to redeem us from death with his own blood. To make us know the difference between the sexes he chose to be born man and not woman.

But if you still want to get an immediate idea of how far man exceeds woman in nobility, consider the Latin terms for them both, and you will see how man is linked with virtue, and woman with filth and ugliness.[3]

Nor can I brush aside the authority of poets and all other authors who say in a thousand places that woman is inconstant and changeable, and finally that all the ills which have befallen the world have originated in woman.

But if these considerations, which are grave enough, should not suffice, the variety and amount of menstrual and other filthy and impure discharges issuing from their bodies are strong enough to ruin any goodness or excellence that they might contain.

Such things, then, written in a thousand places and, furthermore, told, known and seen by nearly everyone, have always convinced everybody that women are less worthy than men, and viler beyond comparison: to wish to affirm the contrary seems both new and as yet unheard-of, and impossible.

1.2 Women are fickle

A successful female poet, Laura Terracina from Naples (1519-?1577) reworks the misogynist poetic tradition to which Capella alluded. In the 27th book of

---

3 The etymological argument links *vir*, man, with virtue, and *foemina*, woman, with *foeditas*, that which is nasty or disgusting.

Ariosto's *Orlando Furioso*, Rodomonte, deserted by Doralice, had railed
against womankind: Terracina expands his lament.

Laura Terracina, *Rime della Signora Laura Terracina* (Venice, 1548), fol. 19r.

> O female sex, how frail you are,
> how mutable you are, how lacking duty.
> So that it's true, imperfect animal,
> that you can have no sense of honour.
> You think you're never wrong, nor live wickedly,
> thus ever demonstrating your high conceit.
> O woman of impatient lust,
> how easily you twist and change.
>
> You're just a woman – could one say worse?
> You are made for nothing but damnation.
> Say it to me, since I indeed must die for you,
> for you, who have tricked me and outraged me.
> This satisfies my heart's desire,
> that you're a woman, from whom all troubles spring,
> contrary to all worthy objects of faith:
> unhappy and wretched is he who trusts you.

THEOLOGICAL ARGUMENTS

The story of the Creation and Fall of man became crucial to Christian
notions of the purposes behind woman's creation and of her characteristic flaws. While one of the two Genesis accounts of creation clearly
proclaims that both sexes were created in the likeness of God (Gen.
5:2), the other, in which Eve was created from Adam's body to be his
'helpmeet' (Gen. 2:18–24), justified notions that women were secondary creations, subservient though potentially dangerous to men.
Theologians with negative views of women tended to base their
arguments on the latter: these were reinforced, after Thomas Aquinas'
absorption of Aristotelian ideas into his very influential thirteenth
century *Summa Theologiae*, by the biological arguments for female
inferiority that will be discussed later.[4]

---

4 For the medieval background, see also E. C. McLaughlin, 'Equality of Souls,
  Inequality of Sexes: Women in Medieval Theology', in R. Radford Reuther, ed.,
  Religion and Sexism: Images of Women in Jewish and Christian Traditions (New York,
  1974), pp. 213–66.

1.3 Vives on women's roles

The Spanish humanist Vives (1492/93–1540) presents theologically based negative views in his 1523 conduct book *De institutione foeminae Christianae*, very influential in Italy even before its 1546 Italian translation. Though advocating education for women, largely in order to improve their capacity to give good moral instruction to their children, he does not envisage a teaching role for them outside the home. St Paul's remarks on woman's subordination to their husbands in I Cor. 11 and, here, in I Tim. 2:11–14, which themselves had invoked the creation story, are used as a guide to correct behaviour in this regard.

Juan Luis Vives, *The Instruction of a Christen Woman*, trans. Richard Hyrd (London, 1529), unpaginated; *The Education of a Christian Woman*, ed. and trans. C. Fantazzi (Chicago, 2000), p. 72.

The apostle Paul ... says, 'Let a woman learn in silence with all subjection. I do not allow a woman to teach or to usurp authority over a man, but to stay silent. For Adam was made first and Eve afterwards, and Adam was not deceived but the woman was deceived and transgressed'. Therefore, since woman is a frail thing and of weak judgement and may easily be deceived (as shown by Eve, our first mother, whom the devil ensnared with such feeble arguments), she should not teach, lest, when she has formed a false opinion or belief on any matter, her authority as a teacher should influence her listeners and easily spread the same error to others.

1.4 An early defence of women

Other writers questioned whether Genesis supported either Eve's prime culpability for the Fall or notions of woman's general inferiority. The defence by the Florentine bookseller Vespasiano da Bisticci (1421–98) in his book of *c.*1480 in praise of women, however, is double-edged, in this following Aquinas: Eve was less responsible for the Fall because less rational.

Vespasiano da Bisticci (1999), pp. 14–15.

Whoever engages in this type of slander against women is basing himself on fictions and fables, not taking note of Holy Scripture. So to damn things created by God – men and women – is to damn and to slander the Creator of the universe who has created all things ...

When God created man in His own image and likeness, He said it would not be good to remain alone, but would be necessary to give him a companion. He chose this companion to be a woman, and created her out of Adam's rib. After this, He said that the two should be one flesh in love, through their affinity and union ... and all was made necessary for human nature so that it could preserve itself.

And if anyone wants to blame woman for the sin of Adam, since she persuaded her husband to disobey the divine commands, I reply that man sinned more than woman, since he, as the head, should have guided her away from such an error ... And to show that the sin of Adam was worse than that of the woman ... when they had sinned, God called Adam and asked him where he was, wishing to lay the blame on the man and not on the woman ... and it follows that this sin should be attributed more to man than to woman, since he was more capable of reason than she.

1.5 The superiority of women

The Venetian writer, Lucrezia Marinella (1571–1653), in her polemical treatise on the excellence of women argues not just for the two sexes' complementarity, but for woman's superiority.[5]

Marinella (1601), fol. 5r–v.

As woman was made from man's rib, and man from mud and clay, she will certainly be more excellent than man, as a rib is incomparably more noble than mud. I may add that she was created in Paradise, and man outside it. Don't you think that the origins from which women are descended are more noble than those for men? And that woman's nature is more precious and noble than man's is also shown in her creation. Since woman was produced after man she must also be more excellent than he since, as the wisest writers say, things produced later are nobler than ones made earlier ... so one can say that man was made to generate woman from his body ... seeking from the nobility of this [second] sex a more worthy material than He [God] had found in man, His creation.

1.6 Mary redeems Eve

Negative views of woman might also be countered by the idea, developing from the second century AD and gaining strength in the Middle Ages, of the Virgin Mary as the New Eve, who effected redemption of the sins of the

---

5 For Marinella and Fonte, see P. Labalme, 'Venetian Women on Women: Three Early Modern Feminists', *Archivio veneto*, ser. 5, 116–17 (1981), pp. 81–109.

first.[6] As will be further shown in chapter 3, Mary's virtues of humility, obedience, modesty and silence seemed the opposite of Eve's presumption, disobedience and beguiling words. Such ideas were communicated to a wider public visually, as in Fra Angelico's Annunciation scenes (Museo Diocesano, Cortona, and Prado, Madrid), or verbally by preachers such as the Franciscan Bernardino da Siena (d. 1444), in a 1427 sermon in Siena, also on the Annunciation.[7]

Bernardino da Siena (1989), vol. 2, pp. 840–4.

When Adam and Eve broke God's commandment through the sin of disobedience ... God said to the woman: 'Under the power of man will you be, and he will be lord over you', and so He left her subject to man. So it will often be said to woman: 'Through your sin, making Adam fall, you caused our expulsion from Paradise' ...

Because it was a woman who said to the man, 'Take this fruit, so we may not die', she could be said to have agreed to disobey and to fall into sin through frailty, lacking any constancy ...

[These accusations are no longer justified] ... because Mary is the one who has restored you from all these disgraces. She has lifted you from shame ... If you say, 'It was woman who made us fall into death', I say you speak truly: but it was also woman who picked us up and revived us. Someone else may say: 'Oh, if you look into it, woman has been the root of all evil'. And I reply: 'Woman has been the beginning of all good'. Another says: 'Still, woman is inferior to man, since she has been placed beneath by God's command'. And I say: 'No more than is man ...' But woman, because I'm saying this, don't rise up in pride! Don't try to rise above man: it's not fitting for you to stand except with your head bent down and low, under the charge of man ...

St Paul has taught you ... woman must keep her head covered in church ... he also says in another passage to the Corinthians, chapter XIV: 'Women should keep quiet in church, because they are not allowed or permitted to speak, but must be placed below, as the law says' ...

The Virgin Mary ... has remedied the frailty given to woman through the frailty of Eve: you are fallen, with no stability, because

6 See H. Graef, *Mary: A History of Doctrine and Devotion* (London, 1963), vol. 1, pp. 37–83.
7 For Bernardino and his audience, see B. Paton, *Preaching Friars and the Civic Ethos: Siena, 1380–1480* (London, 1992).

when you were tempted by the serpent, straightaway you were thrown
to the ground with no resistance. Mary remedies this offence of
woman, so that women can say: 'If Eve was fallen, Mary was stable
and firm'.

1.7 The unique perfection of the Virgin Mary

Another Venetian writer in defence of women, Modesta Pozzo (pseudonym
Moderata Fonte, 1555–92), combines a reinterpretation of Eve's motives with
a traditional invocation of the Virgin's excellencies.

Fonte (1600), p. 50; (1997), pp. 93–4.

Then Helena broke in, 'So who was the cause of our Fall, if not Eve,
the first woman?'

'Far from it: it was Adam,' replied Corinna, 'since she had the worthy
goal of grasping the knowledge of good and evil, and so let herself
be drawn to taste the forbidden fruit. But Adam was not swayed by
this, but by avidity and greed: when she said that it was tasty he
ate it, which was a worse motivation, and more to be censured. And
that is why God did not expel them from Paradise immediately
after Eve sinned, but rather after Adam had disobeyed him. That is,
He was not stirred by Eve's actions, but by Adam's, which immediately made him give both the punishment that they deserved,
which was and is common to all humankind. Besides, how about
the woman chosen above all others for our redemption? God never
created any man (a man who was solely a man, that is) whose merit
equalled that woman who was solely a woman. Search all the ancient
annals and chronicles to find me any man, however holy, who
could attain the thousandth part of the rare excellencies and divine
qualities of Our Lady, the Queen of Heaven. You will certainly find
none.'

BIOLOGICAL ARGUMENTS

Fundamental ideas as to the physical and psychological nature of
women were provided by current biology, dominated by the thought
of Aristotle, especially his *On the Generation of Animals* and *On the
History of Animals*. These expounded ideas of woman as a defective
male, as contributing less to procreation than the male and as cold,
passive and material, inferior to the hot, active male whose sperm
would give form to her matter. The medical, physiological tradition

deriving from Hippocrates and Galen (*De usu partium corporis*), while in some ways affording more positive roles to the female (seeing her as producing her own sperm, for example, rather than merely feeding the embryo with her diverted menstrual blood, and seeing her sexual pleasure as important for conception), also saw her as an underdeveloped man and associated her with the cold and moist humours or temperaments, usually negatively valued.[8]

1.8 The weaknesses of woman

These ideas, and ones flowing from them, are picked up in works for a general readership, such as the following treatise on childbirth, first published in 1596 and often reprinted throughout the seventeenth century and into the eighteenth. The author, Scipione (Fra Girolamo) Mercurio (*c.*1559–1615), a Dominican friar as well as a physician, mingles theological with scientific arguments and repeats dominant received opinions on the nature of females, associating femininity with a range of negative qualities.

Scipione Mercurio, *La commare o riccoglitrice*, ed. M. L. Altieri Biagi et al., *Medicina per le donne nel Cinquecento* (Turin, 1992), pp. 67–9.

It seems most marvellous that man, supremely noble in nature and in wonderful bodily composition, called a miniature world by the Greeks … should still suffer more miserably than any other creature at birth, both the woman giving birth, who endures almost unbearable pains, and the baby being born [...]

The philosophers say that the cause of so much misery and anguish lies in the nature of the mother as well as the child. Since the mother is so very weak and frail, and childbirth is exhausting, great strength is needed, and as her own is not equal to the labour, she inevitably suffers much. Her weakness derives not only from her constitution, but also from womanly behaviour. I say from her constitution because, as Hippocrates and Aristotle maintain in a thousand places, woman is full of much moisture and little heat, and is also colder than men. Coldness and moisture are prone to make her weak and feeble, just as by contrast warmth and dryness are apt to invigorate anyone. To this you may add womanly behaviour, which mostly is idle and pleasure-loving. All this is enough to exhaust the strength of Hercules

---

8 The relevant arguments from the biological and medical traditions are surveyed in MacLean, pp. 28–46; abridged as 'The Notion of Woman in Medicine, Anatomy and Physiology', in L. Hutson, ed., *Feminism and Renaissance Studies* (Oxford, 1999), pp. 127–55.

or of a giant. So, as woman is naturally weak, she suffers greatly in extremely painful childbirth ...

The theologians, too, have much discussed this matter. They have said that at this time both the mother and the child are subject to numerous dangers from death and other miseries through original sin, in which we are all conceived. This not only deprived us of the grace of God, given in custody to Adam, but also causes all the troubles, miseries and woes we suffer in this world as penalties. As the first man, the chief agent, committed original sin for both himself and us, and as woman, the instrument of the Devil, caused him to sin, each of them deserves to suffer. For after that sin, the great Lord said to the woman: 'In suffering you will bear children, and I will multiply your births, but will also multiply your sufferings'.

1.9 Women's reproductive organs

This passage from an encyclopaedia of trades and professions by Tommaso Garzoni shows how women's reproductive organs were understood in terms of male norms, with similarly shaped genitals reversed and inside the body.
Garzoni (1586, repr. 1599), p. 302.

The womb and vulva, or uterus, of woman is placed between the bladder and the upright intestine, like a second bladder. It is extremely sensitive, and contains two ventricles. Also joined to it are the so-called horns of the womb, behind which are testicles broader than man's but not as long, from which come sperm, which flows out of the opening of the wombs. In addition, the womb has a neck which moves outward from the woman's body, and is the equivalent of the penis in man. In virgins, the opening is narrow and creased: in the creases are five veins which are broken when women lose their virginity, and the creases enlarged. In the middle of the vulva is a membrane like a barrier, in which lie the veins that the Greeks call the *hymen*, Romans the *interseptum virginale*, and at the extreme end of the vulva is a high, raised piece of flesh called the *nympha* by the Romans.

1.10 Women's physiognomy suggests their inferiority

Aristotelian notions of the natural weakness, inferiority and disharmony of women pervaded many Renaissance works on both physical science and social matters, often because of the influence of other influential texts from the philosopher or his circle, such as the *Nicomachean Ethics* or the *Politics*.[9] One such 'science', which at times shaped both literature and art, was physiognomy, seeking to connect physical forms to psychological characteristics: one of the fullest physiognomical works, appearing in several editions from the late sixteenth century onwards, was by the Neapolitan Giovanbattista dalla Porta.

Giovanbattista della Porta, *Della Fisonomia dell'huomo* (Padua, 1623), fols 31v–32v.

Woman has a small and narrow head, the forehead sloping back, the eyebrows extended, the eyes small and shining, the nose straight, not projecting from the face much, the face fleshy, the mouth small and always smiling, the chin round and hairless, the neck slender ... the thighs plump ... the shoulders badly connected, the back narrow and weak, the loins fleshy, the buttocks fat and heavy and, to sum up, an entire body smaller, weak rather than strong and sturdy, with very moist flesh, a feebler voice and constricted gait. But her habits are cowardly, enticing and full of tricks ... Plato says that, in all comparisons with men, women are stupider and less perfect, something Aristotle and Galen confirm. They say this arises from coldness, as heat is the principal instrument of nature and lack of heat creates imperfection ... Seneca says that there is nothing more unstable than woman, nor a greater enemy of duty, lacking in faith and ample in infamy, a repository of quarrels and deceits, and that peace and a woman cannot possibly coexist in one head.

BIOLOGY TO SOCIAL PSYCHOLOGY: WOMAN'S TEMPERAMENT AND CHARACTERISTICS

Many non-scientific Renaissance writers drew on current biological theory in exploring woman's general psychological disposition, held to be linked to her physical make-up. Thus her timidity sprang from her bodily weakness, her passivity – or more positively, her temperance – to her predominantly cool or moist humours. It was this innate disposition which was thought to govern her suitability, or unsuitability, for certain social roles.

9 For Aristotelian ideas and Renaissance art criticism, see F. H. Jacobs, *Defining the Female Virtuosa* (Cambridge, 1997), partially reprinted as 'La Donnesca Mano' in Hutson, pp. 373–411, and, for an alleged artistic critique of these ideas, M. D. Garrard, 'Leonardo da Vinci: Female Portraits, Female Nature', in N. Broude and M. D. Garrard, eds, *The Expanding Discourse: Feminism and Art History* (Boulder, Colo., 1992), pp. 59–85.

1.11 **Biological ideas pass into conversation**

In Baldassarre Castiglione's enormously popular *Book of the Courtier*, written in the 1510s and 1520s, a long debate on the nature of woman occupies much of Book 3. Gaspare Pallavicino's Aristotelian view of woman as a defective man is countered by Giuliano de' Medici's view of the complementarity and equal worth of men and women – although he maintains the current norms of men as strong, bold and learned, and women as cautiously conserving goods and nurturing children in the home.

Castiglione, ed. Maier (1981), pp. 359–62.

[Gaspare] ... The wisest of men have left writings saying that Nature would, if she could, continually produce men, since she ever intends and aims to make the most perfect things. So when a woman is born it is a defect or error of nature, and contrary to what she would have wished. The same thing can be seen when an individual is born blind, lame or with some other defect, and when many fruits on a tree never mature. Thus woman can be called an animal produced by chance and by accident: to confirm this, look at the behaviour of men and women and draw your conclusions on the perfection of the one and the other.

... [Giuliano] ... I say that, if you consider nature's doings, you'll find that she makes women as they are not by chance, but adapted to a necessary end. Although nature makes women timid in body and placid in mind, and with many other qualities opposite to men's, the characteristics of both sexes tend towards a single goal useful for both. Though women are less spirited due to their physical weakness, by the same token they are more cautious; thus the mother cares for the children and the father guides them, and with his energy acquires outside the home those goods she diligently conserves within it, something of no less merit ...

... And as you said that nature's intention is always to produce the most perfect things and thus always to produce men, if she could, and that producing women is more an error or defect of nature than an intention, I reply that this is absolutely not the case. I don't know how you can possibly say that nature doesn't intend to produce women, without whom the human species could not maintain itself, something nature desires above all ... As woman is every bit as necessary for this as is man, I cannot see how she can be more a chance creation than he ... So male and female always go together, nor can one exist without the other.

1.12 A general assessment of women

The opinions of the mid-sixteenth-century Sienese writer Alessandro Piccolomini seem influenced by his observation of contemporary women.

Alessandro Piccolomini, *Della institutione di tutta la vita dell'huomo nato nobile, et in città libera* (Venice, 1552), fols 152v–153r.

Although a certain timidity is proper to women, it does not spring from viciousness, but from the weakness of their beings. They are more apt to be miserly than generous; however through their longing for honour, which is very intense in them, this inclination is rendered vain and futile ...

By nature they are somewhat credulous, and easily deceived, something not stemming from vice, but from their goodness, which makes them believe other people are good, judging other characters by their own. Their ready wit means that they debate matters and size things up quickly, swiftly resolving points at issue and deciding almost immediately about the best options before them. Women, for the most part, are very God-fearing, devout, pious and imbued with true religion. In their desires they are very restrained, as witnessed by their chastity, despite having many constraints and obligations, and being more restricted by laws and customs than men. Still, it can clearly be seen that they are more obedient, temperate and law-abiding than men. Again, they have to endure many obstacles, restrictions and burdens which men have imposed on them by force and mastery: still they have born it all most wisely and patiently, with cheerful faces and happy hearts. They are merciful and, as commonly said, charitable, as shown by the alms they often give. They conduct themselves most humbly before God, as witnessed by the prayers and orations they offer all day to the great God: thus it is not hard to believe that they are loved by and dear to Him.

1.13 Aristotle's ideas on women challenged

Lucrezia Marinella, relatively well versed in biological/medical theory because of her physician father, frequently attacks Aristotle's views and their implications.

Marinella (1601), fols 10v–11v.

But few women nowadays devote themselves to learning or to warfare, since men, like impudent tyrants, fearing to lose their dominion and to become servants of women, prevent them and even very often forbid them to learn to read and write. So that our dear friend Aristotle can say: they must always obey their menfolk in every respect, and not seek for anything outside the house. A stupid opinion and a cruel sentence, and coming from a tyrannical and fearful man. But I'll allow us to excuse him, since it was normal for him, being a man, to assert the greatness and superiority of men rather than women. But the great Plato, supremely just and far from ruling by force and violence, wished and ordered that women should engage in military pursuits, in riding and in jousting, and in short that they should go and give advice in the affairs of the republic.

Aristotle's privileging of the male quality, heat, is attacked on several occasions.

Ibid., fols 45v–46r; (1999), pp. 130–1.

So the argument of Aristotle, that men are hotter than women and so more noble, is invalid, since we can see that young men are not thought nobler than men in their maturity, even if they are hotter ...

We surely think that there were and are men hotter by nature than Aristotle and Plato, but are the workings of their minds nobler thereby? Not at all. I would say in this respect, that woman is cooler than man, and thus more noble, and that if any man does something excellent, this occurs because he approaches the nature and temperament of a woman, as his heat is calmed and not excessive. At a mature age, the ardour of the heat that existed in his youth is tempered, and he approaches feminine nature more closely in acting more wisely and judiciously.

There's no shortage of others saying that men are stronger and sturdier, and better at bearing weights and burdens than women ... to which I reply, that women accustomed to labour surpass and defeat men, though indeed this sturdiness is not appropriate to gentle and delicate creatures. However, kings, princes and great personages cannot do the work of porters, nor do I think that Aristotle, who called women weak, like the left hand, was strong, as are peasant men and many women. So was he less noble than these rough men, and many women? By this argument, blacksmiths would be nobler than kings and people of learning and talent.

FROM DESCRIPTION TO PRESCRIPTION: NOTIONS OF WOMANLY VIRTUES

While all types of virtue were advocated in the Renaissance for both sexes, particular virtues or vices tended to be seen not just as 'naturally' characteristic of women, but especially fit to be cultivated, or shunned, by women. Virtues mainly connected with stages in women's lives or with their roles will be looked at in later sections, and concrete exemplars of feminine virtue in the ensuing chapters. Here, brief examples are given of treatise writers trying to explain virtues especially relevant to all women, sometimes referring to ideas charted above, elsewhere guided by social custom or literary traditions.

1.14 A Florentine elder in praise of chastity

The following praise of chastity (*honestà*) attributed in Alberti's *Della Famiglia* (1430s) to the family patriarch, Giannozzo, was spoken to his new wife. However, it was, as stated, meant to apply to all females, in line with the conventional Renaissance prizing of chastity as the supreme virtue for women.

Alberti (1908), p. 209; (1969), p. 213.

[Giannozzo] You should know that in this respect nothing is so important for yourself, so acceptable to God, so precious to me and so advantageous for our children as your chastity [*honestà*]. The woman's chastity has always been the ornament of the family; the mother's chastity has always been a part of the dowry of her daughters; chastity in any woman has always been worth more than any of her beauties. A beautiful face is praised, but unchaste eyes soil it with people's contempt, and it is too often flushed with shame or pale with melancholy or sadness of spirit. A handsome body is pleasing to see, but a shameless gesture or an act of incontinence in an instant renders her appearance vile. Absence of chastity angers God, and you know that God punishes nothing so severely in women as he does this lack. All their lives He makes them notorious and miserable.

1.15 Temperance as a virtue for women

The overlapping, not easily distinguishable qualities clustering around temperance, modesty and restraint could be thought the positive consequences of woman's physiological deficiencies. Capra/Capella concisely explains the importance of temperance.

Capra, pp. 78–9.

Temperance, though it may be fitting for both sexes, is a virtue especially appropriate and paramount for women, since from temperance follow a sense of shame, modesty, abstinence, uprightness, sobriety and restraint: if any one of all these things is absent in a woman, all other virtues are sullied and spoilt, so that all the water of the Arno could not cleanse them.

1.16 Male and female virtues

Renaissance thought could sometimes concede that a minority of women could rise above the norms for their sex, whether from exceptional talent or exalted social status. This was argued by the poet Torquato Tasso (1544–95), who in his treatise on female virtue distinguishes between womanly virtue, to be practised by all women, and ladylike virtue, befitting only women of the highest social ranks or unusual, 'virile' heroism and ability (see 5.4). Most women, though, should exercise virtue only in the limited, Aristotelian sense.[10]

Torquato Tasso, *Discorso della virtù feminile, e donnesca* (Venice, 1582), fols 3v, 5r.

As nature has produced man and woman of very different temperature and complexion, they are not likely to be suited to the same tasks. Man, as stronger, is inclined to some, and woman, as more delicate, to others. So Aristotle concludes, arguing against Plato at the beginning of the *Politics*, that virtue is not the same in men and in women. Thus, bravery and liberality would be male virtues, and modesty [*pudicitia*] female. As Gorgias would have it, silence is a woman's virtue, as eloquence is a man's, or, as Petrarch felicitously put it: 'Speech is prudent and wise when silent.'

Parsimony also is a woman's virtue [since it preserves what man acquires] ...

It is the reputation for modesty which most befits woman. More than any other virtue, this reputation cannot be held generally and still be based on modest behaviour. Genuine modesty, from which it should spring, would favour a retiring life and private and solitary places, and

10 For the sources of Tasso's system and its ambiguities, see Jacobs, pp. 10–14 and 38–40.

shun theatres, parties and public performances ... We will therefore conclude, that man is dishonoured by cowardice and woman by immodesty, since the one is the proper vice of man, and the other of woman. I do not deny, however, that bravery may well be a feminine virtue, but not absolute bravery, but bravery in obeying, as Aristotle says. Still, many deeds which are acts of bravery in women, would not be acts of bravery in men.

2 The discourse of beauty and love

During the Renaissance, women came to be especially valued for their beauty, which not only inspired male love but was, according to some, divine in origin. This emerged from intellectual roots quite different to the Christian and Aristotelian traditions looked at in the previous chapter. Renaissance literature, music and art cannot be understood without some awareness of the ramifications of this cult of women's physical beauty and the related debate on the value of love. How far either affected women in real life, especially women from lower ranks, is debatable, though literary praise of beauty came to colour elegant manners in sophisticated circles in Italy and in Europe, and life imitated art inasmuch as actual women strove to achieve the features of beauty praised by poets.

From the mid-fifteenth century, aesthetic theory had defined beauty, following classical sources, in terms of *concinnitas*, a harmony and concord of parts.[1] Rather later, Florentine Neoplatonism, particularly the commentaries on Plato of the philosopher Marsilio Ficino (1433–99) which appeared from the 1470s, emphasised the divine origins of beauty and the power of earthly beauty to awaken love and lead the lover heavenwards.[2] Beauty did not then necessarily mean female beauty, but from the later fifteenth century Neoplatonic ideas merged with traditional poetic ideals of the beautiful and virtuous lady, associated above all with Petrarch (1304–74). Greater familiarity with antique writings on Venus or other deities and their renderings by famous classical artists also lent prestige to the ideal of feminine beauty. As writers and artists vied to realise this ideal more compellingly, countless evocations or analyses of female charms and their elevating potential ensued.[3]

---

1 Particularly Leon Battista Alberti, in his *c.*1450 architectural treatise *De re aedifica-toria*, Bk I, chaps 2, 3 and VI, 2, following Vitruvius' *De architectura*, Bk I, chap. 2, of the first century AD.

2 Marsilio Ficino, *Commentarium in Convivium Platonis de Amore*, ed. and trans. G. Rensi (Milan, 1992), based on the *De Amore* of 1484. Still helpful is E. Panofsky, 'The Neoplatonic Movement in Florence and the North of Italy', in *Studies in Iconology* (New York, 1962), pp. 129–49.

3 For Petrarchan poetry and Renaissance paintings of women, see E. Cropper, 'On Beautiful Women: Parmigianino, *Petrarchismo*, and the Vernacular Style', *Art Bulletin*, 58:3 (1976), pp. 374–95, M. Rogers, 'Sonnets on Female Portraits from Renaissance North Italy', *Word and Image*, 2:4 (1986), pp. 291–305.

THE NATURE AND VALUE OF WOMAN'S BEAUTY

2.1 Firenzuola analyses woman's beauty

The 1541 *Dialogo delle bellezze delle donne* by the Tuscan novelist and friar Agnolo Firenzuola (1493–1543) gave not the first but the most complete discussion of female beauty. Drawing on ideas from recent debates in Florence and Rome, he gives a Platonic valuation of beauty, followed by a restatement of classical ideals of harmonious proportion, and later he enumerates features of beauty taken from the poetic tradition.[4]

Agnolo Firenzuola, 'Dialogo delle bellezze delle donne', in *Opere di messer Agnolo Firenzuola fiorentino*, ed. P-L. Fantini (Florence, 1763), vol. 1, pp. 259, 264, 266, 303, 307; *On the Beauty of Women* ed. K. Eisenbichler and J. Murray (Philadelphia, 1992), pp. 10–11, 14, 46, 49.

Both beautiful women and beauty deserve to be praised and highly valued by everyone, since a beautiful woman is the most beautiful object one can admire, and beauty is the greatest gift God gave to humankind, since through its power we can direct our souls to contemplation, and through contemplation to the desire for heavenly things. Thus, woman has been sent to us as a sample and a token of heavenly things, one so powerful and valuable that wise men have deemed her the best and finest object of love [...]

... Let us say that beauty is nothing more than an ordered concord, almost a harmony mysteriously following from the composition, unity and mixture of different members – different from each other, and within themselves, and, according to their own qualities and needs, well proportioned and in a certain way beautiful – which, before they are united in a single body are different and mutually discordant [...]

The cheeks should be pale yet radiant [*candide*], being features which possess a certain luminosity, like ivory, as well as whiteness: white alone does not imply shining like snow. The cheeks, therefore, to be called beautiful, should have a shining pallor, while the breast should be merely white [...]

Hair, as those who have written about it explain, should be fine and blond, now resembling gold, now honey, now shining as the bright rays of the sun, wavy, thick and long [...]

---

4 For Firenzuola, see Cropper; M. Rogers, 'The Decorum of Woman's Beauty: Trissino, Firenzuola, Luigini and the Representation of Women in Sixteenth-Century Art', *Renaissance Studies*, 2:1 (1988), pp. 47–88.

The forehead should be spacious, that is broad, high, pale and serene. Its height, which extends from the hairline to the eyebrows and nose, is recommended by many to be the third part of the face, another part being to the upper lip and the third the remainder including the chin. The height [of the forehead], then, should equal half its width ...

2.2 Women's beauty indicates nobility

Women writers such as Lucrezia Marinella took up this notion that their superior beauty demonstrated their nobility in general.

Lucrezia Marinella (1601), fols 10v–11v.

As women are more beautiful than men, they are also more noble, for various reasons. Firstly, because a delicate, blooming face reveals the power of its Creator, in that it has the beauty of Paradise. Also, it elevates minds towards divine goodness. By its nature it is loveable and gladdens every heart, even those unbending and harsh [...] In short women's whole bodies are constructed to be the proper seat of gentleness and virtue.

BEAUTY AND CLASSICAL ECHOES

2.3 Woman as ill proportioned

Theories of proportion derived from classical writers such as Cicero or Vitruvius were debated and reinterpreted by Renaissance artists and archi-tects, predominantly in relation to male bodies. Partly influenced by Aristotelian physiognomical theory, some thought women imperfectly propor-tioned, such as the early fifteenth-century Tuscan artist-writer, Cennino Cennini.

Cennino Cennini, *The Craftsman's Handbook. 'Il libro dell'arte'*, trans. D. V. Thompson (New York, 1960), p. 48.

I wish to give you the proportions of a man. Those of a woman I leave aside, since she lacks any perfect proportions.

2.4 Raphael on women's bodily proportions

Later, women's bodies came to be seen as possessing their own harmonies and beauties, contrasting with those in males. Raphael (1483–1520), studying Vitruvius on the proportions of temples (*De architectura* Bk III, chap. 1, Bk IV, chap. 1) explains how the classical architectural orders relate to women's bodies, in a letter of 1519 to Pope Leo X actually composed by Castiglione.

V. Golzio, *Raffaello nei documenti* (Farnborough, 1971), pp. 91–2.

But in the Temple of Diana they [parts of the Ionic order, usually proportioned like males] change their forms, the columns having the proportion and measure of a woman, with much ornamentation in the capitals and bases, and in all the shafts or shoulders, in imitation of female statuary ... Those called Corinthian are more slender and delicate, and made to imitate a virginal delicacy and grace.

2.5 Different types of beauty

Capella/Capra in 1526 differentiates between male and female beauty, a subject which later writers pursued.

Galeazzo Flavio Capra, *Della eccellenza et dignità delle donne*, ed. M. L. Doglio (Rome, 1988), pp. 96–7.

Of all the gifts bestowed on women, whether by Fortune, Nature, or their own efforts, physical beauty is inexpressibly the most pleasing ...

We can conceive of two types of beauty, one being a dignity and majesty almost inspiring reverence, which is associated with us, and the other a loveliness [*venustà*], attracting much desire and love, and this is special and peculiar to women.

2.6 Striving for ideal feminine beauty

Creating a perfect image of female beauty might involve a method like one repeatedly cited in Renaissance writing: the ancient Greek painter Zeuxis combining different features from five women in his painting of Helen of Troy. Raphael alluded to it in a famous letter of 1514 to Castiglione, who had complimented him on his *Galatea* in the Villa Farnesina, Rome.

Golzio, pp. 30–1.

To paint a beautiful woman, I'd need to see more beautiful women – on condition that Your Excellency came with me to choose the best! But since there's a shortage both of good judges and of beautiful women, I make use of a certain Idea which comes to my mind. Whether this has any artistic merit, I don't know: still, I try hard to attain it.

2.7 Antique authors on women's hair

The discussion of beauty in the 1554 *Libro della bella donna* by the North Italian author Federigo Luigini frequently cites goddesses or nymphs in antique literature, as when he debates different hairstyles. Many earlier painters from Botticelli onwards had enjoyed playing with the contrast between neatly restrained and luxuriantly loose women's locks.

Federigo Luigini, 'Il Libro della bella donna', in G. Zonta, ed., *Trattati del Cinquecento sulla donna* (Bari, 1913), p. 238.

Virgil, describing the meeting between Venus and her pious son Aeneas, who did not know where he was, gave her locks which were loosened and blown out by the wind. However, he then made Camilla's tied back, and also Dido's. Hence one gathers that both styles can make a woman seem beautiful.

BEAUTY AND VERNACULAR POETRY

Descriptions of fictitious beauties – goddesses, nymphs or Arcadian shepherdesses – developed from both classical models and Petrarch's Laura. As well as fair skin and golden locks, gentle eyes and graceful, measured movements characterised Renaissance beauties, influenced by contemporary notions of decorous restraint (see 9.22).

2.8 The beautiful Simonetta Vespucci

The Florentine circle of Lorenzo il Magnifico (1449–92) produced many such visual and literary evocations, whether of fictional or actual women or some blend of both.[5] Giuliano de' Medici's beloved Simonetta Vespucci is described by Poliziano (1454–94) in the 1470s in his *Stanze per la Giostra*, and associated with the muse of Comedy and virtuous classical deities.

Agnolo Poliziano, *Poesie italiane*, ed. S. Orlando (Milan, 1976), pp. 53–4.

> Fair [*candida*] she is, and fair her dress,
> though worked with roses and flowers and plants,
> the loosened locks of her golden head
> fall round her proud yet humble forehead.
> All around her the forest seems to smile,
> and woes become less bitter;

---

5 See most fully C. Dempsey, *The Portrayal of Love: Botticelli's 'Primavera' and Humanist Culture at the Time of Lorenzo the Magnificent* (Princeton, 1992).

her gestures are queenly yet gentle,
and from her gaze alone the storms desist.

Her eyes radiate a sweet serenity,
where Cupid hides his darts,
their expression makes all things pleasing
when she turns her lovely eyes.
Her face is full of celestial joy,
a sweet painting of lilies and roses,
at her angelic speech all breezes calm,
and each bird sings in his own language.

In her bosom sits Modesty [*Onestate*], humble and plain,
who could unlock the key of any heart,
with her goes Gentleness in human form,
teaching her sweet and flowing movements ...

Thalia seems to hold her lyre,
Minerva have her lance in hand,
when she holds her bow, her quiver carries,
she could seem the chaste Diana.
Her face makes gloomy Anger halt,
and Pride soon vanishes before her;
every sweet virtue is her companion,
Beauty she shows, and with it Grace [*Leggiadria*].

2.9 Petrarch's Laura reincarnated

Petrarch's verse evoking Laura's white hands, graceful movements, voice and
chaste virtues served as a rhetorical model all over Renaissance Europe. From
around 1500, Pietro Bembo (1470–1547), his most influential literary advocate in Rome, Venice and the North Italian courts, re-presented Petrarch's
imagery and female ideal.

Pietro Bembo, *Opere in volgare*, ed. M. Marti (Florence, 1961), pp. 456–7.

Hair of wavy gold and amber clear and pure,
swaying and rippling over snow in the breeze;
gentle eyes, more radiant than the sun,
which turn dark night into the clearest day;
smile, which calms all harsh and bitter pains,
rubies and pearls, from which issue

words so sweet the soul is satisfied,
ivory hands, which clasp and bind the heart,
song, which seems like heavenly harmony,
in greenest youth, the ripest wisdom,
charm never yet beheld among us,
utmost beauty matched with utmost chastity,
these are fuel for my fire, and are in you
graces which generous heaven grants to few.

2.10 An enchanting enchantress

Canonical status was achieved by Ariosto's sensuous description of the beautiful magician Alcina in Book VII of his *Orlando Furioso* (1516, revised 1532).

Ludovico Ariosto, *Orlando Furioso*, ed. M. Turchi and E. Sanguineti (Milan, 1982), vol. 1, pp. 142–4.

... only Alcina exceeded every one of them in beauty,
as the sun is more radiant than any star.

She was so beautifully formed
that no painter's efforts could have fashioned her.
Her long blonde tresses were knotted:
gold could not be more shining and lustrous.
Through her delicate cheeks
spread the colour of mingled roses and lilies;
her serene brow was like polished ivory
and of just measure.

Under two of the slenderest arcs
were two dark eyes, or rather two bright suns,
gentle in their gaze, restrained in their movement;
Love seemed to frolic and flutter around them,
and from them let loose his entire quiver
and openly capture hearts.
Next, the nose divided her face,
Envy could not manage to surpass it.

Below this, as if between two little hollows,
the mouth was set, tinted with native cinnabar.

Here were revealed two strings of fine pearls,
when two fair soft lips opened and closed,
from where came gentle words
to soften every rough and uncouth heart,
and here was formed that melodious laugh
which opened up paradise on earth.

Snowy white was her lovely neck, milky her breast;
the neck round, the breast ample and full.
Two young apples made of ivory
rose and fell like waves on the shore,
when a playful breeze sports with the sea.
Argus himself could not see the other parts,
but one could well imagine
that those revealed were equalled by those concealed.

Her arms were justly proportioned,
and her white hands were often to be seen,
rather long and tapering,
marred by no knots or prominent veins.
This marvellous figure was completed
with short, neat, rounded feet.
No veil could have concealed
her angelic and heavenly looks.

All her features were alluring,
whether she spoke or laughed or sang or moved a step.

QUESTIONING AND REVERSING POETIC IDEALS OF BEAUTY

2.11 A novel beauty: a black slave

While many poets merely recycled the Petrarchan imagery of female beauty,
others either parodied it, writing grotesque paeans to hideous hags, extended
their sensuous devotion to accessories like combs, hairnets or mirrors,[6] or

---

6 Examples of comparable playing with accessories in paintings of beauties are the
versions of the *Lady at her Toilette* by Giovanni Bellini and Titian (Vienna and Paris
respectively), for which see E. Goodman-Soellner, 'Poetic Interpretations of the
"Lady at her Toilette" Theme in Sixteenth-Century Painting', *Sixteenth Century
Journal*, 14 (1983), pp. 426–42.

inverted it. No poet did this more ingeniously than Marino (1569–1625), as in his sonnet to an African slave.

Giambattista Marino, *Amori*, ed. A. Martini (Milan, 1982), p. 80.

> Black, yes, but you are fair, a charming prodigy
> midst Love or Nature's beauties;
> dusky is dawn beside you, ivory and roses dimmed
> and made dark beside your ebony.
> When or wherever, in ancient or modern times,
> was ever seen so living, felt so pure a light
> arising from such inky shadow,
> did ever spent coal seem to generate fire?
> As slave of my own slave, I bear
> a dark noose tightened round my heart
> which white hand never can unloose.
> There where you burn most fiercely, Sun, is born
> a Sun that shames you, a Sun who bears night
> on her fair face, who in her eyes has day.

2.12 Beauty is transient

The deceptive or transient nature of beauty could in paintings be implied by the inclusion of transience symbols like flowers[7] or by contrasting young beauties with withered crones. Readers might be urged to *carpe diem* or to repent, as by Antonio Tebaldeo (1463–1537).

Antonio Tebaldeo, *Rime della vulgata*, ed. T. Basile (Modena, 1982), vol. 2:1, pp. 141–2.

> Your hair will not forever golden be,
> your teeth will not forever shine like pearls;
> bright eyes will lose their radiant splendour,
> divine and beauteous face not roseate be.
> Like a flower is beauty: in the morning
> blooming and graceful, but by evening dead.
> We humans can't renew ourselves like snakes,
> who heaven grants a luckier destiny.
> Ah, change your vain behaviour now,
> for days run swifter than the deer or pard,

7 See B. D. Steele, 'In the Flower of their Youth: "Portraits" of Venetian Beauties ca. 1500', *Sixteenth Century Journal*, 28:2 (1997), pp. 481–502.

mere folly is your hope for lasting life.
All things will vanish. Your mirror-image
will show you're not what yesterday you were,
see to it, therefore, you'll avoid regret.

THE DIFFUSION OF POETIC IDEALS OF BEAUTY

Elements from the poetic canon of beauty became part of the rhetoric
of praise for all types of women (see 6.16, 14.13, 14), including saints
and the Virgin Mary.[8] The following excerpts suggest its prestige for
both art and life.

2.13 Painters should emulate poetic beauties

Alcina's beauty was suggested as a model for painters by Lodovico Dolce in
his 1557 art treatise.

Lodovico Dolce, 'Dialogo della pittura', in P. Barocchi, *Trattati sull'arte* (Bari,
1960), vol. 1, p. 172.

The painter should strive not only to imitate but to vanquish nature ...
This means showing in just one body, through his art, all the perfect
beauty that nature usually scarcely shows in a thousand, since no
human body is so perfectly beautiful that it is wholly without flaws.
Here we have the precedent of Zeuxis, who when needing to paint
Helen of Troy for the Croton temple, chose to look at five nude girls,
and by taking some beautiful feature from one which was absent in
another rendered his Helen so perfectly that its fame lives today. But
if painters wish to find a perfect example of a beautiful woman without
trouble, they should read the verses in Ariosto describing the beauties
of the magician Alcina marvellously. They will also see the extent to
which poets themselves can be painters.

2.14 Poetic beauty aspired to in real life

In his collection of beauty treatments, the physician Giovanni Marinelli
constantly refers to classic expressions of the poetic ideal.

Giovanni Marinelli, *Gli ornamenti delle donne* (Venice, 1562), fols 91v–92r.

The eyebrows commended by poets are those resembling ebony:

8 On fusion of biblical and Petrarchan imagery in painting, see M. Vaccaro,
  'Resplendent Vessels: Parmigianino at Work in the Steccata', in F. Ames-Lewis and
  M. Rogers, eds, *Concepts of Beauty in Renaissance Art* (Aldershot, 1998), pp. 134–46.

slender, with short hairs, soft like the finest silk, and tapering from their centre towards their ends with a certain grace [*vaghezza*]. They should reach the hollow or socket of the eye on one side, with the other approach the area near the ear, and end there. For poets' ideas on the eyebrows, you can read in Petrarch's sonnet which begins: '*Quel sempre acerbo, & honorato giorno*', where you find: 'On a golden head, and a face like warm snow,/ebony are her brows ...' And Ariosto says in his 7th Canto: 'Under two dark and slender arcs/are two dark eyes, like two bright suns ...'

IDEAL LOVE

Socially-sanctioned forms of love – filial, marital, and charitable – will be looked at in later chapters: here the focus is on ideal love. This was defined, following Ficino's interpretation of Plato, as a longing to possess beauty, especially higher forms associated with sight and sound, which were meant to elevate the lover, giving experience of the divine.

2.15 Love generated from the enjoyment of beauty

The discussion of love in Castiglione's idealised court of Urbino shows the mixture of Petrarchan and Neoplatonic imagery and concepts found in sophisticated circles, with Pietro Bembo the speaker.

Castiglione, ed. Maier (1981), pp. 522, 536.

[Bembo] I say, therefore, that according to the sages of antiquity love is defined as nothing other than a certain desire to enjoy beauty ... From the senses is born the appetite, which we share with the brute beasts; from reason is born choice, which is proper to man; from the intellect, through which man can commune with the angels, is born will. Man, with a rational nature and placed amidst these extremes can of his free will be drawn by the senses or elevated by the intellect, directing his desires now in one direction, now in the other [...]

... Again, one cannot in any way enjoy beauty or satisfy the desire it excites in our souls through touch, but with that sense of which beauty itself is the true object, namely the faculty of sight. He must therefore detach himself from the blind judgement of the senses and relish with the eyes the radiance, the grace, the loving conversation, the smiles, the habits and all the other attractive enhancements of beauty. Similarly, with his hearing, her sweetness of voice, the harmony of her words, the melody of her music, if the beloved is musical. Thus he will graze on the sweetest food for the soul by means of these two senses, which have little connection with the corporeal and are servants to reason, without desire for the body stimulating any appetite less than chaste.

2.16 Love distinguished from lust

Discussions on love became a fashionable sixteenth-century literary genre, especially after the publication of the Italian version of Ficino's commentary on Plato's *Symposium* in 1544. Often courtesans such as Tullia d'Aragona (*c.*1510–56), who wrote her own love dialogue in 1547,[9] participated, as a predecessor, Diotima, did in the *Symposium*. In this extract from Giuseppe Betussi's *Raverta* (Venice, 1544) the speaker is the Venetian courtesan and poet, Franceschina Baffa, evaluating different kinds of love with reference to classical examples to be discussed in chapter 4.

Giuseppe Betussi, *Il Raverta*, in G. Zonta, ed., *Trattati d'amore del Cinquecento* (Bari, 1912), pp. 138–9, 143.

[Baffa] I consider Love supremely painful: anyone in love is rent by emotion a thousand times a day ... Without a doubt, Love can be very useful and good. However, I also read that Pyramus and Thisbe were violently taken to their death, that Hero and Leander were drowned at sea; I hear that Dido killed herself, and that countless men and women, as would take too long to recount, came to a bad end through love. All the books are full of it. What else could you call the cause of their ruin? Why was Troy razed to the ground, if not for the love of Paris and Helen? What made Samson lose his power and strength if not his too great love of Delilah, from which came the perpetual ruin of himself and the Philistines? What caused Holofernes' death but his excessive love for the beauty of Judith? [...]

[Raverta] All the examples from myth and history you have cited are worthless, because those people did not love perfectly, but lasciviously and unrestrainedly, swayed by excessive lust and desire for the vain possession not of true beauty, but its shadow (since the body is called a shadow), so that they came to a shameful and damnable end.

---

9 Tullia d'Aragona, *Dialogue on the Infinity of Love*, ed. and trans. R. Russell and B. Merry (Chicago, 1997); original in Zonta, (1912), pp. 187–248.

2.17 **Platonic love in poetry**

Lyric poetry became strongly imbued with the imagery of Platonic love: light, flames, celestial harmonies and heavenly ascents, as in one of the many sonnets written to Tullia by her lover Girolamo Muzio (1496–1576).

Tullia d'Aragona, *Rime della Sig. Tullia d'Aragona* (Venice, 1547), fol. 28r.

> When the ray of beauty which shines in you
> pierces the ears and eyes of my mortal frame
> a shining ardour, lady, assails me,
> which all enflames me with eternal longing.
> Then the soul, understanding the new emotion,
> moved by high purposes, each mortal pleasure scorning,
> and beating wings towards heaven,
> takes the path to the beloved light,
> and like an eagle turning eyes to the sun
> rises in ascent to your fire,
> where finally love promises it peace.
> Ah, be generous to it of your lovely splendour,
> and lend prompt succour to its flight,
> lest, weak and blind, it soars too high.

2.18 **A woman poet on her elevating love**

The love of female poets such as Gaspara Stampa (*c*.1524–54) could also be uplifting, if not always unsensuous.[10]

Gaspara Stampa, *Rime* (Venice, 1554), p. 55; ed. R. Ceriello, introd. M. Bellonci (Milan, 1954), pp. 146–7.

> I bless, Love, all the anxieties,
> all the insults and all the pains,
> all the troubles old and new,
> you've amply given me through numerous years,
> I bless the frauds and each deception
> it suits you and your following to devise,
> since, once the two beloved eyes returned,
> instantly all damage is restored.
> All past ills fall into oblivion
> a new and living light is given

10 See F. Bassanese, *Gaspara Stampa* (Boston, 1983).

where my desire alone finds peace.
Ascending straight, inducing me
to contemplate high things, and God:
firm guide, fine escort and a trusty light.

3 The Virgin Mary

Mary's theological status in all Christendom was based on her role as Virgin God-bearer, as shown in countless images of the Madonna and Child. From this were developed in the Middle Ages doctrines like the Assumption of her body and soul after her Dormition, expressing her unique delivery from death, and her Coronation as Queen of Heaven.[1] The doctrine of the Immaculate Conception (meaning Mary's complete exemption from original sin owing to her own miraculous conception) was logically related, and during the fifteenth century was energetically promoted by the Franciscan order, then sanctioned by the Franciscan Pope Sixtus IV and given its office in 1476.[2] Veneration of the Virgin was marked officially by her major feasts, the Annunciation, Visitation, Purification, all three based on Gospel episodes, as well as the Assumption; also important were events such as her Birth, Presentation in the Temple, Betrothal and Marriage which had been recounted in much earlier apocryphal gospels such as the Proto-evangelium of James (second century AD) and were retold in Renaissance devotional writings, many of which had female dedicatees.[3] All of these episodes and themes were given many pictorial renderings. In the later sixteenth century, the Council of Trent reaffirmed the status of the Virgin for Catholics as worthy of the highest form of veneration.

However, her all-pervasive popular cult was mainly based on the sense that she was the most effective intercessor with her son at death and the most powerful protector against life's ills. Miraculous apparitions and relics would demonstrate her presence and her power; prayers and images such as those supposedly painted by St Luke, or the *Madonna della Misericordia*, where particular groups huddle under her protective cloak, sought to channel it.[4]

1 See H. Graef, *Mary: A History of Doctrine and Devotion*, 2 vols (London, 1963) for an orthodox Catholic account of the development of Marian theology and devotion.
2 Graef, vol. 1, pp. 298–306; R. Goffen, *Piety and Patronage in Renaissance Venice* (New Haven, 1986), pp. 73–106. for the Immaculate Conception in Italy.
3 Such as Ippolita Sforza for Antonio Cornazzano's *Del la sanctissima vita di nostra Donna* (Venice, 1471, and several later editions), or the Marchese del Vasto for Pietro Aretino's *La vita di Maria Vergine* (Venice, 1541).
4 See, for example, R. Chavasse, 'The Virgin Mary: Consoler, Protector and Social Worker', in Panizza, pp. 39–164 and L. Marshall,'Confraternity and Community: Mobilising the Sacred in a Time of Plague', in Wisch and Cohl Ahl, pp. 20–45.

Devotional activities that wedded the populace to her cult, such as civic processions and festivities on Marian feast days, or lay confraternities focused on different aspects of her life, were encouraged by both church and state. Thus many groups felt attachment to the Virgin: it was not a specifically female cult. This chapter will try to suggest this breadth of appeal, but also the particular ways in which women approached, or were encouraged to approach, Mary, in public cults and private devotions at different phases in their lives.

WOMEN APPROACHING MARY AS WOMAN AND EXEMPLAR

Although the Virgin's stature could serve as an argument against the inferiority of women generally, as has been seen in chapter 1, it has been claimed that the uniqueness of Mary's combination of virginity and maternity presented real women with an impossible model to follow.[5] However, rather than trying to emulate this paradoxical combination, Renaissance women were encouraged to focus on particular virtues or human experiences of Mary as maiden, wife or mother.[6] Paintings might introduce contemporary elements in setting, costume and accessories, introduce donor portraits, or use pictorial placement or gaze to relate her experience to a female audience, as well as suggest her virtues through symbolism and body-language.

3.1 A female saint on Mary's role in redemption, her selflessness and obedience

Two letters of St Catherine of Siena (1347–80) of c.1375–6 explore different aspects of the Virgin. To an abbess, Monna Paola, she writes of Mary's role as bearer of Christ, here using vegetation metaphors perhaps reflected in Renaissance art, and selfless sharer in His work of redemption.

a. Catherine of Siena, *The Letters of St Catherine of Siena*, ed. S. Noffke (Binghamton, NY, 1988), pp. 117–18; *Epistolario di Santa Caterina*, ed. E. D. Theseider (Rome, 1940), pp. 141–2.

Human pride should well be ashamed to see God so humbled in the womb of sweet Mary, who was the field where the seed of the

5 M. Warner, *Alone of All Her Sex: The Myth and Cult of the Virgin Mary* (London, 1976).
6 See C. Valone, 'The Art of Hearing: Sermons and Images in the Chapel of Lucrezia della Rovere', *Sixteenth Century Journal*, 31:3 (2000), pp. 753–77 for preaching on Marian themes to a female audience in sixteenth century Rome.

Incarnate Word, the Son of God, was sown. Truly, dearest sister, that blessed and sweet field that was Mary absorbed the Incarnate Word into its own flesh, as a seed sown in the earth germinates and brings forth flowers and fruit through the warmth of the sun, while its husk remains in the ground. Truly, the heat and fire of God's divine charity for the human race did the same, when He sowed the seed of His Word in the field that was Mary.

Oh blessed and sweet Mary, who gave us sweet Jesus as a flower! And when did that blessed flower produce fruit? When He was grafted on to the wood of the most holy cross – then we received perfect life ... [Sharing Christ's passionate desire for human salvation, Mary] could long for nothing else save the honour of God and the salvation of creation. Thus the doctors say that, testifying to Mary's boundless love, she would have made a ladder of her very self to help place her Son on the cross, if there had been no other way – all because the will of her Son remained in her.

Keep this is mind, my dearest sister, and never let it leave your heart nor memory nor soul: you and all your daughters were offered and presented to Mary.

To her mother, Catherine encourages her acceptance of her (Catherine's) absence by pointing to Mary's obedience to God's will that her son and His disciples depart from her.

b. Catherine of Siena, ed. Noffke, pp. 252–3; ed. Theseider, p. 338.

I want you to learn from that sweet mother Mary, who for the honour of God and for our salvation gave us her Son, dead on the wood of the most holy cross. Mary, remaining alone after Christ had ascended to heaven, stayed with the holy disciples. And even though she and the disciples had been a great consolation to each other and the parting was wretched, still she willingly agreed to their leaving, for the glory and honour of her Son and the good of the entire world. She chose the pain of their departure rather than the consolation of their staying, and this was only through her love for God's honour and our salvation. So it's from her I want you to learn, dearest mother. You know that my place is to follow God's will, and I know you want me to follow it. It was God's will that I go away.

3.2 Mary as modest, humble and faithful

Bernardino da Siena (d. 1444), preaching at Siena in 1427, sees the behaviour of the Virgin at the Annunciation as demonstrating her twelve virtues, allegorised as 'maidens'– here, enclosure, modesty, humility and faith – which his audience of young women should emulate in their everyday lives.

Bernardino da Siena (1989), vol. 2, pp. 862, 870, 882–3, 885.

[Enclosure] O you girls, learn how you should stay at home, and beware of whoever enters the house, as you see that the Virgin Mary stayed shut away at home, and always wished to see who wanted to come in and why. Girls, you know how powerful a force youth is! Isn't it better if you stay shut away, and don't get familiar with men and even with women: watch for whether they are good, or otherwise.

But we must say where the Angel found her. Where do you think she was? At the window, or involved in some other vanity? Oh no! She stayed shut away in her chamber, and was reading, to set an example to you, my girl, not to enjoy standing or leaning out of the window, but to stay at home, saying the Ave Maria or Paternoster or, if you can read, reading good, pious material. Learn the Office of Our Lady, and delight in that. Oh, what a grave danger for young men to chat where girls are around!

[Modesty] Have you seen that Annunciation scene in the cathedral, at the altar of St Sano, beside the Sacristy?[7] That certainly seems to me to have the finest, the most reverent and modest pose I've ever seen in an Annunciation. Look: she's not looking at the Angel, but is in an almost fearful pose. She knew quite well it was an angel, so why should she be alarmed? What would she have done if it had been a man? Follow this example, girls, of what you should do. Never speak to a man unless your father or mother is present ...

[Humility] The second damsel staying with Mary was called my lady Humility, and it was that quality which made God love Mary. And Mary began to sing with such joyfulness and reverence and humility: 'Quia respexit humilitatem ancille sue; ecce enim ex hoc beatam me dicent omnes generationes'. That's, if I agree, 'all generations will call me blessed'. O why will they call me 'blessed'? 'Because He has regarded the lowliness of His handmaiden.' And then she turned to the Angel, meaning towards God, 'Ecce ancilla Domini. Behold the slave of our Lord God.' Oh, and there is much to say about this. May your father and mother treat their daughter like a slave. Does the house need to be swept? Yes? – Yes, make her sweep up. Are there dishes needing

7 By Simone Martini (1333), now in the Uffizi, Florence.

washing? She should wash them ... Is there laundry to be done? Get her to do it at home. – Oh, but there is a servant! Maybe: get [your daughter] to do it not because it needs to be done, but to give her practice. Make them look after the little ones, wash the swaddling clothes and everything else: if you don't get her used to doing anything, she'll turn into a good-for-nothing.

[Faith] The fourth and last companion of the glorious Virgin Mary was my lady Faith. She had so much faith that she believed all things God willed were possible. *'Omnia opera eius in fide.* All His doings in faith.' And in fact she said to the Angel: *'Secundum verbum tuum.* I am content with what you have said, and consent to no other way.' And so take example from that, you girl, to believe your father and stay content with what he commands, and obey him always.

3.3 Daughters of the Virgin follow her dress

A similar desire to emulate the Virgin, imagined as having spent her early years enclosed in the temple in devotion, informed the rituals and regimes of many institutions for young women, as in a Milanese college for girls from noble but poor backgrounds. Paolo Morigia in 1595 describes the intentions of its founder, the Countess of Guastalla.

Morigia, pp. 61–3.

And she called it the College of the Daughters of the Virgin Mary. The dedication of its fine Oratory was to be to the Nativity of the same Virgin Mary ...

... She wished the girls to be dressed in the clothing of the Virgin Mary herself, so that all these maidens wear a white gown underneath and a blue one on top. The white one warns them they must have purity of life, cleanliness and chastity. The blue one teaches them that all their thoughts must be of heavenly, not earthly matters. I will also mention that the Lady Governor, like the girls, says the Hours of the Blessed Virgin every day.

3.4 A mystic and mother helps the Virgin with childcare

Visions of the Virgin Mary, often crowned, dressed in splendid garments and holding the Christ Child towards the visionary, were common among Renaissance laywomen and nuns. These reflected their knowledge of works of art and earlier accounts of visions, but also were influenced by their individual human experience. Thus, this vision of the birth of Christ on Christmas day

1431 by Francesca Bussa (S. Francesca Romana, 1384–1440), recounted by
her confessor Giovanni Mattiotti, suggests not only the earlier vision of St
Bridget of Sweden, but Francesca's experience as a wife and mother.[8]

Scrittrici mistiche italiane, ed. G. Pozzi and C. Leonardi (Genoa, 1988),
pp. 255–7.

The blessed woman saw how the glorious Virgin took the Lord from
the ground and offered Him in her hands to God the Father, saying:
'O Father omnipotent, I offer and give You Your Son who is the
Incarnate Word' ... Then the glorious Virgin, gazing at the Divine
Word, wished to cover that most beloved and precious humanity
against the cold, but because of her true and holy Poverty had no
clothes to cover Him with: she wished to cover Him not because He
was crying or complaining, but through devoted compassion and exal-
tation. Wishing to cover such excellence, she made as if to take off the
cloth serving as her headdress. Then the divine servant, Beata
Francesca, who was standing close to the glorious Virgin, not waiting
for the great queen to take the cloth off her head to cover her beloved
Spouse, with great promptness and presence of mind took the cloth off
her own head and covered the Lord ... The divine servant in ecstasy
also pleaded with the glorious Virgin that she would deign to lend her
the Divine Mirror, her Spouse, because she wished to cover Him. So
the queen and mother, seeing the blessed servant so concerned ...
agreed to her ardent desire, lending her the Lord. Then the seraphic
servant, taking the longed-for Divine Word, rejoiced with such gaiety
and delight, and was as much melted and enflamed by joyful happiness
as you, reader, can imagine, wishing to take the cloth that served as
her mantle to make a bed for the Lord. And I, seeing such wonderful
actions, brought certain table-linen to the blessed woman, with which
she made a bed for the Lord on top of the bench, remaining in ecstasy
all the while – and she made it so well that she could have made it no
better if she had been in her normal state of mind.

3.5 Vittoria Colonna feels for the lamenting Virgin

Women, particularly older women who had known bereavement, also
empathised with the Virgin sorrowing at Christ's Passion and death, as
evinced in pictorial commissions and in writings like that of Vittoria Colonna
(1492–1547), penned some five years after becoming a widow in 1525.

8 See C. Frugoni, 'Female Mystics, Visions, and Iconography', in Bornstein and
Rusconi, pp. 130–64.

Vittoria Colonna, *Le Rime*, ed. A. Bullock (Bari, 1982), p. 139.

> While the mother embraces her dead
> beloved son, in her faithful mind
> there rises the glory of the different triumph
> that He brings to every spirit elect.
> His terrible wounds and his changed appearance
> increase her bitter, violent torment;
> but the victory for the eternal rule
> brings to her soul a new, exalted pleasure.
> And the supreme Father tells her the secret
> that he has not forsaken His Son, but will strive
> to restore Him glorious and living;
> but, since to a true mother His birth
> is certain, as is His eventual burial,
> her heart was still deprived of any solace.

PUBLIC CULTS

The following extracts convey the flavour of cults whose appeal might cut across all distinctions of gender, wealth or education. Often connected with apparitions of the Virgin, relics or miraculous images, many brought from the East, Marian cults originated locally, sometimes among very humble people, and usually became linked to requests for help with the problems and disasters of life. To the extent that these were different for women than for men, female devotees had their own sets of demands. These cults might then be given official support, ecclesiastical or civic.

3.6 Siena, the city of the Virgin

Several cities in Italy dedicated themselves to the Virgin, most famously Siena,[9] as mentioned in S. Bernardino's 1427 sermon on the Annunciation.

Bernardino da Siena (1989), vol. 2, p. 855.

Aren't you called citizens of Siena? And the city is called that of the Virgin? How should you not have the most special reverence for her? I well know that you have this inscription on your coins: Siena, the

9 See D. Norman, *Siena and the Virgin: Art and Politics in a Late Medieval City State* (New Haven, 1999) and, for Venice, Goffen, pp. 138–54.

ancient city of the Virgin. If you are from Siena, make your actions accord with this description.

3.7 Miracle-working images of the Virgin and their treatment

The diary of the pious Florentine shopkeeper Luca Landucci mentions several miraculous images, in particular the *Madonna dell'Impruneta*, a painting kept in a town outside Florence and later adopted by secular authorities.[10] The Virgin, through the image, was felt to offer help in political trouble or poor weather conditions. Though to an extent seen as a moral exemplar, she is basically a powerful protectress, demanding reverence and, when mistreated, vengeance.

Luca Landucci, *Diario fiorentino*, ed. I. del Badia (Florence, 1883), pp. 41–2, 44, 66, 279, 308.

At this time [12 June 1482] there was much talk of devotion to an image of Our Lady found at Bibbona, in a tabernacle about a bowshot from Bibbona. It is a seated Virgin with the Dead Christ in her arms, after He was taken down from the cross, as is depicted in other *Pietàs*. This worship began on 5 April, when it was transfigured: that is, it changed from blue to red, and then from red to black and different colours. And this is said to have happened many times between then and now, and several sick people have been cured, and many miracles been performed, and quarrels reconciled, so that all the world runs there. Nothing else is talked of at this moment; I have spoken to many who have said they have seen it transfigured themselves, so that one must believe it.

... On 30 May 1483 Our Lady of S. Maria dell'Impruneta was brought so the weather would improve, as it had rained for over a month; and immediately it became fine.

On 17 August 1493 it happened that a certain unbeliever, to spite the Christians, but mostly out of craziness, went round Florence vandalising images of Our Lady, among them the marble one on the pilaster outside Or San Michele. He scratched the eyes of the Child and of Sant'Onofrio, and threw mud in the face of Our Lady. At this, the boys began to throw stones at him, and they were joined by grown men, who in their fury stoned him to death with large stones, and then dragged his body around with much vituperation.

10 See R. C. Trexler, 'Florentine Religious Experience: The Sacred Image', *Studies in the Renaissance*, 19 (1972), pp. 7–41.

... On 13 November 1506, at about 8 in the evening, here at S. Michele Berteldi, people began to say that an image of Our Lady over a door, the one opposite the door of the public baths, had performed miracles and closed its eyes. She seemed not to wish to see the immorality that takes place there. In less than a day, so many candles were lighted and such great veneration paid to it that a wall was built in front of it like a church, and many women would have gone there, had it not been disreputable for women to go near the baths. Despite this, many waxen images were brought to it and many votive offerings.

... On 22 May 1511 the painting of Our Lady of Impruneta was brought so it should stop raining, as there seemed too much water then. And there were many gifts, more than on all other occasions, and there were 8 very rich mantles, and also many chasubles and cloaks, and draperies, 24 in number, and 90 white and yellow tapers, and a fine silver cross.

3.8 A women's confraternity

Most religious confraternities were either all male or male-dominated, but there were some both founded and filled by women, as with this Florentine example at S. Maria del Carmine, Florence, connected with a miracle-working image, the *Madonna del Popolo*. The sixteenth century saw many more female confraternities devoted to aspects of the Virgin's earthly existence, such as her Birth, Presentation in the Temple or Sorrows, which often specialised in charitable work such as giving dowries to poor and virtuous girls or prayer and support for the sick and dying. The Dominican order also promoted Rosary confraternities, promoting the sequence of prayers known as the rosary, and women were especially attracted to them.

N. A. Eckstein, *The District of the Green Dragon: Neighbourhood Life and Social Change in Renaissance Florence* (Florence, 1995), pp. 119–20.

The holy company of the pious and venerable women of S. Maria del Popolo had its foundation and origin on 6 May 1460, and the first prioress was the venerable lady Monna Lisa, widow and former wife of Niccolò Serragli. They were inspired by God and founded this Company in honour of the Virgin Mary with much fine ceremony and devotion. They were about 80 women from the best and most pious families in Florence, and a friar close to God, one of strong devotion and great spirituality, Fra Nicola da Cicilia by name, was its head, principal and founder.

3.9 The miracles of the Virgin's girdle

The Virgin's body could not provide relics, owing to its Assumption into heaven, but her supposed wedding ring, held at Perugia, and girdle, held at Prato, attracted much devotion and were referred to in paintings of related subjects. Although such cults attracted scepticism from some, they could also be defended not just by the naively superstitious but by educated clerics or laymen such as Guido Guizzelmi, whose 1493 book recounts both the Virgin's life on earth and her tossing down of her girdle from heaven to the Apostle ('Doubting') Thomas. This was then obtained in Jerusalem in the twelfth century by a pilgrim from Prato, Michele, and performed many miracles, some with particular appeal for women.

Guido Guizzelmi, *Historia della Cinctola della Vergine Maria*, ed. C. Grassi (Prato, 1990), pp. 119, 138, 158–9.

10th Miracle. There was a noble and rich woman called Beatrice, exceedingly rich, who became sick with a very serious illness and intensely painful chest complaint, so that all the doctors gave up hope for her. Despairing of any temporal aid, she commended herself to the most glorious Virgin Mary, and vowed to give an extremely rich veil to the most precious Girdle, and she did make the offering to the said Holy Girdle. And behold, when the veil was offered, she was miraculously freed and was granted singular health and was healed perfectly. And because the said veil was very fine and exceedingly rich, the not so fine or rich veil in which the Holy Girdle had been wrapped, and in which it had been carried by Michele, was taken away. And this old veil, removed from use for the Holy Girdle, was divided into pieces and given to several people. And the pieces performed many miracles and many graces for those who placed them on themselves.

... 19th Miracle. Another time God allowed a strand from one of the tassels of the said Holy Girdle to come loose, which was given to a noble Florentine lady, who had it woven into a rich veil and held in great reverence, and when any woman could not give birth, it was placed on her, and straightaway she gave birth. And on one occasion it was placed on a woman who was pregnant from an adulterous relationship and had not confessed her sin, and suddenly the strand vanished. Nor was the strand ever seen again, because adultery does not please the Holy Virgin, nor does she have mercy for those unwilling to confess their sin.

... According to old accounts, infinite numbers have been saved through its [the girdle's] merits in war, battles and feats of arms, many from thunder and lightning, many from evil spirits, many from malign spells and witchcraft, many others from strangulation or other torture ... And thus we cannot doubt not only that the Holy Girdle and things which have touched the Holy Girdle can give help through the merits of the most glorious Virgin Mary, but, as we know from countless experiences, that even the tapers and torches, and lights held when the most holy reliquary is shown, have shown themselves of great help to women giving birth.

3.10 Visiting a sanctuary to the Virgin

In 1514, Isabella d'Este prays at one of the numerous country sanctuaries to the Virgin for the health of her husband, to whom she writes.

Translation by J. Cartwright, *Isabella d'Este, Marchioness of Mantua* (London, 1904), vol. 2, p. 69.

Today I have been to Peschiera, stopping to visit the sanctuary of the Madonna of the Ash-trees, which is said to work so many miracles. I saw many images and ex-votos, and the beginnings of a fine church, in which I prayed earnestly for Your Excellency's health.

PRIVATE DEVOTIONS

3.11 The Little Office of the Virgin

The Virgin Mary could form the subject for more personal devotions, aided by images and texts, many particularly directed at women. Official Latin texts such as the Little Office of the Virgin Mary, regarded as a basic devotional manual to be used at home (see 6.10, 11) and one of the most printed books during the Renaissance,[11] received vernacular translations such as that made around 1486 by Pietro Edo, a priest linked to a confraternity of the Virgin in Pordenone. Such combinations of prayers and paraphrases from Luke or the Song of Songs spread awareness of her virtues and associated symbols such as the cypress, rose and palms, shown with many others in Renaissance paintings, some of which would have been viewed in the home.[12]

Pietro Edo, *Officio de Nostra Donna*, ed. F. De Nicola (Genoa, 1977), pp. 29, 40–1.

---

11 See P. F. Grendler, 'Form and Function in Italian Renaissance Popular Books', *Renaissance Quarterly*, 46 (1993), pp. 451–85.
12 See J. M. Musacchio, 'The Madonna and Child, a Host of Saints, and Domestic Devotion in Renaissance Florence', in G. Neher and R. Shepherd, eds, *Revaluing Renaissance Art* (Aldershot, 2000), pp. 149–64.

Opening prayer, and lesson and response for Matins

> Hail Mary, full of every grace,
> your Lord is with you forever more;
> through humility alone, and not through boldness,
> you remain blessed above all other women.
> Free from all female shame;
> you alone bore painlessly
> the blessed fruit of your womb,
> through whom the whole world is saved.
> Pray for us, strong advocate, always,
> but especially in the hour of our death. Amen.
> [...]

Third lesson:

> I am greatly exalted in Israel,
> like dense and lofty cedars
> born, above all, in Lebanon,
> as in Mount Syon the cypresses
> and in Engaddi the palms increase and flourish
> and the roses in Jericho spring low;
> as in the fields are fine olives
> and the plantain planted by the water,
> I am exalted above other goddesses.
> And through the cities, as it pleases the Lord,
> is wafted a sweet and holy scent,
> which descends from me and is born in me;
> and as cinnamon, like balsam,
> sends out its sweetness,
> and fine myrrh its aroma,
> you may inhale the aura of truth.
> Response:
> You are truly noble and blessed
> and more than can be expressed,
> O most holy Virgin Mary,
> worthy of the highest praise,
> since of you was painlessly born
> the Sun of Justice,
> Jesus Christ, gentle and holy,
> and our Lord and God.
> So pray for the people, O Mary,
> and pray for the Church,

and intercede devoutly
for the female sex;
make all who remember
your triumph and glory
always receive and feel your support,
in every ill that befalls them.

3.12 How to pray to and salute the Virgin

Popular texts such as the anonymous late fifteenth-century *Zardino de Oration* ('Garden of Prayer') provided further guidance in the vernacular for private devotions.

Zardino de Oration (Venice, 1494), chap. 5, unpaginated.

And certainly this salutation [The 'Ave Maria'], in which we ask the glorious Virgin to intercede for us with her son deserves to be praised ... And this would suffice for anyone knowing no other verbal prayer ...

Also we should salute the Virgin orally, saying the office made specially for her and her lauds and antiphons, that is *Salve Regina, Ave Regina coeli* and others similar ...

Also we must salute the glorious Virgin with works and deeds and outward signs, kneeling and prostrating ourselves before her and before a figure representing her, with head uncovered, and bowing when her name is said.

3.13 A female poet in praise of the Virgin

Individual poets, most famously Petrarch in the later fourteenth century, also reworked epithets such as the Window of Heaven, the New Eve, or the Woman Clothed with the Sun (Revelation 12:1). From the later fifteenth century, female writers wrote religious drama and poetry, as by Laura Terracina here.[13]

Laura Terracina, *Rime della Signora Laura Terracina* (Venice, 1548), fols 46v–47r.

13 K. Gill, 'Women and the Production of Religious Literature in the Vernacular', in Matter and Coakley, pp. 64–104.

Holy Virgin, immaculate and pure,
sole refuge for mortal misery
where the doubting soul takes assurance,
   Virgin lofty, eternal and immortal,
listener to innocent prayers,
remedy for all affliction, every evil.
   Holy Virgin, to whom I offer
the countless number of my torments,
with great laments and melancholy cries.
   Splendid Virgin, in whom humanity, I pray,
may find mercy, pity, health,
To you I turn and humbly plead.
   Virgin abounding in shining virtue,
whose glorious deeds are in the high choirs
both thanked and praised and known.
   Virgin, pitying our humble prayers,
strong support in human misery
to whom you ever reveal yourself benign.
   Virgin, ineffable and sovereign,
who was crowned by the Eternal King
to give light to our blind and vain lives.
   Virgin, wise and adorned with splendour,
virgin in birth, after birth, before,
you alone blessed among women.
   Virgin, truly abounding in pity,
whose mercy leads heavenward;
chasing the determined, every-ready tempter.
   Virgin full of infinite light,
succour my weakness, I beg you now,
may others not seeking you be given guide:
   pierce gloomy hearts with your shining rays:
show yourself merciful, as you ever are, and gentle,
so I may escape eternal torment.
   Do not harden yourself to the prayers of others,
as ever the advocate for the human race
you were, and always will be, blessed Virgin.
   Succour a heart which, contrite, groans,
benignly gather to you my desire:
give remedy for the eternal punishment,
as much as your Son gave us hope.

4 Female saints

The female saints to whom Renaissance people looked to for protection and help can broadly be divided into figures from the canonical
and apocryphal Gospels (Anne, Mary Magdalene), early Christian
virgin martyrs (Catherine of Alexandria, Lucy, Agatha, Ursula) and
saints of the religious orders (Monica for the Augustinians, Clare for
the Franciscans and Catherine of Siena for the Dominicans). Their
feast days were marked by prayers and liturgies, and might be city
holidays where a saint had patriotic appeal arising from her legend or
the presence of her body. Legends were disseminated by hagiographical writings, the most popular being still the thirteenth century
Golden Legend, by sacred dramas and by poems of praise (*laudi*) to be
recited or sung in groups, and reinforced by the dedication of
churches, altars and confraternities, with related images. Both literary
and visual interpretations varied in their re-presentations of saints to
different audiences. Whether their cults were based on patriotic senti-
ment, prophylactic power or moral example, the saints' appeal was
multi-faceted and cut across gender divisions.

Nonetheless, male authorities considered devotion to female saints
especially appropriate for women. Women, who were usually named
after saints although the fashion for classical names increased during
the Renaissance, felt connections with their name-saints, who would be
represented in altarpieces commissioned by family members. They
evidently responded to saints' general virtues and to aspects of their
stories seemingly relevant to their female experience, though often the
legends were too fantastic or transgressive of social norms for the
saints to serve as close 'role models'. Helena and Ursula were seen as
pilgrims, and Magdalene admired not primarily as the patron of 'fallen
women' but as an ardent follower of Christ, penitent and contemplative.[1]
Female confraternities revered the mother saints Anne and Monica,[2]

1 See S. Wilk, 'The Cult of Mary Magdalen in Fifteenth Century Florence and its
Iconography', *Studi medievali,* ser. 3a, 26:2 (1985), pp. 685–97; S. Haskins, *Mary
Magdalen. Myth and Metaphor* (London, 1993).
2 See K. Ashley and P. Sheingorn, eds *Interpreting Cultural Symbols: Saint Anne in Late
Medieval Society* (Athens, Ga., 1990); C. Lawless, 'Widowhood Was the Time of her
Greatest Perfection: Ideals of Widowhood and Sanctity in Florentine Art', in
A. Levy, ed., *Widowhood and Visual Culture in Early Modern Europe* (Aldershot, 2003),
pp. 19–38.

and Margaret was widely invoked to protect women in childbirth. Stories of the pious companions or relatives of saints like Ursula resonated with female groupings. Nuns or would-be nuns were inspired by young saints' refusal of arranged marriages and determination to remain 'wedded' to Christ, and Renaissance saints found a precedent for their own visionary experience in the story of the Mystic Marriage of St Catherine.[3]

CULTS, PRAYERS, STORIES

4.1 Salutations and prayer to St Agatha

This anonymous later fifteenth-century Sicilian dialect poem conveys the patriotic cult of a female saint. The third century St Agatha's body had been repatriated to Catania from the East; legends of its miraculous 'translation' developed, and the saint became seen as a powerful protector of the city.

Anon., in *Poesie siciliane dei secoli XIV & XV*, ed. G. Cusimano (Palermo, 1952), vol. 2, pp. 116–19.

> Hail, queen of this city,
> O morning star, O sun, O moon,
> true fountain of virginity,
> column and crown of Catania;
> hail, our advocate, holy Agatha,
> through whom God has given us so much grace.
>
> O shining planet, our light,
> O much-loved jewel of Catania,
> our pilot and captain,
> our protection, guide, counsellor, advocate,
> you alone are resplendent among other virgins,
> you are in heaven and so much magnified:
> still we implore you with pious voices
> and recommend your land to you.
> [...]
> You, Virgin, so loved this land
> here where you were born and wished to die,
> and then you asked God
> that you would always favour it,

---

3 For the above, see G. Zarri, 'Ursula and Catherine: The Marriage of the Virgins in the 16th century', in Matter and Coakley, pp. 237–78.

and from Constantinople you came back,
and to your homeland wished to return:
so, if this much love you felt for it,
you would hear our humble prayers.
[...]
And we your citizens, who you love so much,
may you recommend them to God:
guard them and keep them from war and famine,
from earthquakes and disease;
and hearken to the cries and pleas
that every hour the wretched make.
You are our aid and succour:
you are our patron, holy Agatha.

4.2 A drama of St Catherine of Alexandria converted and mystically married

This drama on the life of Catherine of Alexandria (*fl.* 300), the most commonly represented female saint apart from Mary Magdalene, was probably performed by confraternity members. It includes elements both exotic (a procession of wise men from the East) and contemporary (relatives gather to discuss Catherine's suitors and dowry). The role of a painting, prompting visions which convert Catherine to Christianity, is unusual in her legends, though visual art is often recorded as a stimulus to contemporary mystics. More normal is the Mystic Marriage, which female mystics sought to repeat.

La festa et storia di Sancta Caterina: A Medieval Italian Religious Drama, ed. A. Wilson Tordi (New York, 1997), pp. 93, 105–7.

[First Hermit]

This is the figure
of His Mother, the Virgin Mary ...
Hearken, my daughter,
do you see this Child held in her arm
to send you a message soon?
He is the One of whom I have talked with you.

Wise and prudent daughter,
go home with good resolve.
Take this image
With intense reverence and devotion.

Kneel down before it
and pray earnestly to Mary,
that in her kindness
she may show you her sweet Son.

Later, after Catherine's baptism:

[Catherine]

In a vision I saw
The Virgin Mary as queen.
I was kneeling
and she said to me, 'Stand up, Catherine'.
That divine face I saw
of her Son; it gave out
greater splendour than the sun.
O how glorified He seemed to me!

Then the mother of God
with her holy hand took mine
and said, 'My Son,
give her the ring, of your courtesy.'
The Virgin Mary
took my finger, her fair Son
put this ring on me.
I awoke and found it thus.

[First Hermit]

You have received grace
much greater than I could have reckoned,
and have satisfied your mind.
Therefore you should live devoutly
and ever praise God.
Your possessions you will give
with your hands to poor Christians
for love of Him who has married you.

4.3 A pocket book on St Margaret

Narratives of colourful stories were widely read and, rather less frequently, painted. This tiny book (c.1560), easily portable on someone's person, recounts the popular legend of St Margaret, miraculously released after being swallowed by a dragon. It ends with Latin prayers to assist women in childbirth.

Legenda et Oratione di Santa Margherita vergine, & martire historiata (Venice, *c.*1560), unpaginated.

In prison, Margaret is swallowed by a dragon:

> And while she remained in prayer
> her heart humbly devoted to God,
> from one side came a huge dragon
> very fierce, untamed and restive,
> who made his way towards Margaret,
> wild-eyed, his mouth emitting
> flames of fire and stinking sulphur,
> thinking to take Margaret.
>
> Rolling his eyes, and dragging his tail,
> and whistling with his strong tongue,
> and roaring and screeching and twisting his tail,
> he came attacking the girl,
> and he seemed to gnaw at everything
> and struck like a snake with arched neck,
> and his eyes gave out a great light
> which lit the whole prison.
>
> ... The Maiden stayed firm
> all devout in holy prayer
> and while she humbled herself
> her eyes toward heaven, kneeling on the ground
> there moved with horrible malignity
> the dragon, as if in desperation,
> his mouth opened, and with great ferocity
> he devoured St Margaret.
>
> And when this virgin girl
> was in the belly of the fierce dragon
> she turned to her holy star,
> praying, kneeling with humble voice,
> that the confidence of the beast might fail.
> Then she made the sign of the cross:
> as was intended by this sign
> the beast burst open, doing her no harm.

Leaving the stinking, fetid body,
the Maiden, with the cross in hand,
so fair and splendid and shining
seemed a celestial, not human, body;
her body showed no stain at all,
Lest such a marvel be in vain,
when she emerged from his belly
with much humility she praised God.
[...]
O you, Reader, who have yearned for
the legend of this perfect virgin,
pray her that you grasp her with faith,
and hold her in your home like a choice possession,
so that no evil may ever befall you,
because through God she was blessed by heaven,
if your woman is in peril in childbirth,
no better doctor can I recommend you here.

4.4 The penitent Mary Magdalene

The following text by a cleric, Salvestro da Prierio, like much writing and art
from after the Council of Trent, shows concern with penitence and rejection
of worldly vanities, allied to an appreciation of Mary Magdalene's beauty.
After Mary hears Christ's preaching she is converted and does penance.

Salvestro da Prierio, *Vita di Santa Maria Maddalena*, ed. Serafino Razzi
(Florence, 1592), pp. 12–15.

The Magdalene, then, took herself to the sermon adorned with fine
clothing and jewels, with her face most lovely and her soul most vile,
her eyes always wanton and alluring. O you miserable soul, where are
you going now? In truth, happy, since you are going to death for your
sin: go to be reborn as a new woman, and you will be a sinner no more,
but the beloved of Christ ...

And the Saviour enflamed her from all sides, inwardly inspiring her
and outwardly preaching to her. So, returning home from the sermon,
she took off all her finery and divested herself of her wanton clothes.
Dressed in sober garments, with her hair loosened over her shoulders
and arms, and constantly weeping, she went to the Saviour ...

... Then, knowing that Christ was dining in [the house of Simon]
she took with her alabaster ointment ... So the Magdalene came

dishevelled, wearing a sombre dress, and with tears in her eyes and sweet scents in her hands threw herself at the feet of Christ from behind, not having dared to go in front. How much fervour ruled that heart, driving her to go to another's house, and to weep publicly at a banquet. Such was the abundance of tears that they were enough to wash the feet of the Saviour. When these had been washed with tears, she dried with her own hair, and anointed them with precious unguent, and then, as St Luke says, kissed them. But it must not be thought that this kiss was an ordinary one. Thus she embraced the holy feet, and clasped them firmly, and would have willingly placed them in her heart, if she could have done so.

FEMALE SAINTS AND FEMALE DEVOTION

4.5 **Virgin saints as examples**

Female saints were felt to be appropriate subjects for meditation for secular women by both clerical and humanistically inclined writers. This letter by 'Giovanni Napoletano' addressed to 'Silvia, a most chaste virgin', was published with many Italian editions of Thomas a Kempis' *Imitatione Christi*, a text then attributed to Jean Gerson and frequently read by women (see chapter 6).

Giovanni Napoletano, 'Lettere a Silvia', in Iohannes Gerson (*sic*), *De Imitatione Christi et De Contemptu Mundi in Vulgari Sermone* (Venice, 1488), unpaginated.

Run, daughter, to penitence ... Open straightway your closed ears to the loud cries and voices of the martyrs Margaret and Catherine. Remember, daughter, that Lucy divested herself of her most shining eyes lest they offend Lord Jesus; Catherine was carried through blades for God; Margaret consented to enter the poisonous body of the horrible serpent to obey her Creator. The blessed Magdalene, than whom no lovelier a woman was ever born in this rapacious world, left all worldly pomp for love of Christ Jesus. Ah, daughter, lest she further offend her master Jesus in this world she consumed her body for thirty years, nourished by miraculous waters and unknown herbs, in the darkest woods and forests amidst strange and fierce beasts, to attain the heavenly place of paradise. Ah, daughter, what most eloquent orator could express how admirable were the beauties and splendour of these martyrs, who in the end came fearlessly with great suffering to die for God ...

4.6 St Catherine in a book of famous women

A secular author, Vespasiano da Bisticci (1421–98), in his book of *c.*1480 on famous women directed towards female readers, omits discussion of Catherine of Alexandria's visions, stressing her learning and using her and other female saints as exemplars of constancy, contradicting notions of feminine fickleness.

Vespasiano da Bisticci (1999), pp. 50–2.

We come to the marvellous St Catherine, the 18-year-old daughter of a king, learned in all seven liberal arts. Summoned before a tyrant who promised her abundant riches and worldly pomp, she scorned them all. She wished to argue with pagan priests about the supreme faith in his presence, to demonstrate that their religion was false and full of deceptions, and that no other faith existed save that of Christ. She disputed several times with them, converting many to the Christian religion, especially 50 philosophers ...

Seeing this, Maxentius devised torments with horribly cruel wheels made to torture her and others. The angel came and smote them asunder, and over a thousand infidels died. She converted huge numbers to the Christian faith, nearly all of who accepted martyrdom willingly. Though given many types of torture, she always remained constant and steady, without ever wavering. She repeatedly told the tyrant that he could do what he wanted, but she was prepared to accept death for love of God and to preserve her holy virginity ...

... It is apparent from her and from countless women who we will mention or have mentioned how constant their spirit was. This was combined with the most burning faith and hope.

4.7 Catherine of Siena's Agnes and Magdalene

Women, while similarly admiring saintly virtues, often gave their own devotion a particular flavour stemming from their needs and experiences. St Catherine of Siena, writing to female Dominican tertiaries in Siena in *c.*1374, stressed not Magdalene's beauty and penitence but her humble yet fiery love for Christ and for good works. She and another saint, Agnes, are held up as models.

Catherine of Siena, *The Letters of St Catherine of Siena*, ed. S. Noffke (Binghamton, NY, 1988), p. 42; *Epistolario di Santa Caterina*, ed. E. D. Theseider (Rome, 1940), pp. 13–16.

Oh, my dearest daughters, learn from the holy virgin Agnes, that is from true and holy humility, which always seeks to abase itself, submitting to everyone, giving God the credit for every grace and virtue: thus she maintained the virtue of humility inside her. And I say she burned with the virtue of charity, always seeking God's honour and the salvation of mankind, always giving herself to prayer with an ample charity, generous to all: thus she showed her love for her Creator. Her other virtue was her constant care and perseverance, which neither the devils nor anyone else could make her abandon.

Oh sweetest virgin, how similar you made yourself to that devoted disciple Magdalene! See, dearest daughters, how Magdalene knew herself, and humbled herself, with what great love she sat at the feet of our gentle Saviour! And speaking of showing love, we certainly see this at the holy cross: she wasn't afraid of the Jews, and didn't fear for herself, but ran as if in anguish and embraced the cross. Doubtless she was bathed in blood as she beheld her Master. Surely you were drunk with love, O Magdalene! ...

So you see, my dearest sisters, how well these two mothers and sisters of ours agree! So I beg and command you to join their most holy company, where you will find virtue on all sides.

4.8 Margaret as a help in pregnancy

The pregnant Bianca de' Pazzi writes from the country to her mother, Lucrezia Tornabuoni, on 15 July, 1479, for a volume on the saint associated with childbirth.

Translation from Y. Maguire, *Women of the Medici* (London, 1927), p. 116.

My dearest and most honoured mother ... I have frequently sent to your house ... for the book of St Margaret.

4.9 A female writer in praise of saintly virginity

Women both secular and in holy orders came to write works on female saints, many being plays performed by nuns to a female audience.[4] A pioneer was the Florentine Antonia Pulci (c.1452-after 1488), whose plays were later printed. Her *Play of St Domitilla* attests to her happy marriage before entering a convent as a widow, for the early Christian saint can temporarily see the attractions of marriage, before being persuaded of the superiority of virgin martyrdom and marriage with Christ.

4 See *Florentine Drama for Convent and Festival: Seven Sacred Plays*, ed. J. Wyatt Cook and B. Collier (Chicago, 1996).

Antonia Pulci, *La Rapresentatione di Santa Domitilla nuovamente ristampata* (Florence, 1554), unpaginated.

> Holy Virginity, most elevated,
> beloved of God and to the angels dear,
> who lives and reigns eternally
> in heaven with her Maker, shining, clear.
> How blessed are those who under your sign
> take up this path, disdaining
> this bitter life, full of troubles,
> to find another and serener life.
>
> Sins may be expiated by penitence
> but once virginity is lost,
> one never can return to its state.
> Wretched is she who rejects this,
> which surpasses all other virtues,
> and is received joyfully by saints in high heaven.
> Just as the queen is the greatest
> of all other women, this is true honour.
>
> It spreads a sweet scent towards God.
> If you espouse it, you will have as consort
> a young man, gentle, benign and devout
> who never will be parted from you.
> He is Christ Jesus, who with longing
> for His brides makes great celebration in heaven.
> This is certain joy, this true repose,
> blessed is she who turns to such a Spouse.

4.10 Women prize relics of female saints

Relics were eagerly collected generally and by females. An abundant supply of body parts was assured from the supposed 11,000 virgin companions of Ursula, a saint especially meaningful to groups of women. Just one page of Paolo Morigia's 1595 guide to Milan lists many virgin heads in female institutions.

Morigia, p. 44.

In the church of the nuns of S. Bernardino, there is one head of the 11,000 virgins. Another of the same virgin heads can be seen in the church of S. Maria Maddalena, near S. Eufemia. At the Monastero Maggiore[5] another head is honoured, with several bones of the same virgins ... In the church of the Convertite a head of one of the 11,000 virgins is venerated. Likewise, at the Annunziata nuns another is revered, and at S. Vito ... another of the heads is held in great reverence ... In the church of St Catherine, where the maidens live, a head of one of the 11,000 is venerated ... also the nuns of St Catherine have a head.

RENAISSANCE SAINTS AND HOLY WOMEN

During the Renaissance, many women little remembered today attained great fame as living saints or *sante vive*.[6] Their types of sanctity differed from that of contemporary male saints, for women could be neither priests nor popular preachers,[7] though some, if in non-enclosed religious groupings such as that associated with Francesca Bussa (S. Francesca Romana, 1384–1440) in Rome, might exert influence on the secular world through charitable work and miracles.[8] Others might make an impact in political spheres, through prophesying or intervening in civic feuds, notably St Catherine of Siena (Caterina Benincasa, 1347–80, canonised in 1462). Particularly characteristic of Renaissance female saints, however, was their rich visionary experience, mainly with the goal of drawing closer to their beloved Spouse, Jesus Christ. Here the inspiration of earlier female saints such as Mary Magdalene, Ursula or Catherine of Alexandria was important, that of St Catherine of Siena crucial. Printing allowed her letters and her biography, written by her confessor, Raymond of Capua, and later translated into Italian, to be widely disseminated, encouraging many religious women, notably the Blessed Colomba da Rieti (1467–1501) and S. Caterina de' Ricci (1522–90), to imitate different aspects of her sanctity (and others to fake similar visions). Following the tighter enforcement of enclosure for women in religious

5 The convent of S. Maurizio.
6 G. Zarri, 'Living Saints: A Typology of Female Sanctity in the Early Sixteenth Century', in Bornstein and Rusconi, pp. 219–304.
7 For differences between female and male saints of the time, see R. Kieckhefer, 'Holiness and the Culture of Devotion: Remarks on some Late Medieval Male Saints', in R. Blumenfeld-Kosinski and T. Szell, eds, *Images of Sainthood in Medieval Europe* (Ithaca, NY, 1991), pp. 260–305.
8 A. Esposito, 'St Francesca and the Female Religious Communities of Fifteenth-Century Rome', in Bornstein and Rusconi, pp. 197–218.

orders from the mid-sixteenth century, which restricted their social roles, this introverted, ascetic and visionary female sanctity became more marked.

4.11 Lucrezia Marinella on Catherine of Siena

Two centuries after her death, Lucrezia Marinella, who in her later years wrote much hagiography, evokes the range of Catherine's activities.

Lucrezia Marinella, *De' gesti heroici e della vita maravigliosa della serafica S. Caterina da Siena* (Venice, 1624), pp. 232–3.

What deed was so secret, what thought so private, what event so distant, that the celestial girl did not see it, know it, and understand it? She predicted wars, discords and future calamities; she saw inside the hearts and thoughts of others; with the tongue of an angel she put the tranquillity of calm amidst the quarrels, feuds and furies of others; to angry minds she gave the sweetness of peace and concord, both to the troubled breasts and disputes of the appallingly seditious citizens. She sweetened the bitterness of the absence of the troubled people, deflecting the stabs of their piercing sorrows with the hammer of her holy words. She visited and consoled the needy, the afflicted and the distressed with the love of her perfect goodwill. Although she laboured under, and suffered with, a thousand infirmities, no less extensive were her deeds and pilgrimages to lead people to heaven. She was never found wanting in works of charity, and the more she was oppressed and weighed down by various infirmities, the more she brought the light of her divine deeds, like a flame rising to heaven.

4.12 Catherine of Siena's Mystic Marriage sanctions her mission

Catherine's Mystic Marriage is understood by Raymond of Capua as confirming her faith and validating aspects of her activity in the world that were unconventional for a woman.

Raymond of Capua, *The Life of St Catherine of Siena*, trans. G. Lamb (London, 1960), pp. 99–101.

From now on Catherine's soul increased in grace daily. She flew rather than walked along the way of virtue, and a holy desire developed within her soul to attain perfect faith so that, utterly subject to her Bridegroom, she might be utterly pleasing to Him. She began to pray to the Lord ... The Lord spoke to her and said, 'I will espouse you to me in faith'.

Eventually she is rewarded with a vision of Christ, the Virgin and saints.

While David played sweet strains on the harp the Mother of God took Catherine's hand in her own most holy hand and presenting her to her Son courteously asked Him to marry her to Himself in faith. The Son of God, graciously agreeing, held out a gold ring with four pearls set in a circle in it and a wonderful diamond in the middle and with His most holy right hand He placed it on the virgin's second finger, saying, 'There! I marry you to me in faith, your Creator and Saviour. Keep this faith unspotted until you come to me in heaven and celebrate the marriage that has no end. From this time forward, daughter, act firmly and decisively in everything that in my Providence I shall ask you to do. Armed as you are with the strength of faith, you will overcome all your enemies and be happy.'

The vision disappeared but the ring always remained on Catherine's finger and, though no one else could see it, it was always before her eyes ... I believe that this marriage was meant to confirm the divine grace, and that the sign of this confirmation was the ring which she alone could see, so that when she went on to her task of rescuing souls from the swamps of this world she would never be downcast but always trust in God's grace ... Now in defiance of all convention our virgin too was to take part in public life for the honour of God and the good of souls ... and so she had the grace in her confirmed by a visible sign, so that she might be bold and firm in doing the things heaven enjoined her to do ... I believe the Lord willed this because of her sex and the novelty of what she did and the slack condition of our times ... so that she needed special and continuous assistance.

4.13 Colomba da Rieti's asceticism

Leandro Alberti's account of the austerities of the teenage Colomba da Rieti emphasises absence of food and longing for the Eucharist.[9] Colomba modelled herself on Catherine of Siena, and her Dominican hagiographer further stresses their similarities.

Leandro Alberti, *Vita della Beata Colomba da Rieto dil Terzo Ordine di S. Domenego: Sepolta a Perugia* (Bologna, 1521), chap. XI, unpaginated.

---

9 For these aspects of female sanctity, see R. M. Bell, *Holy Anorexia* (Chicago, 1985) and C. Walker Bynum, *Holy Feast and Holy Fast: The Religious Significance of Food to Medieval Women* (Berkeley, 1987).

She tormented her delicate limbs with penitential practices. Apart from the other fasts ordained by the Church, she usually fasted forty days in a year ...

Although her usual food was a little bread and water, eventually leaving the bread, she lightly ate bitter fruits, and unripe grapes, so that the pious neighbours marvelled, and also feared, that poverty made her short of food and drink, and tempted her with tasty pieces to allow her to eat more than usual. But she only yearned for the more delicate food of spiritual life the more strongly and more avidly, that is the true bread of the body of Jesus Christ ...

So our angelic Colomba, having already tasted the food of the angels ... yearned and with all her heart desired spiritual and celestial things, and scarcely maintained the necessities for human life. It happened that when she was in the parish church at the most cele-brated and joyful feast of the Nativity of Our Lord ... and received the holy sacrifice at the sacred altar, she was filled with such sweetness, and enflamed by such love that she almost fainted for holy love and ardour for God, and thought and meditated only on the holy sacrifice, and continually day and night shed tears with such profusion, and cried for her longing for the sacrament, that it was necessary for her good confessor and spiritual father to allow her to take the sacrament every first Sunday of the month, and on the feast days of the Glorious Virgin Mary. Again, she flagellated her frail body with an iron flail, or 'discipline', of five chains bound together, three times per day and at least that per night, following completely our father Dominic and the holy mother, Catherine ... She also wore a hairshirt on her naked flesh. And she prayed for very long periods and was devoutly intent on holy meditation, and often her mind was enraptured in spirit, her actions and the operation of exterior feelings suspended so that her sorrowful body seemed as immobile as the hardest stone. She spent almost all the night without sleep, except for a little rest, rather than sleep. Sweet sermons by the saints consoled her, and she was taught by heavenly visions.

4.14 Saints battle with demons

Saintly women also endured periods of dark travail and struggles with terri-fying demons, as recounted of the Blessed Caterina da Racconigi (1486–1547) by Serafino Razzi.

Serafino Razzi, *Vite de i Santi e Beati, così huomini come Donne del Sacro ordine de' Frati Predicatori* (Florence, 1577), pt 2, p. 128.

Caterina had the most appalling battles with hellish demons. She was attacked sometimes by one, sometimes two; once five, and often by countless numbers. Sometimes they appeared in human form, now living, or sometimes dead. Sometimes they would take the figures of saints, and try to deceive the simple girl: often they changed themselves to look like beasts, birds, or quadrupeds, snakes and other ghastly sights. And they were chased away by her, now with words, and then with argument: often with the sign of the Cross, several times with a stick, and then with wise words.

4.15 Caterina de' Ricci receives the stigmata

The most fortunate were rewarded with stigmatisation, achieving complete identification with their Spouse and Saviour, as described by Razzi of Caterina de' Ricci.

Serafino Razzi, *Vita di santa Caterina de' Ricci*, ed. G. M. di Agresti (Florence, 1965), pp. 133–5.

The raptures of this servant of Christ were so frequent that many times, both day and night, she was found by her supervisor in rapture and outside her normal senses ...

On 14 April in the year 1542, during the octave of the resurrection, Our Lord, through especial grace and favour, deigned to stamp and imprint on the virginal body of this His bride, Caterina, the likeness of His wounds. And although Christ was wounded by the lance on His right side, His servant Caterina was no less wounded on the left side of her heart. And as her supervisor recounted many times, the pain that this wound gave her was so great that it always seemed to Caterina as if she would fall to the ground dead, for all she knew she couldn't die from it.

The wounds on her hands and feet – which at first she only felt on Fridays – from then on she saw and felt at all times, but that on her body she told her supervisor she had never actually seen, not being accustomed nor presuming ever to look at a clothed part of her body that was temporarily naked, pure and holy nun as she was ...

Nonetheless, the sisters in the monastery the following year ... could see the wounds, only on her hands: but those on her feet were seen only by twelve or sixteen of the oldest nuns. They recount how ... it seemed as if she had just been taken down from the cross, and the sweetest, most intense odour issued from them.

4.16 The posthumous fame of Caterina Vigri

While the fame of some *sante vive* was short-lived, others, like St Catherine of Bologna (Caterina Vigri, 1411/13–63), were more enduring. Her devotional writings were reprinted and continued to circulate, her uncorrupted body worked miracles, her fellow nuns spread her cult within and without Bologna, and she was later canonised.[10]

Anon., poem appended to Caterina Vigri, *Le sette armi spirituali* (Bologna, 1500), on her funeral and posthumous miracles.

> As in life she ever taught
> her daughters with a perfect heart,
> so after death she showed them
> her great favour,
> since as a bequest she left them
> holy peace and the fire of charity.
> And also she composed a worthy book
> wherein she showed her divine intelligence.
>
> When the holy body was buried
> a sweet odour issued from it,
> so that it was smelt on every side
> and it was a great marvel to smell it.
> But since this was so
> the sisters decided to make it public
> so it performed great miracles
> and healed many infirmities among them.

Her body was exhumed and found uncorrupted.

> A great miracle was then seen,
> that face, once so worn away
> was now returned to its former state.
> So that anyone who adored the holy body
> would be protected from all sin.
> Sick people came there,

10 See J. Wood, *Women, Art and Spirituality: The Poor Clares of Early Modern Italy* (Cambridge, 1994), esp. pp. 121–44 and 193–204.

and many people
and were completely healed.

Thus our good Jesus demonstrates
how the glorious holy woman
has gone to heaven and remains there,
with gladness and with eternal joy.
...
Rejoice, Bologna, since you are great,
not for pomp or riches or great estate
not for your delicate food
but for the virginal body
through which your name is spread everywhere,
since within your walls it rests.

Be glad, and pray to the worthy saint
that she not deny help to sinners.

4.17 Caterina Vigri in a book of famous women

The late fifteenth-century secular biographer Sabadino degli Arienti, on the
posthumous cult of S. Caterina Vigri: Ippolita Sforza, Duchess of Calabria
(1445–88), goes to visit the body.

Sabadino degli Arienti, pp. 338–9.

She went to the monastery of the nuns of Corpus Christi to make
reverence to the body of the Blessed Caterina, which the nuns had
placed dressed in *damaschino bertino* seated above the altar of her
church; and it is a wonderful thing that a body dead for several years
should remain seated; or rather it is not wonderful, as God sometimes
allows something similar, or truly of greater impact in holy matters.
This most blessed wife, after doing reverence to the holy body with
suitable oblation, with the aid of a high chair placed above the altar
devoutly placed a crown of silver on the head of the blessed lady,
saying: 'The crown well befits her'. And from then on she has always
been crowned with that crown, as one can see.

5 Famous and exemplary women

There is an apparent paradox at the core of some rich and varied strands of writings on women from the fourteenth to the seventeenth centuries – how could women, whose very nature was imperfect, weak and fickle, attain fame and become exemplars of conduct?[1] This chapter examines one of these strands, that of works dealing with the lives and actions of mythical and historical women who achieved fame and exemplary status.

Drawing on a tradition stretching back to antiquity, and especially on the works of Plutarch, Livy and Valerius Maximus, Giovanni Boccaccio wrote *De mulieribus claris* (1361–83), a collection of biographies of famous women from the mythical and historic past.[2] This important and successful work, written in Latin, was soon translated into Italian and expanded twice during the sixteenth century, running into several editions. It was the precursor of a number of compilations of women's biographies dedicated to contemporary famous women: *De mulieribus admirandis* (1467) by Antonio Cornazzano, Vespasiano da Bisticci's *Libro delle lodi delle donne* (c.1480), Giovanni Sabadino degli Arienti's *Gynevera de le clare donne* (1490), and Agostino Strozzi's *La defensione delle donne* (1501), published anonymously. These books constructed explanations for the reputation of famous women, and offered exemplary moral lessons to the reader, according to the Renaissance conception of history as *magistra vitae*. Besides using subject matter from classical historians, they also dealt with characters from the Old Testament and from mythology. The latter were often filtered through another of Boccaccio's influential works, the *Genealogia deorum gentilium* (c.1350), which moralised the gods and goddesses of antiquity and interpreted them as allegories of Christian values.

These historical and mythical female characters not only became exemplars of moral conduct for women, but were also regarded as a strong argument for women's excellence, and appear in treatises, some written by women, praising the female sex. Their stories found their

---

1 See M. Ajmar, 'Exemplary Women in Renaissance Italy', in Panizza, pp. 244–64.
2 See P. J. Benson, *The Invention of the Renaissance Woman* (University Park, Pa., 1992), pp. 9–31.

way also into both general treatises on women and more informal writings.

As well as positive role models, there were also negative ones which alerted women to the dangers of vices such as lust, deceit and disobedience. Finally, some of the exemplars were ambiguous, since they offered women models of behaviour and exemplary virtues, such as fortitude and courage, which might be seen as transgressive. It was therefore less controversial to compare some heroines of the past to contemporary wives of rulers, since their special position allowed them to exercise what were considered to be 'virile' virtues.

Famous and exemplary women were a popular subject for the decoration of *cassoni* and *spalliere*, bedroom furniture commissioned for newly married couples. Their stories were also told in cycles decorating public buildings.[3]

GODDESSES

The three following extracts illustrate how certain female mythological figures could be associated with conventionally virtuous qualities, or even seen as guides for women. This made it possible, later in the Renaissance, for women to be compared to goddesses, as will be seen later in the chapter.

5.1 An embodiment of wisdom: Athena, 1361

Boccaccio's *De mulieribus claris* was known in the second half of the sixteenth century in the Italian translation by the *letterato* Giuseppe Betussi, who also updated it with fifty new biographies of contemporary women (first printed Venice, 1545).[4] Here Boccaccio elaborates meanings for the attributes of the famous statue of Pallas Athena in the Parthenon.

Betussi/Boccaccio (1596), pp. 17–18.

For the number of wonders and works she [Athena] had performed, the ancients believed that the power of her wisdom was a gift of the divine. Because of this, the Athenians, chosen by her because she saw their city was suited to studies bringing prudence and wisdom, took

3 Tinagli, pp. 21–46, with bibliography; and 'Eleonora and her "Famous Sisters". The Tradition of "Illustrious Women" in Painting for the Domestic Interior', in K. Eisenbichler, ed., *The Cultural World of Eleonora di Toledo Duchess of Florence and Siena* (London, 2004), pp. 119–35.

4 The 1596 edition was further expanded by Francesco Serdonati.

her as their patroness, and built a citadel with a large temple dedicated
to her. In it they placed her image, with threatening eyes, because
seldom does one know the intentions of a wise man. She had a helmet
on her head to signify wise men's secret and armed advice. Her breast-
plate signified that a wise man should be always ready to fight against
the attacks of fortune. The long spear in her hand indicated that the
speculative power of a wise man can reach far. She was also armed
with a crystal shield, to which was affixed the head of the Gorgon
Medusa, signifying that all hidden things are clear and evident to wise
men, who are always filled with such serpentine cunning that ignorant
men seem like dumb stones. They placed an owl to guard her,
declaring that wise men can see by night as well as by day. And therefore the fame of this woman and the reverence for this goddess
grew everywhere to such an extent ... that temples were erected and
sacrifices were celebrated in her honour almost everywhere.

5.2 The two natures of Venus, *c.*1469

The Neoplatonic philosopher Marsilio Ficino (1433–99) uses the figure of
Venus, morally dubious according to Christian ethics, to expound his notions
of different kinds of love, inspired by different facets of divine beauty.

Marsilio Ficino, *El libro dell'Amore*, ed. S. Niccoli (Florence, 1987), pp. 36–7.

Pausanias, following Plato, states that Love is the companion of Venus,
and that there are as many Loves as there are Venuses. He tells of two
Venuses accompanied by two Loves: one is the celestial; the other, the
earthly. The celestial Venus was born from Caelus without a mother,
the earthly one was born from Jupiter and Dione ...

Venus has two natures: one is that intelligence which we have placed
in the angelic mind, the other is the drive to procreate, attributed to
the soul of the world ... The first encloses within itself divine splendour, which is then diffused to the second Venus. This second Venus
radiates sparks of the received splendour into the matter of the world.
Because of the presence of these sparks, all the bodies in the world,
according to their capacity, are made beautiful ...

When the beauty of the human body is presented to our eyes, our
mind, which in us is the first Venus, feels reverence and love for such
beauty as an image of the divine. Because of it, this beauty often
awakens to the divine. Furthermore, the drive to procreate, which in us
is the second Venus, wants to generate a form similar to it. So in both

these powers there is Love, which in the first is desire to contemplate beauty, and in the second is desire to generate it. Both kinds of love are honourable, since they both follow the divine image.

5.3 Juno, goddess of marriage

This poem by Isabella di Morra (*c.*1520–46)[5] dedicated to Juno, goddess of chaste love which culminates in marriage, was probably written for a female friend. By the mid-sixteenth century women writers were becoming confident at using mythological figures, but only morally respectable ones, like Juno, Minerva or Diana.[6]

Lodovico Dolce, ed., *Rime di diversi illustri signori* ... vol. 5 (Venice, 1552), p. 213.

> Sacred Juno, if unchaste Love
> be so inimical to your lofty heart,
> make my days and years bright and happy
> with your holy and lawful ardour.
> To you I dedicate my virginal flowers,
> to you, Goddess, and to your propitious thoughts,
> you, who only bring beatitude,
> you, who fill heaven with your sweet perfume.
> Bind my neck with the beautiful golden yoke
> of your dearest and most humble subjects,
> as I endeavour to serve you only.
> Guide Hymen with gentle love
> and make the knot with which I bind myself so dear,
> that one single soul may rule our hearts.

OLD TESTAMENT HEROINES

The heroic actions of women from the Old Testament were a rich source for writers as well as for painters and sculptors. The widow Judith was an *exemplum* of obedience, of humility conquering pride,

---

5 On Isabella di Morra, see L. A. Stortoni, ed., *Women Poets of the Italian Renaissance: Court Ladies and Courtesans* (New York, 1997), pp. 114–27.

6 Morally respectable mythological figures were also represented in works commissioned by women. They can be found, for example, in Isabella d'Este's first *studiolo* in the Castello di S. Giorgio, Mantua (end of fifteenth to beginning of sixteenth century), and in the *camera* painted by Correggio for Abbess Giovanna Piacenza in the Benedictine convent of S. Paolo, Parma (*c.*1518).

and of chastity. She was also seen as an anticipation (antetype) of the Virgin Mary. In fifteenth-century Florence, she personified civic virtue and resistance against tyranny, because by killing Holofernes she freed her people from the enemy.

According to Antoninus, Archbishop of Florence (1389–1459), Queen Esther was a suitable example for the daughters of the Florentine elite, as well as an advocate of justice, and a model for a ruler's dutiful wife. Having delivered her people from peril, Esther could also represent the Church. Furthermore, she was a Marian antetype, since she interceded with Ahasuerus, king of Persia, for the safety of her people.

5.4 Judith: an example of strength, 1552

Domenico Bruni's *Difesa delle donne*, first published in 1552 and dedicated to the Duchess of Florence, Eleonora di Toledo, takes women's side in the debate on the nature of women. Here Bruni uses the story of Judith to praise women's physical strength and courage.

Domenico Bruni, *La difesa delle donne* (Milan, 1559), fols 32v–33r.

Having fully proclaimed, through the examples quoted, how the feminine sex [possesses] a most strong and virile soul, we shall now verify, as we have promised, how women are also equal to men in bodily strength. And to prove this we shall primarily give the example of the most famous Judith who, according to Brunetto Latini, was a woman of the greatest courage, and, in his opinion, stronger and more vigorous than any man. This can be shown to be true because she did not fear the strength of Holofernes but, placing herself in mortal danger in order to save her people, while he was sleeping she killed him with the greatest skill, strength and cleverness, without any damage to herself, and brought his head to the people of Israel. This was the reason for their victory over the enemy.

5.5 An example for the elite: Queen Esther, 1470s

Lucrezia Tornabuoni (1425–82), the wife of Piero de' Medici, highlights Esther's role as intercessor in her *La storia di Hester regina*, which stresses visual qualities and the significance of dress.[7]

---

7 For Lucrezia Tornabuoni, see N. R. Thomas, *The Medici Women: Gender and Power in Renaissance Florence* (London, 2003).

Lucrezia Tornabuoni de' Medici, *The Story of Queen Esther*, in ed. and trans.
J. Tylus, *Sacred Narratives* (Chicago, 2001), pp. 193–4.

> Her eunuchs and handmaidens came to her side,
> and each one attends to comforting her,
> and they brought to her the noblest
> garments that she usually wore
> when she wished to appear every inch a queen;
> without delay she dressed herself in her clothes,
> and they attired her in her regal insignia,
> draping her in rubies, pearls, and infinite treasures
> so that anyone who saw her would be thunderstruck.
> Dressed in this way, she concealed her grief;
> she was royally dressed, adorned, and graceful;
> she well knew it was the right moment to give her all.
> There went with her two ladies-in-waiting,
> one who could support her and sustain her,
> another who attended to her rich garments.
> She had never appeared so beautiful;
> and on this day she seemed to have come truly to this world
> from paradise.
> She went off to the king, pretending to be cheerful,
> concealing from him and everyone else
> her great sadness.
> Not even her beautiful eyes betrayed her sorrow.
> The king was seated on his throne,
> and with his barons he was enjoying his wealth,
> he was spending time in amusements and pleasure,
> there in his palace with a worthy gathering,
> when looking about him, he happened to see Esther.
> He called his Esther to his side
> and held out to her the sceptre of gold,
> with reverence, Esther knelt before him.

5.6 A tale of endangered virtue: Susannah and the elders, 1501

Like Domenico Bruni, Agostino Strozzi denies that women are weak and inferior, and uses exemplary characters in order to praise them. In the *Defensio
mulierum* (*La defensione delle donne*), written anonymously and published only

in 1876, Strozzi tells the story of Susannah, whose virtue was endangered by two elders.[8]

Agostino Strozzi, *La defensione delle donne* (Bologna, 1876, repr. 1968), pp. 124–5.

As the Holy Scriptures bear witness, Susannah would rather have become a prisoner without committing an evil action than sin before God, even if she could have done so in secret. In fact, while she was washing herself in her garden, two lecherous old men, who were judges of the Jewish nation, accused her of adultery. Finding herself in great distress, and forced either to betray her faithfulness to her husband, or be charged and sentenced to death for the false accusation of the two evil elders, she recommended herself to God, and cried out loudly. [At this] her servants arrived, and she was freed from the lust of those shameless old men. Having been accused by the false testimony of the two elders, she was freed with the help of God, who inspired the young Daniel [to defend her]. The two wicked elders having been condemned to the torment they deserved, she was acquitted with the approval of all the people.

FAMOUS WOMEN AMONG THE ANCIENTS

5.7 A faithful wife: Penelope

The story of Penelope, wife of Ulysses, as told in the *Odyssey*, is used by Boccaccio to highlight her exceptional virtues, such as modesty, chastity and constancy. Her weaving made her also an example of womanly industriousness.

Betussi/Boccaccio (1596), pp. 96–9.

Penelope, a most holy and eternal example of modesty and womanly chastity, was the daughter of Icarius and wife of Ulysses, a stern husband. Destiny fought strenuously against her modesty, but in vain. When she was still a young maiden, and worthy of being loved by many because of her great beauty, her father gave her in marriage to Ulysses, and she had a son by him, Telemachus. Then her husband was called by the Greeks to the siege of Troy and was taken there almost by force, thus abandoning her, and leaving her to his father Laertes and his mother Anticlia, together with their small son.

During Ulysses's long absence, Penelope lived chastely as a widow.

8 For Agostino Strozzi, see Benson, pp. 45, 47–56.

Being, however, [a woman] of singular beauty, commendable morals and high lineage, she greatly excited the hearts of many men from Ithaca, Cephalonia and Etholia to love and desire her. [...] She saw that there was no way she could refuse [a new marriage] for long, and feared that her pure intention [to keep chaste] would be stained. By divine inspiration, she cunningly decided to deceive her suitors for some time. She therefore asked them to be allowed to wait for the return of her husband till she had finished weaving that cloth which, according to the custom of royal women, she had begun. Her suitors agreed to this, and she, with feminine cunning, unpicked at night what she had woven during the day. With this trick she held them off for a considerable time, [but] she could not deceive them for much longer. In the meantime, they consumed Ulysses's wealth in banquets and festivities.

[...]

Her virtuous fortitude is the more praiseworthy because it is found only rarely, and because, having been tempted and attacked by many, she steadfastly opposed them.

5.8 A chaste widow: Dido, Queen of Carthage

Dido, whose story is told in Virgil's *Aeneid*, is for Boccaccio an example of chastity suitable for widows.

Betussi/Boccaccio (1596), p. 107.

O, inviolate ornament of chastity, O, honoured and eternal spectacle of widowhood! Dido, I would like widows, especially Christian ones, to direct their eyes towards you, to reflect on your fortitude and, if they can, contemplate in their minds your most chaste body wet with innocent blood. I especially say this to those widows who thought that marrying not only twice, but three or more times is something most trivial.

5.9 An exemplary queen: Semiramis, 1501

For Agostino Strozzi, Semiramis, Queen of Assyria, is an exemplary figure for wives of rulers because of her ability and intelligence.

Strozzi, pp. 102–3.

After the death of her husband Nino, Semiramis obtained the kingdom of Assyria in place of her vile, slothful and worthless son. She achieved many wonderful things in virtue of her great and generous spirit, more than men deem fitting to the female sex. In fact, with extraordinary cunning she occupied the throne which should have gone to her son, and pretended for a long time that she was a man. She valiantly controlled those barbarous and fierce peoples, and ruled over them with great authority. And not only did she keep her empire, which her husband Nino had acquired, with great skill, but she increased it, extending its borders to Ethiopia and India. She enlarged the city of Babylon, and surrounded it with brick walls of wondrous width and height.

5.10 The queens of the Amazons, 1552

Wives of rulers could find suitable role models also in Domenico Bruni's *Difesa delle donne*. Here he writes about Marpesia and Lampo, queens of the Amazons.

Bruni, fols 33r–34r.

These women [the Amazons] lived in Scythia, a very wild country. Two young noble and royal men, Scolapius and Sylisius, arrived there by chance, together with some of their people, and began to loot and kill. The women, enraged, killed them all, and also fought against other enemies, driving them away. During many wars, all their neighbours were humiliated into asking for peace, which they granted them. Those courageous women would never take husbands. At times some of them went to live with their neighbours, and as soon as they were pregnant they would return to their country. Of all the babies who were born, they would kill the boys and keep the girls, whom they would not train to spin, weave or sew, but to make war, handle weapons, joust and do other military drills. They would cut off the right breast [of the baby girls] as soon as they were born, burning [the wound], so that they could then hold well a spear, and would keep the left breast to suckle the female babies who would be born to them. These Amazons were so fierce and strong that they occupied not only the neighbouring towns, but also the whole of Scythia, part of Europe and also part of Asia. One of the two sister queens would go to war, and the other would stay to take care of the government of their nation.

5.11 **In praise of Roman heroines and of the Sabine women, 1528**

The writings of Roman historians were a rich source of exemplars for both men and women. The behaviour of Roman heroes and heroines could be adapted to suit different political systems, so that their stories were admired both by the upholders of Florentine or Venetian republicanism, and by the apologists of aristocratic rulers. Two interlocutors in Castiglione's *Il libro del Cortegiano* praise Roman heroines and the Sabine women.

Castiglione, ed. Longo (1981), pp. 286–7, 297–8.

Book III, xxi and xxii

[Gasparo Pallavicino]: 'If I asked you who are, or were, the great women as worthy of praise as the great men whose wives, sisters or daughters they were, who either benefited them, or corrected their mistakes, I think you would be unable [to answer].'

'Truly,' answered the Magnificent Giuliano [de' Medici], 'nothing else could stop me [from answering], except [their] great number. If I had enough time, with regard to this matter I would tell you the story of Octavia, wife of Mark Anthony and sister of Augustus; of Portia, daughter of Cato and wife of Brutus; of Gaia Caecilia, wife of Tarquinius Priscus; of Cornelia, daughter of Scipio, and of an infinite number of others who are most famous; and not only of our own [Latin] women, but also of the non-Latin.

[...]

Book III, xxx

[Giuliano de' Medici]: 'After a cruel battle between Romans and Sabines, with very great losses on both sides, they were getting ready for another bloody battle, when the Sabine women, dressed in black, and with their hair loose and dishevelled, crying, miserable, without fear of the weapons which were ready for battle, came between their fathers and their husbands, begging them not to stain their hands with the blood of their fathers-in-law and their sons-in-law. If they were unhappy with these family ties, they should turn their weapons towards the women, as it was much better to die than to live as widows, or without fathers and brothers, remembering that their children were born from those who had killed their fathers, or that they themselves had been born from those who had killed their husbands. Many women, moaning and weeping thus, carried their babies in their arms, many of whom were beginning to talk, and it seemed that they wanted to call and greet their grandfathers. The women, showing them their grandchildren, cried: "Here is your blood, which with such vehemence and ferocity you are trying to shed with your own hands". In this instance the women's piety and prudence had such strength, that not only was an indissoluble friendship and alliance born between the two enemy kings, but, even more wonderful, the Sabine men went to live in Rome, and one people was made out of two. This concord greatly increased the power of Rome, on account of those wise and magnanimous women, who were rewarded by Romulus so that, when he divided all the people into thirty Curies, he named each of them after the Sabine women.'

5.12 A tale of rape and death, c.1504

The story of Lucretia, who upholds the good name of her family and commits suicide after telling her husband that she has been raped, was a well-known subject for painters throughout our period. It was also told by many writers, who derived it from Livy, Valerius Maximus and Boccaccio. This version is told by the *letterato* Bernardino Cacciante in a book written c.1504 at the court of Urbino, and dedicated to the Duchess Elisabetta Gonzaga.

Bernardino Cacciante, *Libretto Apologetico delle Donne*, in M. Martini, *Bernardino Cacciante Aletrinate, Contributo alla Storia dell'Umanesimo* (Sora, 1982), p. 67.

They tried to comfort her, telling her that a sin does not carry any punishment if there was no will to commit it, but they could not move her from her resolve. Having decided to die, she first asked everybody to swear that her dishonour would be avenged. She then said these magnanimous, prudent and chaste words to her husband Collatinus: 'What else can a woman lose, after she has lost her chastity? I confess that my body, not my soul, has committed an act that shames you. Therefore I want [my body] to be punished.'

As soon as she had finished this philosophical speech, without delay she courageously plunged a knife, which she was hiding in her right hand, into her left breast, without a moan or a lament. In this way she killed herself, since she wanted to die rather than live under such infamy.

5.13 Lucretia, an exemplar of female industriousness, 1545

Dolce (1547), fol. 11r–v.

When the son of Tarquinius arrived suddenly in Rome together with other young men in order to settle their contest against Collatinus about their wives' chastity, they found the women occupied in festivities and dances. Lucretia, however, sitting with her maids and having apportioned the work among them, was absorbed in her [spinning and weaving]. For this reason she was deemed to be the most chaste, and Collatinus won [the contest].

5.14 Two Roman virgins: Tuccia and Claudia, 1600

Fonte (1988), p. 54.

Since the ancient Romans and all other peoples greatly venerated virgins, regarding and honouring them as holy, the same happens in our times everywhere in the world. The vestal Tuccia carried water to the temple in a sieve because she had not coupled with a man. And Claudia, also a vestal, was able to pull ashore a ship with her girdle only because she was a virgin, while many thousand men had not been able to do it. This is because the woman who keeps apart from intercourse with men is an almost divine creature, and, keeping herself a virgin, can achieve wondrous things.

5.15 Camilla, Queen of the Volsci: beauty, bravery and virginity

Bruni, fol. 34r–v.

Camilla, Queen of the Volsci … was gifted with four worthy qualities: great beauty, a most strong and valiant build, a marvellous lightness and agility (so much so that it is written that she ran through a cornfield without bending or damaging one single earn of corn), and the most pure and intact virginity, so that she was deemed deserving to be called the Honour and Beauty of Italy. With many of her maids she fought against Aeneas as an ally of Turnus, and, fighting bravely, she died during that war.

5.16 A long list of chaste women, 1548

Printed collections of letters became a popular literary genre during the sixteenth century. Purporting to have gathered together letters written by women, the *letterato* Ortensio Lando published a very successful volume in 1548. The following letter is a spoof which satirises the lists of *exempla* fashionable at the time.

Lando (1548), fols 137v–138r.

From Francesca da Correggio Mainolda to Sister Chiara da Correggio:

Some days ago you asked me to write for you an exhortation to chastity, which some nuns who are dear friends of yours had requested, in which I should mention a good number of those who have happily embraced chastity. I have sent you (I do not know whether you have received it) a short Catalogue of chaste men which I put together with great difficulty, so that you yourself could write it without giving me this task, as I am very busy. In order for this undertaking to be successful, more extensive and effective, I would like to let you know that it will be appropriate to include Penelope, even if she was a pagan and even if there are some who do not agree she was chaste. I agree with Ovid who, in the third of his Elegies wrote about Penelope: *mansit, quanvis custode careret, internam multos intemerata procos.* You should also include Daphne, daughter of Paeneus; Biblia, wife of the Roman Duvillus. Remember the Roman Sophronia, and Zenobia, Queen of Palmyris; Etelphrida, Queen of Anglia; Boadicea; Dulo; Etheltruda; Sulpitia, daughter of Patercolo; Rodogune, daughter of Darius; Siritha, daughter of Sinaldus; Uria; the Greek Hippo; Timoclia; the Virgin Ciane from Syracuse; Medullina; Marcia, daughter of Varro, and Eugenia, daughter of the Proconsul of Alexandria, Philippus, who, fearing that the Emperor Commodus would rape her, disguised herself by wearing a monk's habit, hiding her sex and her name. In this way you will write [a work] which is copious and successful, and will free me from much trouble.

ANTI-HEROINES AND THEIR VICES

5.17 A warning for wives: Queen Vashti and Eve as negative examples, 1578

Bernardo Trotto, *Dialoghi del matrimonio, e vita vedovile* (Turin, 1578), p. 85.

Queen Vashti was called by her husband Ahasuerus, lord of one hundred and twenty-seven provinces between India and Ethiopia, so that everybody could see how beautiful she was wearing her crown. She refused to go to him, and, on the advice of his wise men, her husband repudiated her, so that women could learn from her that they have to obey their husband. The king took another wife in her place. Also, you know well that it is written that Adam was created first, and then Eve who, after their sin, turned towards him with humility.

5.18 Delilah, lustful and deceitful, 1588

In his collection of biographies of women from the Old and New Testament, dedicated to Margherita Gonzaga, Duchess of Ferrara, Tommaso Garzoni includes nine biographies of women who did not follow the virtuous path of modesty, chastity and obedience.

Garzoni, (1588), pp. 140–1.

I do not know whether it is possible to read of a more beautiful, a more fraudulent, a more brazen, a more perfidious woman among so many of ancient and modern times than the notorious Delilah. She was worthy of much praise for the beauty of her body, but was utterly odious and detestable to honourable people for the ugly and wicked vices of her soul. She lived (if a consistently dishonourable series of actions can be called 'life') around three thousand nine hundred and seventy-five years [after the creation] of the world. Her gross lust and her life were the opposite of the honour and chastity of two illustrious women of those times celebrated by historians and poets, Eleusina daughter of King Priamus, and Penelope, wife of the shrewd Ulysses, the great conqueror of cities, as Homer calls him. Consider them, rare paragons of chastity. Consider her, foul scum ... She was very skilful and knowledgeable in those arts which are known to all whores, and she could hold on to her lovers with deception and deceit, pretending to be yearning and dying of love. She was second to none in this, as will soon be shown, with damage and shame to her new lover [Samson], as he lost all the honour he had previously acquired and suffered disgrace and ignominy at the hand of his enemies.

5.19 Dido, a negative example of lust, 1544

Different literary traditions and an underlying ambiguity about the nature of women may be the reasons for conflicting interpretations of the lives of some 'illustrious women'. Dido, who was an *exemplum* of chastity in extract 5.8, is here obsessed by lust.

Giuseppe Betussi, *Il Raverta* (Venice, 1544), p. 94.

Dido, unable to hide her burning love for Aeneas, hurried like a fury around Carthage. Now she would lead him with her, showing him the riches of Tyre, now she would begin to speak, and then stop in mid-sentence. Again, she would try to have him present at royal banquets, and, almost crazed, would try to hear yet again the story of the Trojan massacre. If he left, the palace seemed empty to her. When she was with her lover, she would hear him, but think he was not there, and she would hold little Ascanius[9] on her lap and kiss him, as if he were the image [of his father]. The towers, which had begun [to be built], were not rising, nor were other buildings being finished. All work had been interrupted. Young men were not training to fight. All this because, trying to hide her love, and [instead] becoming more inflamed, she had completely changed from what she had been.

FAMOUS WOMEN AND RENAISSANCE WOMEN

Virtuous actions of 'famous women' were used by writers to inspire, describe or praise contemporary women. By the fifteenth century, it had become customary for *letterati*, poets and painters to eulogise aristocratic ladies by drawing elaborate parallels between them and the famous women of the past. Their writings show that it was important to distinguish between womanly virtue (*virtù femminile*), to which all women should aspire, and ladylike virtue (*virtù donnesca*), appropriate only to daughters and wives of rulers.

5.20 A comparison between a Florentine woman and ancient Roman heroines, 1480s

For Vespasiano da Bisticci, the Florentine Alessandra de' Bardi is an example of womanly virtuous behaviour worthy of being included in *De mulieribus claris*.

Vespasiano da Bisticci (1970–76), vol. 2, p. 464.

During these past evenings, you [Giovanni de' Bardi], Alessandro de' Bardi and myself, talked about the men of your House, and not only the men, but also the women, examples of modesty and chastity. We began to praise Alessandra, daughter of Bardo de' Bardi and wife of

---

9 Aeneas's son.

Lorenzo, son of Messer Palla di Nofri Strozzi. She was not inferior either to the Roman Sulpicia, or to Portia, daughter of Cato and wife of Marcus Brutus, conservator of the Roman Republic, about whom Boccaccio writes, together with [the lives] of many famous women. If she had been alive in his times, he would have celebrated her in his writing.

5.21 Examples for a learned woman, 1437

Isotta Nogarola (1418–66), like her sister Ginevra, was well-known by humanists in the Veneto for her learning. She had written to the famous educator Guarino da Verona (1374–1460), who did not reply to her letter. She then wrote to him again, complaining about the disadvantages of being a woman. Guarino finally answered her second letter, encouraging her with suitable examples.[10]

M. L. Lenzi, *Donne e Madonne. L'educazione femminile nel primo Rinascimento italiano* (Turin, 1982), p. 212.

Courage, Isotta, virago with a steadfast soul, compose yourself, and from this moment gather your troops and get ready to direct them against those who caused you offence, using me either as your captain or your comrade-in-arms! And if by chance your womanly modesty restrains you, remember that Dido, who undoubtedly was very chaste, was a woman, and so was Cornelia, the mother of the Gracchi, and who else? The Muses themselves, who instruct, teach and enlighten great men, divine poets ...

5.22 A literary gift to a great lady, 1492

Isabella d'Este, Marchioness of Mantua (1474–1539), thanks Giovanni Sabadino degli Arienti, on receiving a copy of his work, *Gynevera de le clare donne*, a collection of thirty-three biographies of famous and virtuous women, July 1492.[11]

R. Iotti, 'Phenice unica, virtuosa e pia', in D. Bini, ed., *Isabella d'Este, la primadonna del Rinascimento* (Modena, 2001), p. 172.

---

10 On Isotta Nogarola, see M. L. King, 'The Religious Retreat of Isotta Nogarola (1418–66)', in *Signs*, 3 (1978), pp. 807–22.
11 See C. James, *Giovanni Sabadino degli Arienti: A Literary Career* (Florence, 1996); S. D. Kolsky, '"Men framing women". Sabadino degli Arienti's "Gynevera de le clare donne" Reexamined', in M. Cicioni and N. Prunster, eds, *Visions and Revisions: Women in Italian Culture* (Providence, 1993).

Spectabilis et prestans amice noster charissime. Though, because of your fame, we had some previous knowledge of your virtue, in which we took delight, now you have become well-known to us from the work you sent us, *De mulieribus claris,* dedicated to the Illustrious Lady Ginevra Bentivoglio. Therefore not only we are led to hold you dear, but to love and admire you. This work, because it is written with great elegance and deals with a noble subject-matter, has been very welcome. We shall read it with care and we shall attempt to imitate the footsteps of those Illustrious Ladies.

5.23 A sonnet in praise of a woman warrior, Caterina Sforza, 1499

Because of her bravery and courage, Countess Caterina Sforza (*c.*1462–1509), the 'Lady of Forlì', was praised by both Francesco Guicciardini and Niccolò Machiavelli. The poet Antonio Pistoia compares her to the heroines Camilla and Judith in the first of a series of seven sonnets dedicated to her on the occasion of her defence of the fortresses of Imola and Forlì (November 1499–January 1500) against Cesare Borgia.

V. Olivastri, 'Composizioni poetiche di Antonio Pistoia dedicate a Caterina Sforza', in *Caterina Sforza: una donna del Cinquecento* (exhibition catalogue, Imola, 2000), pp. 125–6.

> He wins who, fighting, longer lasts.
> You[12] who guard the fortress of Imola,
> if death wins over you while you defend it,
> your fame will be forever ensured.
>
> Do not give in to bribes or fear,
> as did the traitor Bernardin da Corte,
> but you, Lady of Forlì, do not leave
> through the gates to re-enter through the walls.
>
> Until now the spirit of Camilla
> is united with your fertile body
> as the lively pupil in a human eye.
>
> Your courage is such, Lady,

---

12 The remarks against surrender or betrayal in the first two stanzas are addressed to the captain of the fortress of Imola, Dionigi Naldi da Brisighella, who in fact did surrender in December 1499.

that you make all other strength seem frail.
Fortune is propitious, and the heavens favour you.
In antiquity, Judith killed
with just deception the adulterer.[13]
You by strength and virtue shall defeat the enemy.

5.24 More beautiful than Venus: Lucrezia Borgia as a bride, 1502

On their progress from their native city towards their new home, royal brides were welcomed with ephemeral *apparati* and with floats and chariots carrying allegorical or mythological figures, charged with appropriate symbolism. In their report to Ercole d'Este, Duke of Ferrara, Giovanni Luca da Pontremoli and Gerardo Saraceno describe the celebrations for the triumphal entry into the town of Foligno of Alfonso d'Este's bride, Lucrezia Borgia, during her journey from Rome to Ferrara.

F. Gregorovius, *Lucrezia Borgia* (Rome, 1969, first printed Stuttgart, 1874), p. 226.

[13 January 1502]

[Lucrezia Borgia] was met near the city gate by a chariot above which was a figure representing the Roman Lucretia with a dagger in her hand. She recited some verses, saying that she would give way and surrender to Her Ladyship, who surpassed her in modesty, prudence and constancy. Then, on the square, there was a triumphal chariot with a small Cupid in front of it. On the chariot was Paris with the golden apple in his hand, who recited some poetry. He said that he had already assigned the apple to Venus, who was more beautiful than Juno and Pallas Athena. Now, however, he would have to revoke his judgment, and give the apple to Her Ladyship because she was superior to those three goddesses, since she had more beauty, wisdom and wealth.

5.25 An apartment fit for a duchess, 1562

While painted representations of 'illustrious women' had appeared since the fourteenth century in domestic interiors and in the decoration of rulers' palaces, Giorgio Vasari's cycle of 1561–62 for the apartment of the Duchess of Florence Eleonora di Toledo in the Palazzo della Signoria, which he describes here in his *Zibaldone*, is exceptional for its scope and complexity.

13 Holofernes.

The frescoes are meant both to inspire the Duchess and to praise her, in the context of the virtues of these famous women.[14]

Giorgio Vasari, *Il libro delle Ricordanze di Giorgio Vasari*, ed. A. del Vita (Arezzo, 1938), pp. 86–7.

1562. I note that on January 10, having finished the rooms downstairs, we raised and rebuilt the ceilings of the 4 chambers of the Duchess Eleonora di Toledo, on the same storey as the chapel. First of all we finished the one before the '*camera verde*', where in a large oval we painted the story of the Sabine women bringing peace between their husbands and their kin, with eight small oil paintings with various virtues, and a frieze with putti and *grottesche*. In the next chamber are stories concerning Queen Esther. In the painting in the middle [of the ceiling] she, kneeling in front of King Ahasuerus, asks that she should be forgiven and the Jewish people be spared. Around the frieze are eight gilded ovals with eight medallions with her stories, and a frieze in oil, with putti and the name of the Duchess Eleonora.

In the same year we continued painting the next room, with a large roundel in the middle [of the ceiling], with the story of Penelope dealing with her domestic business while Ulysses is away at the [Trojan] war, with four figures in the corners in oil on wood, and a frieze around the room, with stories of Ulysses, painted in fresco with stucco frames.

5.26 The Duchess of Florence is compared to Juno, 1558–60

In Giorgio Vasari's *Ragionamenti*, a dialogue between Francesco de' Medici and Vasari himself which describes the fresco cycles decorating the Apartment of the Elements and the Apartment of Leo X in the Palazzo della Signoria in Florence, Eleonora di Toledo, Francesco's mother, is eulogised by a comparison with Juno.

Vasari (1906, repr. 1981), vol. 8, pp. 73–4.

Your Excellency knows that Jupiter and Juno, who was not only Jupiter's sister, but also his wife, were born from Ops and Saturn. We can refer [the qualities of these gods] to what is similar in the soul of

---

14 On Vasari's decoration for Eleonora's apartment, see the following essays in Eisenbichler: Tinagli, 'Eleonora and her "Famous Sisters"', pp. 119–35; I. Hoppe, 'A Duchess' Place at Court: the Quartiere di Eleonora in the Palazzo della Signoria in Florence', pp. 98–118; P. J. Benson, 'Eleonora di Toledo among the Famous Women: Iconographic Innovation after the Conquest of Siena', pp. 136–56.

the Lord Duke, your father, and of the most illustrious Lady Duchess, your mother. Certainly, like Juno, she is the goddess of the air, of riches, reigns and marriages. There has never been a lady among the mortals on this earth, who was more serene than air, because with her countenance, majesty, beauty and grace, she always makes the clouds of passion and the winds of painful sighs disappear from her servants and subjects. She made the rain of tears stop in the miserable hearts of the afflicted and of all those who, in their troubles, told her with imploring voices about their difficulties. … As for being the goddess of marriages, nobody more than Her Excellency has favoured marriages among her servants, and has arranged, and every day arranges, marriages among the citizens … And who is similar to her in fecundity and in the happy outcome of childbirth? Juno was called Lucina for this very reason.

5.27 A tribute to the Duchess of Ferrara, 1588

In his dedication of *Le vite delle donne illustri della scrittura sacra* to Margherita Gonzaga, Duchess of Ferrara, Tommaso Garzoni compares her to exemplary biblical women.

Garzoni (1588), unpaginated.

Who will ever be able to deny (leaving aside any adulation) that Your Most Serene Highness could equal, in fact surpass, the Queen of Sheba for nobility of blood, since you belong to two most illustrious houses, Austria and Gonzaga? That in wealth you could contend with Esther, since you are the wife of such a rich lord as the great Duke of Ferrara? That in beauty you could equal the beautiful Abisaac, since you are as welcome to the great Alfonso [d'Este] as she was to King David? That you resemble Rachel in grace and loveliness, since you made your lord burn with love, as she did Jacob? That you are another Susannah in your chastity, since you are praised for this [virtue] by everybody, as she was by the Jewish nation? That you can be compared for your wisdom with the wise Judith, for your sagacious and prudent answers to all who test your lively intellect? And to conclude, [who will deny] that, as far as the various virtues your soul possesses, you are like Sarah in conjugal faith, the Magdalene in piety, Martha in devotion, Rebecca in kindness of heart, Abigail in advice, the Mohabitan in charity, Bathsheba in gravity and in majesty?

Part II
Life cycles

6 Girls

The life of an individual in Renaissance society was circumscribed by gender as well as by the social rank into which he or she was born.[1] While boys were brought up and trained to take their place, according to their rank, in the social, political and economic life of the city, the lives of almost all girls from all ranks were shaped from birth by the expectation that they would marry. They were brought up to be modest, obedient and industrious, since it was believed that virtuous conduct was incompatible with being lazy or wasting time. In order to preserve their modesty and chastity, treatises on the upbringing of girls stressed the need for constant surveillance and the dangers of male company.[2]

It must be remembered, however, that these theoretical writings would have concerned only a small section of Renaissance society, and that the ideals they expound, such as timidity, modesty and chastity, would in reality have been irrelevant in the day-to-day struggle of the majority of the population against poverty and hardship. Sources dealing with the lower ranks of society provide glimpses of girls' lives which were much less circumscribed by parental control, and reveal an existence very different from the protected, ordered lives advocated in treatises on upbringing for the girls of higher social ranks.

The need to safeguard their virtue also conditioned the scope of girls' education, which was imparted at home or within the protective walls of the convent.[3] While at the beginning of the period under consideration literacy, even for girls of mercantile families, was discouraged in

---

1 See S. Chojnacki, 'Daughters and Oligarchs: Gender and the Early Renaissance State', in J. C. Brown and R. C. Davis, eds, *Gender and Society in Renaissance Italy* (London and New York, 1998), pp. 63–86.

2 On childhood and the family, see: J. B. Ross, 'The Middle-Class Child in Urban Italy, 14th to Early 16th Century', in L. de Mause, ed., *The History of Childhood* (New York, 1974), pp. 183–228; C. Klapisch-Zuber, 'Childhood in Tuscany at the Beginning of the Fifteenth Century', in Klapisch-Zuber, pp. 94–116; S. Chojnacki, 'Measuring Adulthood: Adolescence and Gender in Renaissance Venice', in Chojnacki, pp. 185–205.

3 P. F. Grendler, *Schooling in Renaissance Italy: Literacy and Learning, 1300–1600* (Baltimore, 1989); S. Strocchia, 'Learning the Virtues: Convent Schools and Female Culture in Renaissance Florence', in B. Whitehead, ed., *Women's Education in Early Modern Europe: A History, 1500–1800* (New York, 1999), pp. 3–46; G. Zarri, 'Christian Good Manners: Spiritual and Monastic Rules in the Quattro- and Cinquecento', in Panizza, pp. 76–91.

favour of an education based on the teaching of household skills, the realities of family life, as we shall see in the following chapters, required a better education for the women of the middle ranks. This important change was also brought about by the advent of printing, which made books more widely available.

THE BIRTH OF A DAUGHTER

6.1 A notary records the birth of his daughters, Siena, 1382–90

Memorie and *Ricordanze* were written by the head of a household to record important events pertaining to the family. Factual information was noted without comment, but with precision of detail.[4] These extracts from the *Memorie* of the wealthy Sienese notary Ser Cristofano di Galgano Guidini (c. 1345–1410) provide information about godparents,[5] the reasons for the choice of names, and about the very common practice of placing babies with wet-nurses away from home.[6]

C. Guidini, 'Ricordi di Cristofano Guidini', ed. C. Milanesi, *Archivio storico italiano*, VI/1 (1843), pp. 43–4.

My daughter Nadda ... was born on 14 July 1382. Her mother had her till September 28, and on that day we put her out to nurse with Monna Nuta, the wife of Donato di Ruggiero from Rapolano, for 55 *soldi* a month. She had her for 22 months. She was paid in full in many instalments. In addition to that time, she kept her for an extra two months without being paid.

AD 1387, on the 12th day of February, the first day of Lent, in the morning during the sermon, I had a girl born to my wife. She was born in my house at Uvile.[7] She was baptised on the 12th day of February, and was called Agnese, after my mother, who was called that. The godparents were Ser Francesco, the priest, who lived in Chiuslino, and Monna Gemma del Mannaia.

---

4 On *Ricordanze*, see: G. Ciappelli, 'Family Memory: Functions, Evolution, Recurrences', and N. Rubinstein, 'Family, Memory and History', both in G. Ciappelli and P. L. Rubin, eds, *Art, Memory and Family in Renaissance Florence* (Cambridge, 2000), pp. 26–38 and 39–47. See also J. Grubb, 'Memory and Identity: Why Venetians Didn't Keep *Ricordanze*', *Renaissance Studies*, 8 (1994), pp. 375–87.
5 See L. Haas, '"Mio Buon Compare": Choosing Godparents and the Uses of Baptismal Kinship in Florence', *Journal of Social History*, 29:2 (winter 1995), pp. 341–50.
6 Cristofano Guidini married Mattea di Fede in 1375. Between 1380 and 1389 they had three daughters and four sons. Mattea and all the children, except Nadda, died in the plague outbreak of 1390.
7 Ovile, an area of Siena near the city gate which bears the same name.

On the 23rd day of July 1390 Agnese died, and she was buried in St Peter's at Uvile.

AD 1389, on the 19th of July, I had a girl born to my wife Mattia. She was born in my house at Uvile, and was baptised on the 20th day of July. She was called Caterina, in honour of the Blessed Caterina.[8] In her honour the godmother was Caterina di Ghetto, also a Mantellata nun at Camporeggi,[9] who was the special spiritual daughter of the said venerable Caterina.

On the 18th day of August of the said year [1390] we put out the said Caterina to nurse with Monna Pia [...] who lives near Uvile, next to the wall of the Commune, for 4 *lire* a month.

On the last day of August, at the sixth hour,[10] the said Caterina died. God bless her. She was buried in St Peter's. On that day the said wet-nurse had 20 *soldi* and other things, and she has been fully paid.

6.2 The joy of having a daughter, Venice, 1537

While the birth of a son was celebrated as a means of assuring the future of the family name, daughters were by no means unwelcome. After the baptism of his illegitimate daughter Adria, Pietro Aretino writes from Venice to her godfather, the painter Sebastiano del Piombo.[11]

Aretino, vol. 1, pp. 214–15.

[June 1537]

God wanted this creature to be a girl, while I, with a father's inclination, was anticipating a boy. But it is true that females, except for the risk to their chastity which is so highly regarded by the good, give more comfort to us. This is how things are: a boy at twelve or thirteen begins to chafe under a father's restraint, and, having finished with school and obedience, makes those who gave him life and birth regret it. And what matters more are the rude manners, the threats with which, day and night, boys attack their father and mother, which are the cause for curses and God's punishment. But a girl is the refuge where her parents can rest when they are old. No hour goes by without them enjoying her lovingness, expressed as attentive care and

---

8 St Catherine of Siena, who was a good friend of Guidini's.

9 The convent of S. Domenico at Camporegio, in Siena, where St Catherine had been a 'Mantellata'. The Mantellate belonged to the Dominican Tertiary Orders.

10 Approx. 1 a.m.

11 Adria was the first of Aretino's three illegitimate daughters. She was brought up in her father's house until her marriage in 1549.

prompt kindness towards their needs. Therefore, once I had cleared my heart of the disappointment that others feel at having a girl as the fruit of their loins, I was won over by natural tenderness at her resemblance to me, so that in that moment I felt all the sweetness of blood ties. And because I was worried that she would die without tasting life, I had her baptised at home. For this, a gentleman, in your place, held her according to Christian custom. I did not say anything to you, because we thought she would fly to heaven at any moment. But Christ has kept her as a solace of my old age, and as a witness for that life which was given to me, and I gave to her, and I thank him, praying him to give me life till the day we celebrate her wedding. During this time I must become her plaything, because we are our children's jesters. In fact in their simplicity they trample on us, pull our beard, slap us in the face, ruffle our hair, and with these tokens they buy the kisses with which we smother them, and the embraces with which we bind them [...] God save my daughter, because I surely would die if she merely suffered, let alone died, as she has such a lovely nature. Her name is Adria, and I gave her this name because it was God's will that she was born on these shores.[12]

UPBRINGING

All the treatises in this section, whatever their date, insist on constant supervision from a girl's parents, especially mothers, in order to guard her chastity and innocence. The ideal girl needs to be protected from the dangers of the world, while her character is moulded by religious practices and moral exemplars. Particular care is taken to ensure that her companions are trustworthy and virtuous.

6.3 An innocent girl? Siena, 1427

As a preacher in touch with the realities of life, S. Bernardino was well aware that the relentless task of controlling a girl's actions can fail, and that it is easy to fall short of the ideal. In a sermon delivered in the Piazza del Campo in Siena, he comments on the naivety of mothers and on the wayward behaviour of some daughters.[13]

---

12 On the Adriatic Sea.
13 On S. Bernardino, see C. Polecritti, *Preaching Peace in Renaissance Italy: Bernardino da Siena and his Audience* (Washington DC, 2000).

Bernardino da Siena, *Novellette ed esempi morali*, ed. A. Baldi (Lanciano, 1916), p. 129.

And I know there are those who say 'Oh, they are innocent!' And I am telling you that they are mischievous, and pretend they do not understand and do not know, but they understand very well the evil you [mothers] are doing. It is you who make them evil, and then you say 'They are innocent!' Do not say that, but rather 'They are wicked', because they understand more than they [the mothers] see. A woman who had a daughter took her to confession, and said to the confessor, 'Sire, this daughter of mine is so innocent: don't ask her about … you understand my meaning: innocent'. And when the priest asked about her, she was pregnant! This was the good innocent girl!

6.4 Advice to mothers, 1480s

Vespasiano da Bisticci (1999), pp. 124–5.

[Mothers] should bring up daughters in the fear of God. Make them go to confession many times during the year, according to their conscience … Get them accustomed to say, every day, the Office of Our Lady, if they know how to read, and above all, to spend time praying in the morning when they get up, as well as in the evening. Get them accustomed also to fast some days during the year … Do not let them chat with vain girls who are not chaste, and similarly do not allow them to chat with males, not even with their brothers once they are more than seven years old, nor to sleep, chat or anything. Above all, get them accustomed to learn everything expected from a woman: to work with her hands, and to know how to do all things proper to a household, so that she can give orders [to the servants] [...]

While they are still at home, the mother should not let her daughters go away from her till they are married. Do not let them go and stay away from home whether by day or night, whether with friends or relatives. They should be continuously under her care.

6.5 How to bring up a daughter

Dolce (1547), fols 8v, 10v–11r, 12v.

Her first games should be with girls of her own age … I consider that these childish games should in their character almost amount to a blueprint for a chaste and virtuous woman's life. Therefore, I advise that those silly dolls which are fashionable in every house, dressed and adorned with jewels and various clothes, and which almost resemble idols, are removed from her. She should instead be given utensils for every type of housework, scaled down in size, and made of wood and of various metals [...]

Besides this, stories, which innocent children like so much, should not be those which simple and rough women usually tell, but wholesome, imaginative and exemplary. She who has been entrusted, almost like a wise and diligent Architect, with the care of this edifice, should use pleasant inventions, sometimes awakening in the girl the love of God, sometimes alluding to the reverence due to her mother, and sometimes to this or that virtue.

My third consideration is that in the presence of our daughters we must be wary of indulging in any act which is less than honest, or saying any lascivious or inconsiderate word

[...]

As soon as the girl reaches the right age to learn to read and write, I want the father to consider two aims for her: one is religion, the other is the management of the household. Accordingly, he should strive to see that she is trained in virtuous practices and in activities pertaining to a future housewife. Amongst virtuous practices, we would place first the knowledge of God and of chastity. The former is relevant to the formation of the soul, the latter to the actions of the body [...] Two things I would look for in a daughter: timidity and modesty, which should almost be the basis and foundation of the entire fabric with which we intend to construct her. Without these, I believe, the whole edifice would crumble. Therefore, most importantly, both need to be planted in her, cultivated and strengthened from time to time

[...]

A daughter should be able to sew at least sufficiently well, because sewing belongs to woman as writing does to man [...] I would also like a daughter to be trained to do housework ... for example how to equip a bedroom, make the bed, organise the household goods in such a way that they are well ordered, so that the whole house may seem to rejoice and be full of happiness. She should also be trained in the kitchen, learning how to cook and how to present food, which I would like her for the most part to take care of and organise.

6.6 **Strict instructions for adolescent girls, 1546**

Juan Luis Vives gives detailed instructions for the upbringing of a girl approaching puberty, and advises how to curb her awakening sexual desires. Vives, fol. 83r.

Fasting often will be useful to curb the fires of the flesh, but she should not weaken herself. These fasts should be real and holy. Her food should not be too refined or spicy, [as] our first mother [Eve] was driven from paradise because of what she had eaten ... Her bed should not be too soft, and the same [should be true of] her clothes, which should be clean, without stains, because a clean soul enjoys the body's cleanliness. A weak and base soul, on the contrary, enjoys silk garments, believing other clothes to be harsh and intolerable.

APPEARANCE AND DRESS

The preoccupation with girls' virtues, especially chastity and modest behaviour, was also paramount in matters concerning their appearance, in the belief that simplicity and lack of artifice were signs of inner virtue.

6.7 **Unadorned simplicity is best**

Dolce (1547), p. 28.

Our girl should not dirty her face with cosmetics, but should wash it with pure water. She should not colour her hair, but keep it clean and free from dirt. She should not delight in scents, but should be careful that no bad smell comes from her. She should look in the mirror not to dress her braids with exaggerated care, but to wind them [around her head] simply, seeing that, as a modest virgin, nothing in her body could give occasion for criticism. If she is beautiful, she should take care that her soul is not ugly. If she is ugly, she should endeavour to compensate for the ugliness of the body with the beauty of the soul.

6.8, 6.9 **Sumptuary laws in Tuscany**

Sumptuary laws controlled the way in which different social ranks could be distinguished by their clothing, and attempted to limit expenditure and use of precious materials. They were, however, notoriously difficult to implement. In the first extract the legislators are also interested in protecting morals.[14]

Siena, 1437

C. Falletti Fossati, *Costumi senesi nella seconda metà del secolo quattordicesimo* (Siena, 1881), p. 136.

For decorous modesty, and in order not to tolerate any more shameless demeanour from women, it was deliberated and ordered that from the middle of next May no woman or female child from the age of ten, when outside the home, would be allowed to wear and to show more flesh on the front than two fingers from the pit of the throat, so that no uncovered bosom is seen.

Florence, 1562

L. Cantini, *Legislazione toscana raccolta e illustrata*, 30 vols (Florence, 1802), vol. 4, p. 405.

Beside the general prohibitions, it is forbidden to any young unmarried girl, even if she is the daughter of a noble father or of a man eligible for office, to wear gowns or overgarments, either at home or outside, made of velvet, plush, damask or satin, but she is allowed to wear the same type of undergarments permitted for married women. She is allowed to wear on her head a gold garland, worth a maximum of 6 *scudi*, and a chain or a necklace of gold beads or garnet beads without enamel, the said chain or necklace worth a maximum of 12 *scudi*, including the workmanship, and a pair of rosaries made of gold, or of garnet without enamel, worth a maximum of 6 *scudi*, including the workmanship. And she is forbidden to wear shoes or slippers made of *drappo*,[15] but is allowed to wear a beret or a bonnet, and a hat of *drappo* and of straw, each of them worth a maximum of 4 *scudi*.

EDUCATION

Theories

Treatises on education generally stress that moral guidance and religious teaching are fundamental for both males and females, but their emphasis is different with regard to girls. Boys, being trained to take

14 See C. Kovesi Killerby, *Sumptuary Law in Italy, 1200–1500* (Oxford, 2001).
15 A very expensive silk or woollen cloth.

their place in trade, commerce or politics, need skills which are considered unsuitable or even harmful to women, whose tasks are ideally confined to running a household and taking care of the education of their children. St Paul's injunction against women taking on public roles, and the fear that learning could corrupt weak and impressionable female nature, are common to most treatises, both before and after the Counter Reformation. Changes in society and culture between the second half of the fourteenth and the sixteenth century (among which first and foremost is the diffusion of printed books) are, however, highlighted by the difference between the view that all learning is superfluous to women, since they only need practical household skills, and the recognition of society's need for literate women, within clear boundaries of social rank.

6.10 A practical upbringing, c.1360

Paolo da Certaldo, *Libro dei buoni costumi*, ed. A. Schiaffini (Florence, 1945), p. 126.

If you have a daughter, teach her to sew and not to read, because it is not proper for a woman to know how to read unless you want her to become a nun. If you want her to become a nun, place her in a convent before she is mischievous enough to understand the vanity of the world, and there she will learn to read … And teach her how to do all the housework, that is, how to make bread, prepare fowls, sift flour, cook, do the laundry, make the beds, spin, weave bags in the French manner or embroider with silk, cut linen and woollen cloth, repair the soles of stockings and all such things, so that when you marry her off she will not seem foolish, nor brought up in the wilderness. And you who have brought her up will not be cursed.

6.11 Advice on reading matter

From the 1662 simplified edition of Lodovico Dolce's 1545 *Dialogo della institution delle donne*.

Dolce, (1662), pp. 25–8.

I do not believe that a limit should be given either to woman or to man, apart from the fact that knowledge in more disciplines is appropriate to man, since he has to pursue gain not only for himself and his family, but also for the good of his Republic or of his Prince, and of his friends. But I would like woman, who has no task other than the management of her household, to be directed only towards the study of moral philosophy, because she is not to be a teacher to anyone other than herself and her children. It is not fitting for her to teach, nor to debate amongst men, as St Paul very precisely teaches her in his Epistle to the Corinthians, and in his advice to Timothy [...]

Up till this point I have moulded a girl who could be at the head of a kingdom as well as of a private household. Because this cannot be done without books, I think, without any doubt, that the two sacred volumes of the Old and New Testament will suffice, and also enable her to acquire knowledge of God. These she should keep in front of her day and night. As for commentaries, these should be by Ambrose, Augustine, Jerome and such like, and also some of the modern authors, with such understanding as the Lord deigns to give her. [...]

Now, there are many books in Latin, which I would not like chaste women to see and read. Amongst these I mean almost all the poets except for Virgil (though I would not advise them to read all of him) and some parts of Horace, that is, the most chaste and most moral ... Among prose writers, they should be able to look at all the works by Cicero, and all the historians, such as Livy, Sallust, Quintus Curtius, Tranquillus, Suetonius and the others, because from Cicero's lessons one can only gather *exempla* of virtues and good advice, and history is a teacher of life. Amongst the books in the vulgar tongue, they should shun all lascivious books, as one avoids serpents and other poisonous animals ... Among those which must be avoided are all the romances, first among them the great number on knights-errant and all the *novelle* and such [other] vain books. Among those deserving to be read are first of all Petrarch and Dante. In one they will find, together with the beauty of poetry in the vulgar tongue and Tuscan language, examples of the most honest and chaste love, and in the other an excellent portrayal of all Christian Philosophy. To these should be added spiritual works, and the good ones are well-known, from which, in my opinion, she will be able to learn all the virtues and the good and honest morals which belong to a gentlewoman.

6.12 Different learning for different ranks, 1584

The *Tre Libri dell'educazione cristiana dei figliuoli* of Silvio Antoniano (1540–1603), a product of the Catholic Reformation written under the guidance of Archbishop Carlo Borromeo, remained influential well into the nineteenth century. Antoniano is primarily interested in the moral instruction of children. He sees human beings, especially women, as weak and fallible, and needing constant control and correction. Girls are to be brought up segregated within the home until they are married.

E. Cattaneo, 'La cultura di San Carlo. San Carlo e la cultura', in N. Raponi and A. Turchini, eds, *Stampa, libri e lettere a Milano nell'età di Carlo Borromeo* (Milan, 1992), pp. 34–5.

As far as those [girls] of humble and poor rank are concerned, it would be appropriate that they should be able to read some prayer books, while those of middling rank should also be able to write a little. Those noble young girls who are mostly destined to become mothers of distinguished families, besides being able to read and write well, need to be also proficient in the first principles and elements of arithmetic. But I do not approve of them learning languages, oratory and how to write poetry together with male children, and under the guidance of the same teachers, nor can I discern how useful this could be for the common good, or for the particular good of these young girls. In fact, I fear that, since the female sex is by its very nature vain, it would become even more arrogant, and that women would want to teach, which is against the precepts of the apostle Paul ...

Therefore a good father should be satisfied with his daughter reciting the Office of the Most Holy Virgin, reading the lives of the saints and some spiritual books, and in the time remaining she should attend to spinning and sewing, and occupy herself with household duties.

6.13 A defence of women's learning, 1600

The commonly held belief that learning could corrupt female minds is elegantly refuted by 'Leonora', one of the participants in Moderata Fonte's dialogue.[16]

Fonte (1988), pp. 168–9.

Leonora continued: many forbid their women to learn to read and write, maintaining that this is the ruin of many women, almost as if from virtue its contrary, vice, would follow. They do not understand that ... someone who is ignorant can more easily fall into error than someone who is knowledgeable and intelligent, and that therefore experience shows that there are many more unchaste women who are

16 See P. Labalme, 'Venetian Women on Women: Three Early Modern Feminists', in *Archivio veneto*, 152 (1981), pp. 81–109, esp. pp. 87–91.

ignorant than learned and virtuous. How many servants who cannot read, how many peasants and plebeian females there are who, after a short struggle, let themselves be won over by their lovers, because they are simpler than we are. For the examples we have read, the advice we have collected, and [our] love of virtue, we strive to restrain ourselves, even if our senses were to tempt us. Only a few let themselves be carried by their appetites, and those few who err would have done so even without being able to read, because there are always easy ways to do wrong for those who want to, and who are prepared to satisfy their desires.

Realities

From the end of the fourteenth century onwards, girls belonging to the elite and to middle ranking families usually learned to read and write, and were also numerate. They would be taught at home, or less commonly at school, sometimes by female teachers. Convents, where girls from different social backgrounds lived as boarders together with novices, were popular as educational institutions where girls could be kept safe from the dangers of the world until they were married. After the Council of Trent more stringent measures concerning enclosure increased regulations and controls to limit the number of boarders, unless they wanted to become nuns.

6.14 Life in a convent, Padua, 1539

Pietro Bembo (1470–1547) writes from Rome to his illegitimate daughter Elena (b. 1528), a boarder in a convent in Padua.[17]

Pietro Bembo, *Delle lettere di M. Pietro Bembo* ..., vol. 4 (Venice, 1564) fol. 55r.

I received with great pleasure your last letter, in which you write that you are applying yourself diligently to the study of the humanities, but if I want to know how profitably, I should ask your teacher. He writes to me that you are learning nothing. Now, tell me how things are yourself. Then study more, and become as learned as possible, because you will never acquire any faculty which is superior to this. I like [what you say] about sewing, and, since you are under the care of the Lady Laura, I think that she is the best teacher of the art in your city or any

17 Elena was the daughter of Bembo's long-time companion, Faustina Morosina della Torre (d. 1535), who also gave him two sons. Elena was married in 1543.

other. I especially like that you have learned to say the offices, and that you are a good nun, because this will help you to become an abbess, when the time comes. And you will please me very much if you ask Our Lord God to help me to do His will. Thank the Mother Abbess for her greetings, and the Lady Laura, of [the order of] the Discalced Carmelites. Greet for me my Reverend relatives Noali, and take care to grow up following good and holy morals, and in bodily health.

6.15 Advice about devotional reading matter, 1556

The Dominican friar Remigio Nannini writes a dedicatory letter to Lucrezia Bini Giolito, wife of the Venetian publisher Gabriele Giolito, introducing his translation of the *Imitation of Christ*, and recommending it as reading matter for her four daughters.

P. Grendler, 'Form and Function in Italian Renaissance Popular Books', *Renaissance Quarterly*, 4:3 (1993), p. 465.

As during these last months you have been urging me to find some devotional books so that your daughters could learn reading and piety at the same time, ... I have deemed this one to be more appropriate than any other. For in this truly devout book, full of the loving comfort and strength typical of its good and Catholic author, there is a modest level of knowledge attuned to the capabilities of simple and childish minds, which with the fire of divine spirit try to understand things pertaining to God and religion ... I also much praise your loving feeling towards your children, and especially towards your daughters, to whom you are presenting books from which they can learn fear of God and Christian compassion. You do not act as many unwise mothers do, who prefer their daughters to learn a love sonnet rather than a prayer ... Female minds, especially when they are young, are like new vases ... which long retain the smell of the liquid they first contained ... Therefore get them to read good spiritual books.

SOCIAL BEHAVIOUR AND PASTIMES

6.16 Beautiful and virtuous: two young girls in Renaissance Florence

In his *Ricordi* (begun 1393) Giovanni di Pagolo Morelli (1371–1444) describes his sisters, Bartolomea (b. 1365) and Sandra (b. 1369). He praises their unaffected beauty, which is reflected in their frank and open manners. As well as with their physical appearance, he is also concerned with their virtues and with the way they had been brought up, so that they could take their place in the social life of their city.

Giovanni di Pagolo Morelli, 'Ricordi', in *Mercanti scrittori: Ricordi nella Firenze tra medioevo e rinascimento*, ed. V. Branca (Milan, 1986), pp. 153, 156.

[Bartolomea] was of normal height, with very beautiful hair, shining and blonde, with a very beautiful figure, so genteel that she was a delight. And among her beauties, she had hands like ivory, so well-made that they seemed painted by the hand of Giotto. They were smooth, the flesh soft, with fingers long and rounded like candles, the fingernails long and rounded, rosy and transparent. And virtues corresponded to these beauties, because she could do everything she wanted and was required of a woman. In everything she did she was most virtuous: refined and pleasing in her speech, unaffected and restrained in delivery, and eloquent. She was a self-confident, frank woman, with a virile soul, abundant in all virtues. She could read and write as well as any man. She could sing and dance perfectly, and she would have been able to serve at a banquet with men and women as properly as young men used to do at weddings and at similar occasions.

[...]

[Sandra] was of normal height, with olive and yet pale complexion. She was neither fat nor very thin, with a very beautifully shaped face and limbs. She knew what was proper for a well-brought up woman: she could embroider, read and write. She was very eloquent, a great speaker, and she knew well how to say what she wanted with self-confidence.

6.17 Festivities in Florence, 1432

A great number of festivities of various kinds allowed girls of higher ranks to play a public role in the life of Renaissance cities. The extract from Vespasiano da Bisticci's biography of Alessandra de' Bardi (1412–65) describes a reception held in the Piazza della Signoria for the visit of the ambassadors of Emperor Sigismund to Florence, 1432. The girls' beauty and grace, together with their careful training, are shown off as valuable accomplishments.[18]

Vespasiano da Bisticci (1976), vol. 2, pp. 478–9.

18 On public entertainment, see R. C. Trexler, *Public Life in Renaissance Florence* (Ithaca and London, 1980), pp. 235–40, and J. Bryce, 'Performing for Strangers: Women, Dance and Music in Quattrocento Florence', in *Renaissance Quarterly*, 54:1 (2001), pp. 1074–107.

They[19] invited a great crowd of young Florentine women, finely
dressed, most beautiful and seemly in body and mind, splendidly orna-
mented with pearls and jewels, wonderful to behold. Their dresses
were not cut low at the neck as they are today, but cut high in a fair
and modest fashion. Amongst these ladies was Alessandra, who was
the most beautiful and fair of all. Florence had at the time the most
beautiful and chaste women in Italy, and their fame had spread all over
the world. Just think whether nowadays they are still like that.
Alessandra, because she was the fairest and the most dexterous, was
seated next to the chief ambassador. With her was Francesca, the
daughter of Antonio di Salvestro Serristori. The others were seated
amongst the ambassadors. Alessandra had been betrothed that year,
but was not yet married.[20] When she and the other chaste young
women stood up to dance, the ambassadors were invited to join.
Everybody marvelled at the grace with which Alessandra danced.
Indeed, everything she did was well done. After they had danced for
some time a choice banquet was served, which was unusual in entertainments of this kind. On account of her dexterity Alessandra was
chosen to take a dish of sweetmeats to the ambassadors, with a napkin
of fine linen on her shoulder. She offered it to them most gracefully,
curtsying to the ground in a most natural way, as if she had never done
anything else in her life ... After the sweetmeats, she handed them
goblets of wine in a similar manner. She did all this as if she had
always done it, showing how carefully she had been brought up by her
accomplished mother, who had taught her well even in the smallest
things. After eating and more dancing, the ambassadors rose to depart,
as the hour was late, and they left, accompanied by a great number of
citizens together with the young people of the feast. Alessandra and
the most beautiful and noble of the young women walked on either
side of the [chief] ambassador, she on his right, with her hand on his
arm, and another [young woman] on his left. They went with the
ambassadors to the inn where they lodged, and the first ambassador
took from his finger a beautiful ring and gave it to Alessandra, and
gave another ring to her companion. The young men and women said
farewell to the ambassadors, and the men accompanied the ladies to
their houses.

19 The *Signoria*, the government of Florence.
20 Alessandra married Lorenzo di Palla Strozzi later in the same year.

6.18 **A May song, late sixteenth century**

Together with the weeks from Christmas to Lent (a period called *Carnevale*), the month of May was a time for songs, dances, parades and all kinds of festivities, in which girls and young men of all ranks took part. This is a song from Bologna for the 'May Countess', who sat on a decorated chariot for the May parade.

L. Frati, *La vita privata a Bologna, dal secolo XIII al XVII* (Rome, 1968), p. 145.

> Give honour to the Countess,
> You who are walking by.
> Because she should be seen
> We have placed her up on high.
> Give honour to the Countess.

6.19 **Comments on the moral dangers of dancing, 1546**

Vives, fol. 109v.

Why do girls dance so much, leaning on the men's arms so that they can jump higher? Why do they stay on till the middle of the night, till they are tired? If they were told to go to church, they would say that they cannot go, unless by horse or carriage. Does this not show that they are obviously troubled by the furies? I remember hearing that some inhabitants of the distant lands of Asia, seeing our young women dance, run away in fear, saying that [the women] were moved by a new and strange frenzy. And in truth, don't our women appear frenzied to those who have never seen them dancing? ... Christian virgins should keep themselves far from this, because according to a Gentile doctor, nobody dances unless he is mad.

POOR GIRLS

Life in a charitable institution

The precarious and difficult lives of poor girls were often dominated by the presence of charitable institutions, usually financed by private or corporate donations and bequests. Illegitimate children, or children whose parents could not provide for them, were left to the care of *ospedali*, where they were brought up. Babies and young children were placed into the *pila*, an opening in the wall of the *ospedale* housing a cradle (which later in our period was usually fitted with a revolving mechanism called *ruota*, the 'wheel') with some tokens, such as a coin, or at times just a scrap of paper with their name. Once received within the *ospedale*, they were given over to the care of a wet-nurse, sometimes within the institution, but often living outside, and were then returned to the *ospedale* at the age of three. From the age of nine the girls would learn a trade such as sewing or weaving, or work in the *ospedale* as servants. On reaching marriageable age, they were provided with a small dowry so that a husband could be found for them. The *ospedali* were usually founded by laymen, and organised by lay administrators, but the care of children was seen as an act of Christian charity.[21]

6.20 Abandoned girls and a charitable institution, 1480s

These extracts from the records of the Ospedale di S. Maria della Scala, San Gimignano, give indications about the circumstances which led to children being abandoned.

L. Sandri, *L'ospedale di S. Maria della Scala di S. Gimignano* (Florence, 1982), pp. 76, 82, 83.

On Tuesday 3rd October 1458, a little girl was left in the *pila*. We do not know her name because who brought her did not want to tell us, and left quickly. We know she came from Pisa, and is two months old. She had with her an old kerchief, and an old swaddling cloth made of sack, in three pieces, and a small cap for her head, and as a sign she was wearing around her neck half a Pisan *quattrino*.

[1449]

The name of the girl who was brought to us on Wednesday 3rd September ... at the hour of the Vespers, is Maria Agostina. Her father, Santi di Cione from Castelfiorentino, brought her. He said that his wife had died, and he was now alone and so poor that he could not bring her up, and therefore he brought her to the Hospital. He said that the girl was three weeks old, and he brought three linen cloths, one old piece of wool cloth, and a good swaddling cloth. Note that Santi, her father, said that he would like to come here and work as a servant, and would pay for the girl's wet-nurse out of his salary.

---

21 On charitable institutions and *ospedali* for abandoned children, see: P. Gavitt, *Charity and Children in Renaissance Florence: the Ospedale degli Innocenti, 1410–1536* (Ann Arbor, 1990); R. C. Trexler, 'The Foundlings of Florence, 1395–1455', in Trexler, vol. 1, pp. 7–34.

[1418]

The name of the girl who was placed in the wheel on Saturday 28th May at the third hour,[22] on S. Bartolo's eve, is Antonia. She is about two years old, and she is the daughter of Antonio del Conte. She was born in Caggio in the neighbourhood of Colle, and she is legitimate. She has been placed in the hospital because of great poverty following her father's death.

6.21 The adoption of a girl from the Innocenti, 1588

The *guardiani* of the *ospedali* often found adoptive parents for the foundlings. This extract from the journal of the Florentine Ospedale degli Innocenti documents the adoption of a girl.

M. Fubini Leuzzi, "'Dell'allogare le fanciulle degli Innocenti'": un problema culturale ed economico, 1577–1652', in P. Prodi, ed., *Disciplina dell'anima, disciplina del corpo e disciplina della società tra medioevo e età moderna* (Bologna, 1994), p. 883.

4 August 1588

Giovanni di Marco from San Donato a Filetto, who lives in the Podesteria of Poppi in Casentino, and his wife Sandra, nursed and brought up Sandrina, a girl from our Hospital, who today is about 9 years old, and whom they both love as a daughter. Inspired by charity and pity, and considering how God is grateful to those who protect the children abandoned by their own parents and left in this Hospital … the said Giovanni, in his own name and in the name of his wife, of his own free will has asked our Hospital to keep Sandrina in his house at his own expense. As their adoptive daughter, they will teach her virtue and good habits according to her ability, and will put her on the right path, so that she will live honourably. When the time comes, they will marry her or put her into a convent as appropriate, according to her rank, and will give her at least 40 gold *scudi* as alms, and what more they are able or want to give her then. They will take good care of her and will not make her go without anything, according to their abilities, as if she was their daughter.

---

22 Approx. 10 p.m.

6.22 Girls in moral danger, Rome, 1586–92

Girls who lived in morally dubious circumstances, and who seemed likely to become prostitutes, were admitted, sometimes forcibly, to another type of charitable institution. There they were taught religious devotions and such suitable practical skills as sewing. Once a girl reached marriageable age and received an offer of marriage, she was given a small dowry. If no offer was forthcoming, she would continue to live within the institution as a servant or teacher.

The Confraternity of S. Caterina della Rosa in Rome grew from the earlier Compagnia delle Vergini Miserabili thanks to the effort of Ignatius Loyola. After 1555, the confraternity expanded to have under its administration a boarding establishment for girls in moral danger, a refuge for widows and unhappily married women, and a convent of Augustinian nuns.[23] Here, members of the Confraternity of S. Caterina della Rosa record their visits to young girls with a view to admitting them to their institution.

A. Camerano, 'Assistenza richiesta e assistenza imposta: il Conservatorio di S. Caterina della Rosa di Roma', in *Quaderni storici*, 82 (1993), pp. 236–7.

1586. I have visited for the first time Menica, [daughter] of Francesco the armourer ... The girl has been taken in by a neighbour, a poor woman, since her stepmother was driven out at the request of her neighbours because she was living as a whore, as she still is, and this is well known in the neighbourhood.

1592. The widowed mother was left with Cecilia and another daughter who is 6 years old. Since she was extremely poor and knew that she could not support herself and her daughters, and being young and attractive and likely to find something to her advantage, she decided to abandon her daughters and to go looking for her fortune.

1592. We have seen Gentile, daughter of Elisabetta Ronda, who lives with her mother. [The mother] does not live honestly, and while we were in the house all kinds of people came. She lives in a very dangerous place. She is thirteen and six months, and if she has not been corrupted already, which one may well doubt, the mother says that, if we take the daughter, she'll be able to get married, so that we shall save mother and daughter at the same time.

---

23 See L. G. Lazar, '"E Faucibus Demonis": Daughters of Prostitutes, the First Jesuits, and the Compagnia delle Vergini Miserabili di Santa Caterina della Rosa', in Wisch and Cole Ahl, pp. 259–79.

Work

6.23 A Florentine painter hires a servant, 1465

Domestic service was the most common occupation for poor girls, especially
if they were very young and had not learnt a trade. The Florentine painter
Neri di Bicci (1418–92) records the arrangements made for a girl called
Mechera (the diminutive for 'Domenica') who is to live in his house as a
servant. As customary, provisions are made for her dowry, so that she will be
able to marry when she reaches a suitable age.[24]

Neri di Bicci, *Le Ricordanze*, ed. B. Santi (Pisa, 1978), pp. 253, 335.

Monday 7 October 1465.

I took Mechera [Domenica] as a servant. She left on 21 October [*sic*]
1469.

On the day stated above Amadore di Giuliano d'Amadore from
Castello di Gangalandi left his sister Domenica with me as a servant.
She was about 9 years old, [and she is to stay] for eight years or more.
And when the eight years or more are over, if she has been a good,
discreet and honest servant, when she gets married I must give her
one hundred *lire* for her to give to her intended husband, and
whichever linen or woollen clothes she is using then. This was agreed
with Amadore.

Thursday 21 September 1469

On this day Mechera, daughter of the late Giuliano d'Amadore, whom
Amadore left with me as a servant on 7 October 1465, left. He had left
her for a period of eight years when she was a small girl, but she did
not want to stay with me because she was not obedient or prompt in
doing reasonable and honest things. She asked permission to take
those items listed below, that is:

    1 overdress of grey cloth, almost new
    1 overdress of rough grey cloth, used
    1 multicoloured dress, used
    1 dress of rough grey cloth, used
    4 good chemises
    4 caps
    4 handkerchiefs and kerchiefs

24 For comparative material, see D. Romano, *Housecraft and Statecraft: Domestic Service
in Renaissance Venice 1400–1600* (Baltimore, 1996), pp. 118–90.

2 boxes, used
2 ribbons
1 pair of boxes
1 belt, new
1 head kerchief.

6.24 A girl seeks a post as a lady-companion, 1608

An older girl from a respectable but impoverished background, and with a useful skill such as spinning, could hope to find a better position than that of a servant. The Governor of Romagna, Monsignor Annibale Grizi, writes to Father Domenico Marconi to recommend a girl as a paid companion for a lady of their acquaintance.

M. Grizi, *Un prelato italiano del seicento (Annibale Grizio), 1556–1612* (Bologna, 1907), p. 382.

[22 October 1608]

I am taking the opportunity [of recommending] a girl from this area, who was born in a respectable artisan family. She is skilled in the art of spinning silk. She is a fine-looking girl, modest and shy, of about 20 years of age. She has no father nor mother, and only one brother. As it seems to me that, besides being skilful with the distaff, she could be a lady-companion, I have talked about her being taken into service on a salary, according to what the lady [Signora Rusticucci] would decide. If she accepts, it would be appropriate if, as an answer, she could send an old man with a horse, to fetch the girl.

7 Betrothals and weddings

The marriage of members of the political and cultural elite and of the middle ranks was not a love-match, but an alliance of two extended family groups, two lineages. Both bride and groom were the instruments through which networks of client–patron relationships at the heart of the social, economic and political system, were constructed. The personal preferences of the young women and the often not-so-young men were not relevant to this important decision. Choosing a wife or a husband was a matter which involved parents and relatives in prolonged discussions and in skilful evaluations of a number of crucial factors. Moral qualities and good upbringing, as well as a certain amount of education, were of course very important, but so was physical appearance. It was also crucial for the future bride and groom to come from the same social rank. The choice of a future husband or wife was therefore a matter which concerned all the members of the families involved, and which was based on a careful assessment of the prospective 'candidate'.[1] The agreement to marry was formalised with the ceremony of betrothal.

One of the concerns of parents with daughters of a marriageable age was to be able to afford dowries for them all. The dowry, which was paid by the bride's relatives, usually her father, to the groom, was indispensable for a woman to marry. It was her portion of her father's estate, and, though her husband could control it during his lifetime, she retained property rights. Customs and laws regulating the size and administration of the dowry, and its restitution in the case of the husband's or the wife's death, varied from city to city. The amount of money given as a dowry varied according to the status and wealth of the bride's family, but during our period the sum considered appropriate grew considerably throughout Italy.[2] Local customs dictated the

---

1 On betrothals, see A. Molho, *Marriage Alliances in Late Medieval Florence* (Cambridge, Mass., 1994); P. Labalme, 'How to (and How Not to) Get Married in Sixteenth-Century Venice', *Renaissance Quarterly*, 52:1 (1999), pp. 43–72.

2 On different dowry customs, see: S. Chojnacki, 'Dowries and Kinsmen', in Chojnacki, pp. 132–52; C. Klapisch-Zuber, 'The Griselda Complex: Dowry and Marriage Gifts in the Quattrocento', in Klapisch-Zuber, pp. 213–46; H. Gregory, 'Daughters, Dowries and the Family in Fifteenth-Century Florence', in *Rinascimento*, 2nd ser., 27 (1987), pp. 215–37; D. Queller, 'Father of the Bride: Fathers, Daughters and Dowries in Late Medieval and Renaissance Venice', in *Renaissance Quarterly*, 46:4 (1993),

different rituals of the wedding ceremony, which, after the Council of Trent, the Church endeavoured to standardise, bringing it under its control.[3]

CHOOSING A HUSBAND/CHOOSING A WIFE

7.1 The qualities of a prospective wife

This extract from the *Ricordi* of the Florentine Giovanni di Pagolo Morelli (1371–1444), shows the emphasis given to the qualities of a wife, and highlights concerns, such as the political complexion of the bride's family, by a member of the Florentine mercantile elite.

Giovanni di Pagolo Morelli, 'Ricordi', in *Mercanti scrittori. Ricordi nella Firenze tra medioevo e rinascimento*, ed. V. Branca (Milan, 1986), pp. 168–9.

Having thought about this matter, make the decision to take a wife while you are between twenty and twenty-five years old, because God has made this the right age. But be careful not to lose any advantages by rushing into it. If you think that your position would be improved by waiting till you are thirty, so that your status is much greater, then wait. Remember that desire should not blind you, either in this or in any other matter pertaining to honour. Think about it with wisdom and maturity, asking advice about every aspect of this matter from trusted relatives and friends. But if this is not appropriate to your circumstances, take a wife at the age I have mentioned. Above all you should take care of one thing: do not marry down, but rather up, not so much, however, that she will behave like the husband, and you like the wife. Take care to become related to good citizens, who are not needy. They should be merchants, and they should not abuse their power. They should be old citizens of your city, honoured by the Commune, and they should be Guelph. They should have no stain on their name, that is, they should not be traitors, thieves, murderers, neither should they descend from a bastard, nor other despicable and

---

Note 2 continued
pp. 685–71; C. E. Meek, 'Women, Dowries and the Family in Late Medieval Italian Cities', in C. Meek and K. Simons, eds, *'The Fragility of her Sex?' Medieval Irishwomen in their European Context* (Blackrock, 1996), pp. 36–52.

3 On marriage ceremonies, see C. Klapisch-Zuber, 'Zacharia, or the Ousted Father: Nuptial Rites in Tuscany between Giotto and the Council of Trent', in Klapisch-Zuber, pp. 178–212. See also: D. d'Avray, 'Marriage Ceremonies and the Church in Italy after 1215'; and K. Lowe, 'Secular Brides and Convent Brides: Wedding Ceremonies in Italy during the Renaissance and Counter-Reformation', both in Dean and Lowe, pp. 107–15 and pp. 41–65.

shameful things. They should be clean and without stain, and have a reputation as good and affectionate relatives. They should not be miserly about money, but moderate, as wise men and good citizens should be.

Furthermore, you should take care that your wife is well-born, from a mother who was a chaste woman, and from a good family, with honourable kin. Her mother's mother, that is, the girl's grandmother, should also have been a chaste and clean woman, and they should be known by everybody as good women. You should make sure that she is peace-loving, not haughty and proud, and is reasonable and intelligent, as befits a woman. If you cannot find out about these things, look at the fundamentals, that is, that she should be a gentlewoman born from a good man, and that she herself lived with a good and honourable husband. Furthermore, take a girl who pleases you. She should be healthy, unblemished and tall, because of the children who will be born from her. She should have little [free] time, that is, not be idle, since women become immoral when they do not have what nature requires. I do not mean that they should be perfect, but you understand my meaning. Make sure that she is chaste, not too bold and not too vain, interested only in clothes, going to feasts and weddings and other vain things, since today all kinds of dishonest acts take place there, and there is a great deal of chit-chat, so much so that one cannot get away. No woman is so good that in these circumstances she does not become spoilt. Do not dive greedily into her dowry, because nobody has ever profited from a dowry: if you have to give it back, they [her family] will destroy you. Be happy with this: use only what you and your wife need.

7.2 How to choose a good husband for one's daughter

Lodovico Dolce writes for a wider public than Giovanni Morelli, and therefore concentrates on more general matters. What he says about the role of bride's father is particularly interesting: it is to him that recommendations are made to be caring and considerate of his daughter's feelings.

Dolce (1547), fols 31–3.

Since a virgin neither knows nor desires the union with man, our young girl will leave all deliberations in her father's hands, accepting gladly as a husband the one [he] will choose. Apart from the fact that this responsibility does not befit a virgin, she would not be able to make a good choice since she has no experience of the world. It is a father's task to make this choice not only with his usual love, but, in a way, placing himself in his daughter's shoes. In fact [fathers] may fail in this, either because they are unwary or spiteful, or believe that the man they think would make a good son-in-law will also be a good husband for their daughter. For this reason they look at nothing but wealth, nobility, or what could give them more profit, without taking into consideration their daughter's good. It is she who will have to live in the same house with her husband, and lie in the same bed with him till death, the ultimate end of everything, parts them. Other [fathers] expect to become richer, and others, such are the appetites of men, to grow in dignity because of the new relations, or they plan to destroy their enemies. The latter happens in those cities where there are factions which hate each other, while the former may happen in our own city. Therefore these men may be called merchants rather than fathers. But the good father, who is only looking for the good of his daughter and understands how important it is to be bound in an indissoluble knot, will give such a hazardous decision proper attention.

[...]

We must still consider (thinking about what pertains to the body) the husband's age, health and I would also say good looks. The latter is a fragile thing and lasts but a little, and, as long as if he does not look like Baronci del Certaldese,[4] he should be considered handsome by his wife. Health and good bodily habits are necessary, both because the house and the family need to be governed by somebody who is vigorous and healthy, and because of the benefit to wife and children. Were he not like that, he would infect [her] and generate sickly and invalid [children] from his corrupt seed. He should neither be too young, nor too close to old age, so that he can support the burden of the family for a sufficient time, and so that his children will not lack a father before they are grown up. Young age is not prudent enough, but old age is always accompanied by some trouble and impediment which life brings when it begins to decline and to approach its end. But all other considerations, even important ones, pale into insignificance compared to his inclinations and his habits, because a man is valued for his cleverness. Our daughter's husband should therefore be a man of clear intelligence, prudent, learned and good.

---

4 A reference to Boccaccio's *Decameron*, VI, 6, in which the Baronci family members are described as exceptionally ugly.

7.3 A mother looks for a suitable daughter-in-law, Florence, 1465

The letters written by the widowed Alessandra Macinghi Strozzi (1407/8–71) to her son Filippo, in exile in Naples, reveal the intermingling of private and public concerns in a family belonging to the elite of Quattrocento Florence. This letter shows that women were active agents in the process of choosing a wife for their sons and highlights the crucial role played by friends and relatives in this delicate task. It also reveals Alessandra's acute observation of prospective brides' appearance and behaviour.

Macinghi Strozzi (1987), pp. 240–2.

[31 August 1465]

As I have had some very good information from two people, yesterday I talked with Marco.[5] I have had information from four people who are close to her.[6] One of these is Costanza, the wife of Pandolfo [Pandolfini]. Everybody says the same thing: whoever marries her will be glad, because she will make a good wife. As far as her looks go, they tell me what I have in fact seen. She has a good, well-proportioned figure. Her face is long, but I was not able to see it very well, because I think she noticed I was looking at her. After the first moment, she did not turn towards me again, and then she walked away as fast as the wind. But what little I saw agrees with what I have been told, that her face is not one of the most beautiful, but it suits her figure. She will become more beautiful with time, and even more when she dresses as a young woman rather than as a girl. Her skin is not very fair, but not dark; rather, she has an olive complexion. I saw her without cosmetics and in low-heeled shoes. So, what I saw fits with what I have been told, and I don't think I was wrong about it and about her disposition. Pandolfo's wife told me that she can read really well. When I asked whether she was a bit rough, I was told that she is not. She is lively, and can dance and sing. If this is the case, I believe what I have been told about her. Her father was one of the upstanding young men here in Florence, and he is a gentleman. He loves his daughter very much, and it is likely that he has brought her up properly. So yesterday I called Marco, and I told him what I had heard. We talked about it a great deal, and we agreed that he should have a word with her father and give him some hope, but not too much, so that we

---

5 Marco Parenti, Alessandra's son-in-law.
6 Alessandra is discussing a girl of the Tanagli family, whom she had seen in church and described in a letter dated 17 August.

can pull back if we want to. And he should find out from him more than we know about the dowry: I hear that he had a thousand florins or more in the *Monte*.

[...]

As far as the Adimari girl is concerned, we did not say that this was a possibility, but we know that she is beautiful, and has a good dowry.[7] But we cannot think about her because, with such a large dowry, I don't think that they would send her out of Florence as an exile's wife, and they don't need to give her less. So I have not been thinking about her anymore. I have often been to church for morning mass to see her, as everybody says she is such a beauty, but I have never seen her. I saw Francesco's daughter instead, so that I didn't follow that up any more. There is nobody with those qualities a man would want – those who have some good qualities are not beautiful. For me, I would not want to see these unattractive ones around me: it would not be a good thing to have them around the house.

7.4 A bad marriage

Alessandra Macinghi Strozzi writes to her son Filippo, reminding him of a relative, also called Filippo, who, guided by his heart, made a bad marriage.

Macinghi Strozzi (1987), pp. 244–5.

[13 September 1465]

I am not surprised that you are proceeding slowly in choosing a wife, because, as you say, it is an extremely important decision, the most important one can make, because having good company comforts a man in body and soul. The opposite is also true, because when they are silly or hare-brained, or like the one Filippo had, one lives in much tribulation. As to the one Filippo had, it is said that when he was here and he saw her, he liked her foolishness so much, that he didn't want to agree [to marry] anybody else. He wanted to marry her, but her mother didn't want to consent to send her away [from Florence]. There were many well-bred girls available, but he didn't want any of them. Then her mother died, and Messer Manno had her [living] with him [as her guardian]. She behaved in such a way, that they couldn't wait to get rid of her, and she didn't have a dowry, and they gave her to Filippo. So, one should not have been surprised at her, but

7 Fiammetta Adimari, who would marry Filippo Strozzi in 1467.

rather at him, the silly man, who let her do what she liked, and was so infatuated with her, that she brought shame to herself and to him.

7.5 Do not marry an old man!

The merchant and *letterato* Filippo Sassetti, a member of the Accademia Fiorentina, writes from India in 1587 to his sister Maria Sassetti Bartoli, in Florence, discouraging her from choosing a husband who is too old for her daughter.

Filippo Sassetti, *Lettere dall'India (1583–1588)*, ed. A. Dei (Rome, 1995), p. 234.

[27 December 1587]

I have considered all you have told me about your daughter Margherita, and since she is in Florence and I am in India, I cannot give a long answer. I shall only say to you that, having seen in these parts how much wives are unhappy without their husbands, or how much they dislike having one made of wood or stone, which is the same as having a husband who is 57 years old, I exhort you not to go ahead with such a filthy coupling, because in three years' time at the latest it is going to give you more trouble than it does now. And besides, you can imagine how delighted Margherita would be – you'd be placing a child born yesterday to wipe the dribble of an old weakling. In bed, one will want a good time, the other will just tell stories about his grandfather's days. So this is my advice: keep her at home for longer and resign yourself to it, because times are getting harder. If you can read Boccaccio's *novelle*, I advise you to read the one about Messer Ricciardo di Chinzica, and you'll see that I have given you good advice.[8]

THE BETROTHAL

A betrothal was a formal and legally binding promise to marry, made by the fathers of both bride and groom in front of family members, and witnessed by a notary. It was not necessary for the betrothed to be present. This was the first in a series of 'contracts' and ceremonies culminating with the bride finally leaving her parents' house to go and live with her husband. After the Council of Trent, the importance of the betrothal began to change, as the moment of consent to marry

---

8 The *novella* mentioned here, about an old husband with a young wife, is from Boccaccio's *Decameron*, II, 10.

shifted to the actual wedding ceremony, with the bride and groom, rather than their families, taking centre stage in the proceedings.

7.6 A betrothal announcement to the future bride, 1407

Ser Lapo Mazzei, a notary and family friend, informs the fifteen-year-old Ginevra, illegitimate daughter by a household slave of the merchant Francesco Datini (1335–1410), that she has been betrothed. Ginevra had been living in her father's house in Prato since the age of five, cared for by his childless wife Margherita.[9]

L. Mazzei, *Lettere di un notaro a un mercante del secolo XIV*, ed. C. Guasti, 2 vols (Florence, 1880), vol. 2, p. 192.

Blessed be God, from whom come all good and holy things. You should know, dearest Ginevra, that your good father has today promised you in S. Francesco to Lionardo di Ser Tommaso [di Giunta], an honest and good-looking young man, at the presence of a very large and honourable gathering from Florence and from Prato. Praise be to God. Everyone in the area seems very pleased. God bless you. Pray for your loving father. Remember me to Monna Margherita to whom we owe all this, Luca, Barzalone and Ser Lapo, who are like brothers to you.

7.7 A Florentine betrothal, 1447

Financial arrangements and the social status of her daughter Caterina's future husband, the silk merchant Marco Parenti, are the subject of this letter from Alessandra Macinghi Strozzi to her son Filippo. The letter illustrates the Florentine custom of investing money in the *Monte delle doti* (Dowry Fund), established in 1425 in order to lighten the considerable financial burden of providing dowries. At the birth of each daughter a sum of money was deposited in the *Monte*, and after the marriage had been consummated the dowry, made up of the capital and the accrued interest, was given to her husband. Because Caterina's social status was higher than his, Marco Parenti made sure that his presents to her were impressive: the value of the gowns he gave Caterina has been assessed at 1,000 florins, a sum equal to four or five years' salary for a mason.

Macinghi Strozzi (1987), pp. 61–3.

---

9 On the wealthy merchant Francesco Datini, see I. Origo, *The Merchant of Prato, Francesco di Marco Datini* (London, 1957). Datini married the Florentine Margherita Bandini (b. 1347) in 1376.

[24 August 1447]

First of all I let you know that, by the grace of God, we have betrothed our Caterina to the son of Parente di Pier Parenti. He is a good and honest young man, an only son, rich, and twenty-five years old. He is a silk merchant, and his family held offices in the government: it is not long since his father was in the *Collegio*. I shall give her a dowry of a thousand florins, that is, five hundred florins from the *Monte* in May 1448, and another five hundred's worth of cash and *donora*[10] which I'll give him when she marries, which I think will be in November, God willing. This money is partly yours and partly mine. If I had not taken this decision, she would not have got married this year, because he who takes a wife wants money, and I could not find anybody who would wait to have the dowry in 1448 and the rest in 1450. So, since I am giving her these five hundred in cash and *donora*, the 1450 money will come to me, if she is alive. And we decided to do this because she is sixteen, and we should not delay in marrying her. We could have placed her [in a family] of higher rank and status, but only with [a dowry of] a thousand four hundred or five hundred florins, which would have spelt ruin for you and for me, and I don't know how happy the girl would have been, because outside the high ranks there is no choice, and this is a problem. And, everything considered, I decided to place the girl well, without thinking about anything else, and I think I am right [to believe] that she will be as well placed as any Florentine girl. She has a mother- and father-in-law who are so happy that they think of nothing else but how to make her happy. And I am not mentioning Marco, her [intended] husband, who is always saying to her 'Ask me whatever you want'. And as soon as they were betrothed, he had a gown cut for her of patterned crimson silk velvet, and also an overdress of the same fabric. It is the most beautiful cloth in Florence, and it comes from his shop. And a garland made of feathers and pearls, which costs eighty florins, and the headdress has two braids of pearls underneath, which are sixty florins or more, so that when she is dressed for the wedding she will wear more than four hundred florins. And for when she goes to his house [as his wife] he has ordered some crimson velvet to make wide sleeves lined with marten, and he is having a gown made in fine rose-coloured wool cloth, embroidered with pearls. And he can't have enough things made,

10 *Donora* were household and personal objects, gifted by the bride's parents, which the bride took with her when she left her parents' house for her husband's. They were given as an addition to the dowry.

because she is beautiful, and he would like her to look even more so. In truth, there isn't another girl like her in Florence, and many think she has all the [right] qualities. May God give her health and grace for a long time, as I wish.

7.8 A portrait for the Duke of Milan, 1468

Portraits played an important role in betrothals between members of ruling families, when the betrothed lived in different cities or countries. Here Galeazzo Maria Sforza, Duke of Milan (1444–76) writes to his mother Bianca Maria Visconti (1425–68) about his reaction to the portrait of Bona of Savoy (1449–1503) by the Sforza court painter Zanetto Bugatto.[11]

F. Malaguzzi Valeri, *Pittori lombardi del Quattrocento* (Milan, 1902), p. 128.

Most Illustrious Lady my mother, I remember that I wrote to Your Excellency that I had sent the painter Master Zanetto to France in order to paint from life a portrait of the Most Illustrious Lady Bona of Savoy, whom I think we can already call my wife. [I wrote that] if, after receiving the portrait, I thought she was ugly, I would send it to Your Ladyship. If I thought she was beautiful, I would not. Today Master Zanetto returned and brought the portrait of the lady, who seems to me not just beautiful, but very beautiful. Concerning the promise I made to Your Ladyship, I have decided not to send [the portrait] because I want it for myself, and I hope that Your Excellency will forgive me.

7.9 The betrothal of Isabella d'Este and Francesco Gonzaga, 1480

The betrothal between the children of two ruling families, often at a very early age, was a state affair. It took place against a background of pomp and display which was seen as a homage to the status of the guests, and was designed to impress visitors. Betrothal ceremonies were carefully scrutinised, and were reported by ambassadors to other courts. In this account, the Sala Grande of Castel Vecchio in Ferrara is the stage for the betrothal between Isabella (1474–1539), daughter of Duke Ercole I d'Este and of Eleonora d'Aragona, and Francesco (1466–1519), the son of Federico Gonzaga, Marquess of Mantua, and of Margaret of Bavaria. Ercole I succeeded in

11 The wedding by proxy took place at Amboise in May, and then in person in Milan in July 1468. On the various functions of female portraits, see J. Woods-Marsden, 'Portrait of the Lady 1430–1520', in *Virtue and Beauty*, exhib. cat., National Gallery of Art, Washington (Princeton, NJ, 2001), pp. 64–87.

arranging very advantageous marriages for his daughters Isabella and Beatrice, linking the House of Este to the Gonzaga of Mantua and to the Sforza of Milan.

Bernardino Zambotti, 'Diario ferrarese dall'anno 1476 sino al 1504', ed. G. Pardi, in *Rerum italicarum scriptores*, vol. 24, pt 7 (Bologna, 1937), p. 76.

27 May 1480. Messer Francesco Secco, ambassador ... of the Marquess of Mantua,[12] went to the Castello Vecchio to visit our most illustrious Duchess [Eleonora d'Aragona] and the Lady Isabella, her daughter, who is 11 years old,[13] the future bride of the Lord Francesco, his [the Marquess of Mantua's] first born. He gave to the young girl as a present from the groom a gold necklace with gems. The following day, the 28th, at 17 hours,[14] the magnificent ambassador Messer Francesco went into the great hall, accompanied by many gentlemen and knights. The hall was adorned on one side with five gold and silk curtains, commissioned by Alfonso, King of Naples,[15] to the value of 150,000 ducats, together with other *spalliere*[16] and fine tapestries. At one end of the hall there was a stepped *credenza*[17] which reached the ceiling, loaded with very precious gold and silver vases, with a crystal eagle wearing around its neck a necklace with gems and balas rubies. At the other end of the hall there was a dais, on which our Duke ... was sitting, together with his most illustrious wife, the Lady Leonora, with the bride, the Lady Isabella, and the other children and lords of the House of Este, and the ambassador of the King of Naples, the protonotary Monsignor Ascanio Visconti. And Messer Francesco, the ambassador, was received on the dais between our Duke and the other lords, and in front of them Siviero [Sivieri], our Duke's counsellor, officially pronounced and stipulated the promise of marriage as follows. The Excellency our Duke, in order to maintain and preserve the deep-rooted friendship between the House of Gonzaga and the House of Este, declares his legitimate daughter the Lady Isabella to be the bride of the Lord Francesco, first-born of the Lord Federico Gonzaga, and promises to give her to him as his wife when she reaches the legitimate age. And the ambassador promised the Duke that the Lord Federico will ensure that the Lord Francesco at the said time will contract lawful marriage with the Lady Isabella, and will marry her and lead her

12 Secco represented his absent nephew Francesco Gonzaga.
13 Isabella was in fact six.
14 Midday.
15 In fact Ferrante, Eleonora's father.
16 Panels hanging at shoulder height.
17 A sideboard, used to display tableware.

to his house in the praise of God.[18] And to bear witness of this, he touched the hand of the Duke, of the Duchess and of the bride.

7.10 A broken betrothal, 1463

Breaking a betrothal agreement was a very serious matter. In 1450, at the age of three, Susanna (1447–81), daughter of Ludovico Gonzaga, Marquess of Mantua, was betrothed to Galeazzo Maria Sforza, son of the Duke of Milan – a very advantageous match for the House of Gonzaga. Seven years later Susanna, having developed a hunched back, was deemed unfit for marriage and sent into a convent. Her place in the betrothal contract was taken by her younger sister Dorotea (1449–67). In the summer of 1461, because of changes in the political arena, the Sforza began to have second thoughts about the marriage, and rumours started to circulate about Dorotea developing the same malformation as her sister. Ludovico refused to have his daughter examined by doctors, as the Sforza requested, so Galeazzo Maria declared himself free from any obligations. The bitter dispute between Sforza and Gonzaga about Dorotea's health and the validity of this betrothal, however, continued till Dorotea's death in April 1467. In 1468 Galeazzo Maria married Bona of Savoy (see 7.8).

On hearing the sad news about the state of her sister's betrothal, Susanna writes from her convent to her mother, Barbara of Hohenzollern.

Lettere inedite di donne mantovane del secolo XV tratte dall'archivio de' Gonzaga in Mantova (Mantua, 1878), pp. 30–1.

I have learnt with great sorrow from the letter of Your Most Illustrious Ladyship that the betrothal between [the son of the Duke of] Milan and my sweetest sister the Lady Dorotea has been dissolved. This has pained me greatly, even if I know that everything happens according to God's will, and we all have to comply with it because He does everything for the best. But because this marriage would have been very useful and would have brought great honour to my sister and to our house, I cannot help but suffer. I have cried bitterly, both for the warmest love I had and have for her, so that every affliction and tribulation she feels, I feel as my own, and for the damage to our house. The Lady Agata, and all those to whom I have spoken secretly about this, is also grieving and has been crying with me for her great affection for my sister and for the whole family. May God's will be done, and I pray Him to give me patience.

Milan, 7 December 1463,

[your] daughter Susanna, by her own hand.

18 Isabella and Francesco were married in 1490.

DOWRIES, GIFTS AND COMMEMORATIVE ART

7.11 S. Bernardino preaches against dowries, 1427

The most important part of the marriage negotiations centered on the provision for the dowry and the *donora*, personal and household objects the bride brought to her husband's house. In one of his Sienese sermons of 1427, S. Bernardino criticises the excessive importance given to dowries, denouncing them as money accumulated from the exploitation of those who are less fortunate.[19]

Bernardino da Siena, *Novellette ed esempi morali*, ed. A. Baldi (Lanciano, 1916), pp. 128–9.

You are going to give your daughter as wife to a man, and neither the father, the mother nor the groom think about where her dowry comes from. If they were wise, they should think about this first of all: where do these things come from, where do her clothes come from, and from what sort of money her dowry has been made. And in fact, many times, most times, it comes from robbery, from usury, from the sweat of peasants and the blood of widows, and from the very marrow of wards and orphans. If somebody picked up one of those gowns and squeezed it and wrung it, he would see blood oozing from it. Alas, do you not think how cruel it is that you are dressed with the clothes [made from] the earnings of someone who is [now] dying of exposure!

7.12 The *donora* of a wealthy bride, 1419

In the *Ricordanze* of the Florentine Corsini family, Giovanni Corsini lists the *donora* given to his daughter Caterina, and states the value of each object.

A. Petrucci, *Il libro di Ricordanze dei Corsini (1362–1457)* (Rome, 1965), pp. 109–10.

Here I shall note all the *donora* that I, Giovanni, shall give to my daughter Caterina. I have given the value of these *donora* to her husband Nicolò as 130 florins ... which are:

a pair of chests [20]	florins 24
a grey overdress	florins 18
a gown, with 2 1/2 ounces of silver	florins 10
an embroidered overdress of fine wool cloth, with 9 oz of silver	florins 25

19 See R. Rusconi, 'S. Bernardino da Siena, the Wife and Possessions', in Bornstein and Rusconi, pp. 182–96.

20 Painted *cassoni* commissioned for a wedding, which would hold the trousseau.

12 lace-trimmed chemises	florins 10
a rosary	florins 4
a small woman's book [21]	florins 8
a crimson hood with 5 oz of gold, 17 of silver	florins 11
a cap of heavy white silk, with 3 oz of gold, 6 of silver	florins 4
a hood with beads on crimson velvet, with 8½ oz of beads and 4 of silver, all for	florins 16

7.13 Gifts for the bedchamber of a wealthy couple, Florence, 1493

It was customary for the groom's parents to commission furnishings and works of art for the new couple's bedroom. These are some of the gifts given by Andrea Minerbetti's parents to their son and his bride Maria Bini.[22]

G. Biagi, *Due corredi nuziali fiorentini 1329–1493 da un libro di Ricordanze dei Minerbetti* (Florence, 1899), pp. 17–18.

1 bed and 1 day-bed, with a conjoined walnut wainscoting, with chests around it, very well worked and with very beautiful marquetry, 8 *braccia* in height, f[lorins] 50

2 chests, painted and gilded, f[lorins] 18

1 walnut cupboard, decorated with marquetry with unpainted platforms, and with those for the chests, f[lorins] 10

1 painting of Our Lady with its gilded frame, f[lorins] 12

1 childbirth tray, painted, with its gilded frame,[23] f[lorins] 5

1 round mirror with gesso reliefs with a gilded frame, f[lorins] 2

7.14 Jewels for an emperor's bride, Milan, 1493

The total value of the extraordinary jewels given by Ludovico il Moro to his niece Bianca Maria Sforza for her marriage to the Holy Roman Emperor, Maximilian, amounted to 31,373 ducats. Her dowry was set at 400,000 ducats.

---

21 A prayer book.
22 For marriage furnishings, see Tinagli (1997), pp. 21–46; L. Syson and D. Thornton, *Objects of Virtue: Art in Renaissance Italy* (London, 2001), pp. 37–77. See also J. K. Lydecker, 'The Domestic Setting of the Arts in Renaissance Florence', PhD diss., Johns Hopkins University, 1987.
23 For birth trays, see J. M. Musacchio, *The Art and Ritual of Childbirth in Renaissance Italy* (New Haven and London, 1999).

The jewels in the shape of heraldic devices (*imprese*) celebrate the Sforza family and Ludovico il Moro.

F. Calvi, *Bianca Maria Sforza-Visconti Regina dei Romani Imperatrice germanica e gli Ambasciatori di Ludovico il Moro alla corte Cesarea* (Milan, 1888), pp. 131–2.

1: a necklace made in the shape of the device of house leeks, with six large balas rubies, twenty-four diamonds of various types, six emeralds, fourteen large pearls, and thirty-six smaller pearls, ducats 9,000.[24]

Item: a jewel with a very beautiful table-cut emerald; above, a very beautiful table-cut ruby; below, a triangular ruby, and a very beautiful large pendant pearl, set with two horns of plenty, with a crown above. The horns and crown are made with forty-six diamonds. This jewel is attached to a string of thirty pearls, ducats 6,300.

Item: a jewel made in the shape of the device of the bean, with a large table-cut balas ruby, a large faceted diamond above, and a large pendant pearl, ducats 4,000.

Item: a jewel with a large table-cut emerald, a good ruby above, and two good pendant pearls, ducats 3,000.

Item: a jewel with a large faceted diamond, a very beautiful heart-shaped ruby, two pointed diamonds, and a large pendant pearl, ducats 3,000.

Item: a crucifix made of fifty-five diamonds, with three pendant pearls, that is, two round ones and a beautiful pear-shaped one, ducats 1,200.

Item: a jewel with an eight-facet Syrian garnet set in the [device of the] lion with the buckets, with two pointed diamonds above, and three pendant pearls, one pear-shaped and two round ones, to be worn in the hair, ducats 1,000.

Item: a jewel in the shape of a brush, with the handle made by a ruby, a carved turquoise above, a faceted, heart-shaped emerald on top, and the bristles made with nine diamonds and five round pendant pearls, and on the reverse an L made of diamonds, ducats 600.

THE WEDDING AND WEDDING FESTIVITIES

Pre- and post-Tridentine wedding ceremonies

Before the decrees of the Council of Trent (1545–63), weddings followed customs and practices which varied widely according to the

24 The house leek (*sempervivum tectorum*) was the personal device of Bianca Maria Visconti, the wife of Francesco Sforza and the mother of Ludovico il Moro.

social status of the participants and the geographical area in which they lived. Symbolic gestures, such as the touching of hands, the kiss, the giving or exchanging of rings and small gifts, represented the moment of the union. For a marriage to be valid it was necessary for the two parties, sometimes represented by the two fathers, to give their consent in front of witnesses and a notary.

The Council of Trent took weddings away from the sphere of lay and civic life, stressing in 1547, and again in 1563, that the Church had always considered marriage to be a sacrament and not just a civil contract. It also sought to prescribe uniformity throughout Italy, and precise rules were set out for a new religious wedding ceremony. The presence of the parish priest became essential, while the consent had to be given by the bride and groom in front of the priest and two or three witnesses. In practice, however, long-held local customs continued to be followed.[25]

7.15 A wedding ceremony in Florence, 1401

Matteo di Niccolò Corsini gives his daughter Francesca in marriage to Luca di Nicolò de' Falcussi. The extract, from the *Ricordanze* of the Corsini family, demonstrates the various phases of the betrothal and wedding ceremonies during the fifteenth century, according to Florentine custom: first, the betrothal with the drawing up of a document stating the amount of the dowry; then the ceremony of the giving of the ring; and finally the wedding. All these different stages are recorded in writing, and the legal aspect of the agreement is underlined by the presence of a notary throughout.

Petrucci, p. 81.

On the 22nd day of March 1400[26] I promised my daughter Francesca in marriage to Luca, son of *maestro* Nicolò de' Falcussi, and we have to give six hundred gold florins as her dowry, that is five hundred and thirty in cash and seventy florins in *donora*. The document is by the hand of Ser Antonio di Ser Chello.

On 24 April 1401 the said Luca gave her the ring. The document is by the hand of Ser Nicolaio d'Alinari.

We sent her in marriage to the said Luca on the 8th day of May 1401, and very honourably there was a great wedding feast, as needed, and it was a Sunday, the feast day of the Archangel St Michael.

25 See Dean and Lowe, pp. 5–7.
26 The date is in *stile fiorentino*, with the new year beginning on 25th March, the feast day of the Annunciation.

And after this, on 11 May 1401, the said Luca declared the dowry for the said Francesca, and declared to have received on that date six hundred gold florins, to the satisfaction of Luca and his father, *maestro* Nicolò son of Francesco, and Matteo, son of the said *maestro* Nicolò. The document is by the hand of Ser Antonio di Ser Chello from San Miniato, notary in Florence, who was the notary for the Wool Guild, and Matteo di Niccolò Corsini, of the *popolo* of S. Felice in Piazza, declared to have received it from me.

7.16 A Venetian wedding, 1581

Francesco Sansovino's description of the customs and public ceremonies peculiar to the marriages of Venetian patricians shows that local traditions were followed also after the Council of Trent.[27]

F. Sansovino, *Venetia città nobilissima et singolare* (Venice, 1581), pp. 401–2.

Nowadays, the morning after the wedding has been finalised by a third party, with a dowry which among the patricians is usually very large, without having seen the girl the groom goes to the [Doge's] palace courtyard. There the marriage is made public and, accompanied by his relatives, he touches the hand of those going to Court, or they touch his. Then on a specific day, at the hour of Vespers, his friends are invited to the house of the bride's father … And on entering the room where the groom and his relatives are waiting, they congratulate him again, and they touch his hand. When they arrive in the hall, where there are only men, they [all] sit down. The *Paraninfo* leads the bride out of a room, all dressed in white according to an old custom, and with her hair spread out on her shoulders, and her head decorated with gold threads. And after the formal marriage words, she is led around the hall to the sound of pipes, trumpets and other harmonious instruments, all the time dancing slowly, and bowing to the guests. And, having been shown around and been seen by everybody, she goes back inside, and when new people arrive, she again returns to the hall. Having done that various times for an hour or longer, she [then] goes down to the ground floor, and together with many gentlewomen, who have been waiting in various rooms, boards a gondola, and sits on a rather high seat, all covered with carpets, outside the canopy (and this

27 On wedding ceremonies in Venice, see S. Chojnacki, 'Nobility, Women and the State: Marriage Regulation in Venice, 1420–1535', and P. Allerston, 'Wedding Finery in Sixteenth-Century Venice', both in Dean and Lowe, pp. 128–51 and pp. 25–40.

is called 'andare in trasto'), and, followed by a great number of gondolas, goes to visit nuns' convents where she has either sisters or relatives. All this is done with good reason because, since she will have to increase with children the family she has just joined, she shows herself at home and out in the city almost as to witnesses to the marriage. And the people around celebrate as if they were rejoicing at something which touches them, since they are all joined together in the government, as if they all belonged to the same family.

On another day all the gentlewomen go to congratulate the bride, who is called 'Novizza' by the populace, following what their husbands had done not long before. And shortly afterwards a public feast is organised, with pomp and much expense, so that the guests at a wedding often number 300. There are displays of much delicious food, which are, however, regulated by [sumptuary] laws. At this festivity there is one or more witnesses called 'compari dell'anello', who in this case act almost as Masters of Ceremonies, taking care of the musicians and of many other relevant things. And on the morning following the banquet he gives sweets, confectionery and other such refreshments as a present to the bride and groom, and he is also given presents. In the old times it was customary to lead the bride to the Doge as if he were a witness, but in the year 1501 this custom was cancelled from the laws, and it was decreed that any marriage from a thousand ducats onwards should be registered with the *Avogaria.*[28]

7.17 Wedding customs in the Apennines, 1626

During a trial, a witness is asked about wedding customs in his mountain area between Emilia and Tuscany.

Ottavia Niccoli, *Storie di ogni giorno in una città del Seicento* (Rome and Bari, 2004), p. 140.

I know ... that when you go to discuss [arrangements about] a marriage you take a present, you go with love-tokens. Sometimes you take some oranges, sometimes not, according to what seems right to you. Sometimes the bride's relatives prepare food for the groom's relatives, according to their means ... I know that when a groom goes to see the bride and there are formalities, I have heard that in Florence they kiss, but in our parts we don't do that, even if I've heard that there

---

28 The office of Venetian magistrates.

are some who have done it, but I don't know who. But, as I've said, here we don't kiss, but only touch the hand … Most people bring weapons to make merry [firing in the air], when they go to discuss a marriage and see the bride. This is the custom.

7.18 A court case, Bologna, 1556

When is a wedding not a wedding? This transcript from evidence given to the ecclesiastical tribunal of the Bologna diocese in 1556, by a woman petitioning for the annulment of her marriage, highlights the problem of forced marriages, and shows that a wedding could still be carried out without the presence of a priest.

L. Ferrante, 'Il matrimonio disciplinato: processi matrimoniali a Bologna nel Cinquecento', in P. Prodi, ed., *Disciplina dell' anima, disciplina del corpo e disciplina della società tra medioevo ed età moderna* (Bologna, 1994), pp. 918–19.

Camilla Sarti versus Nane Merici:

When I was in their house, Olivia, Nane's sister, called me into her bedroom, which Nane and Berto Rivani, Olivia's husband, also entered, and when Nane was in the room he grabbed my tired hand with force, and I wanted to pull it away, and he was squeezing it so much that he ripped the skin from around my nails, and in the end he pushed the ring down the wedding finger, but as the ring was small it didn't go beyond the first knuckle, and he didn't say anything at all before he married me, and all the time I was saying that he should leave me alone, because I didn't want him to marry me and so he forced the ring on my finger … and as soon as he put the ring on my finger I pulled it off and threw it away … and I told him … that I would make him regret that.

Celebrations

7.19 A wedding feast, Florence, 1466

Festivities for the weddings between members of the fifteenth century Florentine elite took place in public, since marriage alliances between families often had political implications for the city. One of the wealthiest men in Florence, Giovanni Rucellai, describes in his *Zibaldone* the festivities for the wedding of his son Bernardo with Nannina de' Medici, which took place in the street and under the Rucellai loggia near their palazzo, transformed for the occasion into a richly decorated open-air dining room.

G. Marcotti, *Un mercante fiorentino e la sua famiglia nel secolo XV* (Florence, 1881), pp. 83–4.

I record that on 8 June 1466 we celebrated the feast for the wedding
of my son Bernardo and Nannina, daughter of Piero di Cosimo de'
Medici, his wife, who came in marriage to her husband accompanied
by four knights, that is Messer Manno Temperani, Messer Carlo
Pandolfini, Messer Giovannozzo Pitti, Messer Tommaso Soderini.

This feast took place outside our house, on a platform 1½ *braccia* from
the ground,[29] measuring about 1,600 square *braccia* in width,[30] which
occupied the whole of the space in front of our house, the loggia and
the Via della Vigna, up to the wall of our house. [It was] in the shape
of a triangle, beautifully appointed with pieces of cloth, tapestries,
benches and *spalliere*, and with an awning to shade us from the sun.
[This was] made of blue cloth, all decorated with garlands and swags
of greenery, with four shields, two with the coat-of-arms of the Medici,
and two with those of the Rucellai. [There were] other decorations,
especially a very ornate *credenza* with silverware. All this was said to
be the most beautiful and noble *apparato* that had ever been made for
a wedding feast. On this platform there were dances and festivities,
and everything was arranged for lunch and dinner. At the wedding
feast there were 50 beautifully adorned and richly dressed women, and
also 30 beautifully dressed young men. Between relatives, friends and
neighbours of the most important people in the city, 50 had been
invited to each meal, so that at the first tables, counting the women
and girls of the household, the pipe and trumpet players, there were
170 people eating, and at the second, third and fourth tables there were
many people. In all there were 500 people eating that meal [...]

We made a kitchen behind the house, having closed with planks Via
della Vigna at the corner towards [the church of] S. Pancrazio, and
there were 50 people working, between cooks and dishwashers.

7.20 Alfonso d'Este and Anna Sforza go to bed, Ferrara, 1491

Alfonso d'Este, son of the Duke of Ferrara, was betrothed to Anna Sforza (d.
1497), niece of Ludovico il Moro, in 1477, when he was one year old, and his
intended bride three. After the marriage contract was signed in Milan on 23
January 1491, the wedding party left for Ferrara, where the bride arrived on
12 February. The wedding blessing and various festivities took place the
following day. Anna and Alfonso were then accompanied to bed by relatives
and friends, with much merriment and many jests – a popular custom followed

29 Approx. 80 cm.
30 Approx. 800 square m.

by various social ranks. In this letter, Ermes Sforza describes the event to his uncle, Ludovico il Moro.

A. Luzio and R. Renier, *Delle relazioni di Isabella d'Este Gonzaga con Ludovico e Beatrice Sforza* (Milan, 1890), p. 27.

[After the banquet, the wedding party] continued talking for a while, then the groom and the bride were taken to bed. We were all around the bed, making fun of them. On Don Alfonso's side there was the Marquess of Mantua[31] with many others who were taunting him, and he had a stick in his hand, with which he defended himself. The Lady Anna was in good spirits, but they both felt strange to see so many people around their bed. Everybody was saying pleasant things, as is customary in these circumstances. We left, and the following morning we wanted to know how they had got on. We found that they had both slept very well, as we all thought they would.

7.21 An invocation to Venus

The genre of *epithalamia* (poems written to celebrate a wedding) was a fashionable rediscovery from classical antiquity. Here the poet Veronica Gambara (1485–1550) entreats Venus, the goddess of love, and Hymen, the god of marriage, to give happiness to the newly married couple. The poem makes references to the poetry of Petrarch and Virgil.

Veronica Gambara, *Le rime*, ed. A. Bullock (Florence, 1995), p. 94.

Loosen your golden tresses
and crown your forehead with your myrtle and laurel,
beautiful Venus, and may these holy cupids abide with you
in sweet harmony.
You, sacred Hymen, honour this sublime day
with lovely roses and purple flowers,
singing with your golden lyre, with loud and resounding
verses.
And you, great gods, who
govern us mortals, scatter generously
happiness, peace, sweetness and love
so that the chaste kisses and the joyful hours
which these two will have may be so happy,
that heaven could not give them more.

---

31 Francesco Gonzaga.

7.22 A princely wedding in Palermo, 1574

Festivities organised for aristocratic weddings were often described in great detail by *letterati*, and the second half of the sixteenth century saw the publication and circulation of many such texts. These printed descriptions indicate not only a propagandistic intention on the part of princes and rulers, but also the reading public's appreciation of and interest in important contemporary events. This extract, from one such account, written for the wedding of Donna Anna, daughter of Prince Carlo d'Aragona, and Don Giovanni Ventimiglia, in Palermo, Sicily, 1574, describes an ephemeral 'theatre' built for that occasion.

G. Martellucci, *Le nozze del principe: Palermo città e teatro del Cinquecento* (Palermo, 1992), pp. 55–6.

A large wooden hall was built in the courtyard of the *palazzo* of His Excellency the Lord [Carlo d'Aragona] Prince of Castel Vetrano. It was 40 steps in length, corresponding to fourteen Sicilian *canne*, seven *canne* in width, and high in proportion. It abutted onto the wall of the rooms to the north-west, and its floor was built up from the ground, so that the entrance was four steps up on the long side [of the courtyard], towards the south-east. All around the interior, from the middle of the height [of the hall], was a gallery, wide enough for two ladies standing next to each other. It was divided by two tiers of tapestries which covered the walls of the hall. This gallery had a balustrade of simulated white marble with gold decorations, and there were columns reaching the ceiling, covered with velvet in various colours. The ceiling, which reached the gallery walls, was made of cloth. Where the colonnade touched the ceiling there was a wide frieze, carved with foliage painted silver against a red background. Hanging on this frieze were shields with the coats of arms of the bride's and groom's families. Another beautiful frieze covered the edge of the gallery floor.

The size of the hall, the beauty of the tapestries and the way they were placed, the gallery with its balustrade, the colonnade, the friezes, the great roundel in the middle of the ceiling with the royal coat of arms, the pleasant light from the large windows covered with cloth, everything made this hall so enchanting and beautiful, that whoever went inside to look at it did not want to leave for a long time.

8 Marriage and married life

As we have seen in the previous chapter, marriage was not a personal matter involving the preferences and decisions of two individuals, but had major social implications for both families. Throughout our period, the experiences of married women would have been quite different from those of a Western woman in a modern 'nuclear family'. Married women did not live isolated in their homes, but were at the centre of a network of deep-rooted relationships – family, kin, friends and neighbours – so that a couple's private concerns and the events in their lives had public consequences, and vice versa.

The realities of married life would have been as diverse as the circumstances in which women lived, with social rank acting as always as the determining factor. The ideals advocated in theoretical writings, however, are much more constant, as we have seen in the case of girls' upbringing. Throughout the period, for instance, we find similar arguments being used to justify marriage, seen as legitimising sexual relationships and procreation according to Christian ideals, and as providing political and social stability. The same can be said for those treatises dealing with married women's conduct and behaviour, with virtues such as modesty, chastity, obedience and fidelity being praised, and their social importance stressed.[1]

THE JUSTIFICATION FOR MARRIAGE

8.1 The meaning of love within marriage

Fra Cherubino da Siena's *Regole di vita matrimoniale* (*c.*1450–81, publ. 1490) was one of the most popular books on marriage, giving much space to sexuality, conception, childbirth and childrearing. Here he explains the nature of love between husband and wife, stressing parallels between married love and Christ's love for the Church.

---

1 See Dean and Lowe; B. B. Diefendorf, 'Family Culture, Renaissance Culture', in *Renaissance Quarterly*, 40 (1987), pp. 661–81; A. Molho, *Marriage Alliance in Late Medieval Florence* (Cambridge, Mass., 1994); Chojnacki; M. Chojnacka, 'Power, Family and Household in Early Modern Italy', in *Journal of Family History*, 22:4 (1997), pp. 491–95. On marital virtues, see M. Rogers, 'An Ideal Wife at the Villa Maser: Veronese, the Barbaros, and Renaissance Theorists of Marriage', *Renaissance Studies*, 7:4 (1993), pp. 379–97.

Cherubino da Siena, *Regole di vita matrimoniale*, ed. F. Zambrini and C. Negroni (Bologna, 1888), pp. 26–7.

The first thing that you, husband, owe your wife, and you, wife, owe your husband, is called 'heartfelt affection', which means that you must love each other warmly. This is the teaching from the great St Paul, who says: Husbands, love your wives as Christ loves His Church, that is the congregation of Christian souls. As Christ suffered death for the salvation of the Christians, so the husband should, if required, give his life for the salvation of his wife's soul. And as Christ, for the great love He has for us, will always receive and forgive those who sin and sin again, no matter how many times, provided they repent, so you, husband, must so love your wife that if she fell into error, but repented and wanted to make amends, you would forgive her and receive her. Paul also says: husbands must love their wives as much as they love themselves. But for love to be perfect it must not be lame. Love is lame when one loves and the other does not. Therefore you, wife, must love your husband, and you, husband, your wife, and thus, in mutual reciprocation, love will be perfect.

8.2 Leon Battista Alberti on marriage

A social justification for marriage is given in Alberti's *Della famiglia* (*c.*1430s–1440s), in which five speakers voice different opinions on marriage. Here the stability of society and the survival and prosperity of great families, achieved through suitable marriage alliances, are of paramount importance.

Alberti (1960), pp. 106–7.

Book II

Therefore marriage was instituted by Nature, the excellent and divine teacher of all things, with these conditions: man should have a constant companion for his life, and one only; he should live with her under one roof, and never cease thinking of her, never leave her on her own, but return to her, providing for and seeing to her needs and comforts; the woman should safeguard at home what he has provided for her [...]

So that a family should not fall into decline, which, as we said, is most unfortunate, but should grow in fame and in the happy number of its young members, we should urge our young men to marry with arguments, persuasion, rewards, and with every reason, effort and skill. The arguments could be similar to those we have already mentioned, decrying lascivious pleasures and inducing in them the desire for what is honest. The inducements could be these: to show them how pleasant it is to live in the primary and natural partnership of marriage, with children who are pledges and securities of married benevolence and love, and the resting place of all paternal hopes and desires. He who has struggled to acquire wealth, power and land will find it very hard not to have a real heir and keeper of his name and memory. Nobody can be more suited than true and legitimate offspring to enjoy his position and authority, and the fruit and benefit of his labour.

8.3 The holy estate of matrimony

From the published collection of letters by Lucrezia Gonzaga (1522–89), an argument in favour of marriage, based on religous reasons.

Lucrezia Gonzaga, *Lettere della molto illustre Sig. la Sra Donna Lucretia Gonzaga da Gazuolo* (Venice, 1552), pp. 34–5.

To Cassandra dei Polidori, Pisa.

If your daughter does not want to be a nun, but has chosen to be married, you should not have reasons for regret, rather you should consider the excellence and the dignity of matrimony. It was instituted neither by [St] Augustine nor by [St] Basil, nor by that blessed father who gave lustre to the town of Norcia with the innocence of his holy life,[2] but by God himself, who consecrated it with his own words, and did so in the Garden of Eden. Here our first father [Adam] also heard all the high mysteries of the sacrament of matrimony. All this happened in the age of innocence, before the appearance of the stain of sin. Only this estate was kept holy and immaculate, and was preserved from divine wrath in those times when He thought to destroy mankind through the violence of the Flood.

In order to understand even better that your daughter does no wrong in marrying, you should consider that the Son of God delayed becoming human till the Queen of Heaven was bound by such a knot. Not only did Jesus honour a wedding with his own presence, but he also made it illustrious with a wondrous miracle. Besides, I cannot believe that your daughter has not sometime read those holy words written by the blessed Jerome *a vigilantia*: 'If we praise virginity, why don't we greatly love marriage, from which virgins are born?' I cannot

2 St Benedict.

believe that she has never read that passage from Ambrose, which says that marriage not only fills up the world [with children], but heaven as well.

Therefore be at peace, take comfort, and don't be sad, but give her your blessing, praying God that He will let us see offspring worthy of her forebears.

8.4 Why should women marry?

The female speakers in Moderata Fonte's *Il merito delle donne* (Venice, 1600) discuss the merits and disadvantages of marriage from a woman's viewpoint.[3]
Fonte (1988), pp. 170–2.

'I heard so many things about men yesterday' said Virginia, 'and I have heard so much today, that I have almost changed my mind, and all the reasons given by Leonora and by these other [women] have convinced me that I don't think I want to be subject to any man, but to live freely and peacefully'.

'Do not talk like this' said the Queen, 'because it is necessary that you should marry. But I promise you that when the time comes I shall search and search, so that I'll find a companion with whom you shall live happily, because I shall endeavour to find [a man] who is noble, wise and virtuous, rather than rich, weak and idle.'

'Oh, mother' said Virginia, 'I would much better live with you. What would I do if he were arrogant?'

'Then you should be humble' said the Queen, 'because, since we agreed to be subject to them, it is necessary to treat them with blandishments'.

'Oh' said Leonora, 'most of them are pig-headed, and they want to do as they like'.

'Nevertheless there are those' said the Queen, 'who are less proud than others, and if women act right they can be brought around, and even more so if this man is noble, if not by blood at least by soul and manners, because humility is the proper companion of nobility'.

'And if he is strict and intimidating, what shall I do?' said Virginia.

---

3 See V. Cox, 'The Single Self: Feminist Thought and the Marriage Market in Early Modern Venice', *Renaissance Quarterly*, 48:3 (1995), pp. 513–81.

'Be patient and tolerant', rejoined her mother.

'It is not fair' said Leonora, 'because they offend us even if we are silent'.

'If he is wise', said the Queen, 'he will easily and quickly follow reason, and even more so if you do not provoke his anger even more by answering him'.

'And if he is jealous, how should I behave?' added her daughter.

'Do not give him the opportunity to be jealous', said the Queen, 'and since you have to be attractive to him and no one else, if he does not want you to use cosmetics, do not do so; if he does not want you to go out, make him happy. With these means you will be able to move his heart so that he trusts you so that then he will let you do what you want.'

'A jealous man', said Leonora, 'never changes'.

'He will change', answered the mother, 'if you give him reason to, and if he is noble and wise, he will do it for his honour and moderation'

'If he didn't change', said Virginia, 'my life would be too bitter.'

'If you do not like this kind of life', rejoined the Queen, 'just think that if you do not marry you would have to stay always at home all the same, and dress simply without any frills and finery, because a girl who does not want to get married has no other option, and you would be without that companionship which could bring such happiness for the rest of your life'.

[...]

'I say', said Corinna, 'that it is much better to be alone than badly matched'.

'And I say', added Lucrezia, 'that, in spite of men having all those imperfections we have mentioned, since we have to live in this world as it is, it is much better to have their guidance and their company than to be without it, because a thousand accidents, a thousand oppressions may happen to us every day. [Some men] try to defraud us poor women of our possessions, some of our honour or of our life, so that it is better to have one of them as a friend, to defend us from the others, rather than to be alone and to have all of them as enemies. But if by chance, and this does happen, your husband is a good man, either by nature if he was born like that, resembling his mother, or if by his upbringing he becomes an example of goodness and virtue to others, you cannot imagine how great may be the happiness of a woman when she is joined till death to such a companion. Therefore, my daughter, do not lose heart, because you do not yet know what future God has prepared for you.'

CONDUCT AND BEHAVIOUR IN MARRIAGE: THE MARRIAGE TREATISE

The marriage treatise, a new literary genre, was very much a product of the culture of civic humanism. Taking as their starting point Aristotelian writings on the family and the household, the writers in this section discuss the meaning of love, obedience, mutual obligations and sexual relations, and outline the ideal relationship between partners. Marriage should be based on mutual respect, and both husband and wife should fulfil their respective duties. For a woman, following the path of virtue means being chaste and obedient.[4]

8.5 Obedience

The Venetian humanist Francesco Barbaro wrote *De re uxoria* after a visit to Florence in 1415. His treatise was translated into Italian and printed in the mid-sixteenth century. In Book 2, Barbaro describes a wife's duties. Here he discusses one of her required virtues, obedience.

Francesco Barbaro, 'De re uxoria', in *The Earthly Republic: Italian Humanists on Government and Society*, ed. B. G. Kohl and R. G. Witt (Manchester, 1978), p. 193.

The faculty of obedience ... is her master and companion, because nothing more important, nothing greater can be demanded of a wife than this. The importance of this faculty did not escape the ancient wise men who instituted the custom that when a sacrifice was made to Juno, who was called by the name Gamelia because of her governance of marriage, the gall was removed from the victim. They were wisely warning by this custom that it was proper to banish all gall and rancour from married life.

---

4 See B. Richardson, '"Amore maritale": Advice on Love and Marriage in the Second Half of the Cinquecento', in Panizza, pp. 194–208.

8.6, 8.7 Chastity (*Onestà*)

For both humanists and churchmen, *onestà* (chastity, modesty and irreproach-able sexual conduct) is the most important requirement for a woman, and this view does not change during our period. Chastity in marriage did not mean refraining from sexual intercourse. It meant faithfulness to one's spouse, as the following extracts make clear. It also meant restraint and modesty during intercourse.

a. In his *Libro della vita civile* (*c.* 1438), the Florentine humanist Matteo Palmieri states that kinship relations achieved through marriage are at the heart of social structure. He is concerned with the establishment of a stable republic, and his aim is to mould moderate and rational citizens. In this extract he explains how the relationship between husband and wife should be based on honour and mutual faithfulness.

Matteo Palmieri, *Libro della vita civile* (Venice, 1535), fols 74v–75r.

Once the bond of holy matrimony has been tied in this way, the husband will have obligations towards his wife, and the wife towards her husband, and each of them will be required to observe the matri-monial laws. The woman's greatest and absolute care must be both to refrain from copulating with another man, and to avoid the suspicion of such a repulsive wickedness. This error is the supreme betrayal of decency, it banishes honour, it severs the union, brings with it uncer-tainty about offspring, pollutes the family, brings hate and dissolves any connection. The woman no longer deserves to be called married, but corrupt and worthy of public shame. The husband too should not be inconstant and take his seed elsewhere, nor should he shed it into another woman, in order not to lose his own dignity and bring shame to offspring born illegitimately.

b. Following St Jerome, Bernardo Trotto advises moderation and restraint in a wife's demonstrations of love.

Bernardo Trotto, *Dialoghi del matrimonio, e vita vedovile* (Turin, 1578), p. 90.

Whenever [a wife] is with [her husband], also when they are alone, she should never cross the limits of agreeableness, nor should she touch the boundaries of lasciviousness. This is because a lascivious woman, besides giving her husband reasons to be suspicious of her, is held in poor esteem by many. He will not love her much, and others will falsely praise her. And during their most secret caresses, she must hold on to her real reputation, and not offer herself to her husband as a brazen prostitute, but be happy as a chaste wife, and sweetly receive her husband when he seeks her. Nothing is worse for a woman than treating her husband in the way which would allure an adulterer. In fact, if it is seems that the holy bond of matrimony makes many things lawful, it does not however permit any vices.

CONDUCT AND BEHAVIOUR IN MARRIAGE: TWO CHURCHMEN'S VIEWS

8.8 Sexuality between spouses, 1424

S. Bernardino did not avoid controversial subjects, such as sexuality within marriage. In the church of S. Croce in Florence he used a lively, colloquial style to make his message clear to the men and women gathered to listen.[5]

Bernardino da Siena (1934), vol. I, pp. 381, 387.

[There is] among people a great ignorance about things concerning marriage. They say that it is shameful in words and actions to preach about it, or to give advice … Therefore it happens that, since you are not told anything [about marriage] either in confession or in sermons, you are so ignorant about it, that you experience your appetites with malice, like animals and worse than animals, because you do not consider the highest sacrament of matrimony, which was instituted by God in the Garden of Eden, and was the first that he ever instituted. And you turn it into a pigsty. And you think that marriage means only carnal copulation, but in fact it means the faith placed by the husband in the wife and by the wife in the husband.

[…]

Every time the woman is in her time [of the month] one should not have relations with her, under penalty of mortal sin. But two things should be distinguished: either [the bleeding] is continuous, or it happens at intervals. If it is continuous, you can have [sexual] relations, but when it happens at intervals, you cannot, because this is forbidden by the Holy Church, because then monstrous creatures can be conceived, either with two pairs of hands, or with six fingers, or without vital organs, or perverted males or females can be born, full of leprosy or other diseases. And therefore the Holy Church forbids this. But if it is continuous, then one cannot conceive, and it is then not forbidden to husband and wife [to have relations], as and when I shall say.

---

5 See D. Herlihy, 'Santa Caterina and San Bernardino: Their Teachings on the Family', in his *Women, Family and Society in Medieval Europe* (Providence, RI, and Oxford, 1995), pp. 174–92.

If she is in her time, two things can happen. Either he knows, or he does not know. If he does not know, it is not a sin to have marital relations, but the woman must tell him, because of the evil which can ensue. Sometimes because of this husbands may become mad, sodomites, adulterers, and be polluted by a thousand other sins. St Thomas says: 'The woman, when she is in her time, and is approached [by her husband] for marital relations, should not always tell him. If she believes that he will then go elsewhere, and commit a worse sin, she will not sin. But if they both know it, they will both always sin mortally.'

8.9 A wise and tranquil wife, 1577

Agostino Valiero, Bishop of Verona, praises a peaceful, modest and wise wife.

Agostino Valiero, *Della istruzione del modo di vivere delle donne maritate* (Padua, 1744), pp. 19, 21.

It is praiseworthy for a married woman to be peaceful, to keep the peace with her husband, between her husband and [his] brothers and sisters, in the household, and suffer everything rather than break the peace, which is the mother of concord, the sister of happiness, the companion of all virtues, comfort in adversity, and the flavouring of prosperity.

[...]

A married woman ought to be wise and know herself. She ought to know that she is subject to her husband and that the smallest thing may stain her honour. For this reason she must show her modesty through her behaviour: through her eyes, by keeping them always lowered; through her mouth, by not talking if it is not necessary; through her clothes, by inspiring respect in men, rather than desire; through her ears, by listening only to what is useful; by shunning all public feasts, spectacles, comedies, through which the Devil triumphs and continues to gain souls and increase his tyranny ... The saints write that a wise wife is the consolation of her husband, and the care and wealth of the house.

OUTWARD APPEARANCE

The number of sermons and treatises dealing with women's appearance is so large, that it is impossible to underestimate the importance of this aspect of women's lives. As well as signifying modesty and virtuous behaviour, dress was a sign of social rank, and therefore one of the means through which married women could show their status. Because dress conveyed the wealth and position of the family to which a woman belonged, treatises on marriage and the family insist on the importance of displaying clothes and jewels.

Dress and ornaments

8.10 What a good woman should wear

In a sermon of 1427, S. Bernardino recommends modesty and simplicity in dress, reminding women of their duty to be and look chaste, and pointing out the relationship between gaudy clothes and loose morals.

Bernardino da Siena (1989), vol. II, pp. 1070–1, 1073–5.

How does one recognise a good woman? From the way she is dressed … The exterior shows what is inside. On this point I want to say, of a woman who is dressed like a prostitute, I don't know what the inside is like, but from what is outside I think I can see signs of dirt. I think you must be a … I don't want to say it, but you understand me well. How can you wear a dress like that, you silly woman? Don't you have any brains? [...]

So, woman, don't dress or walk so that you look like a prostitute, but rather wear suitable clothes which show you are good and chaste. Just tell me, if somebody said to you, as you walk by, 'Oh, you look like a prostitute!', what would you think? I don't think you would like that. So, avoid the reason why this could be said to you, avoid looking like [a prostitute]. [...]

Oh woman, you who wear so many things which are not yours, if you gave back to the sheep the wool you are wearing, and returned the silk to the worms which made it, and [if] the [false] hair you wear went back to those who owned it and who are now dead, and the horsehair you use went back to the horses, if everything you use to adorn yourself returned where it came from, oh, you would be like a plucked chicken, you would not have so many fripperies and things to smear yourself with, and would not commit as many sins.

8.11 A wife needs beautiful clothes

From the 1427 *Catasto* tax declaration of the Florentine Mariotto di Nozzo Lippi.

E. Conti, A. Guidotti and R. Lunardi, *La civiltà fiorentina del Quattrocento* (Florence, 1993), p. 125.

My wife, who is 15 years old, whom I married this year. I spend a lot of money on her every day, to keep her in clothes and other things, as her peers are accustomed. And I cannot spend any less, because she is the daughter of a well-to-do family, and she wants to show off in front of her peers and relatives. Please, have some consideration for this matter.

8.12 Sumptuary laws, Pistoia, 1558

Sumptuary laws appear in the statute books of Italian cities from the thirteenth century. They sought to regulate dress according to social rank through prohibitions regarding types of cloth, intricate and costly decorations, ornaments and jewellery, in order to highlight the differences between ranks and to privilege the wealthiest and more powerful groups which were exempt from restrictions. At times sumptuary laws also aimed to limit the amount of money spent on clothing, which diverted wealth from more constructive and profitable use.[6]

L. Cantini, *Legislazione toscana raccolta e illustrata*, 30 vols (Florence, 1802), vol. 3, pp. 249–50.

Women in the city of Pistoia … its countryside or its district shall not be allowed to wear any kind of pearls as ornament, except if set in a ring, and as a necklace as specified below. They are not allowed to wear any caps on their head, *etiam* made of velvet, but only a hat made of velvet or other cloth, simple and unadorned, without cords, silver or gold lace, without feathers, gold points, or other similar ornaments.

[They are not allowed to wear] gloves embroidered in gold or silver,

---

6 On sumptuary laws, see: C. Kovesi Killerby, *Sumptuary Law in Italy, 1200–1500* (Oxford, 2001); D. Owen Hughes, 'Sumptuary Law and Social Relations in Renaissance Italy', in J. Bossy, ed., *Disputes and Settlements: Law and Human Relations in the West* (Cambridge, 1983); R. Rainey, 'Dressing down the Dressed-up: Reproving Feminine Attire in Renaissance Florence', in J. Monfasani and R. G. Musto, eds, *Renaissance Society and Culture: Essays in Honor of Eugene F. Rice, Jr.* (New York, 1991), pp. 217–37; C. Kovesi Killerby, 'Practical Problems in the Enforcement of Italian Sumptuary Laws, 1200–1500', in T. Dean and K. J. P. Lowe, eds, *Crime, Society and the Law in Renaissance Italy* (Cambridge, 1994), pp. 99–120.

or gold caps worth more than three *scudi*, nor garlands, *calcami*[7] or other such gold ornament worth more than six *scudi*, which must be without pearls or precious stones, real or false.

[They are not allowed to wear] medals or cameos of any kind. They cannot wear pendant [earrings], or good jewels, or false ones, either in gold or in solid silver. They are not allowed to wear any kind of false chains around the neck, or anywhere else, but they are allowed one gold chain weighing twenty-five *scudi*, without enamel or other stones, worn round the neck, or a string of pearls of similar cost according to the assessment of the *operai* of St James; if they wear the pearls, they may not wear the chain. Or a necklace worth a maximum of eight *scudi*, without the chain; or a necklace of pure silver beads, not gilded, or amber beads, or carnelian, or black amber with gold decoration, worth the same amount, and a chain of pure silver, not gilded, up to eight ounces, worn as a belt; or a belt of amber [beads] with gold decorations, worth a maximum of four *scudi*.

They are not allowed to wear needlework [decorations] or embroidery in gold, silver or silk of any kind on any of their clothes; or silk stockings embroidered with needlework or in any other way, either all over or in part; or slippers and shoes made of velvet or any kind of cloth.

They are not allowed to wear ruffs round the neck, or collars, cuffs or chemises embroidered in gold or silver, either pure, alloyed or false, and they are not allowed to wear pulled or beaten gold in any way, or aprons embroidered in any other material apart from silk or thread: ruffs, collars, sleeves and chemises may be embroidered in such a way. They cannot wear on their clothes, or as lining, or as ornament, Spanish cat, sable, lynx, marten, or other similar valuable furs, but they may wear a marten around the neck without any gold, stones or pearl decoration, but with a pure silver chain of one and a half ounces maximum.

Beauty and cosmetics

Despite universal disapproval of the use of cosmetics from churchmen such as Bernardino da Siena to women humanists such as Laura Cereta, the large number of recipe books which taught how to make

---

7 Variation used in Pistoia of the word *carcami*, meaning diadems or tiaras.

beauty products demonstrate their popularity and their wide use. These books were written in an easily comprehensible language, so that instructions could be easily followed.

8.13 A physician's advice, Venice, 1562

The physician Giovanni Marinelli wrote on cosmetics as well as on medicine. He addresses his treatise to women of the middle ranks and of the aristocracy, considering their health as well as their desire to make themselves beautiful.

Giovanni Marinelli, *Gli ornamenti delle donne*, ed. L. Pescasio (Castiglione delle Stiviere, 1973), pp. 60–2, 92.

To curl hair:

Take equal quantities of beet and myrtle, dry them in the shade and crush into a powder (many squeeze them to make a juice). Mix with olive oil, and rub into the hair, which in a short time will be curly and beautiful.

An excellent potion is made by boiling salt in water and skimming the foam, which will then be mixed with pulverised myrrh. Rub into the hair, which will become curly.

To straighten hair:

To clean and straighten your hair, take one ounce of oil of lily and one of oil of rose, two of oil of violets, and two of finely crushed green leaves of marshmallow. Boil everything together, stirring. Wet your hair with this mixture while combing it.

To remove dandruff:

Bitter almonds, without their skin and crushed, and then tempered in vinegar, when rubbed on the head clean it in such a way that it is wonderful to see. When the hair is dry, wash it in hot water.

8.14 A woman writer's cosmetic recipes

Isabella Cortese was the only woman to write a treatise on alchemy and cosmetics, which she claims to have learned during her travels throughout Eastern Europe. Seven editions of her *I secreti* were printed between 1561 and 1599.

Isabella Cortese, *I secreti della Signora Isabella Cortese* (Venice, 1595), pp. 114, 143, 164.

To beautify your hands:

Take some lemon juice and the same quantity of perfumed water, and place on the fire to boil. While this is boiling, pour in some powdered almond skins, and [stir], turning it into a soap. Wash your hands with it, and it will make your hands white and beautiful.

A face lotion:

Take some lemons and some dried broad beans. Soak them in white wine, together with honey, eggs and goat's milk. Distil the mixture. This lotion makes the face beautiful.

Soap for bleaching hair:

Take three parts of alum, one part of quicklime ... From this take three *bocali*,[8] a small quantity of oil, mix together, and add the white of an egg, a small bowlful of flour, and an ounce of Roman vitriol, and mix for three hours. Leave to rest for one day and the soap is ready. Take it from the container, cut it as you like and dry it in the usual way. Do not expose it to the sun for three days, and it will be perfect. This soap is good for making your hair blond and as beautiful as gold: rub it on the hair in the sunshine, leave it to dry, then rub it again as before.

DOMESTIC SPACES AND FURNISHINGS[9]

8.15 A famous bedchamber, 1529–30

A couple's bedroom furnishings, commissioned for their marriage, were a symbol of their union. Here Giorgio Vasari tells how, during the 1529–30 siege of Florence, Margherita Acciaiuoli courageously defended her famous bedroom furnishings from plunder. Commissioned by Salvi Borgherini for the wedding of his son Pierfrancesco with Margherita in 1515, these comprised a bed, *cassoni*, *spalliere* and day beds, made by Baccio d'Agnolo and decorated with panels painted with stories from the life of Joseph by Iacopo Pontormo, Andrea del Sarto, Bachiacca and Francesco Granacci, from *c*.1515 to 1518.[10]

Vasari (1906), vol. 6, pp. 262–3.

During the siege of Florence, as Pierfrancesco [Borgherini] had gone

---

8 A measurement.

9 On the influence of women on interiors, see P. Thornton, *The Italian Renaissance Interior, 1400–1600* (London, 1990), pp. 348–57.

10 See A. Braham, 'The Bed of Pierfrancesco Borgherini', in *Burlington Magazine*, 121 (1979), pp. 754–65; J. Dunkerton, S. Foister and N. Penny, *Dürer to Veronese: Sixteenth Century Painting in the National Gallery*, (New Haven and London, 1999), pp. 130–4.

to Lucca, Giovambattista della Palla wanted to have the furnishings of that bedroom to add to other things he was taking to France in order to give them from the *Signoria* to King Francis.[11] He was so favoured, and he did and said so much, that the Standard-Bearer and the *Signori* gave orders that [the furnishings] be taken, and Pierfrancesco's wife be paid. So, when Giovambattista and others went to carry out what the *Signori* had decreed, and went to Pierfrancesco's house, his wife, who was at home, insulted Giovambattista as no man had been insulted before. So, she said, you want to be so bold, Giovambattista, you, a lowly second-hand dealer, a cheap little merchant, as to pull out the furnishings from gentlemen's bedrooms, and strip this city of its richest and most precious things, as you have done and are still doing, in order to embellish foreign countries and our enemies? I am not surprised that you, a plebeian and an enemy of your country, can do this, but that the magistrates of this city can allow these abominable wrongdoings. This bed, which you want for your own interest and your greed for money, while you try to hide your malevolence with false piety, is my marriage bed, and my father-in-law Salvi had all this magnificent and regal decoration done in honour of my wedding. I treasure [these furnishings] in his memory, and for the love of my husband, and I intend to defend them with my blood and with my own life. Get out of this house with your thugs, Giovambattista, and go and tell those who sent you here and ordered these things to be removed, that I am the one who does not want anything to be moved from here. And if those who believe in you, worthless and ignoble man, want to give presents to King Francis of France, they can go and send the furnishings and the beds from their own bedrooms, and strip their own houses. And if you are so bold as to come to this house for this, I will let you know at your expense how much respect people like you must have towards the houses belonging to gentlemen.

Because of these words of the lady Margherita, wife of Pierfrancesco Borgherini and daughter of Roberto Acciaiuoli, a most noble and prudent citizen, [who was] a most valiant woman and worthy daughter of such a father, and because of her noble courage and cleverness, these treasures are still kept in their houses.

---

11 The King of France, Francis I.

8.16 **The ideal married quarters in a wealthy household,** *c.*1440

Leon Battista Alberti, *L'Architettura*, ed. P. Portoghesi, 2 vols (Milan, 1966), vol. 1, p. 426.

Book 5, Chapter 17.

The bedrooms of husband and wife must be separate because the wife, when she gives birth or when she is ill, should not disturb her husband, and also because they should, if they so wish, sleep untroubled, especially during the summer. Each room will have its door, and there will be also a connecting door, allowing them to visit each other without being seen. Next to the wife's bedroom should be a dressing room and next to the husband's, a library.

8.17 **Women at home, 1552–3**

Anton Francesco Doni, *I Marmi*, ed. E. Chiorboli, 2 vols (Bari, 1928), vol. 1, p. 136.

Vol. 1, Ragionamento 7.

Chambers are made for sleeping, therefore they only need enough space for this and not for walking or for having banquets or balls. For these, halls are fine, because all the inhabitants of the house will at times congregate there: women will place themselves in the embrasures of windows, so that they can have enough light to do fine needlework and embroidery, and can also look out of the windows. The table is for eating at, and the side table for playing at. Some then walk up and down, others stand by the fire, and there is enough room for everybody.

RUNNING A HOUSEHOLD

Training a wife

Writers on marriage agree on the great importance of training women to carry out all domestic duties in the house, controlling the household goods, and taking care of servants and slaves. This ideal was born out of the needs of fourteenth- and fifteenth-century mercantile society, and from classical sources, such as the *Oeconomica*. A well-run household, where harmony rules and there is no waste, is a happy one, and it is the wife who is responsible for it.

8.18 Rules for a young wife

In Book III of Alberti's *Della famiglia* (written before 1434), the elderly Giannozzo explains how he established strict rules for his young wife.
Alberti (1960), pp. 218–19.

After my wife had been settled in my house a few days, and the longing for her mother and her family had begun to fade, I took her by the hand and showed her around the whole house. I told her that the loft was the place for grain and that the cellar was for wine and wood. I showed her where things for the table were kept, and there were no household goods in the entire house whose place and purpose my wife had not learnt. Then we returned to my room, and, having locked the door, I showed her all my household treasures, silverware, tapestries, garments, jewels, and where each thing was kept. [...]

Only my books and records and those of my ancestors did I want then as now to keep locked away, so that my wife not only could not read them, but could not even lay hands on them. I always kept my records not in the sleeves of my robe, but locked up and arranged in order in my study, almost like sacred and religious objects, and I never gave my wife permission to enter, with me or alone. I also ordered her, if she ever came across any writing of mine, to give it to me at once. To take away any desire she might have for looking at my writings or prying into my private affairs, I often used to express my disapproval of bold and forward females who try too hard to know about things outside the home or about the concerns of their husbands and of men.

8.19 A wife rules over the household, 1547

Dolce (1547), fols 56v–57v.

The wife must be most diligent in the care of everything that comes into the house. Eschewing extravagance, she must not embrace avarice, but rather keep to a certain mean, and follow neither want nor excess. She should be happy to see her husband spend [money] honourably and in charitable works.

She should see that the household does not lack anything, because this is the task that pertains to the woman rather than the man. She should, however, always act according to his orders and his consent, in the way she knows to be agreeable to him, keeping her eye on his wishes, as the helmsman, always steady and determined, keeps his eye to the North ...

The good housewife should take care that no part of the house, no place, no household goods are hidden from her. She should look everywhere, think of everything, go everywhere, so that when she needs [something] she will have what she wants under her eye or under her hand, quickly and without difficulty, just like a captain who often inspects his soldiers. And she should consider the quality of good housekeeping, what is needed for everyday life and for clothing, and while she is sitting working or doing some other duty within her room, she should go over the whole house in her mind, thinking whether there is anything lacking, or anything in excess, what needs to be repaired, bought and sold.

8.20 Advice for a country housewife, 1597

Giuseppe Falcone, *La nuova, vaga, et dilettevole Villa* (Pavia, 1597), pp. 35–8.

On Sundays she should make everyone change into their white shirts. When doing the laundry she should not use too much soap or wood, or employ too many women: all the young girls of the household should do the washing. She should see that torn clothes are mended.

She should set her hens to brood over eggs at the right time. She should know how to castrate cockerels.

Flax should be trampled on at night time, and also at night spinning should be done in the stable.

Bread should be made only for the household, and not too many loaves. Bread must not be eaten fresh, but firm and hard: that is good judgment.

The good wine should never be touched, but always drunk with water added: pure wine should be kept for when it is very hot.

At the table everyone should eat the little that there is in peace and silence, and after saying grace. If there is only one nut, everyone should have a taste of it. No one should sit at the table before everyone in the household has come back home.

[...] She should take good care of the milk, and know how to make butter, *ricotta* and cheese, salted in the proper way.

All kinds of small and medium yard animals should be fed at the right time.

She who has not planted her own vegetable garden, nor sown, hoed or weeded it, is not a good manager of household affairs. No hen, goose or any other animal should at any time be allowed in [the vegetable garden].

She should take good care that lard, sausages and salami do not go bad.

She should take care of the oven, [and] fire for cooking. Bread should be kept before being used.

Every year new linen cloth should be made for everybody in the household.

At night the hen-house must be locked and the eggs must be collected every day from the nests.

Every night she must make sure that hens and chickens are back in the hen-house, and that the bees are not attacked by pests.

It is for the master to buy and sell wholesale, but as for all small domestic affairs, they are the task of the farmer's wife.

Household management and business

Wives of merchants and of men involved in government administration were often left in charge of their family estates, either because their husbands spent long periods away on business, or because the vicissitudes of political life could separate them.

8.21 A merchant's advice to his wife, 1395

The merchant Francesco Datini gives advice from Prato to his wife Margherita, in their Florence house.

E. Cecchi, ed., *Le lettere di Francesco Datini alla moglie Margherita (1385–1410)* (Prato, 1990), p. 135.

[June 1395]

You are wise, so do what you think is best. Look after the household staff in such a way to bring honour to yourself. Do not spend such a long time reading that you will then do everything else badly: first take care of everything else, then you can read as much as you like. At night make sure that the front door is safely locked, and the door which is halfway up the stairs.

8.22 Troubles with the law, Siena, 1482

Camilla Petrucci writes from Siena to her husband, Giovan Francesco Petrucci, in exile in Montepulciano.

Lettere di gentildonne italiane del secolo XV (Siena, 1890), p. 26.

[February 1482]

My dearest, etc. I am writing you this to let you know that Nicolò Buoninsegna came to see me yesterday, and told me that he wanted your cows to be requisitioned by the *Balia*,[12] as directed in a letter from the *Balia*. I told him that I would answer him today that I intend to keep hold of them. And when the *Balia* wants to ask my reasons, I shall be patient, but I want them to be in my possession. If you want me to do something else, let me know what I should do.

8.23 A busy country life in Tuscany, 1535

Isabella Sacchetti (1480–1559) writes from her country estate in Poppiano to her husband Luigi Guicciardini (1478–1551), brother of the historian Francesco, in Arezzo.

I. Del Lungo, *La donna fiorentina del buon tempo antico* (Florence, 1905), p. 256.

[August 1535]

Now we have to think about grape-gathering. We need to put hoops round some of the vats again, and mend the barrel which spoilt all the vinegar ... We need to fell the cherry tree, which, although I gave orders to do it, was never done. I will see all these things get done, if I can, but I think that my leaving will prevent me, because giving orders and not being here does not work out. If I had thought about all the things I have to do, I do not think I would have organised this trip [to Arezzo]. I know that you want me to come, and I do not feel like displeasing you, and if you want me to come, I will, even if I have to let everything go to rack and ruin. I shall not be able to stay more than 15 days, then I shall have to come back, because I have to leave many things [undone]. What irritates me most is that I do not have a servant to leave [in charge] here for 15 days ... I do not see anybody fit to be left here to do all the things that need to be done ...

12 The *Balia* was the governing body of magistrates.

THE LIFE OF MARRIED WOMEN

The letters of Renaissance women often reveal a complex network of relationships, among which first and foremost were their female relatives and friends. In spite of their arranged marriages, many women express in their letters feelings towards their husbands which attest to a rich emotional life and to strong attachments.[13]

8.24 A day trip to Fiesole, 1395

Margherita Datini, in Florence, tells her husband Francesco, in Prato, how she and her friends had organised a trip to Fiesole in June 1395.

D. Toccafondi and G. Cascone, eds, *Per la tua Margherita. Scrittura a distanza: lettere di una donna del Trecento al marito mercante* (Prato, 2001), p. 49.

On Sunday morning I went to the Piaciti house and came back on Monday evening. I could not avoid going because they have been here many times. On Monday night Belozzo's wife, Francesca and Caterina slept here with me, so that we could get up early in the morning. We did just that, and, with all our women, we went to see that holy painting and the relics, and we went all together. For lunch we had the bacon that Fattorino had kept for us. We all had lunch together, and then we went to Fiesole because there was an indulgence [to be obtained], the most important in the whole year. We did obtain it, and we saw the holy image of S. Maria Primerana, which was uncovered. I also went in [to obtain an indulgence] for you. We came back in the evening quite tired, and each of us went back to her own house. We were all at home and in bed by eleven.

8.25 A dance in honour of Lucrezia Donati, 1466

In her letters to her son Filippo, Alessandra Macinghi Strozzi makes frequent gossipy remarks about the wealthy merchant Niccolò Ardinghelli and his beautiful wife Lucrezia Donati (1449–1501), whom Niccolò had left alone in Florence during their betrothal and also after their wedding in 1465, while away on business. The man who kept Lucrezia happy during her husband's absence was none other than Lorenzo de' Medici.[14] Here Alessandra mentions a dance held in Lucrezia's honour on 3 February 1466.

---

13 M. di Leonardo, 'The Female Worlds of Cards and Holidays: Women, Families and the Work of Kinship', in *Signs*, 12 (1987), pp. 440–53.
14 Alessandra comments that Lorenzo 'sees her often' (*'ispesso la vede'*). Macinghi Strozzi, p. 212.

Macinghi Strozzi (1987), p. 307.

[Niccolò Ardinghelli's] wife is here, and she is glad, as she has had a new gown made in her colours,[15] decorated with pearls, few, but large and beautiful. And so at her instance a dance was held three days ago, in the Sala del Papa in S. Maria Novella, which was organised by Lorenzo di Piero [de' Medici]. And he [Lorenzo] was with a group of young men dressed in her colours, with short purple overcoats embroidered with beautiful pearls. And Lorenzo was among those wearing black with a livery of pearls of great quality.

8.26 Family news, 1472

Francesca Pitti Tornabuoni writes from Rome to Clarice Orsini, wife of her nephew Lorenzo de' Medici, in Florence.

E. Plebani, *I Tornabuoni. Una famiglia fiorentina alla fine del Medioevo* (Milan, 2002), p. 58.

[31 July 1472]

If I have not written to you as I should have, it was not from negligence, but so as not to bother you, since you are so busy. Nevertheless, I shall be more diligent from now on [...] I am sending you, together with my letter, a letter I received from Madonna Perna di Romano, who asked me to remind you about her case. You will see what she wants from her letter. I recommend this to you, since it is your business.

Thank God we are all well, and [I hope] He also keeps you in good health. We have just moved into another house, and we have a good and pleasant situation. I cannot think of anything else at the moment, apart from recommending myself to you. I ask you to remember me to Lorenzo, Monna Lucrezia [Tornabuoni] and Monna Contessina[16] and to everybody. [I hope] that God keeps you well. From Rome, 31 July 1472. I have not see your Madonna Maddalena[17] because she was at Monterotondo, but I understand that Her Ladyship is well, and so is everybody else. Please kiss your children a hundred times for me, and I hope they are good ... My Lorenzino[18] asks to be reminded to you. Remind him to Monna Lucrezia and Lorenzo.

15 The Donati heraldic colours.
16 Lorenzo de' Medici's mother and grandmother.
17 Clarice Orsini's mother.
18 Francesca Pitti Tornabuoni's son.

8.27 **An invitation, 1552**

Lucrezia Gonzaga, p. 148.

To the Lady Andriana de Campi:

Now that I am ill with quartan fever, am I to believe that you will not come to drive away the darkness of my sad thoughts with your sweet and pleasant words? In fact it seems to me that the power of your words is such, that those who find it insufficient would also want honey to be sweeter. Please come, my dear Andriana, and don't keep me waiting with your delay. No one dearer to me could come, to whom I could listen more eagerly, who would be more lovingly welcomed by me. Come then, and don't make me long for you in vain any more.

8.28 **Consoling words, 1395**

Margherita Datini writes to her husband, who often suffered from melancholy. Toccafondi and Cascone, p. 44.

[January 1395]

We have received your letter which made me feel very sad because I see that you are so melancholic. Even if I don't know the reason, whatever it may be, why do you take it so badly that your body and soul suffer? Why don't you, on this occasion and on others, do what you say you would if God took away your children (if you had any), that is, accept it? If we entrusted Him with all our cares and were happy with anything that happens, we would not have all the worries we do have. If we thought about death and about the short time we are in this world, we would not suffer as much as we do. We would let Him take care of us, and be content with everything.

8.29 **Isabella d'Este misses her husband, 1492**

Isabella d'Este expresses her feelings for Francesco Gonzaga, her husband of two years.

A. Luzio and R. Renier, *Delle relazioni di Isabella d'Este Gonzaga con Ludovico e Beatrice Sforza* (Milan, 1890), p. 58.

My Most Illustrious Lord. I have been thinking about writing to you in my own hand during all these days, but I never had the time

because I was always in the company of these lords. Now, having with
difficulty stolen a little bit of time, I shall visit Your Lordship with this
[letter] since I cannot visit you in person. I have you always in my
mind, and it seems a thousand years since I saw you, and in spite of
all the pleasure I have here I have no greater one than hearing that
Your Lordship's health is good, something which I desire more than
my own [health] [...] In Vigevano, 22 August [1492].

She who loves Your Lordship as her own life,

Isabella d'Este, in her own hand.

8.30 To a dissatisfied husband, 1542

From their country estate at Poppiano, Isabella Sacchetti gives some
level-headed advice to her husband Luigi Guicciardini in Castrocaro
(Romagna).

Del Lungo, p. 271.

[December 1542]

It seems to me that you very much resent what you are doing and
where you live, since you went unwillingly and with such vexation,
and I think you will be dissatisfied all the time. I would like you to do
what you tell me I should do, and deal with those matters with good
grace. Do you think I enjoy myself and am satisfied being here, with
two servants, and seeing very few others to talk to, and most of the
time writing, and paying what work has been done, and selling, and
keeping the accounts? All these matters are vexing for people of a
certain age. If one wants to be content, one must find pleasure in things
one does not like, otherwise we would be miserable all the time, and we
must think that time flies, and we are already one third of the way along
the road.

PREPARING FOR DEATH

8.31 Thinking of the afterlife, Lucca, 1379

The overriding preoccupation of men and women throughout our period
was to die in a state of grace, ensuring eternal life for their soul and a
speedy passage through Purgatory. A grave commemorating the
deceased, with name and date of birth, was necessary to keep their memory
alive and make sure that prayers and masses would be said for their

soul.[19] Bartolomea di Francesco Boccella gives instructions about her burial in her will, April 1379. It was not unusual for husband and wife to be buried separately.

M. Bacci, *Investimenti per l'aldilà. Arte e raccomandazione dell'anima nel Medioevo* (Bari, 2003), p. 66.

And I want, decide and order that my body be interred and buried in the church of S. Agostino of the Hermit Friars, in the convent in Lucca, in front of the altar of the saint which is there, and which is called 'of the Blessed Nicola da Tolentino'. If my husband Salvuccio does not want to have his grave there, but wants one made for himself, for his burial, I shall be content to be buried there [in his grave]. If however he does not want one made ... I want to be buried there, that is, in front of the said altar, and I choose that place as the grave for my body.

8.32 A bequest to a dear relative, Venice, 1577

Candiana Garzoni (d. 1611), first wife of the patrician Orsatto Giustinian, dictated her first testament in 1577, during a plague epidemic, and another in 1605. Since she was childless, she nominated her husband's cousin as her heir.

O. Giustinian, *Sonetti alla moglie*, ed. S. Mammana (Florence, 2001), p. 20.

In case my dearest spouse dies before I do, and if this is God's will, and in case he leaves me something as a sign of the love he has for me, I want everything he leaves me to go after my own death to Zaccaria Giustinian, cousin of my husband, [who is] like a son for both of us, since we brought him up from the time he was a small child. And I leave this to him as a sign of my love, because he has always been good and obedient to me, as if I had been his own mother.

19 See A. Butterfield, 'Monument and Memory in Early Renaissance Florence', in G. Ciappelli and P. L. Rubin, eds, *Art, Memory, and Family in Renaissance Florence* (Cambridge, 2000), pp. 135–60; S. T. Strocchia, *Death and Ritual in Renaissance Florence* (Baltimore, 1992). See also E. Welch, *Art and Society in Italy 1350–1500* (Oxford, 1997), pp. 138–49.

UNHAPPY MARRIAGES

8.33 A lonely merchant's wife, early 15th century

Margherita de' Banchi, in Florence, writes to her husband Priore di Mariotto de' Banchi, who had been in Palermo for business for a year.

L. Zdekauer, *Lettere volgari del Rinascimento senese* (Siena, 1897), pp. 9–10.

I have not written, nor have I answered because I have not had any signs. Now, seeing that you are not coming back [I am] desperate because you don't want to come. You promised me that you would come back in four months, and [now] you are not here at the beginning of the year, so I will not ask you anything anymore, since you had sworn and made promises. I had taken an oath that I would not write to you again, but I have broken this oath, because Priore Ottavanti came about Bastiano. You will get [this letter] through him, and you will not be able to say that you have not received it.

I am telling you that you must come back, because I don't want to be like this anymore, as I feel the devils' fire. You are the reason why I feel like this, as it is not a month or two, but a year now.

8.34 An unfaithful husband, 1390

In his *Cronaca Carrarese* Andrea Gatari mentions a Paduan lady from the wealthy Scrovegni family, who found her husband with a servant.

'Cronaca Carrarese confrontata con la redazione di Andrea Gatari (1318–1407)', ed. A. Madini and G. Tolomei, in *Rerum italicarum scriptores*, vol. 17, pt 1 (Città di Castello, 1931), p. 416.

And having found her husband with one of the servants breaking the vows of holy matrimony, and having seen such a disgraceful thing, she no longer observed the customs and manners proper to women, but, like her ancestors, decided to take up arms as a brave and virile knight, and, with great courage and strength, to reproach her husband who had broken [faith with] holy and chaste matrimony. But, remembering that she was a woman, she restrained herself, and immediately swore never to lie with her husband for the rest of her life. This vow she kept as long as she lived, which was for about 36 years, and she always observed a true, laudable and resolute chastity.

8.35 Advice to husbands of infertile women, 1546

Because of the importance of procreation, sterility was a serious problem in the life of a couple, with social as well as personal implications. Juan Luis Vives gives advice to husbands of sterile wives.

Vives, fol. 62r.

Husbands should not be harsh towards sterile wives, because sterility often happens with neither party, or both, being at fault. We know that [women] desire having children more than men, just as an unstable wall needs to be supported by pilasters. Anna, wife of Helcana Efratta, was sterile, and her husband comforted her [saying]: 'Am I not better than ten children?' It was fitting that from such a man Samuel, prophet and prince of Israel, would issue.

8.36 An abusive husband and an unfaithful wife, 1548

Ortensio Lando includes in his collection many letters dealing with problems such as adultery, jealousy and violent husbands. Even if these letters were written for publication, they show awareness of marital difficulties and may have provided advice to their readers.

Lando (1548), fol. 53r–v.

Maria de Benedetti to N. R.

If your husband beats you, if he torments you and keeps bad company, you should blame your bad behaviour, your excessive loquacity and extreme obstinacy, which would be enough to make you ugly and unpleasant even in hell. It is now high time to change your behaviour and your habits: do you want to be known for nothing else but your folly, which by now has made you notorious everywhere? I recently met a group of wise and well-behaved ladies, who severely criticised your life and judged you worthy of every torment, because you are more grudging and disobedient towards your husband than any other woman. Others blamed you for having broken your vows and the lawful bonds of marriage more than once, and all this for the un-restrained love you feel towards a most vile scoundrel, guilty of theft and murder, a drunkard and an evil gambler, with whom even the most degenerate prostitute in Rome or in Venice would not associate herself. I am not going to write anything more. I pray God to give you a better mind and a stronger intellect.

8.37 A refuge for the *malmaritate*, Rome, 1543

The Compagnia della Grazia, founded by Ignatius Loyola, was one of the many charitable organisations set up to take care of the *malmaritate* – women who had left an intolerable marriage, or who had been abandoned by their husbands.[20] This is an extract from the Statutes of the Compagnia della Grazia at S. Marta, Rome, 16 February 1543.

P. Tacchi Venturi, *Storia della Compagnia di Gesù*, 2 vols (Rome, 1950–51), vol. 1, pt 2, pp. 288–9.

A house and a monastery have been established for two reasons. Firstly, so that all those married women living apart from their husbands and in the sins of adultery and fornication, separated from God's grace and from their husbands, may convert once they have left behind their sins, and live chastely and reverently. If they want to enter this house, they must continue to live in it chastely and obediently, not leaving it till the time they return to their husbands. Whenever a husband wants his wife, and undertakes to be a good companion, she will be obliged to return to him to live in peace, love and marital fidelity.

8.38 *Song of desperate women running away from home, c.1555*

The writer Anton Francesco Grazzini (il Lasca) (1503–84), was a founder member of the Florentine Accademia degli Umidi (later Accademia Fiorentina). This Carnival song, typical of his satirical and popular work, belongs to a literary genre which invites the reader to make fun of dramatic or violent situations.

C. S. Singleton, ed., *Canti carnascialeschi del Rinascimento* (Bari, 1936), pp. 443–4.

It is only our husbands' fault
if we, wretched and unlucky women,
run away from our homes in desperation.

We all have husbands who are

---

20 S. Cohen, 'Asylums for Women in Counter-Reformation Italy', in S. Marshall, ed., *Reformation and Counter-Reformation Europe* (Bloomington, 1989), pp. 166–88; J. M. Ferraro, 'The Power to Decide: Battered Wives in Early Modern Venice', *Renaissance Quarterly*, 48:3 (1995), pp. 492–512. On unhappy marriages, see L. Guzzetti, 'Separations and Separated Couples in Fourteenth-Century Venice', in Dean and Lowe, pp. 249–74.

jealous of us,
stingy, and – most of all – old and ugly,
ill-tempered and grumpy,
so that at home we hear nothing
but grumbles, screams and rebukes,
and without any reason we are watched
as if we were in prison.

Some of us can scarcely go to church
or to see our mothers.
Some of us cannot tidy ourselves up, or clean up
our beautiful bodies,
because our wretched husbands,
moved by strange urges,
fear that we try to get from this man or from that one
what they cannot give us themselves.

Thus, wretched are we, more than all those
who, even if prudent and fair,
have, or will have such a fate:
they will always have reason to weep.
And not to mention
that none of us will ever taste
what other women like so much:
there is always war at home, not peace.

Well may we complain
about our fathers and brothers,
who wanted us to marry
men who are impotent, who are almost monsters,
so that they could give a tiny dowry, or none at all.
At the end, without any money,
we were not given in marriage,
but were buried alive.

And so, fathers, and you who have
daughters of marrying age,
make them become nuns, or keep them at home,
rather than give them
to a man who is old
or full of disease:
if you want honour for you and benefit for them,
give them wealth and money.

And you women, who have
loving and beautiful husbands,
or – most of all – young and gracious ones,
learn how to enjoy them,
and with great fervour
thank Heaven for such bliss.
As for us, without any further delay
we are off to find our lovers.

9 Conception, childbirth and the upbringing of children

The most important role of married women was to give birth to children, and the great majority of writers agree in emphasising child-bearing as the primary reason for marriage. As was the case for marriage, having children and bringing them up were not meant primarily for individual satisfaction, but for the good of the family and society.[1] The perfect and harmonious society envisaged by fourteenth- and fifteenth-century writers on the family was one where wealth and prosperity were assured by husbands and wives who did the right and useful thing by 'procreating children, increasing the population, and giving citizens to the mother country', as the humanist Matteo Palmieri writes in his *Libro della vita civile* (*c.* 1438). Palmieri compares a wife to fertile earth, 'which, once the seed has been received, will nourish it and multiply it in abundance', and goes on to say that 'human beings desire nothing more [than children], and without them any marriage would be disjointed and lacking'.

Renaissance society expected women to marry at the age of maximum fertility, from eighteen to twenty-five, when the body was strong and fully grown, but obviously women, especially those belonging to the elite, continued to conceive for much longer. Physicians were not usually present at childbirth because of the need to preserve women's modesty, so the care of women was in the hands of midwives, whose expertise and skills varied considerably. In difficult cases, the midwife would resort to the help of a surgeon (a 'barber'), while in extreme need it was suggested that the physician or the surgeon should be admitted into the darkened childbirth room disguised as a woman. The midwife's skill and experience was not the only help offered to women in labour, who relied also on the protection of saints, especially St Margaret, the patron saint of childbirth.

1 See L. Haas, 'Women and Childbearing in Medieval Florence', in C. Jorgensen, ed., *Medieval Family Roles: A Book of Essays* (New York, 1996), pp. 87–99; L. Haas, *The Renaissance Man and his Children: Childbirth and Early Childhood in Florence 1300–1600* (New York, 1998).

Charms, relics, or objects which were believed to have special apotropaic powers were also used.[2]

After the dangers of childbirth, celebrations took place, as seen in some *deschi da parto*,[3] where women visitors are represented in the bedroom of the new mother bearing gifts such as cakes and confectionery. Even in less wealthy houses, nourishing food and drink would be brought, as shown in a lunette in the Oratorio dei Buonuomini in Florence. Baptism also required godparents and relatives to present gifts, according to their means, to the mother and to the midwife.

CONCEPTION

Conception was believed to happen by the union of male and female sperm, in the moist environment of the uterus, according to ideas about the nature of men and women. Advice about the pregnant woman's well-being – the kind of food she should eat or avoid, how she should dress and what she could or could not do during pregnancy – also took into account the theory of humours and of the wet and cold characteristics of female nature.

The writers on obstetrics, Michele Savonarola (1385–1464), Giovanni Marinelli (d. after 1576) and Scipione (Fra Girolamo) Mercurio (*c.* 1559–*c.* 1615), were concerned with spreading knowledge to those who could not read medical treatises in Latin, and therefore wrote in Italian, despite objections that by doing so they were diminishing the authority of medicine.[4]

9.1 How best to conceive, *c.* 1460

After studying medicine at the University of Padua, Michele Savonarola became court physician to the Ferrara court in 1440. In his many writings, which are are based on Arab treatises (Avicenna), on the Greeks (Hippocrates, Galen and Aristotle), and on contemporary medical knowledge, he constantly

---

2 See K. Park, 'Medicine and Magic: The Healing Arts', in J. C. Brown and R. C. Davis, eds, *Gender and Society in Renaissance Italy* (London, 1998), pp. 129–49. See also B. Cassidy, 'A Relic, Some Pictures and the Mothers of Florence in the Late Fourteenth Century', *Gesta*, 30 (1991), pp. 91–9.

3 Painted trays commissioned for the birth of a child. See J. M. Musacchio, *The Art and Ritual of Childbirth in Renaisssance Italy* (New Haven and London, 1999).

4 See H. Lemay, 'Women and the Literature of Obstetrics and Gynecology', in J. T. Rosenthal, ed., *Medieval Women and the Sources of Medieval History* (Athens, Ga., 1990), pp. 189–209.

stressed the importance of experience and observation. His treatise *Ad mulieres ferrarienses de regimine pregnatium et noviter natorum usque ad septennium* (*c.* 1460), circulated in manuscript form. It gives advice for the health of pregnant women and of new-born babies and small children. Here Savonarola explains conception as the union of male and female sperm.

L. Belloni, ed., *Il trattato ginecologico-pediatrico in volgare di Michele Savonarola* (Milan, 1952), pp. 40–1.

A woman cannot get pregnant without feeling great pleasure in the [sexual] act, as she then emits her seed, and the womb is constricted, as it is written [...] Before they begin to copulate, they must talk together about conceiving, and imagine the conception ... After talking like this, they must touch each other, and especially the man [must touch] the woman, touching and rubbing with his fingers the place between her sex and the vagina. This is because that is the place on the outside where women have more pleasure because of its proximity to the neck of the womb, where the pleasure is strongest. With this rubbing, [women] will begin producing their sperm more easily. [Men] can prolong copulation, touching with their hands her breasts and, lightly, the nipples, reaching the cheeks, the mouth and other places, and especially the place below the belly button, and getting closer with [their] member, without placing it inside, but delaying this. All this must be done to induce the woman to produce her sperm. It is also true that some are more ready, others less so, that is, warmer or less warm, so that the man needs to caress them with foresight and measure. Some do not care for such caresses and conceive without them: should the man caress one who is warm by nature and capable of producing seed quickly in the same way as he does a cold one, he would do so in vain.

[...] As soon as the man has poured his seed, the wife must immediately lift her thighs, he must get up, and at once she must hold her thighs, legs and feet together, and keep them lifted for a sixth of an hour, so that the sperm can more easily enter the womb and be retained there, and also because air must not penetrate and spoil the seed. In order to conceive, she must also immediately smell a piece of wadding scented with musk, laudanum, or other perfumed spice, if she does not dislike perfumed things. Having placed it there, she must try to sleep, because the heat inside helps the generative capacity, and the sperm becomes warmer and more inclined to conceive.

9.2, 9.3 **The environment of conception**

The environment in which a child was conceived was believed to influence his or her physical and moral qualities. Leon Battista Alberti, in his treatise on architecture (*c.* 1440s), and the physician Giovanni Marinelli, in his *Le medicine pertinenti alle infermità delle donne* (1563), give advice on this matter.[5]

a. Leon Battista Alberti, *L'Architettura*, ed. P. Portoghesi, 2 vols (Milan, 1966), vol. 2, p. 804.

In those chambers where a husband and wife come together, it is advisable to paint only very beautiful and noble figures. They say that this has great importance for the quality of the conception and the beauty of future offspring.

b. Giovanni Marinelli, *Le medicine pertinenti ...*, in ed. M. L. Altieri Biagi *et al.*, *Medicina per le donne nel Cinquecento* (Turin, 1992), p. 57.

The room where [husband and wife] will copulate should be perfumed with sweet-smelling essences, and hot by nature, as for example musk, aloe wood, civet, amber, perfume burners and such things. If possible, it should be pleasant, beautiful and remarkable, with pleasant paintings representing men, so that they will have similar images in their minds. If they want to have valiant sons, they should have paintings of valiant men, or they could imagine them. Therefore it happens that bastards look more like imagined men than their real fathers, because an adulterous wife, fearing her husband, will continuously think about these during copulation.

9.4 **How to induce erection, help copulation and increase sperm**

Handwritten notes in the 1567 edition of a very popular medical book for apothecaries provide recipes for the cure of some male problems.

Ricettario fiorentino (1567), notes in Biblioteca Nazionale Centrale di Roma copy, 71.3. G. 21

Ad erigendum pene: [Mix] the yolks of two freshly laid eggs, freshly made pine-nut oil and a pinch of cinnamon. Take this before going to bed, and use for many nights.

5 See J. M. Musacchio, 'Imaginative Conceptions in Renaissance Italy', in Johnson and Matthews Grieco, pp. 42–60. On the role of erotic paintings in conception, see R. Goffen, 'Renaissance Dreams', in *Renaissance Quarterly*, 40 (1987), pp. 682–706.

Little cakes to induce copulation and increase sperm:
   clover seeds 3 ij^6
   rocket seeds
   pepper
   refined sugar, dissolved
This makes small cakes of 3 j each, for the use indicated above.

PREGNANCY

Medical advice

9.5 The early signs of pregnancy

La prima parte degli errori popolari, a 1592 Italian translation of the French
court physician Laurent Joubert's 1578 treatise, was one of the most popular
practical texts on medicine. Having stated that ignorance of anatomy is the
cause for many mistaken beliefs, Joubert sets out to explain in clear language
the mechanism of conception, the state of pregnancy, and what happens
during childbirth. Here he lists the unmistakeable signs of pregnancy, having
explained that examining a woman's urine is not a reliable method to discover
whether she is pregnant.

Lorenzo Gioberti (Laurent Joubert), *La prima parte degli errori popolari* ...
(Florence, 1592), p. 111.

How can we then find out whether a woman is pregnant, since no
certainty comes from examining her urine? I would rather listen to
women who know from experience, have conceived often, and are
mothers of many children. One must believe them [when they say]
that they have often felt a change in their body because of their
pregnancy, both in the belly and in their breasts.

There are also other signs ... These are: feeling nauseous and lacking
appetite, or craving strange and absurd things; vomit; debility; heart-
burn; troublesome stomach pains; spitting a lot; headache; lower back
pains; swelling of the legs; weariness and heaviness all over the body.

9.6 Michele Savonarola: the pregnant woman's regimen, *c.* 1460

Savonarola explains how to achieve a healthy life according to the well-known
scheme of the '*regimina sanitatis*', which suggested rules about how to deal

---

6 A measurement.

with the six so-called 'non-naturals': air; food and drink; movement and rest; sleeping and waking; starvation and repletion; and accidents of the soul.

Belloni, p. 82.

Since we have discussed food and drink, let us deal with the other five parts [of the regimen], which are called non-natural, and continue with a discussion of movement or exercise ... the pregnant woman must follow, so that, avoiding mistakes, she does not miscarry. I therefore say, together with our writers, that a pregnant woman must take exercise in moderation, and not in excess, because excess causes miscarriages ... Similarly her movements must be moderate, that is, she must walk slowly, because excess causes miscarriages.

The reason for this is that the foetus is attached to the womb as a flower or fruit to the tree, as we have said. Just as the wind, or shaking the tree, causes a strong movement which detaches the flower or fruit from the branches, so a strong movement will shake the foetus, detaching it from the branches of the veins of the womb to which it was attached ... Note that the greatest danger of excessive exercise is in the first months and the last: in the first months, because, as a flower, [the foetus] is attached lightly; in the last, because the fruit is ripe and about to fall, and could drop for any slight reason.

The trials of pregnancy

9.7, 9.8 Letters to a worried husband, 1478

The humanist Agnolo Poliziano writes from Pistoia to Lorenzo de' Medici in Florence, September 1478, with worrying news about Lorenzo's wife Clarice Orsini, in the late stages of pregnancy. Clarice and her children were in Pistoia, having left Florence after the Pazzi conspiracy. As was customary, she was surrounded by the affection and advice of other women, friends and relatives, who would have helped and encouraged her during pregnancy and childbirth.

a. Agnolo Poliziano, *Prose volgari inedite e poesie latine e greche inedite* ..., ed. I. Del Lungo (Florence, 1867), pp. 62–3.

[7 September, 1478]

Magnifice Domine mi, the Lady Clarice has been feeling a little unwell since last night. She writes to the Lady Lucrezia[7] that she fears she

7 Lucrezia Tornabuoni de' Medici, Clarice's mother-in-law.

will miscarry, or will get the same illness as Giovanni Tornabuoni's wife.[8] After dinner she laid down on the *lettuccio*.[9] This morning she got up late, ate well, and went to lie down after dinner. The Panciatichi women are with her, and Andrea [Panciatichi]'s mother is very expert.[10] Andrea tells me that she told him that the Lady Clarice is still in danger of miscarrying. I think I should tell you all this. But these women say they think she will be fine. To look at her, she doesn't show any sign of illness.

The doctor Stefano de la Turri reports on Clarice's health to Lorenzo de' Medici, 1478.

b. G. Pieraccini, *La stirpe dei Medici di Cafaggiolo*, 3 vols (Florence, 1924, repr. 1986), vol. 1, p. 135.

Yesterday, after my arrival, I let Your Magnificence know what I had been able to gather after my first visit. At 21 hours[11] she had a slight temperature, and I think it was the same on Sunday and on Saturday, so I think that the disturbance of the fever has caused this flux. During the night she had no symptoms, nor pain in the belly like the other night. This improvement lasted three hours, then she had supper with pleasure. I did not let her get up. This morning she has no fever, and from examining her urine it seems she had a slight catarrh.

She has taken heart, and says that since I arrived she does not feel in danger anymore. This is very good for the health she must regain. I hope to direct everything to a happy outcome. It is true that she thinks that this air [of Pistoia] is more noxious to the body that that of Florence.

9.9 What to eat and what to do during pregnancy, 1561

The *letterato* Sperone Speroni writes to his pregnant daughter Giulia, giving advice on her regimen. The insistence on avoiding extremes of heat and cold is linked to prevailing medical theory and to the notion of women's nature as cold and moist.

Sperone Speroni, *Lettere familiari*, ed. M. R. Loi and M. Pozzi, 6 vols (Alessandria, 1993), vol. 1, pp. 139–40.

---

8 Giovanni Tornabuoni's wife, Francesca Pitti, died in childbirth in 1477.
9 A day bed.
10 The Panciatichi women to whom the letter refers were Tita degli Albizzi Panciatichi and her two daughters-in-law.
11 Approx. 4 p.m.

[October 1561]

About your pains, I ask you to think well about which disorder of food, air or clothes could be the cause. Let me know, and see that you avoid them, because they are too harmful. Avoid eating dough, dairy products, goose and duck, and for now drink white wine, if you have any. Don't get cold, and avoid your legs getting cold. Rule out fish, and see that you don't heat up your kidneys, either with your clothes, or by sleeping on your back or by standing. This is all for now. After the delivery I shall give you more advice.

In the meantime, and this is the right season, get some wild rose-hips which can be found on hedges. Now is the right time, because the hedges have lost their leaves, and the rose-hips are clearly visible, looking as if they are stuck on top of little sticks. Better get those from the hills than from the plains, because they are more efficacious. Don't get pale or black ones, but only nearly yellow ones, because they have been more exposed to the sun. Dry them in a shady place, and pound them into a powder which you will use every day with your food, mixing it with some cinnamon. But take just a little, to avoid heating up your kidneys if taken in great quantity. Take it with soups and broths. Garlic and root vegetables, in moderation, are good for you, and the powder will be good with root vegetables in a soup. Use some fennel sometimes with them, sometimes by itself, and sometimes with parsley. Capers are good in a salad, and also radishes, but these should be cooked, and carrots. But not lettuce, or radicchio, or only if cooked, nor endive, because they chill the stomach. Do not eat pears. This is enough for now. Just think about giving birth, and be careful not to get your kidneys hot in bed, but even more avoid the cold, which is the great enemy of pregnant women. I think that linen drawers will be useful to wear in bed and out of bed the whole winter, but they should only be made of linen.

9.10 A miscarriage, 1550

Speroni sends consoling words to his daughter Lucietta Speroni Papafava (1533–63), who had suffered a miscarriage, and advises her to accept God's will. Speroni, vol. 1, pp. 69–70.

[16 April 1550]

My dearest daughter,

The news of your miscarriage which I have just received upset me bitterly, and I grieved that a child carried with so much care for so many months had, in a moment, come to nothing. The fear that you could be unwell, and the fact that I am far from you, added more pain. But I take comfort from reflecting that life's events cannot be changed and from hearing that you are well. Also, as a father who is far from you, I know that you have in Padua as many fathers as there are men in your house and as many mothers as there are women in your house and in mine, and that you had been able to conceive a boy.

I think, indeed I am sure, that what God did to this child of yours is like what is done to flowers of good stock: they are pruned so that one or two may grow and deserve to be carried by ladies to church, or to festivities. It is enough that this child you have miscarried was baptised, and that you have already given your tribute to God and to Heaven. And you can be sure that, if this baby had the power to be reborn and live down here amongst the miseries of this world, without certainty of the health of his soul, he would not want that himself. And even if he were certain to return to Heaven after the troubles of this world, he would still prefer to be up there now rather than wait. Having given your first fruit to God, you can trust that your home will be comforted by the rest of your harvest. You should start another one, and the troubles of pregnancy you have felt before should not weigh heavily on you. Thus you would give peace of mind to your father-in-law, to whom, I know, you could not give more pleasure than by giving him a grandson. But tell your husband that he should not conceive sons elsewhere, leaving the daughters to you, even if the daughters generated by him, if they are like Cassandra,[12] will not be less dear than the boys.

I long to see Cassandra as much as I long to see you, and I hope I shall see her again soon. In the meantime, keep healthy and in good spirits.

CHILDBIRTH

9.11 **A good midwife, 1596**

In this passage from his very successful treatise on midwifery, *La commare o riccoglitrice*, (Venice, 1596), the Dominican friar and doctor Scipione (Fra Girolamo) Mercurio describes what makes a good midwife. He places much emphasis not only on her necessary skills, but also on her psychological and

---

12 Lucietta's daughter.

spiritual assistance. His writing derives from his experiences as a doctor in the small towns, villages and countriside around Ferrara and Rovigo.

Scipione Mercurio, *La commare o riccoglitrice* (Venice, 1601), pp. 87–9.

The wise and prudent midwife is as necessary to pregnant women as the good physician, in fact more so, because, if he helps with advice, she helps both with advice and her hands [...]

The good midwife must be very skilled and experienced, and have safely helped at many births. She should not, however, be so old as to have problems with her eyesight or with weak and trembling hands. If she is, great problems may ensue, since in difficult deliveries she will need great strength to extract the baby, as will be discussed later.

She must also be aware and very careful to know when the birth is close, distinguishing the real labour pains from other pains, and be ready to place the pregnant woman on the bed or on the birthing chair. This is very important because when the waters break she should not waste any time: if there is any delay, the vagina becomes dry, and therefore the delivery will be very difficult. She should never leave the pregnant woman either by day or night, because labour pains may start while she is not there, the waters may break and the delivery begin, and precious time may be wasted while the midwife is sent for [...]

The good midwife should always have an assistant, not only as an apprentice, to be well-instructed in this most important practice, but also because in all circumstances [the assistant] should be ready to help as necessary, for example handing over oils or warm grease, towels, scissors and thread to cut the umbilical chord, or skilfully extracting the placenta, and other such things. Not all women are capable of doing this, and sometimes it has happened that, either because the midwife was old, or because the other [women] were inept, they have let the placenta slip back after cutting the cord, something that means certain death to a woman giving birth.

The midwife should be affable, cheerful, gracious, humorous and brave, and she should always encourage the women, promising them that they will certainly give birth to a boy, that they will not have too much pain, and that she knows this because of many signs she has observed in other women. I think that even if this is a lie it can be said without fear of committing a sin, since it is not said to harm anybody, but only to help and give heart to women in childbirth, even more so since Plato, in the sixth book of the *Republic*, allows the physician to tell lies to comfort the sick.

Besides all this, the midwife must be pious and devout, and must remind pregnant women, before the delivery, that they should not reach the moment of giving birth without having been to confession and to communion, because childbirth is accompanied by obvious danger of death. She must also persuade them of how commendable and beneficial it is amidst danger to resort to prayers for the intercession of saints, especially to the glorious Virgin Mother of God, who, having given birth to her son without sin and without pain, will be well disposed to help those who conceive their children in sin and give birth to them with much pain.

9.12 **Lorenzo Gioberti on the best positions for childbirth, 1592**

Gioberti gives a wide choice concerning the most comfortable position for childbirth. The birthing chair was well known, and described also by Mercurio.

Gioberti, p. 137.

It is necessary to give advice about what position women should take in childbirth. Some of them want to stand up, supported by somebody; others want to sit on a birthing chair, and others want to lie down. When they have tried them all, I leave them to choose the way they feel most comfortable with. The only thing I caution is that the [umbilical] cord should be free, not tight so that it can retract easily. This will be easier when the woman is standing, provided this is done when the baby presents itself, without tiring or troubling the poor woman in vain. This is because, beside what I have said – that the cord, in this position, is free – the baby descends more easily when helped by its own weight, making the birth easier. There are some women and ladies who use beds called birthing beds, because they are used only in childbirth. These are not beds to sleep on, but chairs with a hole in the seat, with arms and legs made in such a way that it is possible to bind and secure the woman's arms, thighs and legs with wide straps without hurting her, so that she can only move the coccyx. This is a good position, but it must be used wisely.

9.13 **A dangerous procedure, 1596**

Mercurio explains how to perform a Caesarean section. He warns against the empirical 'barbers' – practitioners, such as surgeons, who did not have the physicians' philosophical and theoretical culture, nor the knowledge of anatomy required for such a complex operation.

Mercurio, p. 212.

Not every surgeon is able to do a Caesarean section, but only he who is practised in it, who is brave, prudent and, above all, knowledgeable in anatomy, because he must know how deeply to cut, and recognise the omentum, the peritoneum, the abdominal muscles, and make out the uterus. This is certainly the greatest problem, because the art of surgery is practised carelessly, and, even worse, given into the hands of barbers. Once a good surgeon has been found, he must, before anything else, consider diligently whether there is any other way to deliver the baby besides this one ... If he deems that no other way is possible, he should consider whether the woman is strong enough to withstand such a procedure. This he will know from two things: from her pulse, and from the suffering she has gone through [...] If he finds that the woman is strong, with a good pulse, having himself taken heart and encouraged her, and having asked for divine help for himself and for her, he will first prepare the instruments for this cut.

9.14 A recipe to restore strength to a woman after giving birth, 1596

Mercurio gives various recipes for nourishing food to restore strength to women after childbirth, providing also cheaper alternatives for poorer families. This is one of the 'expensive' concoctions – a sixteenth century version of *zabaglione*.

Mercurio, p. 220.

Take the yolks of four freshly-laid eggs and beat them together with some sweet white wine. Add three ounces of sugar and two ounces of fresh butter, and a little powdered cinnamon. Place on a slow fire, and stir the ingredients till they are as thick as cream. This food is then ready, and can be eaten with a spoon.

FESTIVITIES AFTER THE BIRTH OF A CHILD

9.15 Presents for a new mother, Florence, 1468

Giovanni Rucellai lists in his *Zibaldone* the very expensive presents given to his daughter-in-law, Nannina de' Medici, after the birth of a son. The fabrics given to the midwife are also worth a considerable amount.

A. Perosa, ed., *Giovanni Rucellai e il suo Zibaldone. I. 'Il Zibaldone Quaresimale'* (London, 1960), p. 35.

The godfathers gave the midwife as a present 16 *braccia* of crimson silk satin for a gown; 1 1/2 *braccia* of purple damask with gold brocade for the sleeves; a sugared almond loaf.

[Nannina's] father Piero di Cosimo de' Medici gave as a present a silver basin and a silver jug, both weighing [gap] ... lbs, worth florins ... [gap]. The basin was full of small gilt cakes.

From Pier Francesco di Lorenzo de' Medici, a silver goblet full of small cakes. From his brother-in-law Guglielmo d'Antonio de' Pazzi, a silver goblet full of pine-nuts cakes. From my daughter Lena, wife of Domenico Bartoli, a roll of white camlet. From my daughter Caterina, wife of Piero Vettori, ... [gap] *braccia* of red cloth for a gown, and 6 *braccia* of crimson *altobasso*[13] velvet for a small cloak for the child. From Nicolò di Francesco Tornabuoni and his brothers, 16 *braccia* of silk satin for a gown.

9.16 New mothers receive their friends, Venice, 1581

As Francesco Sansovino explains, receiving guests in richly appointed rooms was a demonstration of a family's wealth and social position.

Francesco Sansovino, *Venetia città nobilissima et singolare* (Venice, 1581, repr. 1663), p. 402.

For the birth of a baby, the ceremony of lying-in is of no lesser [importance], because splendour and magnificence are shown in the home in the ceremony of childbirth. So the female friends or relatives who come to congratulate [the new mother] are received in rooms, and in particular that in which the new mother is lying, richly decorated with paintings, sculptures, gold and silver objects, and other valuable things. There is also a great display of confectionery and other fine foods, in gold and silver [vessels], which is noble and beautiful to see. There is such display that the [city] fathers have been forced to deal with this too, with laws [to curb] the great expenses.

---

13 A type of velvet with a pattern made by different depths of pile.

DEATH IN CHILDBIRTH

It has been estimated that almost one-fifth of all deaths of young married women from all social ranks in early fifteenth-century Florence were related to complications in childbirth or ensuing infections.[14] Because of the very real danger of death, pregnant women were advised to make a will and to prepare their soul by confessing their sins and taking communion. Some families also took up insurance policies.[15]

9.17 The will of a pregnant woman, Venice, 1536

The wife of the painter Paris Bordon, Cinzia Spada, draws up her will during her pregnancy in March 1536.

G. Canova, *Paris Bordon* (Venice, 1964), p. 128.

[28 March 1536]

I, Cinzia, daughter of Messer Bartolomeo Spa [Spada or Spata] and now wife of Messer Paris Bordon, painter in the *contrada* of S. Marciliano, for the grace of God healthy in mind and intellect, but, being pregnant, fearing the dangers of this life, asked … ser Alvise Nadal, parish priest of S. Agostino, notary in Venice, … to write this testament, and after my death to carry out my will according to the customary clauses. First I recommend my soul to God and to all the celestial court. I want my executors to be my father Messer Bartolomeo, and my uncle Messer Giovan Alvise Bonrizzo, and my husband.

When it pleases God to call me, I want to be dressed in the garb of the Madonna, and buried where and with the expense which my executors will see fit.

I want one hundred masses to be said before my body is buried. Then for six years every year [I want] one hundred masses for my soul.

I want prayers to be said to God for me at the [church of the] Trinity, at [cross in the text], at S. Piero in Castello and at S. Lorenzo, with the usual almsgiving.

I leave all my personal property free from all outstanding claims and

---

14 See D. Herlihy and C. Klapisch-Zuber, *Tuscans and Their Families: A Study of the Florentine Catasto of 1427* (New Haven and London, 1985), p. 277.
15 On the dangers of childbirth, see Musacchio (1999), pp. 24–31.

obligations to my husband, so that he can pay with this the alms for the hundred masses before I am buried, and the alms for ... the Trinity and to the other churches.

I leave to my father and to my mother, if they are still alive after my death, and after their death to my brothers, sisters and their sons and daughters, all my real property.

9.18 Masses for a dead wife, 1445

The sorrow for a wife's death is movingly conveyed by this extract, from the *Ricordanze* of the Florentine Luca di Matteo da Panzano, even within the conventions of this genre. Masses for the dead were the most important way in which the living could express care and concern for the soul of a deceased.

E. Conti, A. Guidotti and R. Lunardi, *La civiltà fiorentina del Quattrocento* (Florence, 1993), p. 132.

My wife died on 5 November 1445 in childbirth on Friday evening at 2½ hours.[16] God have mercy on her soul, because she was a capable and good wife, and she dies with a good name in the face of God and of the world.

On the 8 [November] I had masses said in S. Croce, with candles and with as much honour as possible, with many relatives and friends. And the death of this woman was a great loss, and the whole population of Florence was saddened, because she was a good woman, a sweet well-behaved woman, and all those who knew her loved her. I believe that her soul has gone to join God's servants, because of her great humility and patience.

I, Luca da Panzano, had 30 Gregorian masses celebrated, beginning on 16 May 1446, one each morning.[17]

9.19 A bereaved husband, 1477

Giovanni Tornabuoni, the head of the Medici bank in Rome, writes to his nephew Lorenzo de' Medici about the death of his wife, Francesca Pitti.

E. Ridolfi, 'Giovanna Tornabuoni e Ginevra de' Benci nel coro di S. Maria Novella in Firenze', *Archivio storico italiano*, 5th ser., 6 (1890), p. 432.

---

16 Approx. 6.30 p.m.
17 Gregorian masses were a cycle of 30 masses for the dead.

[September 1477]

My dearest Lorenzo,

I am so weighed down by suffering and pain for the most bitter and
sudden event [which happened to] my sweet wife, that I do not know
what is happening to me. As you will have heard yesterday, according
to God's will, at 22 hours [18] she passed away from this life during childbirth, and, after she was opened up, we took a dead baby from her body,
which has doubled my suffering. I am sure that, having pity for me
with your usual compassion, you will excuse me if I don't write a long
letter and don't send you any news, because I have not had time nor
chance to do it.

9.20 A tomb for Francesca Pitti Tornabuoni

In Renaissance Italy, it was unusual to commemorate a woman's death in
childbirth with special funerary iconography. Here Vasari describes the tomb
of Francesca Pitti Tornabuoni.

Vasari (1906), vol. 3, pp. 359–60.

Since in those days the wife of Francesco [sic – Giovanni] Tornabuoni
had died in childbirth, her husband, who had loved her very much and
wanted to honour her in death as much as he could, commissioned her
tomb from Andrea [del Verrocchio]. Over a marble sarcophagus, he
carved on a slab the woman, the birth and her death, and also made
three figures representing the Virtues, which were thought to be very
beautiful as his first work in marble. This tomb was placed in the
Minerva.[19]

9.21 The death of Beatrice d'Este, 1497

Ludovico il Moro writes to Francesco Gonzaga, Marquess of Mantua, on the
death of his wife (and Francesco's sister-in-law), Beatrice d'Este.

A. Luzio and R. Renier, *Delle relazioni di Isabella d'Este Gonzaga con Ludovico e
Beatrice Sforza* (Milan, 1890), p. 125.

[January 1497]

Our most illustrious wife, after starting labour pains at 2 hours in the

---

18 Approx. 5 p.m.
19 The church of S. Maria sopra Minerva in Rome.

night,[20] gave birth to a dead boy at 5 hours,[21] and at 6 and a half rendered up her spirit to God. For this bitter and untimely event we are in such bitterness and grief as it is possible to feel, so much so that we would have preferred to die rather than to see her gone, she who was the dearest thing we had in the world. And even if we are feeling such great and extreme grief, more than we can say, and know that Your Lordship will suffer in the same way, we did want to let you know ourselves what has happened, as we felt it was appropriate to our love towards Your Lordship. I pray you not to send anybody to give us condolences, so as not to renew the suffering. We did not want to write about this to the Illustrious Lady the Marchioness [Isabella d'Este], thinking that Your Lordship will let her know in the way which you deem better, and we are sure that together with Your Lordship she will feel great pain.

BRINGING UP CHILDREN

The upbringing of children was recognised by most writers throughout our period as the most important task for women of the middle and upper ranks of society. The first extract shows a concern with civility and manners that is one of the crucial cultural changes in the Renaissance. Bernardo Tasso and Agostino Valiero, on the other hand, give mothers the crucial role of moral instructors of their children. These two writers' emphasis on religious rather than civic morality is characteristic of the Counter-Reformation's thinking on education.

9.22 Good manners, 1548

One of the letters in Ortensio Lando's collection deals with advice about how children should behave in public. The emphasis on the importance of good manners as expressed by the restraint of bodily functions reflects concerns expressed in other writings, such as Monsignor Giovanni della Casa's *Galateo* (1558), the most successful treatise on manners.

Lando (1548), fols 160v–161v.

I would not like your children ever to appear with snotty noses, nor should they wipe their noses on their jackets, but rather hide them from other people's view with their handkerchiefs. You should not let

20 Approx. 6 p.m.
21 Approx. 9 p.m.

them stand in front of important people with their mouths open (as one can read in Aristophanes about the madman Mamacuto). Teach them to refrain from that unrestrained laughter which shakes the whole body [...]

If they are sitting in front of an important gentleman, they should keep their legs together. Their walk should be neither uncertain nor hurried, because the former belongs to those who are effeminate and delicate, the latter to madmen and idiots ... When they are at a feast, teach them that they should be neither too happy nor too sad; they should not be the first to put their hands into their plate, nor should they lick their fingers, or wipe them on their clothes.

9.23 A letter of advice, early 1550s

In a very long letter, Bernardo Tasso (1493–1569) gives his wife Portia detailed instructions about their children's upbringing during his absence. Tasso wants her to be responsible for the manners and for the moral education of the children, but not for their schooling.

B. Tasso, *Delle lettere di M. Bernardo Tasso*, 3 vols (Padua, 1733–51), vol. 1, pp. 396–403.

If God's will, which we must follow uncomplainingly and contentedly, is that [our separation] shall be longer than necessary, you should know ... how to discipline your dear little children ... Since, because of your youth, you lack the experience needed to educate them, I shall give you some guidelines, taken partly from antique and partly from modern philosophers [...] And because education, or upbringing, consists of two parts, that is, manners and literacy, one common concern of both father and mother, the other more suited to the father, I shall discuss only manners with you [...]

Take care not to fall into the error often made by those mothers who corrupt their children's habits by being too indulgent, by pleasing their desires too often ... thus giving their children over to delights, and making pleasure and the senses lord and tyrant of their young minds. I do not say, however, that you have to rely on fear or on corporal punishment. On the contrary: those who beat their children are as reprehensible as if they were beating the image of God. Virtue must be preserved in the souls of children neither with beatings, nor with fear.

9.24 **A moral upbringing, 1577**

Part of Bishop Agostino Valiero's *Della istruzione del modo di vivere delle donne maritate* is dedicated to the important question of children's upbringing. Here he underlines the paramount role of religious practices, and tells mothers what to do.

A. Valiero, *Della istruzione del modo di vivere delle donne maritate* (Padua, 1744), pp. 31–2.

You should punish every smallest lie they [your children] tell, because lying is so much a part of our corrupt nature that he who gets used to it as a child will find it difficult to tell the truth as is proper for a good man and a good Christian.

You should get them used to confessing their mistakes, even if insignificant, because it is a great misfortune, from which almost everybody suffers, to excuse a sin with new sins. You should especially train them to do what they do not want, and many times, because it is very useful in life to know how to yield to the will of others and bend one's own intellect. But you should above all get them to recite the Lord's Prayer well, because it is the prayer instituted by Our Lord Jesus Christ, an example for all prayers and a compendium of all we can ask the Lord God, what should be desired and what should be shunned [...]

You will get them used, as soon as possible, to confession, and to revere the Holy Sacrament of Penitence, and practice it by recommending them to a good priest, through whom you will endeavour to remove from them those vices and miseries to which they are inclined. You will strive to teach them, every day, some new good habit or custom.

9.26 **A caring adoptive mother, Prato, 1398**

Illegitimate children, especially if their fathers belonged to the elite or middle-ranking families, were often brought up in the father's household. This letter shows the concern of the childless Margherita Datini for her husband's daughter, Ginevra (b. 1392).[22]

D. Toccafondi and G. Cascone, eds, *Per la tua Margherita. Scrittura a distanza: lettere di una donna del Trecento al marito mercante* (Prato, 2001), p. 69.

22 See J. P. Byrne and E. A. Congdon, 'Mothering in Casa Datini', *Journal of Medieval History*, 25:1 (March 1999), pp. 35–56.

[December 1398]

Don't worry about Ginevra. I think that her sore throat, with luck, won't get any worse. There is no need for me to tell you more about this, because I know you are sure that I treat her better than if she was my own daughter, and indeed I consider her to be mine. I didn't want to say anything to you because I know that you have other worries, and there was no need. The graze on her head is a small thing, but her sore throat had me worried. The doctor tells me it will have no repercussions. We are following his instructions, and she hasn't had a fever or anything else, and is not eating or drinking any less. May God protect you always.

10 Widows

Widows existed in great number in Renaissance Italy, owing to high death rates and to many husbands' considerable seniority.[1] Their age, financial status and the duration of their widowhood varied vastly. Young widows, especially those without children, would frequently regain their dowry and remarry, having returned to the homes of their father or other birth relatives. Others headed their households and brought up their children alone, living off the proceeds of their dowries or with support from family or charity. Widows beyond the childbearing age, being much less likely to remarry, had different options. Those who were comfortably off might come to enjoy their new-found freedom, occupying their time or expressing themselves with practical, cultural or more frivolous activities. The less affluent might attempt to carry on their husbands' trade, to take other employment for modest reward or to enter domestic service, perhaps in a nunnery. In indigence, sickness or old age, they might be housed in a variety of charitable institutions: both individuals and civic or charitable groups accepted their Christian duty to support widows.[2]

EXEMPLARY WIDOWS; WIDOWHOOD IN GENERAL

10.1 Bernardino da Siena on the good widow

S. Bernardino's 1427 sermon on widowhood gives praise and respect to worthy widows, as do secular writers throughout the period. Paul's words in I Timothy 5 provided the chief scriptural foundation, the prophetess Anna and Judith the main exemplars. The widow must be pious, helpful to her neighbour, and triumphant over adversity, battling against the devil, the flesh and evil company. Unlike the daughter or the wife, she can gain a

---

1 General studies are: L. Mirrer, ed., *Upon my Husband's Death. Widows in the Literature and Histories of Medieval Europe* (Ann Arbor, 1992); O. Hufton, *A History of Women in Western Europe. Vol. 1: 1500–1800* (London, 1995), pp. 217–250; S. Cavallo and L. Warner, eds, *Widowhood in Medieval and Early Modern Europe* (Harlow, 1999); and A. Levy, ed., *Widowhood and Visual Culture in Early Modern Europe* (Aldershot, 2003).

2 See R. C. Trexler, 'A Widows' Asylum of the Renaissance: the Orbatello of Florence', in Trexler vol. 2, pp. 66–91; B. Pullan, *Rich and Poor in Renaissance Venice* (Oxford, 1971).

moral authority by using her freedom well, becoming, as he says, virile and saintly.

Bernardino da Siena (1989), vol. 1, pp. 623–4, 638–9.

Go and read in Luke's second chapter about that manly widow, the prophetess Anna who was inspired and illuminated by God, who when she lost her husband always kept herself in the presence of God in every action. Extremely aged in body, she was far from old in spirit. Her previous fasting did not suffice: now more than ever she undertook fasts, vigils and austerities, and was happier than before in this state, knowing it was better than the married one. And indeed this is so: a widow who can support herself well is half a nun. And if she can't support herself, how wretched is her soul! So citizens, citizens, be willing to help them in their tribulations ...

The widow should think of nothing else save serving God and her children, if she has any. The married woman should think of several things: looking after her husband, children and the whole household, and should think about doing all the things that might please her husband. If she's a widow, she can do more, in her own way ...

Know that the widow, if she can support herself, is half a saint.

10.2 A capable widow

Vespasiano da Bisticci's *c.* 1480 biographies of virtuous contemporary widows sometimes stress prudent management of family affairs, sometimes secluded religious devotions.

Vespasiano da Bisticci (1999), pp. 108–9.

Madonna Francesca, wife of Messer Donato Acciaiuoli, was a lady of most temperate life. She was left widowed very young; was very beautiful, and remained a widow, and resolved to stay a widow, and thus spent sixty or more years in that mode of life. Her behaviour was wonderful: she was the example of her era to all the women of Florence. All held her in the greatest reverence because of her virtues. Her husband died a rebel and in exile, owing to civic discord: with good sense she preserved the assets owned by her sons Piero and Donato, two distinguished young men, and likewise two girl children, two distinguished girls like the men. All was accomplished through the wisdom and goodness of this lady: through her was preserved her household, which had encountered many obstacles. This lady, singular in all things, deserves great praise.

ALTERNATIVE WIDOWHOODS

10.3 **Widowhood as liberty**

In Trotto's late sixteenth-century dialogue, a female speaker praises widow-hood as natural and preferable to the constraints of married life.

Bernardo Trotto, *Dialoghi del matrimonio, e vita vedovile* (Turin, 1578), pp. 14, 16, 32, 50–1.

[Hippolita] ... What grace is more universally longed for by every creature, than fair, sweet, dear and precious liberty? Wherever have you seen an animal, however base or timid, which does not try to gain its freedom and seek escape from all restraint?

... Just compare these words: bound with loosened, confined with free, married with widowed, and suchlike: the first group seems bitter and harsh, the second sweet and pleasing. Then turn to our bodies ... and see if you think that this beauty of face, sweetness of expression, soft-ness of flesh and loveliness of the female form should be put between rough male arms, and left to the will of violent and imperious man? Don't you see that once we get involved with their conceited ways we are fleeing from our own best interests? How about those manly eyes, from which one glance makes you tremble inside? How about that mouth, issuing grim, frightening words? What of those lips, injuring our coral mouths with their lascivious kisses? What of those almost savage looking bristly beards, like thick moss around an ancient ruin, which scratch us, butchering the cheeks we polish with so much care?

... In relation to the widow, Lady Barbara, I see no reason for her to complain. If she's ugly, nobody minds ... If the widow is poor, she can strive to earn her living, without anyone to reproach her that other women are richer or more beautiful than she, nor that she was brought up in an orphanage, or other similar reproofs that husbands make. If the widow is beautiful, her virtue will shine in her fair body as in its proper and fitting place, and will doubly increase the praises for her prudence ... What's more, the widow does not fear those dishonest love affairs that disturb her tranquillity.

... Consider further, Lady Barbara, the many and various benefits that may result from the humility and liberty of widowhood, and the argu-ments which gradually induce me to love its state. See the prudent widow, far from vain pomp and fragile earthly pleasures and strange and fleeting appetites. She despises all weakness, doesn't lower her intellect to vile or futile activities, but lifts it to lofty contemplation.

She is full of holy thoughts, occupies her mind with divine laws and charitable works ... Although she may not enclose herself in a monastery, she will still attend to the health of her soul and the acquisition of eternal life. For all that, she will not neglect the care of her family. Thus, more easily than before, she may expect to make use of any spare moments to elevate her intellect, read entertaining stories, sing charming poems, emulate fine figures of speech and types of argument, study the serious thoughts of philosophers.

10.4 Widowhood as licence

In a 1553 case concerning an alleged broken marriage promise, Francesco Pazzaia, a dyer, testifies in support of his friend against the woman in question and her sister. He claims these young widows, living alone without family protection, are disreputable and untrustworthy.

L. Lazzaretti, 'La donna attraverso i processi', in *Studi veneziani*, 32 (1996), p. 68.

The said Francesca del Prete and Catherine her sister, widows of the *borgo* of Fara, are known by name and ill repute, and that they are too licentious in bringing young men into their house while no one but these two young girls are present, with little caution and concern for their honour, so that they cause gossip about their doings. This I testify and know since I have several times been present there in their house in Fara and outside their house in the said *borgo* of Fara, and here in Feltre, by the Porta Imperial, I have heard and understood word of the doings of the widowed sisters, that is that they spent the entire night partying and dancing and leaping and doing as they pleased ... and it was said that this was not the behaviour of widows or decent women ... they held evening parties in their house and in the public baths and danced and jumped, leaving their weaving and spinning to dance and have fun.

THE AFTERMATH OF BEREAVEMENT

10.5 Alessandra de' Bardi's self-control

It was felt appropriate that a widow's grief should be expressed only in private. Heroic suicides of widows of antiquity were sometimes cited approvingly by theorists, and painted or sculpted. However, it was her Christian morality and control of passion that made the widowed Alessandra de' Bardi admirable for Vespasiano, the one woman whose life deserved inclusion in his *c.* 1480 book of 'Famous Men'. She weeps bitterly after losing her husband, but pain is countered by duty and the memory of stoical precursors.

Vespasiano da Bisticci (1970–76), vol. 2, pp. 491, 493.

'O my God, death would be better for me than life, finding myself in this condition.' There were her sons and a friend who did everything to console her, citing many examples. She, who had such good sense, could console herself only with difficulty. Replying to those who sought to comfort her ... she spoke thus: 'If omnipotent God, the creator of the universe, wept like humans, seeing the two sisters of Lazarus weep, what should I, an unhappy woman, do? ... Had not my religion, in which I was born and which I have tried to observe up to the present, forbidden Christians to take their own life, I would do what Portia, the wife of Brutus, did, who on hearing the death of her husband called for fire, took the burning coal and swallowed it down her throat and killed herself, saying she no longer wished to live. But if I'm not allowed to do this, lest I offend my Creator, I'm not forbidden to grieve ... if S. Paola Romana, as St Jerome writes concerning the death of her husband, who died of natural causes and was himself most saintly, wept and lamented at his decease, how should I behave now that my husband Lorenzo has died a violent death, but likewise weep that his spirit has gone from his body?'

Eventually Alessandra accepts the will of God and prays to Him for her dead husband's soul, Vespasiano commenting:

This is the behaviour befitting the most chaste women at the death of their husbands, to think of God as she did, and to observe St Paul's words, to be a stranger to all pleasures and shrink from lavish clothes – not like some I know – to flee from fancy foods, remain in fasting and prayer as did the prophetess Anna.

10.6 **Proper dress for the widow**

The public funeral was dominated by male family members and associates, but choosing expensive mourning garb, perhaps provided for in the husband's will, might have been a means through which the widow could publicly acknowledge the importance of her marriage, or proclaim her own honour and that of her birth family, within the constraints of custom.[3]

Vecellio (1590), fol. 134r.

3 S. Strocchia, *Death and Ritual in Renaissance Florence* (Baltimore, 1992) discusses mourning customs.

In their dress, the widows of Venice with the death of their husband embrace the death of all vanities and ornaments. Because apart from dressing in black they cover their hair, firmly enclose their bosoms with a heavy veil, gather their mantle up to their forehead, and walk in the streets, with head inclined. When they want to stay a widow, they wear a train, and never ever dress in colours if they do not want to remarry. At home they wear a cap which covers their hair. They always dress in black, both at home and outside. Still, when they wish to remarry they are permitted without stigma to wear some ornament, though not a conspicuous one, and reveal a little more hair, which serves to signal their intentions to others.

10.7 Isabella d'Este plans her husband's tomb

The affluent gained satisfaction from planning a costly tomb or memorial chapel, normally extolling husbands' virtues rather than explicitly referring to their own grief.[4] Isabella d'Este naturally aimed high in her choice of designers for the tomb of her husband, who died in 1519. Castiglione wrote to her from Rome shortly after: nothing remains of the project.

Translation of J. Cartwright, *Isabella d'Este, Marchioness of Mantua* (London, 1904), vol. 2, p. 160.

As to what Your Excellency writes regarding the drawings for the tomb, I hope that by this time your wish is satisfied, and that you have received Raphael's – to my mind – altogether more appropriate design from the hands of Monsignore Tricario. Michelangelo was not in Rome, so there was no one but Raphael to whom I could apply, and I feel sure that his drawing will please you.

10.8 Ostentatious monuments censured

Lodovico Dolce condemned widows who endowed over-lavish tombs and mortuary chapels for their deceased husbands.

Dolce, (1545), fols 71v–72r.

I know that the marbles, bronzes, gilding, intaglios, the grandiose epitaphs and statues with which tombs are adorned are useless to the deceased. I would wish the money which is consumed by these vain pomps and tokens of our pride to be used on works of charity, which

4 See C. E. King, *Renaissance Women Patrons: Wives and Widows in Renaissance Italy c. 1300–c. 1550* (Manchester, 1998), pp. 99–128.

are alms given for the needy, not offerings left to those who are rich.
True alms are assisting widows, wretched orphans, hospitals, or wherever the need seems greatest, not leaving huge bequests to rich
convents, in order to make a sumptuous sepulchre for one's body, or a
memorial chapel with family arms ... But what shall I say about
certain widows, who in order that they can adorn the body of their
dead husband with a more sumptuous tomb, delay in paying off the
debts that he incurred when alive? For this reason they frequently
omit to implement the bequests which he earlier promised in his will.
It's certain that the debts are transferred to whoever is his heir: the
wife as much as the husband is held to these by both human and divine
laws, and whoever does not pay his debts is truly a thief.

10.9 A widow-writer laments

Two well-known Renaissance poets, Vittoria Colonna (1492–1547) and, here,
Veronica Gambara (1485–1550), only published after their husbands' deaths.
While Colonna's 1538 *Rime amorose* sequence was centred on her idealised
dead husband, Gambara wrote only four poems closely related to her
mourning.[5] Both utilised their status as aristocratic widows to gain respect:
Gambara placed an inscription to Dido, the chaste widow, above the entrance
to her palace. The following was composed shortly after Gambara's bereavement in 1518.

Veronica Gambara, *Le rime*, ed. A. Bullock (Florence, 1995), p. 88.

> Torture me, cruel Fortune, with your power,
> make me your plaything as you will,
> relish my harsh, deceptive torment,
> and pile up miseries for me night and day!
> Make me exhausted, let me find
> no respite ever in my too enduring grief,
> but always give me war and never peace;
> heap on me every evil you possess;
> no power that you wield, while I still live,
> can move my steadfast heart from thoughts
> which a thousand times a day both kill it and revive it!
> Nor do I fear your pitiless and savage strike,
> for the source of all my pain is such
> that any blow from you would just seem light.

5 Gambara, ed. Bullock, nos 28–31.

10.10 A commission for a *Lamentation*

Widows, who found it legally easier to act as art patrons than did wives, often commissioned memorial altarpieces, presenting themselves with appropriate religious figures modestly, unidealised and frugally clad.[6] They might also select subjects involving mourning, as with the following, one of Michelangelo's best-documented commissions for Vittoria Colonna, with whom he became friendly in the 1530s, after the death of her husband in 1525. It is a drawing of a Lamentation (perhaps one in the Gardner Museum, Boston, *c*. 1535–40) a subject handled in her poetry, with a measure of identification between the writer and the Virgin (see 3.5).

Ascanio Condivi, *Vita di Michelangelo* (1553), in S. Ferino-Pagden, *Vittoria Colonna: Dichterin und Muse Michelangelos* (Vienna, 1998), p. 426.

He made at the order of this lady [Colonna] a naked Christ, when He was taken down from the cross, who would have fallen at the feet of His most holy mother, like a dead and abandoned corpse, if two angels had not held Him up by the arms. She, however, seated under the cross, her face tearful and lamenting, with arms open raises both her hands to heaven, as if to say what is written on the shaft of the cross: 'No-one knows how much blood it cost!'

COPING ALONE: FINANCIAL AND PRACTICAL MATTERS

Financial arrangements – dowries and provisions in dead husbands' wills – were crucial to the widow's security of life and choice of abode. Both individuals and legislators strove to ensure that her legal right to the restitution of her dowry was actually enforceable: this would either fund any remarriage or allow her to live securely, capital or property being exchanged for an annuity-like income.[7] Husbands thought carefully about how best to provide for their future widows, taking into account temperaments and inclinations.

---

6 For widows' art patronage, see C. E. King, pp. 76–199 and 229–46, also C. Valone, 'Roman Matrons as Patrons: Various Views of the Cloister Wall', in C. A. Monson, *The Crannied Wall: Women, Religion and the Arts in Early Modern Europe* (Ann Arbor, 1992), pp. 49–72; M. Vaccaro, 'Dutiful Widows: Female Patronage and Two Madonna Altarpieces by Parmigianino' and S. E. Reiss, 'Widow, Mother, Patron of Art: Alfonsina Orsini de' Medici', both in Reiss and Wilkins, pp. 177–92 and 125–57.
7 See 'Getting Back the Dowry' in Chojnacki, pp. 95–111, I. Chabot, 'Lineage Strategies and the Control of Widows in Renaissance Florence', in Cavallo and Warner, pp. 127–44.

10.11 **Reluctant bequests to an estranged wife**

From the will of the Florentine merchant Tommaso Spinelli, 4 December 1468, where his estranged second wife is much less generously treated than his nun-sister or daughters.

P. Jacks and W. Cafferro, *The Spinelli of Florence* (University Park, Pa., 2001), pp. 346–7.

Considering that Signora Lisabetta, daughter of Guido Magalotti and wife of the present testator, living in her father's residence and separated from the said testator, and considering that her disposition neither was nor is compatible with that of the testator, and that he neither has had, nor hopes to have, children by her, and that he does not own, nor has ever received anything from her dowry (despite her brothers having promised him 200 golden florins when he married her, which have never been paid), nevertheless, out of a testator's sense of honour I leave and bequeath that the above-mentioned executors should have her dressed in a black cloak, as is fitting, and that for one year from the death of the testator she should be given and consigned 200 golden florins and no more, since when she left the testator's house she took items for personal use belonging to the testator.

10.12 **A painter's widow must do her duty**

The 1573 will of Battista del Moro, a Veronese painter, tries to ensure his widow discharges his obligations to his daughter and granddaughter, perhaps the products of a previous marriage, and reflects the assumption that support should cease when women marry or remarry.

G. Ludwig, *Italienische Forschungen: Archivalische Beiträge zur Geschichte der venezianischen Kunst* (Berlin, 1911), pp. 117–18.

First I wish that my beloved consort Lucretia should have the immediate discharge of her dowry as well as my goods, the dowry being of 100 ducats, that is 100 counted in gold and silver money, and the remaining 300 ducats in moveable goods owned by her. And since my said consort intends to maintain and bring up Paulina my relative, the daughter of the deceased Alessandro my son, I want the said Paulina to be given 25 ducats at her marriage, which I want to be when she is 14 or 15, and a bed with its trappings. And for the maintenance of Paulina and of my consort I want 20 ducats a year from my estate to be allocated to them ... and should my wife perchance wish to remarry, I wish her to have none of this twenty ducats ... I order that each year three ducats should be given to my widowed daughter, Polissena, while she remains a widow, for the rental of a house, and another four ducats a year for her food ... and I wish those seven ducats to cease if Polissena gets married.

10.13 Problems reclaiming the dowry

If it proved difficult to reclaim the dowry, the help of the influential might be enlisted. A Venetian mother, Cornelia de' Martini, in 1480 writes to Lucrezia Tornabuoni, widow of Piero de' Medici, for help for her widowed daughter in reclaiming her dowry from her Florentine in-laws and returning to Venice.

Translation of Y. Maguire, *Women of the Medici* (London, 1927), p. 214.

I am writing these few words to ask you to help my daughter, Francesca, as you have always done. If you do not help her she will be abandoned by everyone there, for those who should help her keep her there unwillingly. We have new proofs of this every day, and I do not know how poor Francesca bears all that is done to her ... I do not doubt that without your help she would have been still worse treated, for they are not relatives but enemies who have been the cause of all her ills, both men and women, in deeds and words. Pardon me, Madonna Lucrezia, if I write too much, but the passion I feel at seeing my daughter treated as she is by her people, makes me say more than I intended. But I hope to be able to act differently with your counsel, and that of Lorenzo, and to take her away from all these troubles, for since they have her dowry I do not want her to stay there, and they keep it so that she cannot do otherwise.

10.14 An artist's widow struggles to manage

The new widow might have to deal with her husband's business commitments or his equipment and stock and collect outstanding debts. Stressing her pathetic situation, she might request support from family members, from her late husband's confraternity, from his former colleagues and influential associates, or from civic authorities mindful of Christian duty to support deserving widows. Giovanna, widow of the artist, Stefano di Giovanni (Sassetta), petitions the Sienese Signoria on 21 April 1451 for payment for a painted Madonna.

S. Borghesi and L. Banchi, *Nuovi documenti per la storia dell'arte senese* (Siena, 1898), pp. 166–8.

Four years ago the said Master Stefano undertook to make the said work ... in which work he occupied all the said time, and when he had done the work and perfectly finished all the drawing on paper, as most of your people have plainly seen, the same Master Stefano ... fell ill with a serious ailment which left him laid up for 2 months. As this was a long period and he was a poor man who lived only from the efforts of his hands, not only was his meagre substance consumed but he incurred further debts besides the previous ones, which were not insubstantial, with the medicine and the doctors ... Finally, as it pleased the Supreme Creator, Master Stefano died, and left me, a poor unfortunate widow with three poor dependants, the eldest seven years old, and God knows in what state; and had it not been for the help of those who had loved Master Stefano in life, it would have been necessary to bury him in the meanest coffin for which I paid two-thirds of my dowry. Nor did I know half my troubles, as I used to leave all the business to be carried out by my husband, as was proper. Now, having seen the wretched state of my poor children, I find there are debts of 187 florins to various people, which they are all, quite reasonably, asking for: I need to have an estimate made of all the extant work of Master Stefano, my husband, among which is the aforesaid Madonna ...

BRINGING UP CHILDREN

10.15 S. Bernardino's competent widow mother

All moralists stressed that the main worldly duty of the widow was the correct upbringing of any children. Here the widow needed to an extent to assume the roles of both mother and father, and, if prudent, could do so successfully, as S. Bernardino claimed.

Bernardino da Siena (1989), vol. 1, pp. 624–5.

It's possible that a son brought up by a good widow could then govern a city or a province, and also the contrary, that he could ruin a province if badly brought up.

10.16 How a widow must bring up her son

The sheltered upbringing outlined in chapter 6 would serve for girls, but the more secular felt that boys needed guidance from actual males in learning necessary worldly skills, and perhaps should go to live with uncles or other family friends, despite dangers from abuse of trust.

Dolce (1545), fols 73v–74r.

[The widow] must in her consort's place, like a prince who succeeds a prince, devote herself diligently to the management of her house. In this the principal concern will be for the children, as it seems that, being deprived of a father, they might find themselves with freer licence to go to the bad, if they do not fear their mother, thus giving rise to the proverb, rare is the son who gains strength under the guidance of a widow. So to avoid this stigma or this danger, I'd think it wise if the males, once they have reached a certain age, go to live with their father's brothers, or hers, or any learned man of good repute: in this matter the widow should be not only liberal, but prodigal with her expenditure. Because there is no capital that produces better interest than that which goes to make our sons virtuous and well-behaved men.

10.17 **Alessandra Strozzi sends her son away**

The Florentine Alessandra Macinghi Strozzi, when a widow of about forty, first procrastinated and then resigned herself to sending away her youngest and favourite son, Matteo, aged thirteen, to learn business and banking with relatives in Naples. Her son-in-law, Marco Parenti, approvingly comments to her elder son, Filippo Strozzi in Naples, on 6 February 1450.

Marco Parenti, *Lettere*, ed. M. Marrese (Florence, 1996), pp. 27–8.

This morning he [Niccolò Strozzi] left, taking Matteo with him, which left Monna Alessandra both sad and glad: she grieved deeply to see not a single one of her three sons remain, yet took great comfort, not with the spirit of a woman but of a man, from the good she hoped must come of it; and indeed I think that all three sons should be very grateful to him and always think of her, as truly I believe you do.

REMARRIAGE

Statistics indicate that a large number, perhaps the majority, of widows under thirty remarried, often leaving children to be raised by paternal relatives.[8] Documents on these unions are largely perfunctory, and little is known about the attendant formalities and ceremonies, which were probably less elaborate than for first-time matches. Almost all

8 See C. Klapisch-Zuber, '"The Cruel Mother": Maternity, Widowhood and Dowry in Florence in the Fourteenth and Fifteenth Centuries', in Klapisch-Zuber, pp. 117–31; G. Calvi, 'Widows, the State, and the Guardianship of Children in Early Modern Tuscany', in Cavallo and Warner, pp. 209–19.

Renaissance moralists were clear that widows, in contrast to widowers, should ideally not remarry, but argued the case on differing grounds. Though ideals of subduing the flesh and fidelity to a beloved husband's memory were extolled, probably concerns for the well-being of children were paramount.

10.18 The dangers of stepfamilies

Cesare Cabei, like many other Renaissance writers, warns in his book of 1574 how children could be threatened by hostile, jealous or miserly stepfathers.

Cesare Cabei, *Ornamenti della gentildonna vedova* (Venice, 1574), pp. 21–3.

The modest woman seeks to live alone and retired; the immodest strives to live amidst people … it is true that one of these modern girls, who are going straight to the devil, may say: 'Woe is me! My living drains away each day, my servants despise me, my advisers deceive me: who will protect my property? Who buy me justice? Who bring up my sons?' And she is forced to take a husband, and thus the wretch, thinking to find a father for her sons, finds them an enemy, instead of a protector, a rapacious tyrant. In order to preserve frail earthly things, which she could have preserved by other means, she willingly abandons her own chastity, something precious above all worldly things. Behold the misery that befalls the new wife of a second husband, if domestic warfare is born together with new children by him. No longer is it fitting for her to love the sons born from the first husband or protect them or look fondly at them with a motherly eye full of just and praiseworthy mercy and love. If she does not dislike them, she shows she loves their dead father. She is thought to love him perhaps more than the second. If through bad luck he has sons by another wife, everyone will call her not a real mother, but a most cruel and unjust stepmother, however just and merciful she might be … The chaste widow must flee a second marriage not just as a blow but as a heavy burden, one that bears down on both body and soul, which perhaps may prove to be the greatest affliction for the disconsolate woman. Our true widow must adhere to the faithful advice of the Apostle [Paul] so that she stays in that new freedom, showing herself zealous for those things that give greatest pleasure to God and are of eternal benefit to her soul.

10.19 A husband envisages his widow's remarriage

While some husbands' wills provided disincentives for their future widows' remarriages, others, especially later in the period, put no obstacles in their way.

From the will of Lodovico Priuli, Venice, 1569, in J. Bernardi, ed., *Antichi testamenti* (Venice: Congregatione di Carità in Venezia, ser. 11, 1892), pp. 11–35.

To Marieta my dearest consort I bequeath that she be given all her entire dowry without the loss of anything, and that should the Lord God send me my death either when she is pregnant, or when she has had children by me, then I wish the residue of all my assets to be given to whatever child there may be ...

... I pray that if His Divine Majesty wills her to survive me, He should grant her to enjoy many more years, exhorting her, if she is still young, to remarry soon after one year, as I don't want her to go to her brother's house, for the reasons she well knows.

10.20 Women happy to avoid remarriage

Moderata Fonte presents differing female views through two of the widowed speakers in her dialogue, the elderly Adriana, and Leonora, the young hostess.

Fonte (1600), pp. 16–17, 24–5; (1997), pp. 53–4, 64.

[Adriana to Leonora] 'But it's a pity you're not going to remarry, as you're so young and lovely.'

'Remarry, indeed?' answered Leonora. 'I'd rather drown than ever again put myself under the thumb of any man! I have just escaped from servitude and misery and you want me of my own accord to get bothered with all that again? Heaven forbid!' All the women agreed she was right, and that she was fortunate ...

[Adriana] ... But when I lost [my cruel husband], I was forced to remarry to have children and I had this one (indicating Virginia). Though I hoped for a better partnership, the opposite happened, for if my first husband was bad, this one was worse, and I didn't much mind at either of their deaths.

INFLUENTIAL WIDOWS

10.21 **Alessandra Strozzi gives business advice**

Shrewd and discreet widows who had adequate means and good relations with their husbands' families and their children could attain considerable stature within their family circles. Alessandra Macinghi Strozzi's letters show not only concern for her children and grandchildren but business acumen: her banker son Filippo consulted her on the financial affairs of her less successful son-in-law Giovanni and her letters imply his deference to her judgement and worldly wisdom.[9]

Macinghi Strozzi (1997), pp. 194–200; to her son Filippo, January 1466, on Giovanni's request for financial help from him.

You say ... you'd like to know two things from me before the business is agreed. The first is my opinion on it [Giovanni's proposed business], and whether I think he would keep careful accounts of it ... I think [Giovanni] would run the business well because he's conscientious and knowledgeable, but if he were responsible for money I'm not so sure he'd be reliable because he still has expenses himself. It's true that as far as I've seen he's done what he ought, and when he's had money of mine, or I've made him loans, though they were only small amounts, still he has always kept careful accounts, and I've heard the same from those who deal with him ... On the second matter of the 200 florins he says he owes, I think it's certainly that or more. He's someone who doesn't talk much about his affairs, but I know he sometimes pawns the few clothes he has and conceals it from me because he's ashamed lest I know ... I would guess that he has more debts than this, as I don't think the figure of 200 includes 40 from you, or 80 from Marco ... I'd like you to help him, but on the other hand I think if you do help him out financially, I don't know if he'll be able to repay you when it's due, because I don't see him being in a position in a year's time to lay his hands on that amount of money. And if he didn't, or couldn't pay, it would cause scandal. So it would be better to leave it alone.

10.22 **Praise for Lucrezia Tornabuoni**

Widows at the highest social levels could exert even wider economic, political and cultural influence. Francesco da Castiglione writes to Lorenzo de'

---

9 See A. Morton Crabb, *The Strozzi of Florence: Widowhood and Family Solidarity in the Renaissance* (Ann Arbor, 2000).

Medici on the death in 1482 of his mother Lucrezia Tornabuoni, widowed since 1469.

Translation of Maguire, p. 220.

What part of the state did the wisdom of Lucrezia not see, take care of, or confirm! She concerned herself with the greater as well as the lesser and the least of all the citizens, and in this way upon occasion her actions, from the political point of view, were more prudent than yours, for you attended only to great things and forgot the less, which nevertheless required attention. She both sought and gave advice to the most important persons and the magistrates, and she also admitted the humblest to her presence, and all she sent away happy and contented. But you know all this better than I do, for you never did anything without consulting her, as she did nothing without knowing your views.

10.23 Two heroic widow-rulers

Aristocratic widows could sometimes exhibit 'virile' virtues, in ruling their states as regents or in their own right. Lodovico Dolce praises both Anna, the widow of Guglielmo, Marquess of Monferrato, and her daughter Margherita, widow of Federico Gonzaga, Duke of Mantua (see 12.5).

Dolce (1545), fols 79v–80r.

And although [Margherita] had few years together with that lord [Federico], in imitation of her mother she has always lived with such chastity, and governed her subjects with such prudence, that one doesn't know whether to admire her more for her religion, her justice, her generosity or her other heroic virtues, befitting not just a princess, but a prince. And as the bravery of one in the last war preserved many places from the sword, from fire, from rapine, murder or rape by enemy soldiers, so the modesty of the other reconciled all the rebel spirits among her people, always obtaining the public benefit and utility that everyone enjoys and will enjoy under her just and peaceable rule. So today the mother governs Monferrato and the daughter Mantua, to the unbelievable satisfaction of all the people.

WIDOWS DISPOSE OF THEIR ESTATES

In both these wills from different centuries and from widows of different social status, patterns typical of women in general can be seen: bequests both of money and of goods of sentimental value to female rather than male relatives, to charities and convents, and to servants, including those of friends and relatives.

10.24 Will of Lucia, widow of the Venetian artist Jacobello del Fiore, 10 November 1463

Ludwig, pp. 94–5.

I, Lucia, widow of Ser Jacomelo de Fiore ... wish as my executors Cataruza my sister, Constantin di Constantini my son-in-law and my daughter Marina ...

First I wish and ordain that my dowry of 600 ducats be disposed and given as follows:

I leave to my daughter Marina 400 ducats ... to my sister Cataruza 250 ducats ... to my three nephews Geronimo, Alvise and Francesco 15 ducats each.

... I leave our slave Nastasia 15 ducats, and while she is waiting for this portion I leave her at liberty and free. And the money from the *Camera de Imprestadi*,[10] which is about 1,200 ducats, I wish and order to be disposed as follows. First, I leave to my four relatives Agostina, Isabeta, Agnesina and Helena 250 ducats each ...

I leave to my son Ercole 15 ducats ... to Catarina my former slave 3 ducats ... to two friends of my daughter Marina, one called Lucia, the other Maddalena, 3 ducats each ...

I leave to my daughter Marina 70 ducats, which I loaned in two portions to my son-in-law Constantin di Constantini ...

I leave all my books to the convent of S. Croce in Giudecca ...

I leave all my share of the houses at Padua to my son-in-law Constantin de Constantini and his male children. I leave to the notary who drew up this my will 3 ducats. The remainder of all my goods I leave to my daughter Marina.

Since I find that I have 200 gold ducats, I wish and order that these be given to my two relatives, Agostina and Isabeta.

I leave to the priest Niccolò of S. Agnese 2 ducats ... to the nuns of S. Daniele, Venice, 3 ducats ... to the nuns of S. Maria della

---

10 An investment institution.

Annunziata 2 ducats ... to the nuns of S. Margarita of Torcello 2
ducats ... to the nuns of S. Croce on Giudecca 2 ducats.

10.25 Will of Elena Barozza Zantani, 11 April 1581

Elena Barozza, a famed beauty in her younger days, was the widow of Antonio
Zantani, a leading music publisher in Venice.

M. Feldman, *City Culture and the Madrigal at Venice* (Berkeley and Los Angeles,
1996), pp. 431–2.

I, Elena Zantana, widow of Messer Antonio ... wish my body to be
buried in Corpus Domini, in the tomb my father-in-law had erected,
where he and my former husband are, without any pomp as my executors think best, but dressed according to the order of the Corpus
Domini nuns. Before I am buried, I wish alms to be given as follows.
First, 30 masses should be said in my neighbourhood and 30 in Corpus
Domini for my soul, and 100 ducats be spent as follow: 10 ducats each
to the Hospitals for Incurables, at SS. Giovanni e Paolo and for
Prisoners; 10 for the Convertite, 10 for the nuns of Corpus Domini, 10
for those of S. Maria Maggiore, 10 for those of the Miracoli, 10 for
S. Servolo, 10 for S. Chiara of Murano, 10 for S. Croce in Venice.[11]

[Executors are named.]

To Madonna Giustina Zantana, my most beloved relative and
companion, I leave 25 ducats a year as long as she lives, namely, 12
ducats six months after my death, and each six months at the same
rate. This is as a sign of love, though I well know she deserves much
more, for the affection she has always shown me ... To my sister-in-
law I leave my mourning dress, and to my relative Helena I leave as a
sign of love 12 of my chemises and 24 scarves: she should choose from
my things the ones she likes best. I leave to three others of my nun-
relatives 3 ducats per year each, which should be given by my heirs
each Christmas as long as they live

[Small bequests to tradesmen.]

To Cornelia, my present servant, 10 ducats for her marriage, to
Margarita, daughter of Anzola Sartora, 10 ducats for her marriage, to
Giulia, daughter of the late Gasparo Zantani's Laura, 10 ducats for her
marriage ... I ask my sister-in-law, together with Helena my relative,

11 The first three are charitable institutions, the last seven nunneries.

to give all my woollen and fur garments to our impoverished relatives, if there are any, and the daughters of the late Gasparo Zantani and Anzola Sartora, for the sake of my soul.

PIETY AND CHARITABLE ACTIVITIES

10.26 A pious young widow

Religious observances and good works were the activities thought most suitable for widows finished with the upbringing of children. A withdrawn, cloistered life and mortification of the flesh was an ideal repeatedly advocated, and thought especially admirable in younger widows such as Vespasiano's exemplary Caterina degli Alberti.

Vespasiano da Bisticci (1970–76) vol. 2, pp. 49–6.

Being young, she adopted remedies to restrain the appetites of youth: she wore a chemise of only coarse grey cloth, denied herself a proper bed, sleeping on a mattress on top of a bench, and only took to her bed in the severest illness. Needing another remedy to mortify the flesh, she fasted on all official vigils and in Lent, and added to these Advent, and other devotions of her own. As another remedy against sloth, the cause of all evil, and to occupy her time worthily, she said the entire Office with the breviary, as priests and friars do ... as she could read. She owned a Bible from which she took great consolation, she had homilies on the year's Gospel readings, which she looked at each day as the Gospels came round, and had other commentators – early Fathers – on the Bible; and all the time that passed she was absorbed in these worthy exercises, and was most devout towards the poor and needy, and in short she succoured in their need both male and female religious institutions and many distressed poor people.

10.27 Piety should not be overdone

Widows often joined religious confraternities or Third Orders (see chapter 11), gaining small fees for charitable acts and perhaps the prospect of support in sickness and old age, as well as companionship and respectability.[12] Suspicious of some of these, Lodovico Dolce counsels against over-ostentatious piety.

Dolce (1553), fols 74v–76v.

---

12 P. R. Baernstein, 'In Widow's Habit: Women between Convent and Family in Sixteenth-Century Milan', *Sixteenth Century Journal*, 25:4 (1994), pp. 787–807.

In respect of her dress, although she may have put aside pearls and gay costume, I would not advise her to wear a hair shirt, or overly severe clothes, but conform to a certain mean; she should avoid ostentation, yet not smell of hypocrisy, for God does not take notice of garments, but of souls. She should not think that donning the habit of St Francis, St Dominic or St Benedict leads souls to paradise, because although humble garments are truly worthy of a Christian woman, placing faith in these vain distinctions is not only idolatry, but madness ... These days people praise a widow who wears the tunic and rough habit of a tertiary, and don't think of whether she is adulterating the bed of some chaste wife, or profaning the cell of another St Monica ... Her prayers should not be like those made by some, who, holding a long strand of paternosters in their hands, mumble through their teeth, make themselves heard throughout the house, and at every little phrase get to their feet, interrupting the sacred words, and cry or curse. Instead she should retire to her room, shut herself in and, with her bodily eyes gazing at an image of the crucifix, and her mental ones turning to God, she should emit more prayers than tears ... She should not concern herself with going to feasts and weddings and suchlike, but only to hear the word of God, and visit her church, where she should be neither the first to enter nor the last to leave ... The churches she attends should not be the most popular, but the most devout, where there is more chance of praying than of sinning: and so I would like her to hold it certain that not this or that church, but rather the whole world, is the temple of God.

10.28 A widow patron of the Jesuits

Many affluent or socially influential widows, especially at the time of mid-sixteenth-century Catholic Reform, espoused a more dynamic interpretation of widowhood, patronising new religious and charitable foundations.[13] Leading churchmen such as Carlo Borromeo (1538–84) in Milan or Ignatius Loyola (1491–1556) in Rome tried to harness their energy, good will and, not least, their money. Letters from Jesuit circles suggest both the successes and the tensions that could ensue. Although the Ferrarese benefactress Maria Frassoni del Gesso received many warm letters from Loyola, she could also irritate, or cause worry about gossip, as in the first letter, to a Jesuit in Ferrara of whom Maria had become too fond. The extreme piety of other widows caused alarm, so that Loyola would not sanction Jesuit houses for women.

13 C. Valone, 'Piety and Patronage: Women and the Early Jesuits', in Matter and Coakley, eds, pp. 157–84.

Saint Ignatius Loyola's Letters to Women, ed. H. Rahner and trans. K. Pond and
S. A. H. Weetman (Edinburgh and London, 1960), pp. 192–3, 199.

a. Pollanco, Loyola's associate, to Father Jean Pelletier, 2 September 1553:

Concerning your frequenting the house of the President's wife [the
widow Maria del Gesso], you have the opinion of our Father
[Loyola]: as servants of God we must always take two things into
account, a clear conscience and the good opinion of those for whose
edification we must work ... It has come to our ears from different
sides that the frequent comings and goings to that house do not
exactly produce an edifying effect – quite the contrary. Our Father
therefore thinks that you must be extremely circumspect in this
matter. Firstly, as you have already been told, you must go to that
lady's house twice a week at most. Secondly, you must try to make
yourself less and less indispensable by introducing her to Father
Filippo, to hear her confession and converse with her from time to
time. This is so that the lady may abandon any untoward affection for
Your Reverence, should one exist, even a spiritual one. Thirdly, Your
Reverence should on no occasion, under any pretext, go alone to that
house, but always accompanied by a fellow religious, as the custom of
the Society demands, so that each one can always keep an eye on the
other.

b. Maria del Gesso to Ignatius Loyola, 30 May 1554:

Although at the present time we are not strong financially, His
Heavenly Majesty has given us so much heart and goodwill that
through his grace we have purchased a new house for the College ...
it cost 5,000 pounds in Ferrarese currency. The house is near the
Ducal Palace and the square in the centre of the city ...

It is very well adapted to the College's requirements. Firstly, it has a
very fine and lovely church; it has very good accommodation for the
College; its garden adjoins that of the Hospital of S. Anna from which
it gets very good air.

... On the twenty-fifth of the present month I solemnly took possession of the house in the name of God. My soul felt enormous happiness
to see [the Fathers] leave the houses of men and enter the house of
Jesus Christ, and to see the Reverend Father Master Jean gather the
fruits of his labours.

10.29 A friar greedy for widows' wealth

Firenzuola (1493–1543), himself a friar, in his 10th *novella* satirises the
cupidity of friars, who exploited the gullible piety of rich widows to win themselves greater luxuries.

Agnolo Firenzuola, 'Novella Decima', in *Raccolta di novellieri italiani* (Florence,
1883), p. 1057.

[News of the death of the wealthy husband of Donna Agnese spreads
to the guardian of the friars] who kept his eye on how this sort of
thing worked out, so that no widow would escape without adopting
the girdle of the Blessed Serafico, St Francis. When she became a
tertiary, going each day to their services, and offering prayers for the
souls of her deceased, she would provide the brothers with fine
Lombard tart. With time, inspired by the zeal for good works of Fra
Ginepro and other of their saints, she might be inclined to endow a
chapel in their church, where she would have painted that wonderful
story of St Francis preaching to the birds in the wilderness, or of the
time he cooked holy soup, or of the Angel Gabriel bringing him his
clogs.[14] And then she would endow them with so many goods that each
year they could hold a feast for the holy stigmata ...

This pious guardian hovered around this widow so much, making such
a row with his clogs that she became willing to enrol in the Third
Order, following which the brethren were regularly supplied with delicate foods and richly worked tunics. But, thinking that all this was
little or nothing, they kept on at her all day long to remember the
matter of endowing the chapel.

14 Invented episodes, of the kind the friars supposed would appeal to the widow.

Part III

Roles

11 Nuns and women in religion

For a woman during the Renaissance, entering a convent was the main respectable alternative to marrying. A large proportion of the female middle- or upper-class population entered convents in their teens,[1] the number greatly increasing in the later sixteenth century, when female exceeded male religious for the first time. More entered in widowhood or old age, and still more older women joined the tertiaries or Third Orders affiliated to the Second Orders, the female versions of the original First Orders of monks or friars. Women from humbler backgrounds who could not afford the substantial dowry customarily donated for a nun's support performed more menial tasks in nunneries, as *converse* or lay sisters.[2]

The older-established nunneries were Benedictine or Augustinian, many having become wealthy, privileged and worldly. Observance of their rules could often be scandalously lax, despite repeated attempts at reform. The new Franciscan and Dominican mendicant orders from the thirteenth century had provided powerful inspiration for change: St Clare (1194–1253), St Francis' close follower, promoted strict observance of poverty, chastity and obedience rather than elaborate liturgy or learning, and emphasised enclosure rather than the public preaching associated with male Franciscans.[3] Dominican female houses also committed themselves more fervently to basic monastic ideals, following the early fifteenth century activity of males such as St Antoninus or Giovanni Dominici and, even more, the inspiration of the Dominican tertiary St Catherine of Siena (1347–80), followed by the Blessed Colomba da Rieti (1467–1501). New female religious organisations more oriented towards charitable work in secular society also arose in the sixteenth century, such as the Angelic Sisters

---

1 Chojnacki, p. 39, estimates that by 1581 three-fifths of all patrician Venetian girls were nuns, and the figure is probably similar for other cities like Bologna or Milan.
2 Overviews are D. Bornstein, 'Women and Religion in Late Medieval Italy: History and Historiography' and R. Rusconi, 'Women and Religion in Later Medieval Italy: New Sources and Directions' in Bornstein and Rusconi, pp. 1–27 and 305–26. For convents within different cities, see R. L. Trexler, 'Celibacy in the Renaissance: the Nuns of Florence', in Trexler, vol. 2, pp. 6–30 and M. Laven, *Virgins of Venice* (London, 2000).
3 For Franciscan convents and their traditions, see J. Wood, *Women, Art and Spirituality: The Poor Clares of Early Modern Italy* (Cambridge, 1994).

of St Paul, part of the Barnabite order, and the Company of St Ursula,[4] as did women's confraternities.[5] Whereas attempts at reform had waxed and waned in earlier centuries, after the Council of Trent (1545–63) abuses in female religious houses were more consistently and energetically attacked by the church hierarchy. Privileges, lax observance and scandals were controlled, but in the process much creativity from religious women – whether in the form of cultural expression or of new types of organisation – was repressed.

ENTERING A CONVENT: PROCEDURES, MOTIVATIONS, PERSONNEL

Economic pressures or familial piety meant that many girls were intended for convent life from early childhood or even before birth. As funding a nun's entry endowment was cheaper than a marital dowry, a family with several daughters might marry only the most attractive or healthy, and place the others in nunneries. Though this practice was clearly open to abuse, many girls who had boarded in convents in their youth, perhaps with family members, may have preferred to remain in this familiar, often comfortable environment, perhaps to pursue learning, than to undergo an arranged marriage and hazardous childbirth.

11.1 A child accepted as a future nun

S. Caterina de' Ricci writes to her father on 24 April 1544 about the acceptance of her sister, then aged 6, into her convent at Prato.

Caterina de' Ricci, *Santa Caterina de' Ricci, Epistolario*, ed. G. M. di Agresti (Florence, 1973), vol. 1, p. 53.

I want also to give you some good news. That is, yesterday, the 23rd of this month, with the firm agreement of all the chapter of nuns, your dearest daughter Lessandra, together with the other girls, was accepted, and it was a fine decision, so that you should thank the Lord – and I with you – for the many blessings that He continually bestows.

---

4 See R. De Molen, ed., *Religious Orders of the Catholic Reformation* (NY, 1994).
5 See later essays in Wisch and Cole Ahl; N. Terpstra, 'Women in the Brotherhood: Gender, Class, and Politics in Renaissance Bolognese Confraternities', *Renaissance and Reformation*, 24 (1990), pp. 193–212.

11.2 A Ferrarese girl's entry

Girls commonly entered convents at thirteen or fourteen, an age when families would be considering futures for their daughters, and, after adopting the habit and spending about a year as novices, formally took their vows. The following entries by a Ferrarese diarist describe typical economic settlements and ceremonial procedures for girls from middle-class families.[6]

Bernardino Zambotti, 'Diario ferrarese dall'anno 1476 sino al 1504', ed. G. Pardi, in *Rerum italicarum scriptores*, vol. 24, pt 7 (Bologna, 1937), pp. 82–3, 116.

On Saturday 18th [of November 1480] ... Ser Jacomo Zambotto, notary and Ferrarese citizen, my father, gave a donation to the monastery of S. Agostino for my sister Eufroxina, who on the following day was to enter the monastery. And he sent a sack of bread, eggs, cheese, two pieces of veal, chicken and fish, the bed and a chest of possessions, and wine, and he consigned them the dowry, debited against 300 *lire* of *marchesini* the monastery had for spices from our shop ...

On the 19th, Sunday morning: Suor Eufroxina, my sister, was accompanied by other gentlewomen on foot and young men in front, to the monastery of S. Agostino, dressed in silver brocade with her hair loosened on her shoulders, with the devotional image [*anchona*] and a lavishly decorated holy doll,[7] and with a candle of white wax in the fashion of a bride. And after mass was said by Don Zoanne da Carpi, chaplain to the sisters, she was blessed and received, with singing by the nuns and the abbess with great devotion ...

On the 3rd [of November 1482], Sunday morning: my sister, Suor Eufroxina, this morning made her profession, after mass had been sung in the church of S. Agostino ... And several relatives and friends offered her candles, according to custom, together with my father ... And they gave the donation due to the pious women for her living costs as is usual.

11.3 Older women enter convents

For older women, the need for protection in old age and to make a good death

---

6 For convent entry ceremonies, see K. Lowe, 'Secular Brides and Convent Brides: Wedding Ceremonies in Italy during the Renaissance and Counter-Reformation', in eds Dean and Lowe, pp. 41–65.

7 Devotional statues of the Infant Jesus, often lavishly dressed.

must have been powerful factors, as suggested in these passages from the Necrology (record of deaths) at the reformed Dominican house of Corpus Domini, Venice, written by Suor Bartolomea Riccaboni.[8]

Riccaboni, Bartolomea, *Cronaca del Corpus Domini* and *Necrologio del Corpus Domini*, in Dominici, Giovanni, *Lettere spirituali*, ed. M-T. Casella and G. Pozzi (Friburg, 1969), pp. 299, 302, 327–8; *Life and Death in a Venetian Convent: the Chronicle and Necrology of Corpus Domini*, trans. D. Bornstein (Chicago, 2000), pp. 68–9, 72, 99.

In the said year [1403] departed from this life Suor Maruza Bonzi, the mother of Suor Franceschina da Noal. She was of the Third Order of St Francis and lived to almost 100. Becoming infirm and near death, out of respect for her daughter she was brought here and vested in our habit, and lived 22 days very piously. This blessed woman was like a good tree which bears good fruit, since her daughter, Suor Franceschina, and two of her daughters and a relative, belong to our order; the monastery has over two thousand ducats from her property. I believe that through the good fruit issuing from her she will enjoy the gifts of eternal life.

Suor Franceschina da Noal entered the monastery seven days after it was enclosed and was a widow of 49. She lived devoutly in the secular world with her husband and always wore a hair-shirt under her velvet. When she was left a widow she dressed humbly and coarsely. When she became a nun, she entered the order, desiring greater perfection, bringing with her one of her daughters, aged 7 [...]

On the 10th day [of May 1431] Suor Geronima Cancillieri of Pistoia, a widow, died. She entered the monastery aged 51 and lived there 26 years. This lady was the daughter of the Count of Pistoia, all her brothers were counts and of high rank. The wife of a knight, she was left widowed young, and always wished to serve God. She wished to go where she would not be known or honoured, and, as it pleased God to grant good wishes, she was converted as a result of the preaching of our father,[9] then preaching in Tuscany, and hearing the good reputation of this monastery she made an agreement with him and came to Venice. Learning this, her two sons, who were highly esteemed knights, and two of her married daughters tracked her steps to Rimini to prevent her. As it pleased God, she overcame everything and came to enclose herself here out of love.

8 For these chronicles, see K. J. P. Lowe, *Nuns' Chronicles and Convent Culture in Renaissance and Counter-Reformation Italy* (Cambridge, 2003).
9 Giovanni Dominici.

11.4 Girls tricked into entering convents

While convents' necrologies describe pious girls longing to become nuns while their relatives dreamed of advantageous marriages, a commoner stereotype was the girl forced into a convent owing to economic pressures.[10] This phenomenon became particularly marked during the later sixteenth century, when secular dowry inflation contributed to a huge increase in nuns, and gave great concern to reformers. The bitterest critic of such forced entry was the Venetian nun and polemist Arcangela Tarabotti (1604–52).[11] In her *L'inferno monacale* of the 1640s, unpublished during her lifetime, Tarabotti describes the deceptions used by parents, aided by nuns, to get their daughters' consent to enter.

Arcangela Tarabotti, *L'inferno monacale*, ed. F. Medioli (Turin, 1990), pp. 31–2.

The greed and tyranny of fathers, together with the naiveté, ignorance and untimely obedience of daughters, produce these terrible consequences ...

With blandishments suited to the age of the girls, sweetly they [older nuns] solicit them ... To little girls they describe wondrous places little different from the Earthly Paradise, even tricking them so that they imagine trees which out of season bear sweetmeats and sugared fruits, so that their childish simplicity is led to believe that the monastery orchards produce sweetness and succulence.

But our gardens only abound in thorns, tribulations and unhappiness!

To older girls they promise delightful games, freedom from work and rich foods. To the even more mature, they promise considerable freedom, and that in entering they will gain lovely dwellings, comfortable rooms and handsome refectories ...

Such are the schemes cooked up by these tyrants, miserly with their meagre money but prodigal with the liberty of others. Instead, they should explain in sensible discussions with their relatives destined for the cloister what they must agree to, and teach them the virtues a true nun must display.

10 S. K. Cohn, 'Nun and Dowry Funds: Women's Choices in the Renaissance', in S. K. Cohn Jr, *Women in the Streets: Essays on Sex and Power in Renaissance Italy* (Balitmore and London, 1996), pp. 76–98.
11 See introduction in Arcangela Tarabotti, *Paternal Tyranny*, ed. L. Panizza (Chicago, 2004), pp. 1–31.

THE MONASTIC WAY OF LIFE:
IDEALS AND PRACTICES

11.5 Catherine of Siena writes to nuns

All institutions subscribed to the basic monastic ideals of prayer and poverty, chastity, obedience, humility and a contempt for worldly things. These were fervently advocated by the most committed men and women of the day, here by Catherine of Siena, writing to the nuns of S. Gaggio and of Monte San Savino in *c.* 1376.

Catherine of Siena, *The Letters of St Catherine of Siena*, ed. S. Noffke (Binghamton, NY, 1988), pp. 196–7; *Epistolario di Santa Caterina*, ed. E. D. Theseider (Rome, 1940), pp. 258–62.

Dearest mothers and daughters in Jesus Christ,

... I yearn to see you hidden and shut away in the side of Christ crucified. Otherwise it would be useless to be enclosed within [convent] walls; in fact, it would be like being in prison. So, just as you are enclosed physically, let your affection and desire be securely enclosed, turned away from worldly ambition and pleasure to follow your Bridegroom, gentle Christ Jesus ...

Do you know what path your Bridegroom walked? One of freely chosen poverty and obedience. Out of humility, utter exaltedness descended to the baseness of our humanity. Because of that humility and His boundless love for us He gave up His humanity to the shameful death of the cross, choosing the way of torment, scourging, torture and insults. You must imitate that humility. But know that it cannot be achieved except through real self-knowledge and by contemplating the deep humility and meekness of the Lamb ...

I said that He walked the way of true poverty. He was so poor that He had nowhere to rest His head. At his birth gentle Mary didn't even have a little blanket in which to wrap her son. So you, His spouses, must follow this way of poverty. You know you have promised to live in such poverty until you die, and I beg you, for love of Christ crucified, to keep that promise. If not, you would be adulteresses rather than wives, since you would be giving your love to something apart from God – just as a wife is called an adulteress if she loves another man more than her husband.

So it is that obedience follows closely upon poverty and humility. The more a spouse [of Christ] freely embraces poverty of spirit, and the more she renounces worldly riches and ambition, the more humble she is. And the more humble she is, the more obedient she is. Proud people are never obedient because their pride makes them unwilling to bend or submit to anyone. I want you, then, to be humble, despoiled in heart and affection until death. You, Mother Abbess, must be obedient to the rule, and the rest of you must be obedient to the rule and to your abbess.

11.6 Advice on nuns' communal behaviour

Prayer primarily meant the arduous round of saying and singing the eight canonical offices, explained in detail in Benedictine rules. This encouraged musical excellence and learning, but required a good proportion of nuns to be literate and versed in Latin, reinforcing their tendency to be of upper-class origins. Less fervent sisters evidently found communal services tedious, as implied in a 1568 advice book by a Franciscan friar, which also counsels behaviour at mealtimes, when sacred texts would be read.

Bonaventura Gonzaga da Reggio, *Alcuni avertimenti nella vita monacale ...* (Venice, 1568), pp. 13–14, 15–16.

How to behave in Choir

Since of all your doings, those in God's service must be the most important, disciplined and best performed, you should not, therefore, be slothful or sleepy in celebration of the Divine Office, but vigorous, with the body forced to obey the spirit. Stand or kneel reverently as the occasion demands, speaking the psalms cheerfully and devoutly, in the presence of the angels of God who are close beside you. Scorn giggling and gossiping before One whom all creation should serve with fear and reverence. Try to enunciate the words of the lessons or psalms or whatever comes up clearly and distinctly. Do not swivel your eyes now here, now there, unless required. Do not wander about the choir unless forced to, and never leave before the Office is completed ... When Divine Office has been celebrated, avoid rushing straight into trivial and mundane conversations, but try to maintain the devotion you have gained by psalm-singing and prayer. If through any evil inclination you feel yourself lacking in inner devotion, at least outwardly show signs of humility and good behaviour, in reverence to God, and to set a good example to your neighbour.

How to Behave at Meals

Be circumspect in the public refectory, and do not try to look at everything, except what is beside you. Keep your attention either on God, or on the reading. Eat timidly, politely, and silently, not impatiently, as

though you wanted to gulp down everything on the table in the blink
of an eye, nor look as though you are intent on the best, most delicious
food, but eat as much as suffices you, always praising God and His
infinite bounty ... You must always steer between two extremes,
neither eating so little that you lack the natural strength to perform
communal tasks, nor so much that you can only wearily and with great
difficulty read, pray and do all the other things you are commanded.

11.7 Personal devotions in Venice

Apart from private reading of texts stressing monastic virtues and the
following of Christ, the Virgin and female saints and those of their order, nuns
meditated intensely on the Eucharist and on the beautiful face or suffering
body of their beloved Spouse. Meditation and prayer was, in more devout
houses, frequently rewarded by visions: Suor Bartolomea Riccaboni describes
several at Corpus Domini.

Riccaboni in Dominici, pp. 299, 301; ed. Bornstein, pp. 69, 69–71.

In 1403 ... Suor Felicitas Buonio passed from this life aged 18 years,
a most pure virgin, as she was in spirit and was evident in her deeds.
She was so mild and gentle that she seemed like an angel; all who
looked on her were devoutly acknowledged; her whole life was a
holy meditation, truly observant and obedient. Once, standing in the
choir for the octave of the body of Christ, when the door of the [taber-
nacle of the] sacrament was kept open, looking towards the Host
she saw a most beautiful male infant, who seemed to her to greet her
and promise her eternal life; a few days later she became ill, and spent
a year in infirmity and was blessed and received all the holy sacraments, and with utmost devotion rendered her soul to her beloved
bridegroom.

... In 1405 Suor Diamante passed from this life on the 24th of March;
she was 20 ... She would study Holy Scripture constantly and had the
greatest aptitude at reading and singing. She was most devout and had
a great revelation from God. One time she remained rapt in spirit for
a day and night without bodily movement. She had a great longing for
martyrdom; my lady St Ursula with all her company appeared to her
and it was revealed that she would be of that company.

11.8 Devotion to the Passion of Christ at Prato

From the Dominican chronicler and hagiographer Serafino Razzi's 1594 description of the religious devotions of nuns at S. Vincenzo, Prato.

Serafino Razzi, *Vita di santa Caterina de' Ricci*, ed. G. M. di Agresti (Florence, 1965), pp. 51, 53.

Suor Domitilla di Piero Coppini, from Prato, was vested nun in 1522. She was most observant in religious matters and much devoted to Holy Communion. She used to say that looking after the sick with loving care was a devout preparation for receiving it. She took great delight in meditation on the Passion of Our Lord. When roses were in bloom she would place five red ones before her while she worked, the better to meditate on the Five Wounds.

11.9 The dangers of involvement with men in religion

Rules also laid down the internal government of the institution, the house-keeping practicalities, and the relationships with superiors within or without the particular order. Chaplains or Visitors were needed to say Mass, act as confessors, and generally oversee the nuns. Selecting suitable individuals, and avoiding undesirable relationships developing, caused continual problems, implied here in the restrictions on Visitors' entry added by the Blessed Battista da Varano (1458–1527), writer, visionary and Franciscan reformer at Urbino and Camerino (Marche), to the Rule of St Clare.

Battista Varani, *Le opere spirituali della beata Battista Varani dei signori di Camerino fondatrice del monastero delle Clarisse*, ed. M. Santori (Camerino, 1894), pp. 335–6.

I counsel and advise, and as far as possible order and dispose, that the visitation be done diligently and charitably, without entering the monastery but at the grille ... The visitation should be made only once a year in all diligence and fear of God, and also with proper modesty, and then carried out as swiftly and promptly as possible. And none of the sisters entrusted to my care should dare to send letters to any friar or other person, nor receive any letter sent them ... Nor should any presume to make pieces of embroidery or needlework or suchlike for any friar of our order. Also no sister should presume to speak with any friar of our order ... except in the presence of the Vicar, the Visitor at the visitation, or in the presence of the nuns' confessor.

11.10 **Work: printing**

Work was carried out during appointed hours both to avoid idleness and to earn necessary money. Apart from domestic duties and tending the kitchen garden, this meant spinning or doing needlework, perhaps making ecclesiastical vestments, or producing illuminated manuscripts and, from the later fifteenth century, printed illustrations and books.

From the business diary of the Dominican convent of S. Jacopo di Ripoli, Florence, in M. Conway, *The 'Diario' of the Printing Press of San Jacopo di Ripoli 1476–1484* (Florence, 1999), pp. 156, 225.

... The abovementioned 10 florins from Bartolo are put aside for the salary of our nuns who work as compositors in the printing-shop of the said Bartolo. (1478)

... To Suor Marietta of our house, for all of February 1481 [1482], two large florins for her help in setting the *Morgante* ... And on 16th April 1482 she had a half ducat, to be payment for the help given. (1482)

11.11 **Work: illumination**

A letter from the nuns of S. Marta to the nuns of S. Abondio, Siena, requesting payment for books illuminated by them, *c.* 1500.

Appendix by G. Milanesi, in S. Borghesi and L. Banchi, *Nuovi documenti per la storia dell'arte senese* (Siena, 1898), pp. 361–2.

We send you this example of a service book [*comune*], which you requested, and is supplied. We would like you to say which you would like next, and not give us difficulty. And we would like you to send the remaining payment for the writing of this small psalter, for which you have already paid 24 *lire*, and give the remaining 6 *lire* for the other manuscript, that is for that service book we have now written. We will not speak of the miniature now: we will do this another time ... We would like you to do us the great favour of sending us one of the good pens for writing, since we have been told that you have geese. Greet Suor Cornelia on behalf of her niece, Suor Orsola de' Sozzini, who also asks if she could also send two or three pens as she is learning to write,[12] and says she will write a psaltery.

---

12 Probably implying that Orsola was learning to write elegantly, not that she was previously totally illiterate.

PROBLEMS AND ABUSES

11.12 Nuns request help to buy new tunics

Poverty and enclosure (*clausura*) were the areas that caused nuns most problems. Well-endowed institutions ran the risk of luxurious worldliness, the less
affluent of excessive indigence. Petitioning family members, or influential
outsiders, for gifts (often reciprocated with offerings of biscuits and sweets,
needlework, and certainly the promise of prayer), was common in all cases.
Here, the prioress and sisters of the monastery of S. Agostino at Pisa ask
Lucrezia Tornabuoni for new tunics on 22 October 1474.

Lucrezia Tornabuoni, ed. P. Salvadori, *Lettere* (Florence, 1993), p. 134.

Allow us the spirit and the confidence to write to Your Magnificence,
that your clemency and charity might condescend to comfort us with
your pious visitation and observe our needs, which are great in many
things and especially in the tunics, or rather wool shirts of these
sisters, which are so torn and worn out that they cannot be mended.
So again we call on your mercy, most compassionate lady, towards the
poor and especially towards nuns who seek to do good, that it should
please you to remember us in this our misery and need, providing us
with the heavy cloth called *savonese* for at least two tunics each,
rendering us ever obliged to your charity to pray to our Spouse, Lord
Jesus, for you and your children and family.

11.13 Nuns fail to observe *clausura*

Other nuns became embroiled in managing the assets of their house, involving
trips outside the convent, which conflicted with ideals of *clausura* advocated
both within stricter orders and by ecclesiastical authorities. The energetic and
influential reforming archbishop of Milan, Carlo Borromeo, writes to
Monsignor Spiciano from Brescia in November 1580, on reform of convents.

A. Rivolte, *San Carlo Borromeo. Note biografiche* (Milan, 1938), p. 315.

They no longer observe *clausura*; the recently deceased Bishop had
permitted a few nuns – although certainly with conditions – to go out
on occasions. So a large number of them abuse this to visit their families, one of them busying herself with the domestic affairs of their
confessor. They often go to visit their properties and lands; they look
into and execute the business of the convent with strangers. All these
things exceed the limits of the permission granted by Monsignor
Domenico Bollani, and this is why these wretched virgins are weighed
down with offences and misdeeds.

11.14 Adverse economic consequences of enclosure

Stricter observance of *clausura* impeded nuns in maximising proceeds from their work, as pointed out by the Commune of Prato in a letter of 27 May 1571 to the general of the Zoccolanti Franciscans about the plight of nuns of S. Giorgio.

Caterina de' Ricci (1973) vol. 3, pp. 141–2.

The poor, indeed mendicant sisters of this land of Prato, who are 130 mouths, have, contrary to their custom, been shut in so that they cannot go out to earn their living, nor benefit from their work, since they cannot show it to merchants as they used to do when they were less restricted, and they may die of hunger if Your Reverence does not do anything about it.

And as we must look after these holy virgins, our creatures, we make a heartfelt plea that you deign to allow them at least to send out their servants, and also to exhibit their works in certain rooms, close to the gate of their monastery, to secular women, who at present cannot go in to see it – so that they lack work – and thus prevent them from dying of hunger.

11.15 An abusive confessor

Scandalous absences of chastity in nuns were not fictitious: documents confirm the existence of long-standing liaisons between nuns and their lovers, sometimes producing illegitimate children who might be brought up within the convent, further diluting the devotional atmosphere. This episode of 1561 at the Monastero delle Convertite, Venice, involved a lecherous and sadistic priest and his charges, repentant prostitutes. The papal Nuncio Capilupi writes to Carlo Borromeo.

R. Canosa, *Il velo e il cappuccio* (Rome, 1991), p. 63.

[The priest] held in his hands the reins of that convent, where there were 400 nuns, mostly young and beautiful. He succumbed to his desire to satisfy all the debauched appetites of his lust, and did it in such a way that when one of them who attracted him confessed, in the very act of confession he tried to bend her to his will with various arguments thought up in advance, and by touching them with his hands to excite their carnal appetites more easily. If he found one at all resistant to such approaches, he praised her greatly as constant and strong, and tried to make her think he had been moved to tempt her to test her goodness. But a few days after making passes at confession, taking advantage of an opportune moment, he would have her put in prison and beaten and fiercely tormented in different ways. And he often obtained by cruelty what he could not by flattery, since some of them were inclined to consent to him, rather than being kept in chains and in the stocks.

11.16 General slackness thought endemic

A perennial problem perceived as more acute from the mid-sixteenth century, when nuns hugely increased in number, was general laxity, as described by Caterina Visconti in a letter of *c.* 1548 to her daughter, who had considered becoming a nun.

Lando, fols 39v–40v.

Today so little profiting from things spiritual takes place in female monasteries. Truly, I see few mortifying themselves, few who are unwilling to engage in secular practices ... I go to nunneries and I see their parlours and their grilles full of talk – a marketplace has not so much. If you want to hear any news, go to the sisters: there you'll learn at what time priest Gianni dell'India sleeps with his wife, there you'll learn if the Venetians are rearming this year, if the pope will make many cardinals, if the Protestants will come to a Council ... At the sisters', marriages are contracted for unfortunate women and divorces for unhappy husbands.

THE PHYSICAL ENVIRONMENT OF NUNS; THEIR USE OF ARTEFACTS

The scale and physical splendour of nunneries naturally varied according to their wealth and history of patronage. Important benefactors might wish to support their nun-relatives in style, provide appropriate settings for relics, or acquire prestige and merit from building new premises. In planning new buildings, nuns might show themselves well informed about current architectural developments within their own order or elsewhere, known through letters or outside visits.[13]

---

13 Differing views in M.-A. Winkelmes, 'Taking Part: Benedictine Nuns as Patrons of Art and Architecture', in Johnson and Matthews Grieco, pp. 91–110, and G. M. Radke, 'Nuns and their Art: the Case of San Zaccaria in Renaissance Venice', *Renaissance Quarterly*, 54:2 (2001), pp. 430–59.

11.17 A traveller's impression of Venetian convents

Canon Pietro Casola wrote an account of his visit to Venice in 1494.

Translation in Pietro Casola, *Canon Pietro Casola's Pigrimage to Jerusalem*, ed. and trans. M. M. Newett (Manchester, 1907), pp. 136–41.

I went – also in company – to visit a few of them [nunneries], especially the convent of S. Zaccaria. There are many women there, both young and old, and they let themselves be seen very willingly. They have a beautiful church and many relics in the altar. I think it is their first church, because they have their choir there. They are said to be very rich, and they do not trouble much about being seen ...

In the said Murano there are 7 convents for women, and among them one where building is continually going on by order of the present Doge, the Lord Agostino Barbarigo, who has 2 of his daughters in the same convent [S. Maria degli Angeli]. Much more might be said about this place and its beauty and pleasantness and how it is situated in the water and has beautiful gardens.

11.18 Devices to maintain *clausura*

The concern to enforce *clausura* led to the evolution of architectural devices that both limited access and dramatised the nuns' separation from the secular world: high walls, fortifications and, here described by Battista da Varano in her additions to the Rule of St Clare, grilles, bars and the communication wheel or *ruota*.

Battista Varani (1894), pp. 319–20.

None of the sisters may speak to anyone in the parlour or at the grille without the permission of the abbess.

Only rarely may permission to speak at the grille be granted. Since the Rule makes no mention of the wheel, be it known that two sisters must be given permanent custody of the wheel, who can reply to whoever comes, either jointly or singly. The wheel should be set up and arranged so that the nuns within can see nothing outside, nor the outsiders anything within, and no-one can enter or leave by means of it.

No sister is granted freedom to speak with anyone at the door.

A curtain should be placed over the grille beside it, which should not be moved.

The gaps in the grille should be well secured and the exit locked with wood and bolts and padlocks, with two keys in the padlock firmly fastened.

Of these keys, one should be held by the abbess, the other by the sacristan.

11.19 Building a fine new convent

The new convent at Prato built from 1558 with the donations of Filippo Salviati is well described by Serafino Razzi in 1594. It catered both for the visionary Caterina de' Ricci and for the needs of secular visitors, the church maintaining the usual distinction between a nuns' choir – either a screened-off adjacent area or a gallery – and a lay persons' church.

Razzi (1965), pp. 74–6.

The foundations of the aforesaid church were laid: in which, three *braccia* wide and eight deep, were placed by the servant of Christ Suor Caterina (as Messer Filippo wished) many holy relics of saints.

And first there was built ... the new church for use as the nuns' choir, 37 *braccia* long and 17 *braccia* wide, and vaulted above and with lunettes below. At the head of it was made the church for the secular people, with a big door on to Piazza S. Domenico. And the said church is 16 *braccia* long and wide, and 15 high; on its right, towards the road going to the Pistoia gate, was built a fine sacristy. And beside this, a room with chambers and antechambers and other rooms for the wife of Messer Filippo and his daughters, when they came to Prato. And on the left of the said church for secular people, towards S. Niccolò, were built rooms for the father confessors, with two confessionals. And beside this Messer Filippo had built several rooms for himself, for when he would come to this district, which after his death were incorporated into the monastery and were used by the nuns, as was also done with those used by his wife and daughters.

Above the nuns' new church a beautiful terrace was constructed, supported by pilasters and architraves of wonderfully thick fir; and above the new church for secular people, he had a drawing room built the same size as the church. And above the rooms for his wife and daughters, he built a dormitory of 13 cells, also stretching out above the new sacristy. And above the nuns' church, the same in size up to the presbytery, a very fine room was made, intended to serve as chapter house, although it was later not used as such, and it is thought that one day it will serve for the burial of the nuns, as the place already made under the presbytery is not sufficient.

Finally, he had built between the dispensary and the church, between two gardens, a new room where the nuns were to work in common, 13 *braccia* wide and 32 long, with five stone columns in the middle, as ... it would not have stayed up without them owing to its great size. And this new room was carried out due to Monna Margherita Strozzi ne' Serristori, also a great benefactor of this house.

... And the said building works were completed on the 22nd of September 1565. The expenses Messer Filippo wished no man to know, it being enough that God would know, from Whom he said he awaited recompense; but it is estimated that it was over 30,000 ducats.

11.20 A Passion scene for nuns

Nuns' churches and communal buildings might contain high quality paintings and sculptures, donated or commissioned when nuns from leading families felt imperatives of 'honour' and 'magnificence' like their secular relatives. In line with nuns' piety, subjects were often Passion scenes or images of the Virgin Mary or female saints. If strictly enclosed, they might not see much of works of art in churches open to the public.[14] Here, Giorgio Vasari writes in 1568 in praise of Perugino's *Lamentation* (Florence, Uffizi), then in the Clarissan nuns' church in Florence, which articulated nuns' devotion to the body and wounds of Christ (see 11.8 above) in a way felt moving to laymen.

Vasari (1984), vol. 3 Testo, p. 599.

For the nuns of S. Chiara he painted a picture of the dead Christ with such beautiful and novel colouring that it made artists think it wonderful and excellent. In this work several very fine heads of old men are to be seen, and also certain Maries who have just stopped weeping, and gaze at the dead Christ with extraordinary admiration and love ... It is said that Francesco del Pugliese wanted to give the nuns three times the price they had paid to Pietro, and have him make one just like the one he had painted for them, and that they would not agree, since Pietro said that he did not think he could equal it.

---

14 J. Gardner, 'Nuns and Altarpieces: Agendas for Research', *Römisches Jahrbuch der Bibliotheca Herziana*, vol. 13 (1995), pp. 27–57.

11.21 **Nuns commission an altarpiece**

The document below, from a nunnery in the Venetian lagoon, shows the use of a male intermediary to deal with negotiations with artists.

G. Ludwig, *Italienische Forschungen: Archivalische Beiträge zur Geschichte der venezianischen Kunst* (Berlin, 1911), p. 105.

29th June 1563, in the parlour of the Nunnery of Santa Eufemia, Mazzorbo. The present document declares that the reverend nun, Suor Eufemia, Abbess of the nunnery and in the name of the nunnery, has met with the painter Master Niccolò Frangipane, son of the deceased Matheo, living in Contra' S. Canciano in Biri, and that Master Niccolò must paint them the high altarpiece, with all the expenses for colours and other necessities for the altarpiece and painting. This is to be priced at 40 ducats ... In the painting there should be four female martyr saints and a Madonna above them on a cloud with angels and Christ in her arms, the Madonna to be from life. And Master Niccolò is obliged to hand over the painting by next August. The said Reverend nun now gives him as advance payment 10 ducats and 6 grossi ... as is shown in a receipt signed by Master Niccolò in the account book of the nunnery.

The colours of the painting should be the finest possible, the blues ultramarine. And in assurance of this I, Claudio Aleveno, doctor of this nunnery have written this in my hand, with the consent of all present: the reverend priest Messer Leonardo Vio, confessor, and Messer Lorenzo de Motoni, procurator of the nunnery.

11.22 **Gifts for a young nun**

Individual nuns would either bring with them, or over time acquire, various devotional images and books, and sometimes lavish furnishings for their cells. The Venetian painter Lotto notes his gifts to Lucrezia, the nun-daughter of Mario d'Armano, with whom he lodged in Venice between 1540 and 1542.

Lorenzo Lotto, *Lorenzo Lotto. Il 'Libro di spese diverse'*, ed. P. Zampetti (Venice, 1969), pp. 212, 214–15.

[30 December 1540] Given to Lucrezia in the
convent of San Bernardo   L- 12 *soldi*
to buy her a bound copy of the Lives of the
Holy Fathers   L 3, *soldi* 2

for a psalter with an Italian commentary,
bound in paper L2 s12
a book in quarto, Gerson's *Contempt for the World* L- s4 ...
January 1542 for a picture of the Madonna with
three little angels, which Mario wanted to have
ready for when Lucrezia took the veil L74 s8 ...
July 1542, for the frame and the cover of the little
Madonna picture for Lucrezia. The woodwork cost
3 lire 5 soldi, the gilding with its cover ie the metal
frame with its cloth worth L11 s3 L14 s8
For Lucrezia, the wooden crucifix, polychromed
and with a gilded frame L34 s-

NUNS' SOCIAL CONTACTS AND CULTURAL ROLES

Renaissance nuns were not necessarily cut off from the outside world. Rules might allow nuns to leave convents temporarily if circumstances required. Nuns, within limits, corresponded with and were visited by relatives and friends, and received and made gifts. Several groups of non-professed people might respectably live within convents, particularly young girls being educated and older women ill or on retreat. Orphanages, hospitals or female confraternities might be linked to nunneries.

11.23 Nuns receive a gift of food and wine

Caterina de' Ricci, from her convent, thanks a woman friend for gifts of food, on 1 December 1543.

Caterina de' Ricci (1973), vol. 1, pp. 38–9.

The goods we have received from your charity are, as you say, 2 bushels of walnuts, 1 bushel of chickpeas, half a bushel of large beans, 6 flasks of white wine, a basket of wonderful fruit, the large pumpkins, a pot of fine olives. You have supplied me not only for Advent, but for Lent! God be praised for it all! And I thank you once again.

11.24 A nun-diarist

The diary of the Modenese nun Lucia Pioppi (1537–1619) demonstrates continual awareness of political and social events and shows the ties between convents and their communities, as in this sample from 1557.

Lucia Pioppi, *Diario (1541–1612)*, ed. R. Bussi (Modena, 1982), pp. 31–2.

[11 January]: Messer Francesco Crivelli brought news to the monastery here of how Pope Paul V from the house of Caraffa made our most excellent Lord Duke of Ferrara general of all the forces in Italy, and was also made general of the sacred King Henry, the Most Christian King of France ...

In this same time all the villages of Bazovano and Saliceti were full of soldiers of the sacred King Henry of France, and because of these troubles they brought all the peasant women from our lands with their daughters, and also their poor little boys, to Modena to our monastery of S. Lorenzo, with many chests full of their possessions and with two dairy cows, to the great damage of our poor monastery. May God in His mercy help them.

... 21 February. Due to divine grace, the magnificent Commune of Modena, which had been sent a large quantity of baked bread made for the camp of the sacred King Henry ... ordered it to be given to sacred institutions, and 40 *mano* of bread to our monastery, which Our Lord has granted us in His mercy.

11.25 Nuns' theatrical activities

Nuns could be aware of cultural developments, and might publish writings, eventually not only on religious topics or for circulation within their order. In Milan and other North Italian cities, plays and entertainments were produced, though the less decorous of these were challenged by stricter enforcement of *clausura* during the Counter-Reformation period.

Visitation records for S. Agnese, Milan, 1576, in R. L. Kendrick, *Celestial Sirens: Nuns and their Music in Early Modern Milan* (Oxford, 1996), p. 440.

Each year at Carnival time there are very many masquerades with nuns dressed in different sorts of garments, friars' habits and those of secular men, and they eat in the refectory dressed like this, with daggers and swords ... They put on plays for themselves of the most illicit sorts of love ... the nuns, in different sorts of male dress, dance with the friars at the window.

11.26 Nuns' concerts

Concerts by nuns were famous in several cities, such as Milan, and an important source of patronage.

Morigia, pp. 186–7.

In this our city almost all convents practise music, both playing musical instruments and singing. In several convents there are voices fine enough to seem angelic, serene enough that the nobility of Milan delight in going to hear them. Among others, there are two who deserve praise, inferior to none in their musical excellence, which are the Monastery of S. Maria Maddalena, near S. Eufemia, the other that of the Assunta, called del Muro; these venerable nuns, apart from observing the holy apostolic life, are also highly talented in the practise of music, both playing and singing: one hears a range of voices brought into harmonious concord, with a blending of divine voices in concert, with a mingling of sounds seemingly like angelic choirs, which sweeten the ears of their listeners, and are praised by men with knowledge of this art.

11.27 A venerable Venetian nunnery

While pious houses commanded attention through the fame of a saintly inhabitant, or the perceived efficacy of their prayers, older convents might host public, quasi-political ceremonies.[15] Francesco Sansovino describes the Easter procession of the Doge to the famous Benedictine nunnery of S. Zaccaria, Venice.

Francesco Sansovino, *Venetia città nobilissima et singolare* (Venice, 1581, repr. 1663), fol. 196r.

Having heard the sermon in S. Marco, [the Doge] leaves in triumph, and is led with the *Signoria* to the aforementioned church. There he is ceremonially welcomed by the nuns and abbess, and solemn Vespers are sung, and there is a major indulgence that day, so that all the population of the city come there.

---

15 For Venice, see J. Sperling, *Convents and the Body Politic in Late Renaissance Venice* (Chicago, 1999).

THE THIRD ORDERS AND OTHER
NON-ENCLOSED RELIGIOUS GROUPINGS

11.28 Colomba da Rieti: a charismatic tertiary

A burgeoning of religious organisations for women outside the formalised
orders occurred throughout our period, with women forming or joining
groups for devotional or charitable purposes and for mutual support.[16] Some
of these, the tertiaries, became affiliated to established orders, following
modified forms of their rules, and lived together in communities much like
convents, as with those established by Colomba da Rieti, the most influential
of Renaissance tertiary reformers, in S. Domenico, Perugia, in 1488.

Anonymous chronicler, in G. Casagrande, 'Terziarie domenicane a Perugia',
in G. Casagrande and E. Menestì, eds, *Una santa, una città: atti del convegno
storico del V centenario della venuta a Perugia di Colomba da Rieti* (Spoleto, 1991),
p. 143.

This bride of Christ, enthused by divine love, joyfully made profession
of the said rule of penitence of St Dominic and of the collegial way of
life with the three sacred vows, that is obedience, poverty and
chastity ... in front of all the people who were in the church, a great
number of men and women, with such great devotion and tears that it
moved all those standing there in an indescribable way. Then many
pious ladies, both mature and young in age, followed her; and many
who were sisters in the city earlier renounced their own way of life
and joined with her in that common life and form of profession. In this
way within a short while there grew up a great number of sisters from
the upper classes and nobility of the city, and devotion increased so
that all the pious and generous women loved and honoured her, and
so frequently did the populace come to listen to her as if she were an
angel from God. And thus with her loving words she drew each
person to God, such was the sweetness of her speech.

11.29 Female tertiaries in Venice

Usually tertiaries were older women, who whether remaining in their own
homes or joining communal houses were relatively free of institutional

---

16 See J. Pennings, 'Semi-Religious Women in Fifteenth Century Rome', *Medelingen van
het Nederlands Historisch Institut te Rome*, new ser. 12, 47 (1987), pp. 115–45;
A. Esposito, 'St Francesca and the Female Religious Communities of Fifteenth-
Century Rome', in Bornstein and Rusconi, pp. 197–218; P. R. Baernstein, 'In
Widow's Habit: Women between Convent and Family in Sixteenth-Century Milan',
Sixteenth Century Journal, 25:4 (1994), pp. 787–807.

control, spending their time on socially useful charitable activities or on pilgrimages, as the following extracts suggest.

Vecellio (1590), fol. 147r–v.

In Venice there are many different types of tertiary, which are the female religious of the Mendicant Friars, to whom they conform, at least in colour. In this city of Venice, as in others cities of Christendom, a certain type of women, mostly widows, retire, either through devotion or through necessity, in certain places reserved for them. And thus retired they live from alms or from other honest tasks, being subject to the authorities of the religious order whose habit they dress in. As they do not observe the strict vows of cloistered women, they cannot really be called nuns, but still they live under obedience, observing some of the rules and regulations of their superiors, and living chastely. And since they are free from husbands they can serve God, usefully visiting the sick, dressing and accompanying the dead to burial, and participating in prayers and other pious works.

11.30 A peripatetic tertiary venerated

Protected by their habits, tertiaries could enjoy freedom to go on pilgrimage, as recorded in this hagiographical collection.

Serafino Razzi, *Vite de i Santi e Beati, così huomini come Donne del Sacro ordine de' Frati Predicatori* (Florence, 1577), pt 2, p. 108.

Beata Anna Spagnuola, a sister of penitence or, to be accurate, of the Third Order of St Dominic, because she took delight in visiting holy places, with permission, as it is believed, from her superiors. She went twice to the Holy Sepulchre of Our Lord in Jerusalem; once to St James of Compostela; once to France to visit the tomb of St Mary Magdalene; and once to Rome. Finally, ending up at Mantua, she was much loved for her sanctity by the most illustrious Princess Isabella and her consort. After dying in that city, an honourable sepulchre was made for her, in our church of St Dominic.

11.31 Precepts for the Company of St Ursula

Of the new women's religious groupings of the sixteenth century, the most successful was the Company of St Ursula, envisaged by its founder, St Angela Merici (1470/4–1540), as a familial band of professed virgins and widows living in the world devoted to good works and the moral elevation of society, though later having more nun-like regulations imposed by church authorities.[17]

Advice of Angela Merici in 1540 to the designated leaders of her Company, older married or widowed women who supervised and encouraged the younger Company members who lived in their city districts, usually with their families, from T. Ledochowska, *Angela Merici and the Company of St Ursula*, trans M. T. Neylan (Rome and Milan, 1967), vol. 1, pp. 239–40.

Second precept

Be gracious and humane to your young daughters. Make sure they are motivated solely by their love of God and fervour of soul ...

Fourth precept

You should often (as time and convenience permits) visit your daughters and sisters, especially on feast days, and greet them, see how they are, comfort them, inspire them to be constant in the life they have begun. Encourage them to long for heavenly joys and blessings ... Remind them that they should behave well in their homes, intelligently, prudently, and that they should be modest and sober in all things. They should eat and drink not for enjoyment or to satisfy the appetite, but only so as to sustain nature, the better to serve God. They should sleep sparingly, sleeping only as is needed, and similarly they should be restrained and sober in laughing. They should only enjoy listening to modest, legitimate or necessary talk. In speech, their words should be prudent and well-behaved, not biting or coarse, but humane and conducive to harmony and kindness. Tell them they should try to set a good example where they can. And that they should have a good reputation for all the virtues. And that they should be obedient and subject to their superiors. And that they should strive to foster peace and concord where they can. Above all, they should be humble and agreeable. And all their conduct, all their deeds and words should be charitable, and they should bear all things patiently: with these two paramount virtues you can break the head of the devil.

11.32 The growth of the Ursulines

Father Francesco Landini writes on 21 December 1566 on the growth of the Ursulines.

Ledochowska, vol. 2, p. 407.

---

17 See C. J. Blaisdell, 'Angela Merici and the Ursulines' in De Molen, pp. 99–136.

After her [Angela Merici's] blessed death [the Company] became finer, greater and more glorious ... and today goes forward more freely and fruitfully, with a better reputation and the satisfaction of all the city.

Now it serves all the hospitals in Brescia, it serves all the schools for the Christian instruction of girls, it serves God in the conversion of souls and in drawing the many houses where the members live to the service of His Divine Majesty. It would be difficult to give an idea of the great general good which God dispenses through this holy Company in all sorts of works of pity and mercy; the Company members frequent the holy Sacraments, sacred prayers and the holy worship of the Lord. In this the ornaments of the sacred virtues of poverty and obedience radiate and shine forth, so that all the congregation wishes to be present at the Supper of the Father of the Company ... It is a marvel above all marvels to see these three girls, still young virgins, not burning in the furnace of Babylon, but like so many Agneses or Agathas remaining unharmed and intact amidst the brothels and the flames. I will say only this, that the Father who governs them praises them much and takes great satisfaction from the virtues of this virginal and angelic choir.

12 The court lady

We know more about *donne di palazzo* and *donne di corte*, that is, the women of the ruling houses and their female companions, than about women from any other rank in society. Letters, documents about every aspect of their lives, contemporary biographies and writings on history provide us with detailed pictures of rulers' daughters and wives and with an understanding of life at court, even behind the idealisation of much contemporary writing. Furthermore, recent work and re-evaluation has established the extent of these women's significant political and cultural roles. The adoration of the lady evolved from medieval poetry, especially Petrarch's work. The latter, fashionable throughout our period, is at the root of a number of extremely influential writings on court life. These, like the two dialogues by Pietro Bembo and Baldassarre Castiglione included below, place the court lady at the centre of the stage: around her, and for her, courtiers engage in whatever can demonstrate their refinement and elegance, such as discussions about philosophy, love, poetry, music and dance.

THE COURT LADY AS AN IDEAL

12.1 The garden of love at Asolo, 1503

An idealised vision of the court of the deposed Queen of Cyprus, Caterina Cornaro (1454–1510), at Asolo in the Venetian mainland territories, is the setting for Pietro Bembo's *Gli Asolani* (Venice, 1503). In this very successful, often reprinted dialogue, three young gentlemen conduct discussions on the theme of love in the presence of three court ladies. Rooted in Bembo's personal experience, this work helped to shape later ideas of court life and the literature of love. In this extract, the ladies' beauty and graceful manners inspire men's love and admiration, and days are spent in delight and pleasure.

Pietro Bembo, *Gli Asolani*, ed. G. Dilemi (Florence, 1991), pp. 13–14.

Once they had sat down on the grass, some near the beautiful fountain, others at the feet of the shady laurel trees on both sides of the small stream, Gismondo carefully placed himself and looked at the beautiful ladies around him, and then began to talk in this way: 'Gracious ladies, we have all heard, while we were still sitting at table, the two young ladies who sang so gracefully before the Queen, answering each other with many songs. If I can remember the first two, which I liked very much, today we shall have a beautiful and ample subject for our conversation [...]

When the two young ladies arrived before the Queen, they greeted her with reverence. Then they stood and, having made sure she was in tune with the sound of the lute played by a musician behind them, the eldest one begun to sing in this way:

> Love, why do you teach me to fall into the fire
> where my heart burns,
> following him who runs away from me,
> loving him who makes fun of my pain?
> I believed that being in love
> would make any toil sweeter.
> Alas, enemy of my love,
> there is no pleasure, and torment is renewed.
> Ladies who have not yet felt love,
> you are most lucky,
> If you don't know it,
> look how great my pain is.

12.2 The qualities of a court lady, c. 1513–24

The Urbino court of Guidobaldo da Montefeltro and Elisabetta Gonzaga is the setting for the most famous of all dialogues and treatises on court life, Baldassarre Castiglione's *Il libro del Cortegiano* (c. 1513 to 1524, published in Venice in 1528). This extremely successful book set out the ideal behaviour for courtly life for the whole of Europe.[1] Book III reports a conversation, supposedly taking place in March 1507, dedicated to the court lady. She should be, like all women, a good wife and mother, her comportment guided by modesty and authority. As well as being able to conduct learned and accomplished conversations, she should know and understand literature, music, painting, dance. In everything she does she should possess that elusive quality, *grazia*, which both men and women at court must have and which allows them to do everything perfectly, elegantly and apparently without effort. Here Giuliano de' Medici, son of Lorenzo il Magnifico, a guest at the Urbino palace while exiled from Florence, describes his ideal court lady.

Castiglione, ed. Longo (1981), pp. 264–5.

---

1 See D. A. Trafton, 'Politics and the Praise of Women: Political Discourse in the *Courtier*'s Third Book', in R. Hanning and D. Rosand, eds, *Castiglione: The Ideal and the Real in Renaissance Culture* (New Haven and London, 1983), pp. 29–44, and D. Knox, 'Civility, Courtesy and Women in the Italian Renaissance', in Panizza, pp. 2–17.

Book III, iv.

[Giulano] The Lord Gasparo [Pallavicino] said that the same rules which apply to the courtier also apply to the lady, [but] my opinion is different. Although some qualities should be common and necessary to the man as to the woman, there are some which befit the woman rather than the man, and others which are more fitting for the man and must be absent in a woman [...] Above all, it seems to me that, in the qualities she possesses, her manners, words, gestures and deportment, the woman should be very different from the man, because, while he should show a certain solid and steady virility, it is fitting for her to have a sweet and delicate tenderness, thus giving every movement a feminine sweetness, so that in all circumstances she always appears as a woman, without any similarity to a man. Having, therefore, added this qualification to the rules that these gentlemen have taught to the courtier, I think that she can make use of many of them, to adorn herself with excellent qualities, as the Lord Gasparo says. In fact, I think that many of the virtues of the soul are as necessary to the woman as to the man, that is, nobility, avoidance of affectation, being naturally graceful in all one's actions, having good morals, being clever, prudent, not conceited, not envious, not speaking ill of people, not being vain, or contentious or foolish. She should be able to gain and keep the good will of her lady and of everybody else, and to do well and gracefully those exercises which are suited to women. It seems to me that in a lady beauty is more necessary than in a male courtier because, in truth, a woman without beauty lacks much. She must also take more care and consideration not to give others the opportunity of speaking ill of her, so that not only she is not guilty, but she is not even tainted by suspicion of guilt, because a woman has not as many means as a man to defend herself from slander.

THE COURT LADY

Accounts of aristocratic women's lives developed from the model set by Boccaccio's *De mulieribus claris*. Taking as a starting point factual information about events in the lives of rulers' daughters and wives, these usually short biographies eulogise, with appropriate variations, qualities and virtues fitting for all women, while stressing others which were seen as suitable only for *donne di palazzo*, such as learning, justice, prudence and the patronage of artists and *letterati*.

The image of the court lady in dialogues and biographies is always a paradigm of perfection. Another perspective is provided by sources written with a different function: ambassadors' reports to their governments are full of gossipy, detailed descriptions of events and people. Their sharp observations break through the adulation and idealisation of much writing on court life.

Biographies

12.3 Paola Malatesta Gonzaga, Marchioness of Mantua (1393–1453)

Sabadino degli Arienti, pp. 139–44.

Paola [was the] beloved daughter of the most happy prince Malatesta from Pesaro and spouse of the glorious Gianfrancesco Gonzaga, first Marquess of Mantua, a most splendid prince. This most excellent lady was very beautiful, of lovely and dignified appearance, most eloquent, most kind to those great and small and of any rank. She was most charitable in giving alms, in comforting the afflicted, and was an enemy of avarice, the root of all evil. She was beloved by her people. Her counsel was most prudent and esteemed not only in her own dominion, but also in foreign ones [...] In her youth, this most worthy lady of flawless virtue became a hunchback, so that, according to some, her descendants still suffer from this. She was also oppressed by pains in her hips, gout and various other illnesses, so much so that she could not bring her hands to her mouth. Being very patient, she thanked God for everything, as if she was a martyr for Jesus Christ. Being very devout, she had a building erected near the monastery of St Clare in Mantua, where as a faithful Christian she ended her life, four years after the death of her husband, at the age of sixty.

12.4 Battista Sforza, Countess of Urbino (1446–72)

Betussi/Boccaccio (1596), pp. 363–5.

After the death of her mother Costanza [Varano] while she was still a young girl, her father, Alessandro [Sforza] brought her up with the greatest care and good morals. Being also instructed in the humanities, and full of many other virtues, with time she acquired a most famous and immortal name. From her girlhood, while learning grammar, she began to recite orations so gravely and fluently, and with such facility of speech, that everybody was astonished by this maiden's virtue. When she reached a more mature age, she progressed so much in the study of the humanities and eloquence, that at that time there was not a single orator with whom she had not dared to test herself and her skills, so that her great fame grew. She was small in height, but well formed, and she showed in her demeanour a certain magnanimity which made her loved and honoured by all. She was very generous in all her actions, and greatly loved learned men and *letterati*, always wishing to get to know them and associate with them. After she married, she governed her husband's state almost all the time as, being away at war, he could not attend to it. Being clement and just towards her subjects, she always behaved in such a way to be much praised by everybody [...] She was very caring towards the poor. She had such a good memory that, on her husband's return to his dominion, she would give him an account of everything that had happened, point by point, with the greatest order.

Ambassadors' reports on court ladies

12.5 Margherita Paleologa di Monferrato, Duchess of Mantua (1510–66)

The Venetian Ambassador, Bernardo Navagero, writes to the Venetian Senate about the widow of Federico Gonzaga in 1540.

A. Segarizzi, ed., *Relazioni degli ambasciatori veneti al Senato*, 4 vols (Bari, 1912–16), vol. 1, pp. 57–9.

The Duchess is the last remaining member of the Paleologi, a most noble and ancient family, from which many and virtuous emperors were born [...] She certainly reveals herself to be the descendant of such noble lineage and illustrious blood ... I cannot say anything about her height, her figure or her beauty, since when I was sent by Your Serenity at court for the first time ... I found her in such a dark place that in truth I cannot say what she looks like [...] From what I have heard, she is rather plain, or perhaps in fact very plain, but she certainly does not lack virtue. In fact, when her husband was alive, she always bore with great patience abuse and insults from [Isabella] Boschetti,[2] who wanted to compete with her in many things. She is so devout that she takes communion on all the most important feast days.

---

2 Federico Gonzaga's mistress.

She gives much to charity and, more importantly, she does so secretly and without any ostentation, not wanting anybody to know [...] She brings up her maids of honour in such saintliness of life and morals, that he who can marry one of them is thought to have made a good marriage.

This lady is so close to the Cardinal[3] that one could not ask for more. His Lordship communicates with her about everything, important or not, and he wants her as a partner in all his actions, and he told me that he very much trusts this lady's judgment and prudence.

12.6 Eleonora di Toledo, Duchess of Florence and Siena (1522–62)

Vincenzo Fedeli, secretary to the Republic of Venice, reports about the wife of Cosimo I de' Medici in 1561.

Segarizzi, vol. 3, p. 149.

The Duchess, a lady of rare mind, follows her husband in educating their children to live in this way [without superfluous expenditure]. This Duchess has an income of her own of more than 40,000 ducats, which she administers as she likes, and with this she marries her maids of honour, giving each of them a dowry of 10,000 ducats after they have been in her service for a few years. She gives much to charity, as far as one can know and see from the gathering of the poor. This lady is always unwell. She vomits her food every morning. She gambles as a pastime, but she always wants to win, and plays for high stakes.

THE *DONNA DI CORTE* OR LADY-IN-WAITING

Court life was based on a very complex network of relationships between people of different social rank and upbringing. For a well-educated girl from a good family the position of lady-in-waiting or maid of honour to an aristocratic lady could be a profitable career, even if learning how to behave properly and wisely and to prosper in the competitive atmosphere of a court, was quite a difficult task. Manuals teaching rules on behaviour became very popular during the second half of the sixteenth century, when Spanish manners and customs made more elaborate court rituals fashionable.

---

3 Her brother-in-law and co-regent, Ercole Gonzaga.

12.7 A prospective lady-in-waiting, 1603

Vittoria Landriani, Countess of Carpegna, writes to Countess Zambeccari in Bologna about a suitable girl from a respectable family as a prospective lady-in-waiting.

G. L. Masetti Zannini, *Motivi storici dell'educazione femminile (1500–1650): scienza, lavoro, giuochi* (Naples, 1982), p. 362.

[June 1603]

I remember that Your Ladyship once told me that you were looking for a maiden as lady-in-waiting, and that you wanted a young girl so that she would be brought up and instructed as you like. I therefore propose to you a well brought-up eleven-year-old girl, the daughter of an honourable man, who shows a good attitude and will learn all kind of good manners. Her father belongs to the household of the Count my husband, and since his wife died recently, he would willingly place his daughter in such [a household] as Your Ladyship's. I believe she would be a success, and the Count my husband would gladly accompany her to your house.

12.8 Advice for a young lady-in-waiting, 1586

Annibale Guasco gives moral and practical advice on how to behave at court to his daughter Lavinia, aged twelve, who had just been accepted as a lady-in-waiting to the daughter of Philip II of Spain, the Infanta Caterina, Duchess of Savoy, at the court in Turin. The extract points out the difficulties a young girl might find in such circumstances.

Annibale Guasco, *Ragionamento del Sig. Annibale Guasco a Lavinia sua figliuola della maniera di governarsi in corte …* (Turin, 1586), fols 12v, 14r, 21v.

You should think first of all that, leaving your paternal home to go [and live] in the palace of such a great lady, you will have to alter the way you live in the way which such changed circumstances require. Your condition will be different: from that of daughter with a father and a mother, to that of servant to a mistress. Therefore you will have to transform yourself completely. This transformation will not be too difficult, since you are entering service at an age which is not so mature that it would be difficult to graft new habits, but not so green that you cannot accommodate yourself to it sensibly [...]

I do not want to forget to advise you that whenever you are with her, either in her chamber, or serving her at the table, or in any other place or occasion, you should always carry yourself properly. If you are standing, you must stand evenly on your two feet, still as a statue. You must not sway about, twisting this way and that perhaps sometimes yawning, because nothing is more annoying to those who are served, as it seems that this [attitude] is born out of discontent with being in service, and from little reverence or affection for those whom you serve.

[...]

Even if in your father's house, through the grace of God, you lacked nothing, yet you did not have such varied or abundant food as there is in the house of princes, and particularly of such a great lady as your mistress. For this reason you will have to restrain yourself somewhat and not let your appetite and the variety of food carry you to excess. Get up from the table hungry rather than too sated, so that the quantity of food and the lack of exercise, since you will have to remain most of the time inside a chamber, will not cause you to become ill. You will have to abstain from foods forbidden in our household as noxious to children, and beware of eating too rich food outside mealtimes. To keep you going in your growing age, some bread and an apple for breakfast and afternoon refreshment should be enough, as it used to be at home [...] Remember to be moderate also in the use of wine, because you will have before you the example of Spanish ladies, who, according to the Spanish habit, are used to drinking water. I am not saying that you have to do the same, since neither you nor others in Italy are used to this. What is natural and useful for those ladies, for you would be not only harmful but dangerous.

12.9 A bitter view of court life, 1586

Tommaso Garzoni dedicated a chapter of *La piazza universale* to *cortigiani* and *donne di corte*. His view of court life is the opposite of the ideals of Bembo and Castiglione.

Garzoni (1586, repr. 1599), p. 531.

Court ladies have all the faults and vices of male courtiers, combined with their own pride: luxurious clothes, pampered soft bodies, idleness which is the enemy of all virtues, the artfulness taught by courtly books on love, plays, *novelle*, jests, songs fashionable at court from which they learn very harmful habits, vanity, impudence, arrogance, intrigue, insolence, filthiness, contentiousness, contrariness, obstinacy, vengeance, cunning, malice, loquacity, immodesty, impertinence and a dishonest tendency towards lust. All this, and what they learn from older women, who teach the young ones all that is bad, and who are an example of all kinds of wickedness. They teach them to make themselves beautiful, to use cosmetics, to be all refined, to do their hair, curl it, make ringlets, rouge their faces, perfume, embellish and admire themselves. [They teach them] to steal, ensnare, charm, bewitch their lovers, since (as St Jerome says against Gioviniano) these arts are the familiars of women, together with deceit, fraud, poisons, sorcery and vanity of charms. Courts nourish all these, and obvious misery, unhappiness and misfortune for all those who love [court life], as the Lady Vittoria Colonna writes in that poem, which begins:

> Others, wasting their young lives'
> Most beautiful flower at some great court,
> While seeking profit and honour
> Only find envy, insults and injuries,
> Thanks to evil princes, who have banished
> All virtues, and have only deceit
> And ugly avarice in their heart,
> A public injury and dishonour to the world.

THE ROLES OF A RULER'S WIFE

Life at court was not just a succession of pleasures, since a ruler's wife was supposed to occupy herself with many tasks, within and without the palace. The most important of these was the complex and difficult role as regent in her husband's temporary or permanent absence. Charity was also a crucial duty, bringing fame and spiritual merits to a princess, while at the same time helping to alleviate social problems in the city. Patronage of literature and the arts was one of the aspects of *magnificentia*, a quality much admired in the Renaissance, which a ruler and his wife demonstrated by using their power and wealth for the good of their family and of the city.[4] Finally, a ruler's wife was responsible for all the needs of her ladies-in-waiting.

---

4 On the patronage of court ladies, see E. Welch, 'Women as Patrons and Clients in the Courts of Quattrocento Italy', in Panizza, pp. 18–34, and S. E. Reiss and D. G. Wilkins, eds, *Beyond Isabella* (Kirksville, Miss., 2001).

a. Political and civic duties

12.10 Advice to a new duke, 1466

In the dangerous circumstances of the transfer of power after the death of her husband, Francesco Sforza, the Duchess of Milan, Bianca Maria Visconti, gives vital advice to her son Galeazzo Maria, who was in France.

V. Ilardi, ed., *Dispatches with Related Documents of Milanese Ambassadors in France*, 3 vols (Dekalb, Ill., 1981), vol. 3, p. 391.

Galeazzo, you will have heard from our letters and messengers about the tearful event concerning the late most illustrious lord your father and our husband, and therefore we shall not repeat any of it in this letter. We can inform you, for your consolation, that nothing else has happened. Our people keep the same reverence, obedience and faith towards us and our State, as they did to the good memory of our husband. Every day things are better and quieter, and nothing new has happened in any way, and I can say the same about the Genoese, who have written what you shall read in copies of letters I am enclosing to help you. We shall attend to all those measures appropriate for the safety of our subjects and our State, and in fact we have already done a good deal of this, and day and night we do not cease taking care of what is needed. We believe that before receiving this you will have already left to come here, and that even before beginning your journey you will have considered everything with prudence, and taken every care to come safely. You must take special care about this, and use your brains and take great care in travelling, to ensure that you will not meet any mishap.

12.11 A wise regent, 1478

Eleonora d'Aragona, Duchess of Ferrara, acts as regent for her husband, Ercole d'Este.

Bernardino Zambotti, 'Diario ferrarese dall'anno 1476 sino al 1504', ed. G. Pardi, in *Rerum italicarum scriptores*, vol. 24, pt 7 (Bologna, 1937), p. 57.

When His Excellency our duke left Ferrara and went to Florence, he left the most illustrious lady Eleonora d'Aragona to govern in his place and to give audience, together with some gentlemen and secretaries. She carried this out most wisely, with the love, benevolence and obedience of all the subjects of the state, doing everything that every wise ruler would need to do.

b. Charitable acts

12.12 Eleonora di Toledo dispenses charity

Betussi/Boccaccio (1596), p. 656.

She much wished to help the needy, and she particularly relieved [the poverty of] the holy virgins dedicated to God. At different times, and during several famines, she gave alms to many monasteries, not only in Florence, but also in other cities and lands of the [Florentine] dominion. She had some good men who, in her name, also gave alms to the nuns of those places, and to other needy and good virgins.

12.13 A charitable princess

The Jesuit priest Sebastiano Morales, confessor of Maria of Portugal, Duchess of Parma and Piacenza, describes some of her good deeds.

Sebastiano Morales, *Vita e morte della Serenissima Maria di Portogallo, Principessa di Parma, e Piacenza* (Rome, 1602), pp. 46–7, 52–3.

Her Highness used to say that one of the greatest [moments of] happiness she ever had was when a young woman of easy virtue threw herself at her feet in church, imploring her to help her to live well and leave sin behind in order to serve God. Having heard this, [the princess] publicly embraced her, and did not fail to comfort her, allowing her, after the usual probation, to enter the religious life [...]

Apart from her usual [charity], her special devotional care was to provide clothes for some poor people, especially members of religious orders. Every year on Thursday in Holy Week she used to clothe thirteen women, twelve God-fearing old widows of good virtue and one young girl of about fifteen. She would wash their feet with her own hands with great humility. She would then sit them at a sumptuously prepared table, offering them to eat, and serving those poor women herself with her own ladies. If there was a blind one, Her Highness would feed her with great pleasure.

c. Literary, artistic and musical pursuits

12.14 A dedication to a dancing princess, 1455

While some educators considered dance to be an essential accomplishment for a court lady and also a beneficial physical exercise, others believed it to be fraught with moral dangers. Despite the negative connotations it had for some writers, dancing was one of the most important court entertainments, and the fifteenth century saw the circulation of treatises, such as Gugliemo Ebreo's *De Pratica seu arte tripudii*, completed in Milan in 1463 and dedicated to Galeazzo Maria Sforza, and Antonio Cornazzano's *Libro dell'arte del danzare* (1455). Stating that he is only describing those dances which are suitable for a court environment, Cornazzano dedicates his treatise on dance to the nine-year-old Ippolita (1445–88), daughter of Bianca Maria Visconti and Francesco Sforza, who had just been betrothed to Alfonso, Duke of Calabria.

Antonio Cornazzano, *The Book on the Art of Dancing*, eds. and trans. M. Inglehearn and P. Forsythe (London, 1981), p. 16.

Amazon nymph, illustrious goddess,
daughter not of Leda, but of Diana,
following whose chaste and pure example
infinite beauty resounds to the farthest shore!

Love justly ordered me, lest it be lost,
to write down the art I have taught you,
since I understood how much courteous human virtue
flourished in such a young heart.

With the study of this work I write for you,
The more mature age you will reach
will make you a goddess amongst the others, noble Lady.

Here you will learn the graceful movement
of dancing feet, and if my work is accepted,
whatever my worth, I entirely dedicate myself to you.

12.15 Music for Isabella d'Este, 1496

Isabella d'Este commissions a clavichord from the instrument-maker Lorenzo da Pavia (Lorenzo Gusnasco). Gusnasco, who was living in Venice, was one of Isabella's trusted friends. Beside providing her with musical instruments, he also helped her to find books and art works, such as paintings and cameos.[5]

A. Luzio and R. Renier, *Delle relazioni di Isabella d'Este Gonzaga con Ludovico e Beatrice Sforza* (Milan, 1890), p. 122.

[March 1496]

Egregie, you will remember that, when we were in Pavia, you gave a

---

5 See W. F. Prizer, 'Isabella d'Este and Lorenzo da Pavia, "master instrument-maker"', in *Early Music History*, 2 (1982), pp. 1261–79.

very beautiful and most perfect clavichord to the most illustrious lady the Duchess of Milan, my sister. Since I wish to have one which cannot be bettered, we have thought that there is no other person in Italy who can serve me better than you. Therefore we pray you to make one which in beauty and quality corresponds to your fame and to the hope we have in you. We do not give you any other particular instruction, other that it should be easy to play, because our touch is so light that we cannot play well when the keys are stiff. You will understand our need and desire; for the rest, make it as you wish.

12.16 A commission for Raphael, 1515

Isabella d'Este asks Baldassarre Castiglione to act as intermediary between her and Raphael.

R. Iotti, '"Phenice unica, virtuosa e pia"', in D. Bruni, ed., *Isabella d'Este. La primadonna del Rinascimento* (Modena, 2001), p. 176.

[November 1515]

Magnifice Eques carissime noster ..., we thank you a great deal for your attempt on our behalf to persuade Raphael of Urbino to work for us. In order to bring your kind task to completion, we send you the canvas for the painting by our horse drover. Enclosed are details of the illumination and measurements, which you should send to Raphael, writing to him that he should begin, and work as is convenient for him, but stating that the sooner he does the work, the more agreeable it will be to us.

12.17 A commission for Bronzino, 1550

On behalf of Eleonora di Toledo, Sforza Almeni, *cameriere* of the Duke and Duchess of Florence, writes to Pierfrancesco Riccio, Majordomo, on a commission for Bronzino.

Archivio di Stato, Florence: Mediceo del Principato, vol. 1176, insert 1, fol. 6 (www.medici.org).

[April 1550]

My Lady the Duchess told me that I should ask Your Lordship to ask Bronzino to make a cartoon for an altar tapestry which she plans to send to Spain, similar to the one which was in her chapel, with the same figures, surrounded by a beautiful garland border. Because she worries that it may be small, she would like to have all the measurements, that is, how large it will be with the garland border added.[6]

12.18 Eleonora di Toledo deals with building work, 1550

Tommaso de' Medici, Treasurer, writes to Pierfrancesco Riccio, about some work to be carried out in the Duchess's apartment in the Palazzo della Signoria.

Archivio di Stato, Florence: Mediceo del Principato, vol. 1176, file 3, fol. 2 (www.medici.org).

[March 1549 (1550)]

The most illustrious Duchess this morning ordered me to write to Your Lordship, as she wants new floors in the green chamber, and in the one where the Lady Isabel de Reinoso works. Also, master Mariano should make that door where the Duchess ordered, in the room where the Lady Isabel de Reinoso works. I am writing this just as the Duchess told me.

d. Domestic relationships

12.19 A wedding gift for a maid of honour, 1423

Parisina Malatesta, wife of Niccolò d'Este and Marchioness of Ferrara, asks the court administrators to pay for a gift of *cassoni* for one of her maids-of-honour.

A. Franceschini, *Artisti a Ferrara in età umanistica e rinascimentale: testimonianze archivistiche. Parte I dal 1341 al 1471* (Ferrara, 1993), p. 119.

[January 1423]

We want you, our factors, to give and pay Master Giovanni della Gabella, painter, 25 ducats in coins for his expenses and labour for two painted and gilded chests, which Pellegrina, our maid of honour and daughter of Zoexe, is having [as *donora*] for her wedding.

---

6 Tapestries could be used as altarpieces. See J. Cox-Rearick, *Bronzino's Chapel of Eleonora in the Palazzo Vecchio* (Berkeley, 1993), p. 82.

12.20   Eleonora di Toledo takes care of her ladies' wardrobe, 1544

On behalf of the Duchess of Florence, Francesco Pretino writes to Pierfrancesco Riccio.

Archivio di Stato, Florence: Mediceo del Principato, vol. 1171, file 3, fol. 115 (www. medici. org).

[September 1544]

The most illustrious lady, the Duchess, since she wants her ladies and the Lady Julia to stop wearing mourning, asked through the Lady Caterina that Your Lordship should send her the things listed below. First of all, for the Lady Maria: the pearl and gold necklace which is in a small box tied with a black ribbon ... also the diamond earrings and the gold belt of the Lady Maria ... her gown of *lucchesino*[7] fabric, the green satin gown, a silk ribbon for garters, the hat and her cap, a gold necklace, one of the small chains and a garland and two pairs of earrings ... some nets and some raw silk to make nets and silk ribbons for head-dresses for the Lady Isabella; the cloak and the short mantle which is in the chest in the room of the Lady Isabella.

LUXURY AT COURT

Members of the ruling family and of the court showed their wealth, power and *magnificentia* through lavish expenditure on furnishings, clothes and jewellery. Display at court was therefore a serious business, as well as a pleasure and a privilege. Members of the aristocracy and courtiers were exempt from sumptuary laws regulating dress and celebrations.

a. The court environment

12.21 The bedroom of Lucrezia d'Este, wife of Annibale Bentivoglio, in the Palazzo Bentivoglio, Bologna, 1487

C. James, 'The Palazzo Bentivoglio in 1487', in *Mitteilungen des Kunsthistorischen Instituts in Florenz*, 41 (1997), pp. 188–96.

Her room, which faced east, was hung with fine silk tapestries all around, with figures of beautiful nymphs, animals and birds in pleasant

---

7 A bright red luxury cloth, originally made in Lucca.

greenery. The matrimonial bed was very beautiful, lovely and pleasing, covered with purple satin, and the floor was covered with carpets. The ceiling was not high, well worked in wood, painted in [various] colours and gilded. The chimney breasts and the windows were also decorated with gold, and with many other rich adornments.

b. Clothes and objects:

12.22 The gown of Beatrice d'Este, 1493

Isabella d'Este's agent, Bernardo Prosperi, describes the gown worn by her sister Beatrice for her entry in Ferrara on her way to Venice. The gown was probably a gift from Ludovico il Moro, since it was embroidered with one of Ludovico's devices.

F. Malaguzzi Valeri, *La corte di Ludovico il Moro*, 4 vols (Milan, 1929), vol. 1, p. 374.

The duchess was wearing a gown of crimson washed silk, embroidered with the lighthouse of the harbour,[8] and on each sleeve were [embroidered] two towers, two more on the front and two on the back. On each of these towers was a large balas ruby. On her head she was wearing a cap with very large pearls, as large as Your Ladyship's largest ones, with five more very beautiful balas rubies.

12.23 Isabella d'Este sets the fashion, 1509

The daughter of Count Niccolò da Correggio, Eleonora, asks Isabella d'Este for used head-dresses (*zazare*).

A. Luzio and R. Renier, 'Il lusso di Isabella d'Este, Marchesa di Mantova', in *Nuova antologia*, 5 (16 Sept. 1896), p. 667.

When I was in Locarno, I heard that some gentlewomen in Milan wear a new type of silk *zazare* devised by Your Ladyship's remarkable ingenuity, and since at the moment I am almost bald, with the greatest desire I pray you to deem me worthy of having one [...] So I pray Your Most Illustrious Ladyship, if you have some spare head-dresses that Your Ladyship does not use anymore, could you send them to me, so that I should not be excluded from the group of your most faithful followers.

---

8 The harbour of Genoa, which was in Milanese hands.

12.24 Special fans from Milan, 1511

Lucrezia Borgia asks her sister-in-law Isabella d'Este to send her some fans.
Luzio and Renier (1896), p. 686.

I am sorry I am troubling Your Ladyship again, as I have already written about having some new kinds of fans from Milan. I worry that because of the present situation they would not arrive as quickly as I would like. With the trust I have in Your Ladyship, if you find some black ones, without any decoration, but lovely and beautiful, I very much pray you to send them to me. The sooner it will be, the greater the obligation I shall have towards Your Ladyship.

RELAXATION AND PASTIMES

12.25 Cecilia Gallerani visits a spa

Cecilia Gallerani (c. 1473–1536) was the mistress of Ludovico il Moro from c. 1489 to 1492, when she married Count Lodovico Carminati. In his *Novelle* (1554), Matteo Bandello describes her visit to a spa in terms which recall Bembo's *Gli Asolani*.
Matteo Bandello, *Novelle* (Milan, 1990), p. 138.

While the most gentle and learned Lady Cecilia Gallerani, Countess Bergamina,[9] was in these past days bathing at the Acquario spa[10] in order to strengthen her stomach, she was constantly visited by many gentlemen and ladies, both because this lady is pleasant and virtuous, and because the best and most interesting minds from Milan and from elsewhere gather every day in her company. Here military men discuss the art of war, musicians sing, architects and painters draw, philosophers question the natural order, poets recite their own compositions and those by others. All who enjoy either discussing or hearing important matters about virtue can find here food suitable for their taste, because in the presence of this heroine one always talks about what is pleasant, significant and civilised.

12.26 Hunting in the countryside, 1491

Beatrice d'Este writes to her sister Isabella about the delights of Villanova, one of the hunting retreats of the Sforza, north-west of Milan.

9 Cecilia's husband was known as Count Bergamini.
10 Near Milan.

Luzio and Renier (1890), p. 43.

[March 1491]

At the moment I am here in Villanova where, because of the beauty of
the countryside and the sweetness of the air, temperate and balmy as
if it were May, I ride every day with hounds and falcons, and the lord
my spouse [Ludovico il Moro]. I never return home without having
enjoyed infinite pleasures hunting herons and other river birds. About
this I will say no more. There are so many hares which jump here and
there that we do not know where to turn for pleasure, because the eye
is not able to see all that we wish to see, and all the animals the countryside offers. Again, I will not say how much the most illustrious
Messer Galeazzo[11] and I, together with other courtiers, enjoy playing
pallamaglio[12] after lunch, and we invite and often desire the pleasure of
Your Ladyship. I am telling you all this not to decrease your pleasure
when you come by letting you know what you can expect, but because
you should know that I am well, and the lord my spouse fills me with
kindness, and I could not enjoy any recreation or happiness if I could
not communicate it to Your Ladyship. I am letting you know that I
have had a field planted with garlic, so that when you are here we shall
be able to have the garlic sauce Your Ladyship so loves and longs to
taste.

12.27 A dance in Rome, 1501

Isabella d'Este's agent 'el Prete' describes an evening in Lucrezia Borgia's
Roman palace, near the Vatican, at a particularly important time in the life of
Pope Alexander VI's daughter. Lucrezia's wedding to Alfonso d'Este had been
celebrated by proxy in Ferrara, and the ceremony had then been repeated in
Rome. Between 26 December and 6 January 1502, the date of Lucrezia's
departure for Ferrara, the Pope organised a series of dances, plays, horse races
and other spectacular festivities.

F. Gregorovius, *Lucrezia Borgia* (Rome, 1969), pp. 214–15.

On Sunday evening, St Stephen's Day,[13] I went to [Lucrezia Borgia's]
rooms. Her Ladyship was sitting near the bed, and in a corner of the
room there were some Roman ladies, about twenty of them, dressed in

11 Galeazzo Visconti, a courtier.
12 A ball game.
13 26 December.

the Roman fashion, wearing a veil on their head, and also her maids of honour, about ten of them.

A gentleman from Valencia began the dance with a maid of honour called Nicola. Then Her Ladyship danced very gracefully with Don Ferrante.[14] She was wearing a gown of black velvet with gold stripes, and black sleeves. The cuffs were tight, the sleeves decorated with slashes up to the shoulders, [so that] the chemise was visible. Her breasts were covered up to the throat with a veil hemmed in gold. She had a beautiful string of pearls around her neck, [on her head] a cap of green veil and a fillet of small rubies. [She had] an overdress of black velvet, with a beautiful coloured lining.

12.28 Entertainment in Ferrara, 1502

Leaving her husband Francesco and her beloved son Federico in Mantua, Isabella d'Este went to Ferrara for the celebrations for her brother Alfonso's marriage to Lucrezia Borgia. From 29 January to 7 February 1502, Isabella wrote to her husband a series of lively, descriptive letters about life at the Este court during a period of uninterrupted festivities: Carnival had exceptionally been extended into Lent by Papal decree in order to pay homage to the bride and groom.

'Notizie di Isabella Estense moglie di Francesco Gonzaga', *Archivio storico italiano*, vol. 2 (1845), Appendix 2, pp. 308–9.

My Most Illustrious Lord,

[...] The play entitled *The Bacchae* begun at twenty three hours and a half,[15] and it was so long and boring and without danced *intermezzi*, that I often wished I was in Mantua. I cannot wait to be there, to see Your Lordship and my little boy, and also to get away, because here there is no pleasure. Your Excellency should not envy me because you did not come to this wedding, because I lack enthusiasm to such an extent, that I am the one who envies those who remained in Mantua. If I had time to write to Your Lordship in my own hand, I would pass the time with less bother. But as soon as I am up, my brothers come to see me, and do not leave me during the whole day, and furthermore [there is] the concourse of all the ladies who fawn on me since they cannot see the Lady Lucrezia till she comes out into the hall. At five hours[16] in the

14 Alfonso d'Este's brother.
15 Approx. 3.30 p. m.
16 Approx. 9 p. m.

evening we dine, and at seven or eight we go to bed.[17] Now just imagine, Your Lordship, how much I am enjoying myself. You should feel sorry for me.

There were only two *moresche*[18] during the play. In one there were ten men, who seemed naked, wearing a veil across their body, with tin-foil on their head and horns of plenty in their hands with four torches inside, full of varnish, which blazed up when the horns were moved. Before them a young girl came out, walking silently, and she went to the front of the stage. Then a dragon came out, and went to devour her, but near her there was a warrior on foot who defended her and fought against the dragon. Then the young girl and a young man, walking arm in arm, were followed by the bound dragon. Around them were the naked men, dancing and throwing the varnish into the fire.

In the second *moresca* some madmen, wearing a shirt and stockings on their head, with a bundle and a blown-up bladder in their hand, and beating one another with it, were a sorry spectacle. The first *moresca* was after the first act, the second after the fourth. At the last one there was nothing else but yawns and complaints from the spectators, because it had gone on for four and a half hours. There is nothing else worthy of notice, apart from the fact that I recommend myself in good grace to Your Excellency, and I pray you not to forget to kiss Federico with love from me.

12.29 How a court lady should invite a gentleman to dance, 1600

Marco Fabrizio Caroso (?1526–?1605) was a well-known dancing master. His *La Nobiltà di Dame*, dedicated to the Duke and Duchess of Parma and Piacenza, Ranuccio Farnese and Margherita Aldobrandini, is the first treatise on dance to be widely circulated, since the works by Antonio Cornazzano and Guglielmo Ebreo were circulated only in manuscript form. While in Book I Caroso deals with questions related to manners – how to move elegantly while dancing, how to bow, how to greet equals and superiors – in Book II he describes the movements for forty-nine different dances, each dedicated to a court lady.

M. F. Caroso, *Nobiltà di dame* (Bologna, 1970), pp. 82–3.

At dances, there are some married ladies and other court ladies who keep their eyes lowered, so much so that the gentlemen, not knowing

17 Approx. 11 p. m. or 12 midnight.
18 A Moorish dance.

which among them is the one [the lady] is inviting, [make mistakes], and one gets up rather than another, or sometimes, keen as they are to dance, they all give their hand to her, so that she does not know which one to take. Therefore it is good not to keep the eyes too lowered, and when [a lady] invites a gentleman, she should look at him, so that the others, who are sitting next to him or behind him, do not get up ... When the gentleman she has invited stands up, he should take off his right glove while bowing to her, and she must pretend she is adjusting her gown, wriggling and flaunting herself in some way, turning slightly to the side of the gentleman she has invited. And because sometimes gentlemen wear tight gloves, and it takes them longer to take a glove off than to recite a Hail Mary, it is not good that the lady should stand facing him, because like that it looks as if they are making love. This is why gentlemen should wear their gloves a little loose rather than tight.

There are some ladies who invite a gentleman [to dance] while he is talking to somebody else, and another gentleman, sitting behind or next to him, will then get up, and the lady will offend him by saying that she did not ask him, but the other. This should not be done, because when a gentleman gets up, she must dance with him on her honour. Other ladies, if the gentlemen are sitting or standing far behind, make certain gestures with their hands or with their head when they invite them to dance, and sometimes they even call them by name. All these are very bad manners, because when ladies are dancing they have to be prudent, modest, graceful and well-mannered, otherwise they will be deemed badly brought-up by all those present and by other ladies.

MISTRESSES AND CONCUBINES

It was common for princes to have their mistresses living at court, so that often their wives would have to share the limelight with them.[19] A wife, even if she objected, could do little about this situation, and would be encouraged to accept, even to bring up, her husband's illegitimate children. As in the case of Lucrezia d'Alagno at the court of Naples, and of Cecilia Gallerani at the Milanese court of Ludovico il Moro, the position of a mistress could be socially acceptable. Furthermore, being a ruler's mistress could bring great power to a

19 See H. S. Ettlinger, "'Visibilis et invisibilis": The Mistress in Italian Renaissance Court Society', *Renaissance Quarterly*, 47:4 (1994), pp. 770–92.

woman and to her family. Not having a mistress was something worthy of note: Cosimo I de' Medici, who had been faithful to his wife Eleonora di Toledo till her death, was considered an exception to the rule.

12.30, 12.31 Lucrezia d'Alagno and the King of Naples

a. In his *Commentarii* (late 1450s) Enea Silvio Piccolomini, the future Pope Pius II, writes about Lucrezia d'Alagno (1428–79), the 'virgin mistress' of Alfonso I d'Aragona, King of Naples.

Enea Silvio Piccolomini, *I Commentari*, ed. L. Totaro, 2 vols (Milan, 1984), vol. 1, pp. 171–3, 189–91.

She was a beautiful woman, or young girl, the daughter of poor but noble Neapolitan parents. The king loved her desperately, so that in her presence he was as if beside himself, and could not see nor hear anybody else apart from Lucrezia. He could not take his eyes off her. He praised her words, admired her wisdom, praised her gestures, and thought her beautiful figure to be divine. And having given her many gifts and ordered that she should be honoured as a queen, finally he gave himself totally to her, so that nobody could obtain favour from him without her consent. Wondrous is the power of love!

Lucrezia travels to Rome to ask Pope Callistus III for the annulment of Alfonso's marriage to Maria of Castile.

At that time [October 1457] Lucrezia ... went to Rome accompanied by such a retinue as if she had been a queen. Callistus received her with all the cardinals, and honoured her in many ways. Enea [Silvio Piccolomini] and many others did not like this, thinking that it was not very decorous that she, whom the king loved in such a scandalous way, should be so honoured by His Apostolic Majesty. And even if Enea was very fond of Alfonso, he did not visit his mistress in Rome. Many other cardinals did, among them Pietro [Barbo], Cardinal of St Mark, who showed himself to be not only master of ceremonies, but also a great collector of secular favours.

b. After the death of Alfonso in 1458, Lucrezia d'Alagno lost much of her influence. Here she writes to Francesco Sforza, complaining about the way she has been treated by Alfonso's son and successor, Ferrante.

B. Croce, 'Lucrezia d'Alagno', in *Storie e leggende napoletane: scritti di storia letteraria e politica*, vol. 11 (Bari, 1967), pp. 87–117.

Certainly I would deem it vile-hearted to love [King Ferrante], who has tried to deprive me of my honour, because I value little else in life. In fact, to let you know completely what I think, I wish nothing else but death, which will end my adversities, since, after the sinister death of that most happy King [Alfonso], I now live my life in constant sorrow and misfortune. Nobody could hate more strongly the world, in which I am forced to live against my will.

Therefore, for these reasons, and also for many others about which I cannot write, it is necessary that I should think highly of nothing else but my honour, which is dearer to me than a thousand lives. Since he has employed all his might, in full consciousness, in staining it and in slandering me, without any fault of mine, and has caused me much damage, this is what I have decided: either he returns my fame and my things to me, ... or I will complain about him to God and to the world. I will not do this willingly, but I shall be forced by him to do it.

12.32 A poem by Sigismondo Malatesta on leaving Isotta degli Atti

Sigismondo Pandolfo Malatesta, Lord of Rimini, fell in love with Isotta degli Atti (1432/3–74), a merchant's daughter, when she was ten years old. She became his mistress in 1446, and lived at court while Sigismondo's wife, Polissena Sforza, was still alive. After Polissena's death in 1449, Isotta continued to be Sigismondo's mistress, while at the same time he had a number of illegitimate children with other women. They finally married, probably in 1456. Isotta ruled as a regent during Sigismondo's absences and after his death.

A. F. Massera, 'I poeti isottei', in *Giornale storico della letteratura italiana*, 57 (1911), p. 11.

> Adieu, with a sad voice and with sighs
> I say, weary, O beautiful and serene countenance,
> My dear sweet place, beautiful ground
> Which was the beginning of my lofty desire!
> You bring me to death,
> Oh painful parting!
> O my sweet pleasure
> Where am I leaving you?
> My sorrowful breast
> Will always be full of pain.
> No woodworm ever gnawed

As this great pain, bitter evil destiny,
Is gnawing at my sad senses.
Tears will be my food and my nourishment
Till I come back to see
Her, to whom I have pledged my heart.

12.33   A close friendship, 1572

Isabella Medici Orsini (1542–76), daughter of Cosimo I de' Medici and
Eleonora di Toledo, writes to her brother Francesco's mistress, the Venetian
Bianca Cappello (1548–87). The letter, which shows the close relationship
between the two women, refers to the attempt of Bianca's father to persuade
her to leave Florence and return to Venice after the murder of her husband
in August 1572. Bianca and Francesco were finally secretly married in 1578,
after the death of Francesco's wife, Joanna d'Austria.

G. Pieraccini, *La stirpe dei Medici di Cafaggiolo*, 3 vols (Florence, 1924, repr.
1986), vol. 2, p. 169.

Most magnificent sister of mine ... you know well that I love you
much more than a sister, and that I shall never give you advice which
is not for your advantage and your honour. I have been told that your
father has sent somebody here with the intention of taking you back
to Venice. I do not want to fail to remind you how little he has cared
for you in these eight years, and that with his strange way of behaving
he has astonished the whole world [...] Now just think whether it
would suit you to place yourself in his hands, and how you would be
treated!

I remind you, as a loving sister, that [here] you are in your own home,
as your own mistress, while [in Venice] you will have to be subject to
a father who, from past indications, loves you but little, and to a not
very loving brother, and to a brother-in-law! Think about it well, and
consider that everything I say to you I say only because I love you as
much as I do. Remember that I have sworn to be your sister ... God
help you, and open your mind's eyes so that you will do what is best
for you, which is to take pleasure where you are adored, which is here,
without looking for another place.

Written from my bed, 24 September [1572], your loving sister, the
Lady Isabella Medici Orsini.

13 Women and work for gain

In our period lower-class women worked for direct or indirect economic gain at all stages of their lives. Mostly this involved such traditional female skills as laundering, cooking, cleaning or sewing, or helping in farms, shops or inns, but there are also records of women working in a huge range of urban trades.[1] They might slip into the gaps in the male labour market, as when a widow continued her dead husband's business, when a new industry arose (printing)[2] or expanded (silk production), or indeed when there was a general labour shortage. The best established and documented areas, apart from prostitution (the most frequently mentioned female profession in some city records), were textile production, domestic service, wet-nursing, and caring for the sick and infirm, which will be emphasised in this chapter. Despite all this activity, however, Renaissance treatise writers found it difficult to envisage women supporting, let alone fulfilling, themselves through work: even writers advocating women's autonomy or education assumed they would have private means, not need to earn their livings.

WOMEN IN THE MARKETPLACE

13.1 Women traders and inn-workers

Though earlier than the period covered in this book, this conduct book (*c.* 1320) vividly suggests the variety of retailing trades pursued by women. Detailed studies of districts in urban centres such as Rome or Venice confirm the presence of many such women, whether country women coming in to sell their produce or city dwellers, whether girls, wives and widows, or those of indeterminate marital status.

Francesco da Barberino, *Francesco da Barberino. Reggimento e costumi di donna*, ed. G. E. Sansone (Rome, 1995), pt 15, pp. 169–71.

---

1 General studies are S. K. Cohn, *The Laboring Classes in Renaissance Florence* (New York, 1980); J. C. Brown, 'A Woman's Place Was in the Home: Women's Work in Renaissance Tuscany', in M. W. Ferguson, M. Quilligan and N. J. Vickers, *Rewriting the Renaissance: The Discourses of Sexual Difference in Early Modern Europe* (Chicago, 1986), pp. 206–24; M. Chojnacka, *Working Women of Early Modern Venice* (Baltimore, 2001).

2 D. Parker, 'Women in the Book Trade in Italy, 1475–1620', *Renaissance Quarterly*, 49:3 (1996), pp. 509–41.

If you'd be a market-woman
Don't put green leaves on musty fruit,
Nor place the best fruit in front,
Nor grease figs to make them ripen,
Nor keep them in water to fool people.
Don't buy bread, bran, or wine,
Nor salt, nor oil, nor salted meat
From menservants who've pilfered it ...
If you're a poultry or cheese-seller
Don't wash the eggs or cheese
So they look fresher to customers.
      ...
If you want to be a saleswoman
Tell the truth to all
Make your claims true,
And don't be deceiving women
Who don't know what jewels are worth,
Don't talk about others' business with them ...
If you're an innkeeper, a waitress or barmaid,
Sell your goods and not your person,
If you're at all attractive
Don't make this part of the merchandise.

TEXTILE WORKERS

Fundamental to women's work was the economically crucial production of cloths in linen, cotton, wool and silk, which involved numerous
women of all ages, secular or religious. They mostly worked from
home, though some travelled to business premises, spinning or, less
frequently, weaving raw materials provided by entrepreneurs. Women
were sometimes admitted into guilds, often with different provisions
than for men, salary figures suggesting they were mostly unskilled.
Later in the period, expertise in embroidery or lace-making was felt
desirable for elegant ladies, and such skills evidently had commercial
value since they were taught to girls in orphanages and convents
where income was needed.

13.2 Spinning and weaving at home

Ability to spin and weave were considered basic feminine skills, as is implied in numerous documents, such as the Florentine *Catasto* entry of 1427 for Giovanni di Michele, a carpenter.

E. Conti, A. Guidotti and R. Lunardi, *La civiltà fiorentina del Quattrocento* (Florence, 1993), p. 63.

Monna Tonia his wife weaves linen cloth and sews linen cloths.

An elder girl of 13, Benedetta by name, his daughter, helps her mother with the weaving.

A girl of 9 named Nana, his daughter, helps them with weaving.

13.3 Passages from guild regulations, Treviso, 1416

The language of guild documents often disguises the sex of workers.[3] However, the passages below from the regulations of the Guild of Wool-Workers at Treviso clearly use female forms when referring to spinners, while using the masculine for weavers (among whom females could have been included). As is usual in such regulations, a desire both to protect and to control workers is evident.

L. Pesce, *Vita socio-culturale in diocesi di Treviso nel primo Quattrocento* (Venice, 1988), pp. 345, 349–50.

19. We desire that if any woman [*alcuna filiera*] spinning at the mill or the wheel spins poor-quality thread, or makes any falsification either in the wool or the thread, or indicates a weight other than that which the wool or thread could reasonably produce, this spinner should be condemned at the discretion of the guild authorities and should make up the loss noted through the officials of the guild, and if she is found out in deception on three occasions, she should be banned from spinning, with a fine of 18 *soldi* for whoever gives her further spinning work. [...]

44. We order that no-one from our Guild be allowed, either in person, or through an intermediary or any third party, to take, or have taken from, to give, or have given to, any wool to spinners [*filiere*] or from spinners, under pain of 10 *soldi* for each reel, and three *soldi* for each pound from the spinning-wheels.

---

3 On this and other matters relating to women in guilds, see R. Mackenney, 'The Guilds of Venice: State and Society in the "longue durée"', *Studi veneziani*, 34 (1997), pp. 15–44.

13.4 Women rearing silk worms around Vicenza

The silk industry expanded rapidly in many regions of Italy, involving many women workers, such as those noted by Casola in 1494 around Vicenza.[4]

Pietro Casola, *Canon Pietro Casola's Pigrimage to Jerusalem*, ed. and trans. M. M. Newett (Manchester, 1907), pp. 121–2.

The city has a great trade in silk. As I rode through the country I was shown the whole process of making the silk, which was very interesting. Very few other trees are to be found there save mulberry trees, which are stripped of their leaves to feed the worms that make the silk. I saw many women looking after the worms, and they explained to me the great care they needed by day and by night. It was a very pleasant thing to see such a great quantity and in so many places.

13.5 Women inventors and entrepreneurs

While the vast majority of women in the textile industry were humble employees, a few records exist of females attempting to benefit from their own technical innovations by petitioning the Venetian Senate.

R. Berveglieri, 'La produzione di manifatture tessili non laniere a Venezia', in G. Ericani and P. Frattaroli, eds, *Tessuti nel Veneto* (Verona, 1993), pp. 122–3.

6 May 1556. Pulisena Vincenti petitions, successfully, to be able to:

... enjoy, together with her children, the benefits from her invention in manufacturing in Venice *veriselli* or *surian* cloths, both white, black and all colours, of all the varieties made in the regions of the Levant, and designed with every sort of device or other pattern and in any colour.

9 March 1623. Laura Lunaga and her relatives obtain a privilege lasting 10 years:

... to make use of the method for piercing veil cloth invented by them.

13.6 Women's textile work and classical lore

Garzoni's encyclopaedic *La piazza universale*, categorises only a few trades as women's work, linking them with classical mythology.

Garzoni (1586, repr. 1599), pp. 731, 826, 908–9.

4 L. Mola, *The Silk Industry of Renaissance Venice* (Baltimore, 2000).

On Wool-workers

The pagans claim ... that it was Minerva who invented the craft of working with wool, and that she was the first to weave cloth and colour wool as wool-workers do today.

On Spinners

For women spinners the spindle and the wheel seem to be used as the main tools, and so for spinning they need the distaff and the spindle, the spool, the wheel, the winding-frame with the bobbin and the shaft ... and thus they make the strand or the thread thick or fine, of high or low grade, and make the low-grade into stuffing ... This craft is honoured by the three poetic Fates, one called Clotho, another Lachesis and the third Atropos, of whom one is supposed to hold the wheel, the other to spin and the last to break the woven threads of our life.

On Silk-workers

The silk is extracted from the cocoons placed in a cauldron on top of a stove, and rolled up on a sort of scraper, and then is sent to a carder, who combs it with combs, and cards it with cards, and then to the mistresses, who double the strands and the twists, and the reels and the spindles, and, putting it on the reels, both double it and wind it. Then it goes to the reeler, who puts it on the spools, and to the male spinner ... and once spun it returns to the women's hands, who double it again on the reels, and it returns to the spinner to be twisted. It then goes to the dyer, after the merchant has seen it, and the dyer first heats it up with water and soap, then dyes it a particular colour. It returns to the merchant, who puts it to the winding spools – hence these masters are called winders – with which they stretch it well, and make it appear lustrous and polished. And then it goes back to the mistresses, who treat it according to the instructions of the weaver who wants the work done, and who then weaves it, as he pleases.

13.7 Spinning and weaving comes to be seen as lower-class

The textile arts were also connected with Eve and the Virgin Mary, and also, as here, with the virtuous or ingenious heroines of antiquity (see 5.13).

Dolce (1545), fol. 13r–v.

You should know, my Lady Dorothea, that the work of women in antiquity was to spin and weave: two activities very useful for the maintenance of the family. Today, both are done by lower-class women, with small benefit for those of them who support their poor families. O empty vanity, O damnable snobbery of the noblewomen of our century that they should be ashamed to do what has in all ages been held honourable by ladies of high estate ... I do not think it much matters whether our ladies work with wool or with linen, when both are equally useful, and were always the most respectable occupation for worthy young girls.

13.8 Handiwork for elegant ladies and their protegées

By the later sixteenth century, many pattern-books of embroidery and lace designs for women, and used for clothing and household objects, came to be published. Cesare Vecellio's book of lace designs communicated with illiterate readers through illustrations, and with a more aspiring clientele by incorporating mythological or allegorical designs, making flattering parallels to painters, and mentioning aristocratic practitioners.

Cesare Vecellio, *Corona delle donne* (Venice, 1591–1617), unpaginated dedication.

With this work, noble and talented ladies delighting in the profession of sewing will have patterns of laces both large and small, such as rosettes, friezes and suchlike in the modern fashion of all Europe: all sorts of *punti tagliati, punti in aria, punti a reticello,* and other kinds, doing with the needle what the finest painters do with the brush. The needle can serve them as an ornament, and like a crown make them stand out above all others, thus justifying the name of the present book: it will turn out suitable works, either useful or intricate, to their utmost delight and glory. I have, then, judged no-one more fitting to be presented this in print than Your Illustrious Ladyship,[5] who is worthy and excellent above all others both in her expertise in all these techniques, and in the pleasure she takes in encouraging their execution by the women of her household, which is a shelter for the most virtuous young girls living today in that city.

13.9 A 1595 guide to Milan on embroiderers

The chapter on male and female embroiderers mentions women from different social backgrounds, starting with Caterina Leuca Cantona.

Morigia, pp. 299–300.

---

5 Viena Nani.

This honoured gentlelady has with needle and colours of silk and gold imitated, to universal astonishment, every finest painting or miniature, as can be seen in the marvellous cloths she gave to the Infanta Donna Catherina of Austria, Duchess of Savoy, which were used at the solemn baptism of her firstborn. Also the stupendous works made by her divine hand can be seen in over thirty churches in this city, and elsewhere … Equally, there is a very large number of women, both the ladies of the prime nobility and other gentlewomen, citizens, and craftswomen, who need not envy any women in Italy in needlework, in embroidery and in other skilled professions.

SERVANTS AND SLAVES

Women doing domestic work for private households, businesses or institutions formed the largest section of women workers. Most households ranking from prosperous artisans upwards employed at least one servant or slave, usually female.[6] They were hired mainly through personal connections, and came often from country districts, or, in the case of slaves, whose presence decreased in the sixteenth century, from eastern Europe or west-central Asia. Relationships between masters or mistresses and servants were in some cases short-term, cash-based and mistrustful, in others characterised by loyalty and apparent affection over a long term, supported by notions of honour and Christian duty. Slaves would commonly be freed and provided for in their employers' wills; younger long-serving female servants given contributions to a dowry (see 6.21, 22, 33; 10.24, 25). Sometimes called 'familiars' (*famigliari*), employers to an extent thought of them as members of their extended family. Women bequeathed money, gifts of clothing and personal items both to their own servants and those of their relatives or neighbours; servants' wills might make bequests to females in their mistresses' families or express the wish to be buried with them.

13.10 **Caution in selecting a slave**

Alessandra Macinghi Strozzi to her son Filippo, 1465.
Macinghi Strozzi (1997), pp. 169–170.

You told me in your letter of 28th September that you'd noticed a slave

---

6 D. Romano, *Housecraft and Statecraft. Domestic Service in Renaissance Venice 1400–1600* (Baltimore, 1996).

there who used to be with Leonardo Vernacci, and that you'd have bought her if you hadn't got the old one at home. To which I say that she's not for you, in my view. Leonardo's wife had her for four or rather five years; and because she was ill-looking and had bad blood, so that people thought she might somehow harm herself or others, they turned her out of the house – and she was dishonest. They sold her to Antonio della Luna, and she stayed only a short time as they didn't want her and sent her back, so they sent her there [to Naples]. Leonardo's wife made her do the sewing, but she didn't have the brains for it: if she'd been a good servant she'd have hung on to her. You say you have another in the house, who used to be with Filippo degli Albizzi. She was thought highly capable, but they sold her because the wine was starting to cause problems and make her always tipsy – and also she was immoral, and as the wives had daughters, they didn't want her in the house.

13.11 Doge Agostino Barbarigo (d. 1501) provides for domestics in his will

Noteworthy are the origins of the serving women, from territories subject to Venice, and the request that Donna Giacoma should pray for her master's soul at the miracle-working shrine of the Madonna dei Miracoli. The affluent were well aware that God loved the poor and lowly, so their prayers could be particularly efficacious.

F. Nani-Mocenigo, 'Testamento del doge Agostino Barbarigo', *Nuovo archivio veneto*, 17 (1909), p. 249.

We order that Caterina our slave be freed and all her possessions be given her and a bed furnished as our daughters think fit and she should have 15 ducats for her marriage and 5 for other expenses. If our daughters think she does not wish to marry because of possible changed circumstances we leave it to them to do what seems best. We leave to Rosa the Slav, because of all the time she has spent with us, 20 gold ducats and all her possessions and a bed furnished as our daughters think fit, so she may go and live in the Hospital of Ca' di Dio,[7] as she has had a place allocated to her by the Prior. To Donna Giacoma of Vicenza should be given the remainder of her salary and 5 ducats for the love of God, so she may go and live in the hospice of the Hospital of S. Marco, in the place we have reserved; we commend

---

7 A hospice for the old or infirm.

the said Donna Giacoma to our sons and daughters since she deserves all the best, and that they have her go, at the time they think best, to Our Lady of the Miracoli and to S. Fantin to pray to Our Lord and His most holy Mother for our soul. To Maddalena should be given 10 ducats for the time she spent with us and, should she wish to marry, she should have another 10 ducats and a bed fitted out as our daughters think suitable.

13.12 The servants of the Venetian painter Lotto

This extract from Lorenzo Lotto's accounts book for 1546–7 conveys the importance of personal connections between lower-class women, whether relatives or neighbours, in finding suitable employment, and of spinning to supplement their incomes.

Lorenzo Lotto, *Lorenzo Lotto. Il 'Libro di spese diverse'*, ed. P. Zampetti (Venice, 1969), pp. 126–7, 140, 305.

Donna Lucia, brought up in Ca' Venier, at S. Maria Formosa, came to live with me as a housekeeper, aged more than 60 years, and I promised her 4 ducats a year as salary, with no other obligations from me. She was to spin for me, leaving it up to her conscience to do a little spinning for herself; this was in the presence of her relative, Donna Maddalena, the widow and my landlady, the wife of Messer Giovanni de la Volta of the Corona where I live ...

The said Donna Lucia was not able to continue working because of her great age. She had to leave and I paid her for the month she was here ...

On 16 August 1546, Donna Maria from Montagnana came to live with me, to be in charge of the house and in service with a salary of 4 ducats a year, through Donna Lucia of Cadore, a washerwoman in the court-yard of Ca' Barozzi at S. Moise, and I made the above agreement with her.

On 1 October 1547, having given permission to the said Donna Maria, my housekeeper, as she hadn't met my requirements, with no bad feeling on either side I set her free to fend for herself elsewhere.

From Lotto's will of 25 March 1546:

10 ducats should be given to Donna Lucia the Cadorine, washerwoman at S. Moise, in the courtyard of Ca' Barozzi, either to her or her son Giovan Maria who today is aged about 10: this for having been faithful to me in Christian charity.

13.13 **Young female servants must beware of their masters**

Fourteenth century advice, directed towards the servant, discusses a problem experienced throughout the Renaissance period.

Francesco da Barberino, pt 12, p. 139.

I believe it's not well suited for a young girl to live in service with any man who hasn't a wife ... If a woman serves a man on his own ... she should stay all the more cautious, and take care as she goes around to watch out for his flattery and false promises, which will quickly turn out to be jests, taken seriously by few. She should take special care lest the master touch her, which will lead to deadly war with the mistress, which she [the servant] will end by losing. In cooking and in her other duties she should be as clean as she can. She should watch out for men-servants and boys, and, whatever friends or relatives she might have, should not let them have any household item. She should not go around made up and dressed up, which ill suits her station.

13.14 **A servant girl harassed**

Agnoletta, a fictional but credible servant girl, complains about the sexual advances of a range of men.

Alessandro Piccolomini (Lo Stordito), *L'Amore Costante* (Venice, 1540), pp. 39–40; performed in Siena, 1536.

Oh St Agatha, I could tell you what it's like when a maidservant comes across those messenger boys who fool around with her: my flesh is all bruised! Jesus, how I loathe their pinches and their stupid catcalls on the street: 'I'm ready for it, are you? Hey, girl, would you like a peach? Gather your shirt, put it on ...' And with these words this one pokes me here, that one prods me from there, one puts his hands behind, the other touches in front. Quickly they grab us and pull us into a shop, and argue over us in a way that drives us mad ... But I know how to protect my honour, because when I was in a shop, the perfumer, who was alone, began to make phoney eyes at me, and say he thought me a fine piece of goods, and how long was it since I'd had it, and lots of other smarmy bullshit. I, having heard the same rubbish several times from other men, who then wanted to ruin my reputation, replied that I might be fine goods, but I wasn't his. With that he dragged me by the arm into the shop and put his hands on me, one on my breasts and one on my neck, and wanted to carry on with the rest, but fortunately

he heard his wife come downstairs, and quickly he pulled himself
together and I took myself off.

13.15 Proper behaviour of the housewife towards her servants

Lodovico Dolce directs the mistress on how to achieve a harmonious household.

Dolce (1545), fol. 57r–v.

[The wife] should not be harsh or cruel to the members of her household, but benevolent and agreeable, since obedience and esteem from
servants arise from the mildness, not the severity of masters.
Competence, good judgement, serious speech and behaviour carry
greater weight than frowning faces, shouts or beatings. It's better to
rule wisely than irascibly: power that is temperate, not over-severe, is
stronger ... I would like it to be rigorous but not harsh, painstaking
but not violent, bearing in mind that those who by the injustice of
fortune have been assigned to servitude are men, and thus rational
beings and creatures of God with immortal souls, as much as are kings
and emperors.

WET-NURSES

Of the heterogeneous group of women who earned their keep caring
for the young, sick, old or infirm, the largest and best-documented
sector were the wet-nurses (*balie* or *nene*) hired by more affluent
townspeople (see also 6.1). They either lived with these families, or
took the infant to their own homes, sometimes in the countryside. As
lactation could last up to three years, choosing a trustworthy wet-
nurse was of immense importance for the parents, and wet-nursing,
which was better paid than other forms of female domestic service,
was a considerable money-earner for lower-class or peasant women.
Other wet-nurses stayed after weaning to become general nursemaids,
or even trusted retainers with close and enduring relationships with
their 'milk children' (*figli di latte*).[8] Numerous wet-nurses also worked
for orphanages and foundling hospitals: larger institutions employed
hundreds of these, who might live within the building complex.

8 C. Klapisch-Zuber, 'Blood Parents and Milk Parents: Wet Nursing in Florence
1300–1530', in Klapisch-Zuber, pp. 132–64.

13.16 A Florentine hires wet-nurses for his daughters

The employer is careful to stipulate what he requires of the wet-nurse, who in turn receives a generous gift of clothing.

Francesco di Matteo Castellani, *Ricordanze*, ed. G. Ciappelli, 2 vols (Florence, 1992–5), vol. 1, p. 128.

1450. I record how on the —th day of May of the above year, Caterina —, the slave of Monna Ginevra, the wife of Filippo, or rather of Donato the son of Filippo del Tinta the furniture-maker, came to stay with me as wet-nurse for Maria, my daughter, at a rate of 18 florins a year, beginning on the same day and continuing for two or three years as we wish, and more or less as the child needs, giving her healthy milk.

1460. I record how in the name of God on 3 December I gave my daughter Giovanna to be breastfed with Monna Orsina, the wife of the shoemaker Michele di Domenico and relative of Monna Caterina da Brozi through whom we've hired her, at a salary of 5 *lire* a month, if she gives good and healthy milk and looks after her with all the care reasonably required, and in the event anything proves unsatisfactory or that Monna Orsina gets pregnant or anything else we must retain part of our money, following reasonable usage.

On 23 May of the same year I gave Monna Caterina da Brozi 5 *lire*, 8 *soldi* in one big florin; she said she wanted it to give to the husband of Orsina, who had come for part of her salary.

On 8 March of the same year, 25 lire for a green dress with sleeves of purple cloth I bought for the said Monna Orsina.

13.17 A foundling hospital in San Gimignano employs wet-nurses

Note the involvement of the wet-nurses' husbands in the transactions, and also the evidence of one woman's demand for more satisfactory terms of employment.

L. Sandri, *L'ospedale di S. Maria della Scala di S. Gimignano* (Florence, 1982), p. 140 n. 5, p. 144 n. 11, p. 145 n. 15.

Monna Piera, wife of Mignano del Gesso, took the said Andrea to nurse on Sunday 2 March 1426, and is to have 25 *soldi* a month and a bushel of grain ... this agreement satisfies us and also her ...

Maria Agostina, as the child is called, was taken to nurse with our workman at Montorsoli, Michele di Lorenzo, called Calandriello, on 19 November of this year, and the same girl was formerly put to nurse with Piero di Luca da San Quirico ... to be given the breast and well brought up ...

Giovanni da Luparello and his wife, from Monteacuto, a workman for Ser Agnolo di Ser Bartolomeo of San Gimignano, on 1 July of this year took our child Maria Agostina to nurse, who formerly was with Michele di Lorenzo ... and he should have as salary and for their child-rearing efforts 3 lire a month ...

Monna Nanna, wife of Giacomo di Macallo, at present residing in San Gimignano, took the said Niccolò to nurse, on Tuesday 8 February of the same year [1445], to have 50 *soldi* a month while at the breast ... as she was not satisfied with the said rate, she was given six *soldi* more per month.

13.18 A Milanese infants' hospital, 1595

The Hospital of S. Celso, Milan, like several large hospitals in sixteenth-century Italy, catered for infants on an almost industrial scale.

Morigia, p. 54.

Here all [children] of both high and low estate are received, and also nursing infants ... And besides, all infants are nursed with great love and care. At the time of writing, there are eighty women who carry out these pious tasks, and all obey a chief Matron like a Prioress. The number of mouths at present in this Hospital is six hundred or more; besides this there are over a thousand little girls and babies, who are given to nurse to wet-nurses outside the Hospital, so that its expenses exceed ten thousand *scudi* each year. And during 1593 the Deputies spent three thousand a hundred and sixty-six *scudi* and four gold *lire*, to pay the wet-nurses giving milk.

HOSPITAL STAFF

Former wet-nurses might be employed in different jobs for hospitals later in their lives. There are also many, if brief, records of female nursing staff working in almshouses, hospices and hospitals. Those in positions of authority might be linked with the founders or bene-factors of these institutions (who were often women), those with more menial duties drawn from lower classes, and from religious tertiaries.[9] The humble tending of the poor and sick was a standard element in Renaissance definitions of female (and sometimes male) sanctity.

13.19 The *Ospedale* at San Gimignano employs women workers

The records show different ways of employing women: some were hired to do various menial tasks for a salary or payments in kind; others, such as Monna Chiara, came to live at the hospital with their husbands as oblates, dedicating their goods and labour to the institution in return for a room and care in future sickness or old age.

Sandri, pp. 44–5, n. 13; p. 45, n. 14; p. 43, n. 9.

Monna Leonarda, the wife of the deceased Fabiano di Ghezo, shoe-maker from Siena, came to serve in the hospital on 10 November 1394, at a salary of 24 *lire* a year.

Monna Leonarda, the former wife of Fabiano of Siena and our employee and convent woman, needs to have 12 *lire* a year to clothe and shoe herself, like the other women of the household, beginning on 10 May 1398.

Monna Piera di Biancalana, who came to serve in the hospital a year ago, beginning on the 15 March 1419, must have in the same year 4 florins and a chemise for her back of new fine linen and a pair of new shoes for her feet. Monna Piera re-engaged herself for the fourth year of 1423 and must have in that year 6 florins for her salary … The said Monna Piera left, going in February 1426. She was at that salary 2 years and eleven months …

Monna Maddalena … came to serve the hospital and care for the household together with the women and Monna Chiara and to look after her as she is sick and thus care for the children and do the other housework, and her salary began on 1 June 1426 and the year finished the 1 June 1427.

13.20 A Venetian confraternity hires women to tend plague victims

One of the rules (*Mariegole*) of *c.* 1481 of the Scuola Grande di S. Rocco in Venice (St Roch was popularly invoked against the plague) provides its female care-workers with both salaries and accommodation.

9 J. Henderson, 'The Hospitals of Late-Medieval and Renaissance Florence: A Preliminary Survey', in L. Granshaw, L. and R. Porter, eds, *The Hospital in History* (London, 1989), pp. 63–92.

F. Tonon, *Scuola dei Battuti di San Rocco* (Venice, 1998), p. 76.

We must permanently employ four good women, for whom a house may be rented by our confraternity, which should pay up to six ducats per annum in time of plague. And each month they should be given twenty *soldi* each as alms by the confraternity. The women should and must at a time of plague (which immortal God through the intercession and merit of the glorious confessor, Messer S. Rocco, may decide) visit our sick brothers in the confraternity and those outside it, and if they find any others without anyone to care for them they should serve them and tend them with all care and diligence.

13.21 A Turin hospital appoints a woman teacher

The 1541 regulations of the Ospedale Maggiore di S. Giovanni Battista, Turin, appoint a Master to teach boys to read and perform a trade, and a woman to instruct the girls as deemed suitable.[10]

T. M. Caffaratto, *L'Ospedale Maggiore di San Giovanni Battista e della città di Torino: sette secoli di assistenza socio-sanitaria* (Turin, 1984), p. 48.

Also a woman of the highest repute to take care of the girls, both to instruct them in right living, true religion and the fear of God, and in spinning, sewing and other proper female tasks, keeping them neat and clean.

10 N. Terpstra, 'Work in the Orphanages of Florence and Bologna', *Sixteenth Century Journal*, 31:4 (2000), pp. 1063–79.

14 Prostitutes and courtesans

Prostitution was the occupation apparently supporting the largest number of women during the Renaissance outside family homes or convents, and one which took very different forms. Lower or more casual prostitution overlapped with menial female labour at the disreputable bathhouses or inns where sexual assignations took place. Most cities possessed these by 1400; some had prostitute districts or well-known brothels, often regulated by government.[1] After 1500 the number of prostitutes seemingly grew, perhaps initially as a consequence of political disruptions. In particular Rome, with its large number of affluent single males, and Venice, with its commercial wealth and trading activity, acted as magnets for women and girls unable to find work in their homelands. Prostitutes, with their procuresses and pimps, may have amounted to 5–10 per cent of the entire population of these cities, the numbers perhaps increasing in subsequent decades.

However, from around 1500 much prostitution came to be perceived differently, even if mostly the reality continued as before. An elite group of prostitutes became known by the euphemistic name of *cortigiane* (female courtiers), rather than *meretrici*, with a super-elite dubbed *cortigiane oneste*. Ambitious girls, sometimes aided by their mothers, acquired graceful, lively manners and often talents in music and literature, and aspired to richer rewards and to fame and respect like the *hetairae* of ancient Greece and Rome.[2] Though circumstances varied, the classic *cortigiana onesta* occupied her own premises, financed by one or more lovers, entertained in lavish style, and expected to be wooed with gifts and rhetoric rather than simply hired for cash. This chapter will be weighted towards this better-documented group, who as inspirations to authors, artists and musicians, and sometimes as writers or performers themselves, contributed to the cultural life of Renaissance

1 Surveys of different aspects of prostitution are R. Trexler, 'Florentine Prostitution in the Fifteenth Century: Patrons and Clients', in Trexler, vol. 2, pp. 31–65, J. K. Brackett, 'The Florentine Onestà and the Control of Prostitution, 1403–1680', *Sixteenth Century Journal*, 24:2 (1993), pp. 273–300, and E. S. Cohen, 'Seen and Known: Prostitutes in the Cityscape of Late-Sixteenth-Century Rome', *Renaissance Studies*, 12:3 (1998), pp. 392–409.

2 Studies emphasising this type of courtesan are G. Masson, *Courtesans of the Italian Renaissance* (London, 1975) and L. Lawner, *Lives of the Courtesans: Portraits of the Renaissance* (New York, 1987).

Italy. Idealised courtesans seemed like paragons of beauty, charm and talent to some, like symbols of corruption to satirists, moralists and outraged civic authorities.

Both successful courtesans and less fortunate, and more typical, prostitutes were urged to repent by moralists, and some did so, perhaps joining semi-monastic institutions. Others might not escape the ravages of age, venereal disease and poverty, seen by many as their just deserts. Especially from the mid-sixteenth century much effort in many cities was expended in rescuing, rehabilitating and generally supervising members of 'the oldest profession' and their offspring.

PROSTITUTES IN CITY SPACES

Brothels, inns, streetwalkers

This section evokes the range of venues where prostitutes practised, and the areas from which they originated.

14.1 A Renaissance sex district

When describing an ideal city layout in his 1464 treatise, the architectural theorist Filarete assumes that sexual services will be part of the goods for sale, in areas adjoining the main mercantile district. This is doubtless moulded by what was observable in contemporary Italian cities.

Antonio Averlino (Il Filarete), *Trattato di architettura*, ed. A. M. Finoli and L. Grassi, 3 vols (Milan, 1972), vol. 1 (book VI), p. 166.

On the market square will be, as I have said, the Captain's palace, and on one side the butchers' and poulterers' and also sellers of fish at the appropriate time. And beside the square ... will be the pleasure quarter [*luogo venereo*] and also the bathhouses or stews, and public inns or taverns, from the eastward side as far as you please.

14.2 The origins and careers of Roman prostitutes

The author of *Il Ragionamento dello Zoppino* (1534) provides vignettes of the early careers of successful Roman courtesans. Some came from the Roman lower classes, others from elsewhere in Italy, or abroad, perhaps having originally sought more respectable work, a pattern found in other sources and confirmed by studies by modern historians.

Zoppino, *Dialogue de la vie et généalogie de toutes les courtisanes de Rome* (Paris, 1883), pp. 80–4.

These pretensions don't come from her parents, any more than Lorenzina's come from the bakery, where I have seen her a thousand times, barefoot and carrying a dish of stewed apples on her head; I have seen both her and her mother sitting on a servants' bench, and then going to dance in an inn ... Nor do Beatrice's, who was the daughter of a poor washerwoman in the Campo Marzio with several daughters, who would go semi-naked, with baskets of clothes on their heads, to do the laundry in the Tiber. She fell into the hands of a dissolute doctor during Julius II's time, the brother of Gianpietro of Cremona. He put her to service dressed as a boy, and took his pleasure as if she were a youth, the unnatural way ... Angela the Greek came to Rome in Leo X's time, and was carried off by certain pimps to Lanciano and brought to an inn in Campo dei Fiori covered in rash ... in the end, as she was a beautiful and honourable woman, graceful and lovely, she fell in love with one of Leo's chamberlains, who brought her into favour. Cecilia the Venetian (so-called, though she is from Friuli) was Jewish twenty years ago. She was baptised, married a rogue, then left him to return to Rome with a gluttonous priest who was sent to the galleys: she then took up with a Sienese banker who put her on her feet again.

14.3 A catalogue of Venetian prostitutes, c. 1566

Later Venetian sources document both prostitutes working from home, perhaps controlled by procuresses, and streetwalkers. From the *Catalogo di tutte le principal et più honorate cortigiane di Venetia, c.* 1566, listing 210 women with prices, some (Baffa, Franco, Zaffetta) known from other sources. Typical charges of 2–3 *scudi* would correspond to 2 weeks' work for a skilled worker.

A. Barzaghi, *Donne o cortigiane?* (Verona, 1980), p. 166

201 Vienna Borella, near S. Trovaso, at the boatman's beneath — *scudi* 15
202 Vassalea, at S. Apostoli, in the buildings round Ca' Bembo, with Chate the Slav woman — *scudi* 2
203 Vicenza from Burano, at S. Tomà, with the same woman — *scudi* 2
204 Vienna, at the Madonna dell'Orto, with her housekeeper — *scudi* 6
205 Veronica Franca, at S. Maria Formosa, with her mother — *scudi* 2
206 Vittoria Bellaman, at S. Barnaba, at the silversmith's nearby — *scudi* 3

207 Violante from Siena, at the Maddalena church, with Costanza at the Storto bridge — *scudi* 4

208 Viena, at S. Felice where you take the boat for the new houses, beside the lower window — *scudi* 1

209 Viena, at S. Caterina, in a house on the main street, with Chate the Slav woman — *scudi* 2

210 Zanella from Burano, in S. Trovaso, with her mother Catarina — *scudi* 2.

Legislation

The perceived increase in prostitution moved several states to repeated legislation. Concern was expressed less at the spread of syphilis than at the blurring of boundaries between the respectable and the otherwise, the loss of honour to the city and its religious institutions, the corruption of the young and the misuse of economic resources. Two extracts from different cities provide samples.

14.4 **Prostitutes to be distinguished in dress**

This 1511 decree of the Florentine Magistracy for Decency makes a distinction between public prostitutes and those maintained in brothels, attempting to mark the former from respectable women.

M. S. Mazzi, *Prostitute e lenoni nella Firenze del Quattrocento* (Milan, 1991), p. 231.

Seeing that much disorder arises from street prostitutes going about in a fashion undistinguished from other women, and that it would be well to do away with such impropriety, we therefore establish and order that, after the present provision, none of these street prostitutes may or should go outside their dwelling houses to any place dressed in a *cioppa*[3] for any reason. Should they want to wear a cioppa like other women, let them be required to wear on their head a square veil of at least one *braccia*, either coloured red, green, yellow or a pastel colour, as they please.

14.5 **Prostitutes invade holy places**

A Venetian law of 16 September, 1539, from the Magistracy for Public Health. Barzaghi, pp. 133–4.

---

3 An overgarment.

No prostitute or courtesan of any kind may live or maintain herself anywhere near a church or holy site, setting a bad example and causing scandal to men and women coming to hear the word of God. Nor can the said courtesan or prostitute attend any church on feast days and principal services, lest with lascivious movements, gestures, words and deeds she sets a bad example to those visiting the churches in good faith, giving shame to this city and dishonour and contempt for holy places, and offence to God's majesty. When going to church on other days, the aforesaid must not stand, kneel, or lean over the church seating where there are nobles and citizens of a good and upright kind, but should remain separate and removed from them and take care not to cause scandal to other respectable people.

DIFFERENT METHODS AND BEHAVIOUR

14.6 Bandello on early sixteenth-century Venetian prostitutes

In one of his novels of *c.* 1520, to an extent based on fact, Matteo Bandello describes the *modus operandi* of Venetian prostitutes.

Matteo Bandello, *Novelle*, ed. F. Flora (Milan, 1935), vol. 2, pp. 417–18.

One more feature of Venice is that there is a vast number of prostitutes, who are called by the respectable name of 'courtesans', as is also done in Rome and elsewhere. There is also a custom in Venice, which I have never heard of elsewhere, namely that a courtesan would normally have six or seven Venetian gentlemen as lovers, each of whom has one night a week when he goes to dine and sleep with her. The daytime is free for the woman to spend serving whoever comes her way so that her mill never lies idle and perhaps goes rusty through lack of use. If occasionally some foreigner whose purse is well-lined wishes to spend the night with her, she accepts, but first tells the client whose night it is, so that if he wants to grind grain, he can do so by day since the night is occupied with another. If this is done, the lover pays by the month and it is expressly written into the agreement that the woman can entertain and give overnight accommodation to foreigners.

14.7 Prostitutes use classical names

Prostitutes in their attempts to rise socially often adopted pretentious new names, sometimes suggesting the goddesses, nymphs or famous courtesans of classical antiquity, as mentioned in this letter in Ortensio Lando's 1548 volume.

Lando, fol. 109v–110r.

I've never liked it that for some time you've been living in districts where many prostitutes live, not without infecting respectable women ... Maybe it would be enough if your neighbours only led wretched and lustful lives, without also imitating the names of fallen women from antiquity. They re-christen themselves: instead of Maria, Francesca, Ursula, Helena and Antonia they call themselves Glyceria, Phryne, Thais, Flora, Lydia, Philena and Callidena. So take my advice, and move from this neighbourhood.

14.8 A transvestite prostitute

Other courtesans sought to intrigue through baffling changes in appearance or spicy conversation. Pietro Aretino writes to the transvestite courtesan from Pistoia, La Zufolina, in 1547.

Aretino, vol. 2, pp. 789–90.

Twice my good fortune has sent your fair person into my house, and others', once as a woman dressed like a man, the other as a man dressed like a woman. Certainly, nature has made you of both sexes, so that one instant you appear male and then all of a sudden female, so that Duke Alessandro wanted to have sex with you just to see whether you were genuinely a hermaphrodite, or only one in jest. You see, you talk like a girl, but behave like a boy, so that someone who didn't know which you were, would take you now for the rider, now for the steed, that is both nymph and shepherd, active and passive. What more can I say? Even your clothes, which you change continually, leave it unclear as to whether you're a male or female gasbag. Even dukes and duchesses are amused by the entertainment of your exceedingly piquant and salty chatter. From your mouth and your lips escape tasty aromas, like pine-nut tarts, like honeycomb, like marzipan to those who find your gossip diverting.

14.9 A resourceful procuress

The last day of Aretino's *Dialoghi* or *Sei giornate* shows how older women could share the spoils of venal sexual activity. In what is in part a parody of conduct literature, his fictional midwife explains how to be a successful procuress or bawd. She should not be a brothel-keeper but a fixer of profitable assignations, seemingly respectable but actually a wily and quick-witted trickster.

Pietro Aretino, *Sei giornate*, ed. A. Romano (Milan, 1991), pp. 300–10.

[Midwife] The procuress and the whore, dear wet-nurse, are not only sisters, but born from a single body: and Mrs Lust is the mother, and Mr Brothel the father ...

Nevertheless, the bawd needs to be more shrewd ... the bawd can't make her way if she doesn't have a hundred tales on her tongue ...

Being a bawd is fine work: she makes herself everyone's friend and companion, stepchild and godmother, she pokes her nose into every hole. All the new fashions of dress in Mantua, Ferrara and Milan follow the model set by the bawd; and she invents every different style of hairdressing found in the world ... She tries to chat with all the passers-by on the street, not to mention those who doff their caps at her or make signals, nudges and winks ...

By night the bawd is like a bat that never rests; and just as owls ... leave their nests, so the bawd leaves hers and goes flitting through the monasteries, convents, courts, brothels and every single tavern. Here she picks up a nun, there a monk. To one man she brings a whore, to another a widow, to the third a wife and to the fourth a virgin. She satisfies the manservant with his master's maids, and consoles the steward with somebody's wife. She casts a spell on wounds, gathers herbs, exorcises spirits, breaks off the jaws of dead men, takes footwear off hanged men, performs rituals with cards, controls the stars, dissolves the planets, and sometimes gets a good beating!

THE SUCCESSFUL COURTESAN

Material worlds

14.10 Imperia lives like a princess

Courtesans with wealthy clients could live opulently in dwellings surrounded by gifts or by works they had commissioned themselves.[4] Matteo Bandello's description of such a courtesan in the Rome of the 1510s in his *Novelle* III, 42 is thought to be based on Imperia (d. 1522), famous in the 1500s, and may only be slightly exaggerated.

Bandello, vol. 2, pp. 461–2.

4 For the courtesan as possible taste-maker in furnishings, see P. Thornton, *The Italian Renaissance Interior 1400–1600* (London, 1991), pp. 348–58.

She lived in a most honourably appointed house, with many servants, men and women who continually waited on her. The house was equipped and provided with everything, so that any stranger who entered and saw the furnishing and the ranks of servants thought a princess lived there. Among other things, there was a reception room and a chamber and a smaller chamber so grandly decorated that there was nothing to be seen but velvets and brocades, and the finest carpets on the floor. In the little bedroom where she withdrew when some great personage visited, there were hangings covering the walls, all of cloth-of-gold *riccio sovra riccio*,[5] ornately and delightfully worked. Then there was a cornice, all picked out in gold and ultramarine, masterfully made: on it were exquisite vases made of a variety of precious materials, alabaster stone, porphyry, serpentine, and thousands of other kinds. Then all around were to be seen many coffers and chests richly incised, so that all were very precious. Then in the middle was a little table, the finest in the world, covered in green velvet. On it were always a lute or a lyre with music books, and other musical instruments. There were also several little books in the vernacular and in Latin, richly decorated. She greatly delighted in vernacular poetry, having been much enthused by Messer Domenico Campana, called Strascino, and already so profitably, that she composed rather fine sonnets and madrigals.

14.11 The possessions of a Venetian courtesan

The household goods in the 1569 inventory of Julia Lombardo, a courtesan flourishing in the Venice of the 1520s and 1530s, compare with those in upper middle-class households, though, unusually for a woman, she had her own *studiolo* for prized objects.[6] The parrot cage suggests a penchant for exotic pets often noted among courtesans.

C. Santore, 'Julia Lombardo, "Somtuosa Meretrize": A Portrait by Property', *Renaissance Quarterly*, 41:1 (1988), pp. 68–9, 72–3.

In the chamber facing S. Caterina:

A painting of Our Lady in a walnut frame, with gilded columns

---

5 An elaborate fabric, with patterns of looped threads.
6 For a comparable household inventory, see A. A. Smith, 'Gender, Ownership and Domestic Space: Inventories and Family Archives in Renaissance Verona', *Renaissance Studies*, 12:3 (1998), pp. 387–91; for the *studiolo*, see D. Thornton, *The Scholar in his Study* (New Haven, 1998).

Another large painting with Christ and various figures, with fittings of gilded stucco

A painting with the head of St John the Baptist

A large lamp of gilded bronze

Five paintings with three different figures, imitating bronze

A small painting on panel with a head sketched in

A parrot's cage, gilded all over, with a red cover

A walnut writing desk

A walnut bed, with columns for curtains gilded with several motifs, which the maids say comes from Madama Cecilia Colonna ...

Two small lady's chairs of old gilded leather

A green harpsichord ...

Pieces of *spalliere* panelling for the said chamber, with fragments of figures

Gilded leather to furnish the said room

Carpeting for the chests ...

... and several chests containing chemises, scarves and other clothing, bed-coverings and household linens, carpets and furnishing fabrics, silversmith's work and coins. The adjoining *studiolo* included:

A bronze figure, with a bow in hand

A casket banded with steel, covered with black velvet, with a tin box with trinkets inside ...

A bag with pearls ... a bag containing a little gold crucifix, with four rubies, not very valuable, with five pearls

A gold needlecase

A small gold container, formed like a small dolphin ...

A crown of blue enamel, with olive motifs and gold motifs

A crown of cornelian

An ebony crown, small with motifs in gilded Perugia work

On the shelves of the said *studiolo*:

Vases and flasks of various kinds of *reticella*[7] glass, 50 pieces

7 With complex patterns made from white threads blown with the glass.

...

Three porcelain dishes, and two smaller dishes

Five porcelain bowls

...

A painting of Piera

A painting of Dante

Books, old

Three large majolica dishes, two painted and one white.

14.12 Presents of luxury lingerie

Several of the letters to various mistresses of the Venetian writer Andrea Calmo detail his lavish gifts, here of embroidered undergarments.

Andrea Calmo, *Delle lettere di M. Andrea Calmo* (Venice, 1572), fol. 57r–v.

To Madama Orsolina

My most beloved mistress, it is the first day of the year, when all courteous people send gifts to those to whom they wish well, so I have tried to buy you something which will please you and do me honour. First, I send you two chemises of Rheims cloth[8] embroidered by a Jewish woman in Crete. One you will see is done in the Apulian style in crimson silk, with the wedding of Cupid and Psyche celebrated in the clouds on its front. At the stomach is Priapus' infatuation with the nymph Lotis in a cypress grove; on the shoulders, Mars and Venus copulating, caught under Vulcan's net; on the left sleeve, the triumph of Neptune, and Thetis with Glaucus, Triton and Galatea in the sea; on the right, Orpheus on a hilltop playing his lyre and singing, surrounded by different animals.

The courtesan as a paragon of beauty

Numerous poems and prose writings, whether or not tongue-in-cheek, extol individual courtesans as exemplifying current ideals of beauty and surpassing beauties of antiquity.

---

8 Fine linen, a status symbol.

14.13 A courtesan compared to antique beauties

The Venetian writer and musician Girolamo Parabosco writes to his mistress, using the elegant rhetoric with which courtesans expected to be wooed in a letter probably always intended for publication. The females mentioned were well known as some of the loves of Jupiter.

Girolamo Parabosco, *Lettere amorose* (Venice, 1545), fols 6v–7r.

My life's sweetness, can you imagine how much suffering I endure through my envy for the luckiest of lucky papers, that soon will be worthy to touch those whitest of hands, to be admired by those charming eyes without which Love would be neither feared nor revered? I swear to you, I am so tormented by what might happen to this letter I write you, that I have written a thousand others this very hour and burnt them all ... Alas, I remember all those tricks the gods used to employ to enjoy their object of love, and turn icy-cold for fear lest Jupiter changes himself into this sheet so as to touch those beautiful hands and those fair breasts which you used for a while as a dear and blessed lodging for other of my writings. Well might I fear this, for I am sure that neither Leda, Europa, nor Danae, for whom he changed himself into a swan, a bull or a golden shower, could compare with you in beauty, grace or virtue.

14.14 A Roman courtesan like a goddess

In Pietro Fortini's *Novella XI*, Ippolito, a young Sienese gentleman in Rome, is befriended by the maid of a successful courtesan (perhaps Lucrezia da Clarice, known as 'Matrema non vole', who flourished in 1520s Rome), who takes him to her mistress.

Pietro Fortini, in *Raccolta di novellieri italiani*, 2 pts, (Florence, 1834), pt 2, pp. 1180–1.

She led me up through an ample, spacious staircase, in order to conduct me into a decorated reception room, looking out on one side to the river, and on the other, towards the Belvedere and the Vatican Palace. This room was entirely decked out in gilded leather wall-hanging, with the finest pictures, and in it, on a rich chair, there was a beautiful and charming young woman of eighteen years, dressed in the richest clothes, with an infinite number of gold trimmings and clusters of pearls, with jewels and gold chains, so that she seemed like the most radiant sun. When I had thus arrived, I remained transfixed for a time, not knowing if I was dreaming, or if what I saw was true;

and, overwhelmed by so much beauty from the lady adorning the
room, from the superb clothes she was wearing, from the rich jewels
with which she was bedecked, I remained as if stunned ... The courteous lady, all charming and gentle, rose to her feet, and with
unassuming grace placed herself before me, and with many dainty and
affable words made me welcome. When I heard her speak so sweetly,
so close to me, it seemed to me that though the dark night had fallen,
day was breaking, as when you begin to see the sun, when all the
green hills lighten up, the birds begin singing, the hares burst out
running, the deer begin to leap, and all animals give signs of joy ...

After supper and conversation:

Then the lady took me by the hand, and led me to a rich and lordly
chamber, all decked out in silk draperies, where there was a bed with
the most superb curtains and a truly royal coverlet and, above all, such
delicate, fine, and lustrous sheets, that they seemed like delicate, fine
and lustrous white of egg ... She took off her outer clothing, and
remained in a skirt of crimson silk all figured with gold thread, so that
she certainly seemed as beautiful as she did fully garbed. Also there
was a hairnet worked with gold and pearls, with a border made with
the finest gold work, bound with a thousand rich jewels of great price,
which she wore as a headdress, as it's usually called, and beneath it her
golden wavy tresses were lovely to view. And thus, taking off her cap
and hairnet, she put on a little hair-band embroidered with different
sorts of flowers and golden stars. Then she took from her neck a
precious and extremely costly necklace of oriental pearls, bigger than
the biggest chickpeas you could find. When she had placed these on a
table serving as furniture in her bedroom, she took off her underskirt
as well, since spring was in mid-bloom, stripping down to her chemise
to enable her to go to bed, and also taking off her shoes. So beautiful
and finely made was this lady that she seemed like a divine being, like
nothing more than an exquisite rose, plucked fresh under the warm
rays of dawn, as she revealed her well-fashioned flesh of rubies and
pearls, which could be seen under the flimsiest of undershirts. When
I saw her undressed like this, with the splendour of her charms, I was
stupefied, having never seen a sight more rare or beautiful ... I
certainly maintain that even the woman to whom Paris, in his false
judgement, gave the apple[9] was not as beautiful, nor do I believe an
equally beautiful woman could be found ... and so that night, when I

9 Venus.

had thought myself lost, stuck in a dark inferno, in my good fortune I found myself in blissful paradise.

The courtesan's social world

Numerous courtesans who mastered 'courtly' skills were praised for reciting poetry and singing and playing music. Their salons attracted the socially eminent and the artists and writers of their day, who were not necessarily their lovers. Some famous courtesans feature in chapters 2 and 15: here brief extracts suggest social and cultural worlds and friendships of these and others.

14.15 Praise for Tullia d'Aragona

A letter from Battista Stambellino to Isabella d'Este on 13 June 1537, praises Tullia d'Aragona (c. 1510–56).

J. Cartwright, *Isabella d'Este, Marchioness of Mantua* (London, 1904), vol. 2, p. 384.

Your Excellency will hear how a courteous Roman courtesan, named Signora Tullia, happened to come to this country, coming to stay for a few months as I understand. She is pleasant, discreet, shrewd and endowed with very great and outstanding talents: she can sight-read any motet or *canzone*, she is peerless in discussion and speaking, and comports herself so agreeably that there is no man or woman in this land who equals her ... Her house is always full with distinguished men, and one can visit her at any time, and she is rich in money, jewels, necklaces and rings, and other goods of note, and in short she is well set up in everything.

14.16 A singer-courtesan portrayed

Vasari's 1568 *Life* of Domenico Puligo attests to the talents of Machiavelli's musician/actress mistress Barbara Raffacani Salutati, who, like several other courtesans, was portrayed by major painters.

Vasari (1984), vol. 4 Testo, p. 250.

He also drew a portrait of Barbara of Florence, a notorious and beautiful courtesan of the time, beloved of many for her beauty and fine manners, and because she was a good musician and sang divinely.

14.17 A supper party for a reformed courtesan

Many of Pietro Aretino's letters show not only amorous but respectful or comradely relationships between himself, various courtesans, and writers and artists of his acquaintance, as where he writes in December 1548 to Angela Zaffetta.

Aretino, vol. 2, pp. 881–2.

You are in my affections what Adria [10] is in flesh ... though I have been your adviser and mentor and patron since your tender girlhood, you have never experienced my love as other than what I feel for Austria,[11] born of my own blood. But if in my lascivious youth the conduct arising from the affection I bear you always kept within due limits, you may be sure that my respect for your honour is twice as great now, in my entirely chaste old age. So come to supper tomorrow with your long-standing supporters, Titian and [Jacopo] Sansovino: that's because their affection has doubled, inasmuch as you have changed your licentious way of life to a more continent one.

COURTESANS SPEAK

The following letters between courtesans and their lovers, or would-be lovers, suggest a range of relationships and motivations.

14.16 A profession of love

Alessandra Fiorentina was one of several women inhabiting a private brothel in Florence for Filippo Strozzi and his circle of male friends, whose intimate letters have fortuitously survived. In 1515–16 she writes to her lover, Francesco del Nero, expressing seemingly genuine affection.

Lettere di cortigiane del rinascimento, ed. A. Romano (Rome, 1990), pp. 90–1.

Illustrious and lofty lord, countless greetings!

Your last letter, received yesterday, was enormously welcome, and in thanks I'd like to mention a small trifle I've sent you. I marvel greatly at your words. Just as I've given you my heart, so also my possessions and all my living faculties are consigned and placed in your most precious of hands. Your Lordship may dispose of them as you yourself please, for I seek no other reward or recompense from your kindness

10 His elder daughter.
11 Another daughter.

than reciprocal love. Although the obligations we owe to you are countless, it is above all your favour which makes me indebted to you, and I value and hold it more dear than a gift of all the most precious treasures in the world. And I am certain, my most delectable lover, that I love you more than my own health, and long to please you more than myself.

... I grieve, my sole protector, that I can no longer see you as I once used to. At least, since the day is ruled out, let me enjoy the night, so I may take much consolation from the honeyed words issuing from your adorable mouth.

14.17 Penitence is hard

Others in the group at Florence moved to other cities, but stayed friendly with their former male associates. Here Beatrice of Ferrara writes from Rome in April 1517 to Lorenzo de' Medici, Duke of Urbino, then wounded in Ancona. Romano, pp. 143–5.

So that Your Excellency may know everything I've been doing, I want to write to you quickly and be accused of temerity, rather than not write, and be accused of negligence ... Certain cheeky men have worn me down so much, day and night doing you know what ... that I haven't had a minute to remember myself to you, I've been so busy ... I'll tell you another time! ... I resolved to give myself to spiritual things, and let it be known to all my lovers that they'd have to wait until another time ... Thus, half contrite, I went to confession with our preacher at S. Agostino.[12] I say our preacher, because however many whores we are in Rome, we all come to listen to him. So, seeing such a distinguished audience, his only concern is to convert us all. Ah, what a hard task! He'd have to preach a hundred years for me! Still, he's had some success, as Gambiera has become a nun and calls herself Sister Sophia ... and Tadea soon will too. As for me, I could well have done it, but every time I thought of not being able to do you know what, it just wasn't on. Still as I said I confessed to the preacher and for his troubles gave him 2 golden ducats, full weight, which I now bitterly regret ... On the same day as me, Gambiera and Tadea also confessed to the preacher – just think of what good stories he must have heard in one go! ... Having confessed, I straightaway gave myself

12 A Roman church well known as the haunt of courtesans.

up to spiritual matters, and began to pray to God for Your Excellency that, though I may be a sinner and a whore, I would wish above all other grace to be worthy of your health, and to be able to see Your Excellency in the same pristine state as before, vowing that if this were granted, I would make a pilgrimage to S. Maria di Loreto.[13] And so I've decided to go and carry out my obligation, and if it doesn't bother Your Excellency, will move to Ancona to kiss the feet of Your Excellency. Eight days, My Lord, I've been in a state of sanctity, and have never suffered worse!

14.20 A courtesan proclaims her integrity

By contrast, the letters of the Venetian courtesan Veronica Franco were published in her lifetime. She adapted the pre-existing genre of intimate letters to her own purposes, partly to demonstrate her literary ambitions and ethical aspirations. In this example from her *Lettere familiari* (1580) rejecting a lover's suit, she rebuts the charges of avarice and falsehood regularly levelled against courtesans.

Veronica Franco, *Lettere*, ed. B. Croce (Naples, 1949), pp. 29–31.

I cannot reward you with an equal return of the love you profess to bear me, as I have already fixed my thoughts elsewhere ... I could, with feigned adulation, something neither impossible nor difficult, have implanted an untrue opinion in you, in order to take advantage of you as the occasion arose, since you are a high-ranking gentleman, from whom I might have expected help and favours in many ways ... Lest I deceive you, I did not wish to do this, since I cannot love you. And when on other occasions I have happened to indicate this resolve discreetly to you, you have shown that you did not believe my words were true. Your belief was influenced by your desire: you interpreted my words as meaning that I was resisting your demands to make you keener and to encourage you to please me by making gifts ... You are quite wrong in imputing avarice to me, in thinking you can buy my love with rewards. Such a love would come from a woman who cannot compete in richness or other advantages with you, but still is not a vile woman who for a suitable price ransoms any part of her body, let alone her mind ... And the reason why I am displeased, why I feel you have upped the bidding for me, almost bargained for me (as though I were greatly enamoured by a self of so little worth), is this: if you would be

13 The supposed site of the Virgin's house; a very popular pilgrimage.

happy for it to be known and talked about that you love a woman you think venal, I too would be unhappy to be thought such by you.

NEGATIVE VIEWS OF COURTESANS

As well as government regulation and physical attacks, the sixteenth century saw much satire, invective, and moralising writing against courtesans and prostitutes, with a variety of ethical stances or motivations.

14.21 The courtesan as witch and grotesque

Zoppino's 1534 *Ragionamento* shows the association between prostitutes and witchcraft common at the time,[14] as well as a disgust with the physical realities of women's bodies that is much influenced by the misogyny in ancient Roman and early Christian writing.

Zoppino, pp. 18–22, 36–46.

If perchance they see the flow of gifts is slowing, they straightaway resort to Jewish witches and sorceresses ... I've seen so many in the paths [of cemeteries] laden with bones, heads and clothing of dead men! Many with pincers, scissors or clips extract teeth from skulls and putrefied jaws of hanged men, and also take their hats or shoes! And I've seen them carry off whole pieces of rotten flesh, which they give you to eat, saying words they know ... And I have met them by the light of the enchanting Moon, now with dishevelled hair, now naked, with the strange gestures and behaviour of witches, speaking words that I tremble to utter, the most devout of which are their calls to the Devil ... and some anoint themselves with holy oil ...

Indeed, you see cesspits, graves, harpies and carrion ... Since their faces are painted, do you think that their bodies are natural? Through excessive use, they are wrinkled and creased; their breasts floppy, like empty vessels hanging down. The ones you think most beautiful ... wear gloves when they sleep alone at night to heal hands covered with scabs and rashes ... so they can have soft hands to help make impotent men erect, and lead the blind to drink at the fountain. What's more, they make pastes with wax, honey and figs for their stomachs, or they smooth out their bellies with pine lotion ... and then with

14 Some real-life cases are discussed in G. Ruggiero, *Binding Passions* (Oxford, 1993), pp. 24–56, 90–4.

depilatories and baths ... darken their hairy limbs stinking with infections ... Most of the time they need to wear napkins or rags among their underclothes, so that corrupt discharges don't flow down their heavy thighs. Some always wear a sponge, and many keep it in place when you have your way with them, so as to seem a better catch since their slit is smaller, because when rubbing against these sponges you think it is narrower. I've seen so many caught out like this! ... And if you knew how they put powders, and ground glass, up their sexes, to mop up the humidity within, which scrape against a thousand unfortunate young men and make them cut their members! If you knew the thousandth part that I know, you would never desire them again, if you've seen them, as I have, in their domestic surroundings. I've seen them going to the privy in the evening making a noise like all the guns in Castel Sant'Angelo going off, or at least like fireworks: that's the loud shriek of unborn souls descending from their rears. With their thick thighs, and their hands soiled with the bloody discharge cascading from their cunts, do you think they can have any sense of right? ... When you're in bed with them, and have had a bit of sport, lift the sheet a little, and sniff it ... Make them walk around a bit in the bedroom naked, you'll see lots of things that disgust you ... This is the remedy for love.[15]

14.22 The courtesan as robber

By contrast, the *Trentuno de la Zaffetta* (late 1530s), a vicious pornographic satire on Aretino's friend, is marked by the disdain of the aristocratic author, Lorenzo Venier, for the pretensions of courtesans. Zaffetta's false airs, avarice and gluttony are seen as undermining the patrician order, and will be punished by a humiliating multiple rape, graphically described.

Lorenzo Venier, *Le Trente et un de la Zaffetta* (Paris, 1883), pp. 10–15.

> In Venice, by grace of God, sir,
> are three or four legions of whores
> ruining patricians and plebeians alike,
> some in grand houses, some in the brothel district ...
> [Among the top few] there's just one
> behaving as if the best of this damned crew.
> ... Her Highness is named Zaffetta,
> claims to be born of royal blood ...

15 A reference to Ovid's *Remedies for Love*.

Suffice to say, Zaffetta goes perfumed,
in silk and gold, in stately pomp and splendour
... Her grand, exalted state,
which corrupts our gentlemen each hour,
comes from a sort of self-indulgence
born of effeminacy, competitiveness and folly,
which seeks now this, now the other idler.
To this Harpy, who despises who best loves her,
they have given, without desert nor pleasure,
their souls and money, to their rotten regret.
Avarice is the great force which clutches at a whore,
so that for a coin, a farthing,
an old glove, a piece of shoe-lace,
anything of lesser price,
she'll always rob you, with deceitful, flattering words.
So avid is her appetite for thieving
that even in the brothel where she lives
she'll pinch this or that.

14.23 The dangers and miseries of the life of a courtesan

Veronica Franco gives an insider's view of the hazards of life as a courtesan, writing to a friend ambitious to make her daughter one.

Franco, p. 38; A. R. Jones and M. F. Rosenthal, *Veronica Franco. Poems and Selected Letters* (Chicago, 1998), p. 39.

It is too wretched, and too contrary to human reason, to subject one's body and one's efforts to a servitude such as one dreads to think of. To make yourself the prey of so many, with the risk of being despoiled, robbed, killed, deprived in a single day of so much that you have accumulated from so many over so long a time, with so many dangers of injury or of catching horrible contagious diseases; to eat with another's mouth, sleep with another's eyes, move according to another's will, always clearly rushing towards the shipwreck of your faculties and your life. What greater misery! What riches, what comforts, what delights can compensate for this? Believe me, of all the world's misfortunes, this is the worst, and then, if you add to worldly matters those of the soul, what perdition and certainty of damnation is this?

ATTEMPTS AT REFORM

Prostitution concerned many reformers, particularly as part of the drive for moral and social improvement of the mid-sixteenth-century Catholic revival. Both laypeople and religious orders, especially the Jesuits and the Barnabites, involved themselves in such work. As well as preaching and writing against prostitution, reformers built up institutions all over Italy for the rehabilitation or support of penitent, needy or sick fallen women, and also (see chapter 6) for the instruction of their children.[16] Varying in strictness, these houses combined features of hospitals, workhouses, schools and convents, and frequently received charitable donations from more affluent members of society.

14.24 **An Imperial ambassador's widow rescues fallen women**

Letter of 1545 on the activities of Donna Eleonora de Vega, widow of Don Giovanni de Vega, recruiting prostitutes for the house of S. Marta in Rome, founded by Ignatius Loyola.

P. Tacchi Venturi, *Storia della Compagnia di Gesù* (Rome, 1950–1), vol. 2, p. 169

Dona Eleonora, wife of Don Giovanni de Vega, the Imperial ambassador, has put such effort into that house [of S. Marta, Rome, for reformed prostitutes] as to make news worthy of praise to Our Lord God, and cause confusion to many. She takes a servant woman with her, solely to accompany her on rounds of the houses of fallen women to try to convert them. Only yesterday it was heard she caused yet another to do this ... She seeks to speak with those she meets in churches and streets and then brings them to the house, where she welcomes all those wishing to convert to good living, so that they are placed in S. Marta or the Convertite. Two days ago they encountered one of the most famous courtesans in S. Agostino, and begged and exhorted her to leave sinning, and they induced her to recognise her faults and misdemeanours with deep penitence, and took her to the palace. Already through her efforts five or six such women have been placed securely in S. Marta, and Our Lord has so filled her bosom with love, that she seems almost drunk with her holy service. Often she

16 See S. Cohen, *The Evolution of Women's Asylums since 1500: From Refuges for Ex-Prostitutes to Shelters for Battered Women* (New York, 1992), and L. Ferrante, 'Honor Regained: Women in the Casa del Soccorso in San Paolo in Sixteenth Century Bologna', in E. Muir and G. Ruggiero, eds, *Sex and Gender in Historical Perspective* (Baltimore, 1990), pp. 46–72.

comes to visit the house of S. Marta and admires the penitents in the service of Our Lord, so that Rome is full of news of such an edifying example.

14.25 Establishing a refuge for former prostitutes in Venice

Veronica Franco in 1577 petitions the Venetian government to establish a House of Refuge, the Casa del Soccorso, for repentant prostitutes that would be less strict than the existing, quasi-monastic, Convertite.

M. F. Rosenthal, *The Honest Courtesan. Veronica Franco, Citizen and Writer in Sixteenth-Century Venice* (Chicago, 1992), p. 131.

There are many women, who through their poverty, or inclination, or some other reason, have led an immoral life, who are sometimes moved by the Spirit of the Divine Majesty. Thinking of the end to which such a life most usually leads, miserable both for body and soul, they would readily turn away from their wrongdoing if they had a decent place to repair to, where they could support themselves and their children, because they are not allowed to enter the Zitelle[17] or even the Convertite since they have mothers or children or husbands, or other obligations. Besides, it would be hard to make them change suddenly from such great licentiousness to a strict and austere way of life, such as at the Convertite. From this lack of provision stems their persistence in their habits ... and the still worse abomination of needy mothers secretly selling the virginity of their own innocent daughters.

17 For children of prostitutes.

15 Writers, artists, musicians and performers

One incontestable change during the period covered by this book was the emergence of a significant number of women who wrote, made and composed music, acted, or practised the visual arts. Lack of space prevents this chapter from providing adequate analyses of their individual achievements or extensive samples of their works. Rather, it will try to suggest the diversity of the women involved and of the contexts in which they operated, and their reception in their different fields, each with its own conventions.

The increased female audience fostered by changes in women's training and education was clearly a very important factor. Literacy had been encouraged among at least some women from the later fourteenth century, and the advent and expansion of printing (including music publishing) from the late fifteenth century onwards made both much more, and more diverse, material available more cheaply to a wide readership, including literate women. Although women were frequently urged to limit their reading matter (see 6.11), and to show modesty in intellectual ambition, this increased material could broaden tastes and encourage emulation of other practitioners. Furthermore, by the later fifteenth century the evolving ideal of the court lady encouraged female participation in music and dance, and awareness of literature and the visual arts. By the mid-sixteenth century this seems also to have been true of some women from upper mercantile and professional backgrounds, and also *cortigiane oneste*.

To turn readers, listeners, or viewers into practitioners, other conditions were needed (other than innate talent). Important were sympathetic family environments; helpful education or training; influential associates; and awareness of female precedents. Finally, art genres needed to be of a kind to which women could contribute, given the sort of training or education society allowed them, and which they could reshape in fresh ways: lyric poetry, letters, dialogues, madrigals and portraits are the outstanding examples.

BACKGROUNDS, SETTINGS, TRAINING, MENTORS

The excerpts in this section are intended to show the range of intellectual, creative and performing women at different times and places, where possible giving insight into how they were trained and fostered, with family encouragement and the help of teachers, mentors or patrons.

Humanist women, writing in Latin

15.1 Battista Malatesta

The revival of antique learning in the late fourteenth or early fifteenth centuries allowed a few women, initially solely aristocratic, to learn Latin letters with the help of parents, family tutors or learned nuns. This skill might be maintained through personal contacts with humanists and displayed in letters for circulation among friends, or, in rare instances, in public speaking.[1] Giuseppe Betussi's additions in his 1545 translation of Boccaccio's *De mulieribus claris* cite several aristocratic learned women, here Battista da Montefeltro Malatesta (1383–1450), married to the lord of Rimini.

Betussi/Boccaccio (1547), fols 158v–159r.

Battista Malatesta ... had an almost divine intellect and was very well versed in letters, so that she had such clear, precise speech in both Latin and the Italian that she was held to far surpass any other person of those days. She wrote such numerous excellent and skilful Latin speeches, both to the Emperor Sigismund and to many cardinals, and recited parts of them herself so gracefully and to such universal wonderment, that she was thought a new Demosthenes. Moreover, she was not unfamiliar with good Philosophy. She had many arguments to overcome those several men who disputed with her in philosophy. She took divine precepts much to heart, and composed a book in Latin on human frailty based on Holy Scripture, and another on true religion. She also wrote many letters to different people, in which her purity and polish, and her calibre, were evident. She made an oration to Pope Martin ... that not only Pope Martin but all the College of Cardinals praised to the skies, and he recorded it in a letter. This most distinguished lady also wrote many other things seemingly futile to record, since time has consumed most of them.

15.2 Laura Cereta

The case of Laura Cereta (1469–99) shows how two generations later an

---

1 For women humanists, see M. King and A. Rabil Jr, *Her Immaculate Hand* (Binghamton, NY, 1983).

exceptional girl from a professional background in Brescia, given family support, might acquire a knowledge of Latin language and literature, as described in a letter of 5 November 1486.

Laura Cereta, *Laura Cereta: Collected Letters of a Renaissance Feminist*, ed. and trans. D. Robin, (Chicago, 1997), p. 27 (translation of Diana Robin, with permission of University of Chicago Press).

My father ... soon sent me back to my instructress in liberal studies [a learned nun], since I had already begun to be bored with childish pursuits ... With all the vigor of my genius depending on her, my teacher, I immersed myself night and day, blinking back my fatigue, in long vigils of study. Then in my eleventh year, after I had entered into this dry diet, I was removed from the discipline of the rod ...

At home, as though starving for knowledge, I diligently studied the eloquence of the tragic stage and the polish of Tully[2] in so far as I was able. But when scarcely a year had gone by, I assumed the responsibility for almost all of the household duties myself. Thus it was my lot to grow old when I was not far from childhood. Even so, I attended lectures on mathematics during the days when I was free from toil, and I did not neglect those profitable occasions when, unable to sleep, I devoured the mellifluous voiced prophets of the Old Testament and figures from the New Testament.

Women writing in the vernacular

Only a few female writers in Italian are known from the later fifteenth century. Some, such as Lucrezia Tornabuoni and Antonia Pulci (see chapters 4 and 5), had links with the vernacular devotional writing that produced *laudi* and plays for confraternities and convents;[3] others came from sophisticated circles in which lyric poems in the Petrarchan/Platonic tradition circulated. In the next century such exchanges of letters and poems with literary men gave encouragement and led to publication.[4]

---

2 Cicero.

3 K. Gill, 'Women and the Production of Religious Literature in the Vernacular', in Matter and Coakley, pp. 64–104.

4 For overviews of women writers in Italian, see K. Wilson, ed., *Women Writers of the Renaissance and Reformation* (Athens, Ga., 1989), L. A. Stortoni, ed. and trans., and M. Prentice Lillie, trans., *Women Poets of the Italian Renaissance* (New York, 1997).

15.3 Veronica Gambara: a literary exchange

The aristocratic Veronica Gambara (1485–1550) was a pioneer in achieving wide fame for her verse, though she never published a volume under her sole authorship during her lifetime. Her correspondence with the very influential Pietro Bembo over several decades suggests the value of personal contacts for an aspiring writer.

Pietro Bembo, *Opere in volgare*, ed. M. Marti (Florence, 1961), pp. 857–8; Francesco Sansovino, *Lettere da diversi re e prencipi e cardinali e altri uomini dotti a Mons. Pietro Bembo scritte*, ed. D. Perocco (Ferrara, 1985, reprint of Venice edn, 1560), fols 23r–v, 25v–26r.

Bembo to Gambara, 11 September 1504:

Your charming and delightful sonnet has been so dear to me, that I can declare that I am sending one I wrote in reply, not without much envy for your creation: it will be happy, inasmuch as it will enjoy your presence, and uncertain, inasmuch as it fears your verdict.

Gambara to Bembo, 22 January 1531:

Today I have written two sonnets on the death of Sannazaro.[5] I am sending them to your lordship, as my light and escort. Had I had the ability to phrase them better, I would have done so. Excuse me for being a woman and ignorant.

Bembo to Gambara, 27 May 1532:

I am having my *Rime* reprinted, and have collected two sonnets which I once wrote to you, and want to include them with the others. My printed verse was in reply to poems similar to one you wrote me when still a girl, which began: '*S'a voi da me non pur veduto mai*'. By chance I have mislaid this sonnet – I have only the first line I've mentioned – and I cannot find it anywhere. So I beg you to be so good as to search for it among your papers and send me it, so I can also put it in this book being reprinted.

Gambara to Bembo, 19 October 1540:

I have resolved, as I am writing to you, to send you a sonnet seen by no-one, born I don't know how, as it has been completed for many days. You will see what I have tried, but not succeeded, to express ... Just as I dedicated my first efforts to Your Reverence, so I

---

5 Jacopo Sannazaro, the Neapolitan writer (d. 1530). 'Occasional' poetry was an important part of the oeuvre of Gambara and other sixteenth-century poets.

am sending you this, which I think will be the last, and once again kiss
your hands.

15.4 Women's poetry printed with male endorsements

By mid-century, a few women's writings appeared under their own names, an
important precedent being the collection of poems by Vittoria Colonna
(1492–1547) in 1538.[6] Support from male associates in the literary coteries or
informal academies that were springing up at this time was important psycho-
logically and practically. Volumes by Tullia d'Aragona (c. 1510–56) in 1547,
Laura Terracina (1519–77) from 1548 and Gaspara Stampa (1524–54) in 1554
were accompanied by endorsements from such men.

Simone dalla Volta, in Tullia d'Aragona, *Rime della Sig. Tullia d'Aragona*
(Venice, 1547), fol. 40v.

> TULLIA, a prodigy, a miracle, a Sibyl,
> at whom the world both marvels and rejoices;
> a sea of knowledge, bottomless, unbounded,
> carrying joyful, tranquil waves,
> from which such gentle moisture, such lucid drops
> of virtue true, and rarely found today,
> which fortune cannot spoil nor time erode;
> less than with Sappho or Camilla ...

15.5 Women writers and their literary worlds

Support also came from the *poligrafi*, the productive literary all-rounders
involved in treatise-writing, translations and editorial work. Aware of women
as readers and as dedicatees, they might see the potential of women as writers,
if only for their novelty value. Such men – Dolce, Domenichi, Ruscelli and
others – edited the nine successive volumes, variously entitled *Rime diverse* ...
or *Rime di diversi* ... of an important poetry anthology appearing from 1545
to 1560, where many women writers featured (see 5:3).[7] Other literary men
also encouraged women to experiment with genres other than lyric, occasional
and religious verse, and in a few cases, such as Veronica Franco (1580), to
publish their own letters and to do editorial work. Franco's most important
literary mentor was Domenico Venier: here her correspondent is unknown.

Veronica Franco, *Lettere*, ed. B. Croce (Naples, 1949), p. 39.

---

6 G. Rabitti, 'Vittoria Colonna as a Role Model for Cinquecento Women Poets', in
  Panizza, pp. 478–97.
7 L. Dolce, L. Domenichi *et al.*, *Rime diverse di molti eccellenti autori*, 9 vols (Venice,
  Bologna and Cremona, 1545–60).

And I beg you to indulge me by agreeing to use your most refined skills in the composition of whatever number of sonnets that time and my entreaties permit you, on the occasion of the death of the illustrious Count Estore Martinengo, whom I hold in great respect. And in addition to the sense of duty I feel to commemorate him and the surviving members of his whole family, I've been asked by a man whose wish is my command to compose some sonnets myself and to have all my friends and lords write on this subject. So, not dawdling at all in the task of commissioning such works, I've begged many other noble spirits to favour me by writing, and many whom I've asked have already written.

Female musicians and singers

Though barred from participating in major church choirs or court chapels, women made music in many other settings.[8] Inventories show that possession of musical instruments spread down into the urban artisan class; all types of people might sing. By the earlier sixteenth century musical skills had become not only desirable for court ladies and courtesans (and, working within different musical traditions, for nuns) but for the middle classes. Thus a broad base was established from which talented individuals might rise to give public performances, in differing contexts.

15.6 Singers for a play in Florence

Machiavelli, from Florence, to Francesco Guicciardini, on working with the singer/actress Barbara Raffacani Salutati, his mistress but clearly a professional performer heading a troupe of singers.

Niccolò Machiavelli, *Tutte le opere*, ed. G. Mazzoni and M. J. Casella (Florence, 1929), pp. 907–8, 911.

October 1525: Lodovico Alamanni and I dined these last evenings with Barbara and discussed the play, so she has offered to come with her singers and perform the choral work between the acts. I have offered to write songs appropriate to the action, and Lodovico has offered to give her and her singers lodging ...

3 January 1526: As for Barbara and the singers ... I believe I can

8 Several relevant essays are in J. Bowers and J. Tick, eds, *Women Making Music. The Western Art Tradition, 1150–1950* (Urbana, 1986).

attract her for fifteen *soldi* to the *lire* – I say this since she has various lovers who might prevent her, but they can be calmed down with careful handling. And you have this assurance that she and I have decided to come: we have composed five new songs relating to the play, and they have been given music to be sung between the acts, so that you can consider them.

15.7 A concert in Venice

Venice had a lively musical life, helped by the presence of a vigorous publishing industry with many writers who could produce or adapt words for madrigals and other songs. Music was an important element in middle-class social gatherings and in more public concerts.

Anton Francesco Doni, 7 April, 1544, appended to his *Dialogo della musica*, in M. Feldman, *City Culture and the Madrigal at Venice* (Berkeley and Los Angeles, 1996), pp. 32–3, n. 38.

There is a gentlewoman, Polisena Pecorina, consort of a citizen from my native town, so talented and refined that I cannot find words high enough to praise her. One evening I heard a concert of *violoni* and voices in which she played and sang together with other excellent spirits.

15.8 Girl choirs from orphan hospitals

Large-scale choral or orchestral music-making needed institutional support, which for women was provided, apart from convents, by houses for orphans and for girls in moral danger. Many became known for their choral singing; the excellent training eventually produced women, often from very humble backgrounds, who could earn fame, or at least a living, through their musical talents.[9]

Vecellio (1590), p. 148v.

And among the other wonderful and praiseworthy things one observes about them [the orphan girls in Venetian hospitals], not the least is the sweetness of their choral singing for their divine services, so harmoniously that many quit the main churches and go eagerly to their churches to hear them sing. These girls accompany the dead to burial, and leave the house for other reasons, but in pairs, with such modesty and chastity, and always singing, that one should indeed

9 J. Baldauf-Berdes, *Women Musicians of Venice: Musical Foundations* (Oxford, 1993).

thank God for the original founders of such holy institutions, and for present-day people giving them a helping hand.

15.9 Two girl musicians

Professional female musicians who received a regular salary or other payments at court certainly existed from at least the early sixteenth century. Only decades later is information fuller, however, as their participation in the increasingly elaborate court musical entertainments became more significant. They seem overwhelmingly to have been the daughters or other relatives of male musicians, like the girls Lucia and Isabella from the Pellizzari family of musicians employed at the Mantuan court and at the Teatro Olimpico, Vicenza, in the later sixteenth century.

I. Fenlon, *Music and Patronage in Sixteenth-Century Mantua* (Cambridge, 1980), vol. 1, p. 128, n. 20; p. 132.

The listeners were especially astonished by the sound of the cornet and trombone made by two young daughters of Pellizzari, the custodian [*custode*] of the Academy [...]

The following madrigal was sung[10] with exquisite style and skill, by two young girls in service with the Most Serene Duke of Mantua, with no small envy from lovers of such eminent talent.

15.10 A Jewish singer

Several Jewish musicians are known, working not only within their community but for urban or courtly audiences, such as Europa Rossi, employed by the Mantuan court in the 1580s and 1590s, and described by an observer, Federico Follino, in 1608.

Federico Follino, *Compendio delle sontuose feste ...*, in D. Harrán, *Salamone Rossi. Jewish Musician in Late Renaissance Mantua* (Oxford, 1999), p. 37.

A woman understanding music to perfection, she sang to the listeners' great delight and great wonder, in a most delicate and sweet-sounding voice ... delightfully modulating her mournful tones which caused the listeners to shed tears of compassion.

---

10 At the wedding of Christine of Lorraine and Grand Duke Ferdinand of Tuscany in 1589.

15.11 A woman composer

Rather later, the daughters of the musician Giulio Caccini attained great fame at Mantua and elsewhere. Settimia (*fl.* 1600–20) has been estimated to have been the highest paid of all musicians in Italy of her day. Francesca (1587–after 1626) also composed, as is mentioned in a letter by her father of 1607.

Giulio Caccini, from W. Kirkendale, *The Court Musicians of Florence during the Principate of the Medici* (Florence, 1993), p. 314.

Over several years she has rewritten 300 works by her hand in three books, with all those passages of inventions that others can imagine, and with them the finest emotions that could be produced by anyone practising solo singing. Finally she has banished the fear of poetry that inhibited her, and has composed both the words and the music for several madrigals and *canzonette*, which have much pleased those who have heard them.

Visual artists

Drawing was often taught in the home or the convent in conjunction with making embroidery designs or embellishing manuscripts. However, women aspiring to paint in oils and to do large-scale public commissions needed further training, explaining why so many successful women artists were the daughters of painters, like Marietta Tintoretto and Lavinia Fontana.

15.12 Lavinia Fontana and her protectors

The support from a range of males helps explain why Lavinia Fontana of Bologna (1552–1614) became the most wide-ranging and successful female artist of the period.[11]

Giulio Mancini, *Considerazioni della pittura*, ed. A. Marucchi (Rome, 1956), vol. 1, pp. 233–5 [published Bologna, 1620]; M. T. Cantaro, *Lavinia Fontana bolognese 'pittora singolare'* (Milan, 1989), p. 319.

So our Lavinia, born in this homeland and of that father, had natural talent and family training to enable her to progress as she evidently did, since she had already become famous for her works and especially

---

11 See C. P. Murphy, *Lavinia Fontana: A Painter and her Patrons in Sixteenth-Century Bologna* (New Haven and London, 2003).

for portraits, which were valued highly, as seen in her self-portrait done as a virgin in the year 1578. She was then married by her father to [Giovan Antonio Zappi], also a painter, though more with words than with brushes, as he did not practice himself, but he had good judgement and knew it, so that this helped his wife greatly in the profession.

She was brought to Rome with her husband and family and protected and favoured by the Cardinals of Ascoli and of Este: by the first she was commissioned to do the altarpiece in S. Sabina and the other allocated her comfortable rooms in his palace.

15.13 Marietta Tintoretto

Carlo Ridolfi's short biography of Marietta Tintoretto (d. 1590), published in Venice in 1648, suggests the importance not only of paternal protection but of the polite social accomplishments acquired by middle-class girls of the time.

Carlo Ridolfi, *Le maraviglie dell'arte*, ed. D. von Hadeln (Rome, 1965), vol. 2, p. 79.

There lived in Venice Marietta Tintoretto, the daughter of the famous Tintoretto, and the dearest delight of his genius, and taught by him in drawing and colouring, so that she produced works that made men marvel at her lively intellect. When she was a little girl she was dressed as a boy, and taken with him by her father wherever he went ... She was especially talented at doing portraits well ... She portrayed many Venetian gentlemen and ladies, who came to her willingly, as she had genteel manners and entertained them with music and singing.

15.14 Plautilla Nelli, a nun artist

Other female artists picked up skills as best they could. Vasari's passage on one such, the Florentine nun Plautilla Nelli (1523–88), within his 1568 'Life' of Properzia de' Rossi, stresses the limitations of such autodidacticism, even if Suor Plautilla was helped by existing convent traditions of illumination.[12]

Vasari (1984), vol. 4 Testo, p. 404.

---

12 See *Suor Plautilla Nelli (1523–1588): The First Woman Painter of Florence* (Florence, 2000).

Of these women [comparable to Properzia de' Rossi], the first is Suor Plautilla, a nun and currently prioress in the monastery of St Catherine of Siena in Florence ... Having begun little by little to draw and to imitate in colour panels and paintings of fine masters, she has with much effort finished several pieces that make connoisseurs marvel ... And since this venerable and talented sister, before she executed panels and important works, used to do miniatures, there are many fine paintings by her as well as others by various others who don't deserve mention. But those by her hand are better than those she modelled them on, which shows that she would have done wonderful work had she had the opportunity to study and pay attention to *disegno* and depict living, natural things, as men do.

15.15 A print-maker

The new phenomenon of printing provided opportunities for female print-makers, as well as writers, editors and publishers.

Francesco Peranda in 1609 to the husband of the print-maker Diana Mantovana (*c.* 1547–1612), from M. Bury, *The Print in Renaissance Italy 1550–1620* (London, 2001), no. 67, p. 107.

That *Feast of the Gods* [after Giulio Romano] is an amazing piece, so that even I, who had the warmest opinion of her, remain overcome by her talent, and I confess that I underestimated her worth.

POSITIVE CRITICAL REACTIONS

Positive reactions to learned or creative women were often framed with reference to appropriate famous practitioners mentioned in antique sources. However, the fact that authors often feel the need to emphasise the virtue of the women practitioners implies doubt about this novel phenomenon, an issue to be explored later.

Learned or humanist women

The prestige of the scholarly tongue made it easy for humanist women to be accommodated within the evolving 'famous women' tradition.

15.16 Isotta Nogarola

Giovanni Sabadino degli Arienti, writing around 1490, stresses the chastity, as well as the learning, of Isotta Nogarola (1418–66) from Verona: later lack of acceptance may have forced her retreat into a convent.

Sabadino degli Arienti, pp. 174–7.

Isotta ... dedicated herself to this virginal state as did Varro's Marcia, a perpetual virgin ... Isotta to avoid sloth devoted herself to learning, and in these divine studies was not less excellent than Marcia was in the knowledge of painting. This Isotta, then, was a woman of religion and piety, abstinent and inclined to fasting, full of gravity and so much learning and eloquence, that I believe she surpassed any other famous woman of antiquity, as demonstrated in her brilliant speeches, written for Popes Nicholas V and Pius II ... She was learned in theology and philosophy, in which she composed a major dialogue on whose was the greater sin, Adam's or Eve's, when they ate the forbidden fruit of the all-powerful God in the earthly paradise. She learnt almost all the Bible by heart, and was excellently versed in sacred literature, with which she came to be so familiar that she could scarcely utter a word without some eloquent allusion to the works of Augustine and of Jerome ... her dress was like that of a widow: she wore a black mantle, with which she kept her head covered.

15.17 Cassandra Fedele

Cassandra Fedele (1465–1558) attained fame from the late 1480s, giving orations at the University of Padua and before doges, and corresponding with many learned and distinguished men in northern Italy, most famously with the Florentine poet Poliziano (1454–94). His eulogy to her was published and became widely known.

Agnolo Poliziano to Cassandra Fedele, in *Cassandra Fedele. Letters and Orations*, ed. and trans. D. Robin (Chicago, 2000), pp. 90–1 (translation of Diana Robin, with permission of University of Chicago Press).

O maiden, glory of Italy ...

... In our own time when few men have achieved much in literature, only you, a girl, exist, who would rather comb a book than wool, paint with a quill rather than rouge, stitch with a pen rather than a needle, and who would rather cover papyrus with ink than her skin with white powder ... You will, Cassandra, write subtle, elegant, articulate Latin missives, and although with a certain girlish grace, a certain virginal simplicity, they will still be very sweet and also serious and prudent. I have also read your oration, which is erudite, eloquent, sonorous, brilliant and full of felicitous talent. Nor have we heard that you lacked the ability to compose extemporaneously, a gift that even great orators sometimes lack. You are also said when you practice dialectics, to tie knots that cannot be unknotted and to explicate mysteries that others have never before solved. Thus you so comprehend philosophy that you quickly and vehemently defend all questions posed and formulated and you dare, though a maid, to run with the men. Thus it was in the playing field of scholarly studies that sex did not stay in the way of your mind, nor mind in the way of modesty, nor modesty in the way of genius. And though no one would fail to praise you, still you restrain your own and your audience's opinion of you modestly and respectfully when you cast your virginal eyes down on the ground.

Women writing in the vernacular

When publishing made Gambara, Colonna and Terracina generally well known, unlike earlier women vernacular writers, all three were further helped by elevated backgrounds, respectable lives and uncontroversial subject matter.

15.18 Ariosto on Vittoria Colonna

Colonna's pious widowhood and largely religious writings fused into a lofty ideal.

Ludovico Ariosto, *Orlando Furioso*, ed. M. Turchi and E. Sanguineti (Milan, 1982), vol. 2 (XXXVII), p. 1000.

> Not only has she immortalised herself
> with her lovely style, which the best of men would not despise,
> but can drag the one of whom she speaks or writes [13]
> out of the tomb, and give him eternal life.
> As the pale sister of Phoebus [14]
> spreads more light, and is more admired
> than Venus or Mercury or any other star
> which turns with the heavens or by itself,
> so she of whom I speak breathes eloquence
> above all other women, and sweetness too,
> and gives such power to her lofty words,
> as makes our age adorned by another heavenly sun.

13 Her dead husband.
14 The moon.

15.19 **Betussi on Gambara**

Gambara's elegance of style was frequently commended.
Betussi/Boccaccio (1547), fol. 214 r–v.

It can be said that in our language she has far excelled what Sappho and many other antique women did in their time. And she has been so graced by heaven, that she has expressed her concepts divinely, with a sweet, soft, fluent and grave harmony of style, so that all those features which are judged to be necessary in good poetry have been rediscovered, and we see in her a true light of our century.

15.20 **Lucrezia Gonzaga praises Gaspara Stampa**

By the mid sixteenth-century, several women writers praised or encouraged each other in verse or prose, as when a woman pioneer in publishing her own letters, Lucrezia Gonzaga, wrote to Lando on Gaspara Stampa.[15]

Lucrezia Gonzaga, *Lettere della molto illustre Sig. La Sra Donna Lucretia Gonzaga da Gazuolo* (Venice, 1552), p. 325.

I have read over a thousand times the sonnet written in your praise by the talented Madonna Gaspara Stampa, which seemed to me so wonderful, and to have issued from so fine a vein, that I could not believe that any woman could have written it, now that the Marchioness of Pescara[16] and Signora Veronica Gambara have gone to heaven. And I would still doubt it, had I not heard the kind of talk of her that I must believe. I will stay silent about the many testimonies I have had from other parties of her remarkable intellect, so that I greatly rejoice for you that you have someone so learned to trumpet your praise.

Women musicians and performers

Of all creative women, it is female singers who seem to have received the most fulsome and unqualified praise for their interpretative skills and expressive powers. They made significant contribution to the development of the madrigal and to the music-dramas that would evolve into opera.

---

15 See F. Bassanese, *Gaspara Stampa* (Boston, 1983).
16 Vittoria Colonna.

15.21 Gaspara Stampa as singer

Gaspara Stampa, today best remembered as a poet, was in her own day as much praised as a singer in Venice,[17] as when the madrigalist Girolamo Parabosco wrote to her in 1545.

Girolamo Parabosco, *Lettere amorose* (Venice, 1545), fols 24v–25r.

Who has ever seen such beauty elsewhere? Who such grace and such charming behaviour? Who has heard such sweet and gentle speech? Who listened to such lofty thoughts? What can I say of that angelic voice, which when it fills the air with its divine sounds makes such a sweet harmony as would ... infuse spirit and life into the coldest stones, making them weep from its overpowering sweetness? So you can be sure, most fair and talented lady Gasparina, that any man seeing you would remain your servant forever.

15.22 A female ensemble

A trio of female singers, Laura Peverara, Anna Guarini and Livia d'Arco, performing around 1575 at the courts of Mantua and Ferrara, were probably a professional ensemble. Their fame popularised a new style of singing for two to three trained female voices, making it possible for subsequent women to aim at a career in music.

Vincenzo Giustiniani, *Discorso sopra la musica* (1628), in I. Fenlon, *Music and Patronage in Sixteenth-Century Mantua* (Cambridge: 1980), vol. 1, p. 192.

These ladies of Mantua and Ferrara were highly competent, competing with each other not only in the tone and range of their voices but also in the ornamentation of exquisite passages delivered at appropriate places, without being overwhelming ... Furthermore, they lowered or raised their voices, loud or soft, making them light or heavy, according to what occurred in their pieces; sometimes dragging on, sometimes breaking off with a gentle interrupted sigh, sometimes with long drawn-out passages, followed by brisk, detached ones. Now there would be groupings, now jumps, now with long, then with short trills, or again with passages which were sweet and sung softly, to which one might sometimes hear an improvised echo in reply. Above all, they accompanied the music and its theme with appropriate facial movements, glances and gestures, with no unseemly movements of the mouth or hand or body which were not directed towards the character

17 See Feldman (1996), pp. 104–8, for Stampa as a performer.

of the song, and articulated the words well, so that one could hear even the last syllable of each one, which were never interrupted or obscured by passages and other embellishments. They employed many other particular effects which will be known to persons more experienced than I.

15.23 Settimia Caccini casts her spell

Settimia Caccini (*fl.* 1600–20) is described singing roles to music by Monteverdi at performances for the wedding of Margherita de' Medici and Odoardo Farnese at Parma in December 1628.

Buttiglij Marcello, '*Descrittione dell'apparato ...*' (Parma, 1629), in Kirkendale, pp. 343–4.

The illustrious singer, with superhuman grace and angelic voice, made the air resound singing the following verses, and filled the whole theatre with accents of supreme sweetness ... At the first sound of Signora Settimia, playing Aurora, all murmured conversation among the audience ceased ... their ears were so consoled by the smoothness of her voice and the divinity of her song that there was not a single one among the ten thousand people sitting in the theatre, however feeble in discernment he might be, who was not moved at her trills, did not sigh at her sighs or be driven to ecstasy by her phrasing and who was not almost stupefied or turned to stone at the sight of a miraculous beauty and the sound of a celestial siren.

15.24 Three outstanding actresses

Female actresses in *commedia dell'arte* became common by the 1560s. Little is known about most of them: some may have started as semi-courtesans, though the sexual morals of Isabella Andreini, from an acting family, were never questioned. Garzoni praises Andreini (1562–1604), Vincenza Armani (d. 1569) and Vittoria Archilei (d. 1610s).[18]

Garzoni (1586, repr. 1599), pp. 753–4.

The gracious Isabella, the honour of the stage, the ornament of the theatre, a superb spectacle not only of beauty but of virtue, has also illumined this profession so that, while the world endures, while the

18 See R. Andrews, 'Isabella Andreini and Others: Women on Stage in the Late Cinquecento' in Panizza, pp. 316–33, and T. Carter, 'Finding a Voice: Vittoria Archilei and the Florentine "New Music"', in L. Hutson, ed., *Feminism and Renaissance Studies* (Oxford, 1999), pp. 450–67.

centuries exist ... every voice, every tongue, every cry will resound with the famous name of Isabella. I will not speak of the learned Vincenza, who, imitating Ciceronian fluency, has placed the art of comedy in rivalry with oratory, and partly through her marvellous beauty, partly with her inexpressible grace, has made herself enormously successful in the theatrical world, showing herself the finest comic actress of our age ... But above all divine Vittoria seems to me worthy of the utmost honours, who transforms herself on stage, a beautiful magician of love who gladdens the hearts of a thousand lovers with her speech, a sweet siren, who enchants with seductive spells the souls of her devoted spectators. And without doubt she deserves to be deemed a compendium of art, her gestures being well proportioned, her movements harmonious and concordant, her demeanour pleasing and majestic, her words gentle and soothing, her sighs crafty and bewitching, her smiles piquant yet sweet, her bearing proud yet liberal, and all her person having everything that befits and belongs to a perfect comedy actress.

Women visual artists

15.25 Sofonisba Anguissola

The references to antique female painters in the chapters on painting in the *Natural History* of Pliny the Elder could provide precedents not just for the existence of, but for the types of painting produced by, modern women artists. Here, the Milanese Gian Paolo Lomazzo, using famous artistic mouthpieces, speaks in *c.* 1563–4 of Sofonisba Anguissola (1532/5–1625), a portrait and self-portrait specialist.[19]

Gian Paolo Lomazzo, *Ragionamento Quinto*, in R. P. Ciardi, ed., *Scritti sulle arti*, vol. 1 (Florence, 1973), p. 95.

[Leonardo da Vinci] ... I should give you news of the miracles of a woman from Cremona, whose name is Sophonisba, who to the amazement of everyone throughout Europe impresses all important princes or learned men through her paintings. These are none other than portraits, which seem so natural to those who see them and which display so much skill that many fine painters have thought that she has lifted the paintbrush from the hand of the divine Titian ...

19 For the self-portraits of Sofonisba Anguissola, see J. Woods-Marsden, *Renaissance Self-Portraiture* (New Haven and London, 1998), pp. 187–213; for critiques of her and other Renaissance female artists, see F. H. Jacobs, *Defining the Female Virtuosa* (Cambridge, 1997).

[Phidias] Truly she is a great miracle of nature. But I also could inform you of several women of antiquity who in their time caused immense astonishment among people ...

The virgin Cizicena painted her own portrait in the mirror, together with many other portraits of women in Rome: through them she surpassed the finest painters living in her day.

15.26 Praise for the Anguissola sisters

In his 1568 'Life' of Benvenuto Garofalo and Girolamo da Carpi, Giorgio Vasari links the talents of the Anguissola sisters, Sofonisba, Lucia, Europa and Anna, to women's procreative powers.

Vasari (1984), vol. 5; Testo, pp. 428–9.

And since Anna, the fourth sister, also studied *disegno* with much profit, though still a small child, I can only say that one needs a natural bent towards achievement, and then add the effort and study that these four noble and distinguished sisters have put in, sisters so enamoured with every rare talent and in particular with matters of *disegno*, that the house of Signor Amilcar Anguissola – the most fortunate father of an honest and honourable family – seems the very home of painting, as of all the virtues. But if women know so well how to make living men, why marvel that those who wish could also paint them so well?

15.27 Fede Galizia as portraitist

Arguably, Morigia's commendation of Fede Galizia (1578–1630) implies a slight talent, connected with the lesser artistic virtues of diligent copying from life, rather than utilisation of the creative imagination termed *invenzione*.

Morigia, p. 282.

Great praise should be given to the very courteous and talented Fede Galizia, the virgin, unmarried daughter of the virtuous and honourable Nontio Galizio. This young woman, apart from her other distinctions, has such a natural inclination for painting and drawing, that she has already provided clear and obvious signs that she must be one of the truly noblest painters of our time, since in this her tender young age one sees many very fine and precise drawings by her. This most praiseworthy girl has also portrayed from life her father and mother as nobly as one could wish. She has also made a small portrait of the most excellent Lady Maria Giron de Velasco, Duchess of Frias, and one of Signora Camilla, wife of Ercole Ferrara, both showing resemblance, and great diligence.

NEGATIVE REACTIONS: ISSUES OF DECORUM

15.28 The vices of learned women

Though the semi-mythical 'famous women' to whom women writers, artists and musicians were so often compared provided valuable precedents, some of them were also felt morally dubious.

Bartolomeo Taegio, *La villa* (Milan, 1559), p. 120.

V. Hence, learned women are commonly thought suspect.

P. And why is that?

V. Because an artificial malice is added to the malice natural in women. If you wish to see how rarely learning and chastity go together, look at the example of Sappho, so renowned for poetry, who so lustfully loved Phaon. No less censure is given to Sallust's Sempronia, both condemned for immodesty and praised for erudition. I'll pass over in silence Leontia, the concubine of Metrodorus, from whom he learned Epicurean philosophy. And lest I bore you with a mass of examples, I'll just say that learned but unchaste women were infinite.

15.29 The passion of Properzia de' Rossi

Adapting Vasari's earlier remarks about a relief made of Joseph and Potiphar's wife by the Bolognese sculptor Properzia de' Rossi (*c.* 1490–1530), Gian Paolo Lomazzo in his *Sesto Ragionamento* interpreted the scene as pure self-expression, placing the sculptor in a line of over-passionate female suicides.

Lomazzo, in Ciardi, vol. 1, pp. 155–6.

Being like most pre-eminent women in love with a young man whose favours she could never obtain, to console herself and to assuage the ardent passion which burned in her, this woman made a figure of Joseph, his cloak torn off by Pharaoh's wife. This done, she diverted herself somewhat, being reluctant to throw herself from the mountain as Sappho did, or go mad as Medea did for Jason, or kill herself out of bitter passion as did Thisbe and other women.

15.30 Art is against women's nature

Paolo Pino, in his *Dialogo della Pittura* (Venice, 1548) presents an argument echoing Aristotle, that in practising their art women are acting contrary to their nature.

Paolo Pino, *Dialogo della Pittura*, in P. Barocchi, ed., *Trattati dell'arte del Cinquecento* (Bari, 1960), vol. 1, pp. 95–139.

[Lauro] I dislike hearing women compared to men's excellence in ability to paint, and I think art is denigrated thereby. Art draws the feminine species away from its proper sphere, for women are fit for nothing but the distaff and the reel.

[Fabio] You are right, but those women [mentioned by Pliny], famous for different talents, were women with masculine qualities, such as the mythical hermaphrodites were said to possess.

15.31 Those dreadful blue-stockings!

One of the possibly fictional correspondents, Aurelia Magi, in Ortensio Lando's letter anthology of 1548, proclaims herself unattracted by the prospect of study.

Lando, fol. 125 r–v.

It would be better if I were to leave them [theology, grammar and philosophy] in peace, and devote myself to the tasks women have performed up to now ... I don't want to be a female poet, since I see that women devoted to letters don't know how to mend a pair of stockings or wash a handkerchief. I know of no other way of making myself admired and honoured by the world than to be chaste, modest, silent and humble, lacking literary learning or philosophy.

15.32 Virtue in danger

The Angelic (Barnabite) nun Paola de' Negri warns Gaspara Stampa in a letter of August 1544 of the spiritual dangers from the misuse of her musical and poetic gifts in consorting with dishonourable men.

In Gaspara Stampa, *Rime* (Venice, 1554); ed. B. Ceriello, introd. M. Bellonci (Milan, 1954), pp. 55–6.

Those talents that the world honours give the soul nothing but the slight and temporary satisfaction that the praise of flatterers gives us ... but true virtues, holy virtues, Christian virtues, divine virtues, embellish the soul, give it lustre, enrich it, adorn it, bless it both in the present and the future lives ... O beloved soul, put your efforts into being truly chaste, truly patient and filled with other holy virtues ... don't believe the flatterers, those that love you physically: don't deceive yourself, I beg you, and distance yourself from those habits or associations which are foreign to Christ, and place you in danger.

15.33 Playing music modestly

Certain instruments, as well as overly forward behaviour, could be deemed unsuitable for women, according to Castiglione's Magnifico.

Castiglione, ed. Maier (1981), pp. 353–4.

[Giuliano] [The court lady should make music decorously] ... and with that gentle delicacy we have declared suits her. When dancing, I would not like her movements to be violent and forceful, nor in singing or playing music to employ those emphatic, repeated ornaments which show more skill than grace. Similarly, in my view her choice of instruments should conform to this. Imagine how ungainly a sight it would be for a woman to play drums, pipes or trumpets, or suchlike instruments, since their harshness obscures and removes that mild sweetness which so greatly enhances a woman's every act. So when she comes to dance or make any sort of music, she must let herself reluctantly be persuaded and coaxed, doing so with a certain timidity which betrays a fine modesty, the opposite of impudence.

15.34 Composing unsuited to women

A singer at the royal chapel at Naples comments on Maddalena Casulana (c. 1540–after 1586), the first woman to publish her compositions, books of madrigals appearing in 1568 and 1570.

B. Pescerelli, *I Madrigali di Maddalena Casulana* (Florence, 1979), p. 16.

The other [of two female singers] is Maddalena Casulana: not only are the two charming in their singing, but she much enjoys composition, indeed more so than is fitting for a woman to do.

SELF-PRESENTATION AND JUSTIFICATION

Women wishing to engage in artistic disciplines could adopt various strategies to protect themselves against negative responses. Retiring to

convents, moving towards uncontroversial subjects and seeking protection from the influential, often an aristocratic lady, were all tried.
Modest statements about their efforts were often made: these
were expected generally during the Renaissance, but tend to be particularly characteristic of creative women, deflecting accusations of
presumption.[20]

15.35 Laura Terracina's 'unpolished' verse

Laura Terracina published several verses denigrating her literary efforts, here
to the Neapolitan poet Luigi Tansillo.

Laura Terracina, *Rime della Signora Laura Terracina* (Venice, 1548), fols
12v–13r.

> You, who are kind, learned and courteous
> And who see my feeble woman's rhyme,
> You have not given me insidious words of praise
> So I may entrap you with my ignorant snares,
> I grieve I have made this obvious to another
> With my replies, which have no value.
> Polish my verse, prune all of it
> As a good gardener renews his fruit.
>
> If I write further, cease to listen,
> For I know my style is weak and foolish:
> And when I speak to myself, I lack
> All help in singing little or much.
> When I write or speak, it makes me fearful,
> And my hand trembles and my face pales.
> And as I fashion and compose myself
> I straightway show it to you and keep silent.
>
> You, fount of Parnassus and of Nature,
> Write, then; writing is granted you:

20 Of the many studies on creative women's self-presentation and the need for an
appearance of modesty, see also L. Lawner, 'Gaspara Stampa and the Rhetoric of
Submission', in *Renaissance Studies in Honor of Craig Hugh Smyth* (Florence, 1985),
vol. 1, pp. 345–62; M. Garrard, 'Here's Looking at Me! Sofonisba Anguissola and the
Problem of the Woman Artist', *Renaissance Quarterly*, 47 (1994), pp. 556–622;
C. King, 'Looking a Sight: Sixteenth Century Portraits of Women Artists', *Zeitschrift
für Kunstgeschichte*, 58 (1995), pp. 381–406.

I, a woman devoid of art or measure,
Order and weave the thread I hold in me.
And rightly does my intellect fear,
Since the female sex does not persist in ventures.
If I write no more, do not blame me
But rather my modesty, I pray you, praise.

15.36 Lavinia Fontana claims to be too greatly honoured

Lavinia Fontana writes in 1579 to Fulvio Orsini, who wished to acquire one of her self-portraits for his collection of images of illustrious personages.
Cantaro, p. 306.

You do me too much honour, both by your over-abundant praises, and by giving my portrait such an honoured position. The one I attribute to your excessive benevolence, the other makes me think that you have wisely decided that the talent and the merit of Signora Sophonisba[21] and suchlike distinguished people (who I am unworthy to serve let alone to equal) would shine more brightly thereby. For just as good musicians sometimes insert dissonant notes to produce sweeter harmonies, and just as the odd cloud makes the splendour of the heavens seem more radiant, so Your Excellency has judged that the imperfection and shadows of my portrait would make his most noble museum shine more brightly.

15.37 The moral value of the classics in translation

Another approach stressed the moral value of their writings. Ippolita Clara, from a professional background in Alessandria (Piedmont), who attracted praise for her poetry and for her translations from Latin, dedicates her translation of books I–VI of the *Aeneid* to Francesco II Sforza, Duke of Milan, on 10 August 1533.

In S. Albonico, 'Ippolita Clara', in C. Bozzetti, P. Gibellini, E. Sandal, eds, *Veronica Gambara e la poesia del suo tempo nell'Italia settentrionale* (Florence, 1989), pp. 367–8.

So I, an unimportant woman of no learning must dare do what so many worthy men do not ... This my small effort I dedicate and send to Your Excellencey, though I am certain that the Latin language

21 Anguissola.

pleases you more than any vernacular or learned style, and also that my work is not in polished Tuscan speech and perhaps has thousands of mistakes that my feeble eye cannot see ... Such a work is made to be an example for unlearned women, those who do not understand Latin, so that in the First Book of the *Aeneid* they can see how one must always (as far as one can) avoid the wrath of the gods ... Again, in the Fourth, they should clearly know that never for any reason should one love a man other than one's own husband: that is how love can besmirch the modesty a true woman should have, because the fate of Dido, abandoned and worse, mostly came from it.

15.38 Laura Cereta's pleasure in literature

Laura Cereta, writing in March 1488 to ask favour and protection from Cardinal Ascanio Sforza, strikes a more confident note.

Translation of Robin, pp. 37–9, with permission of University of Chicago Press.

Though I was untrained and scarcely exposed to literature, through my own intelligence and natural talents I was able to acquire the beginnings of an education. While my pleasure at embarking on such a journey of the mind and my love of study were strong at the outset, the weak seeds of my small talent have grown to such a degree that I have written speeches for public occasions, and these I embellished grandly, painting pictures with words in order to influence people and stimulate their minds. My love of reading caused me to sample different kinds of subjects, and only in study did I feel a sense of inner contentment ... I have found satisfaction in literature that would give me not smoke and darkness but something perfect, secure, and lasting.

15.39 A composer asserts her intellectual gifts

A distinctly defiant tone is heard from Maddalena Casulana when dedicating her *Il Primo Libro de madrigali a quattro voci* (Venice, 1568), to Isabella de' Medici Orsini, Duchess of Bracciano, herself a noted musician and composer.

Pescerelli, p. 7.

I am well aware, most illustrious and excellent lady, that these my first-fruits cannot through their feebleness give birth to the effect that I would wish, which would also, apart from bearing witness to my devotion to Your Excellency, be to show the world … the vain error of men who deem themselves so much the masters of the lofty gifts of the intellect that they think these cannot be shared by women.

15.40 An actress and writer seeks to fulfil her talent

Introduction to Isabella Andreini, *Lettere d'Isabella Andreini Padovana, comica gelosa et academica intenta* (Venice, 1607), unpaginated.

Since I have been sent by the bounty of the Supreme Creator to be a citizen of the world, and as that thirst for knowledge happened to be born more powerfully in me than in many other women of our age, in which though many are found talented in learning, and many have become famous and immortal, still others only want to … stick with the needle, the distaff and the reel. Born with the most intense hunger for knowledge, as I said, I wanted with all my power to feed it; and though Fortune was miserly with the ingredient at my birth … nonetheless, so as not to betray that talent which God and Nature gave me, and because I did not want my life to seem like one long slumber (as I knew that a citizen is thought good inasmuch as he benefits his homeland) scarcely could I read, so to speak, before I set to work to compose my *Mirtilla*, a pastoral fable, which came out in print, and can be seen in the theatre of the world.

THE PLATES

1. Palma Vecchio, *La Bella*, c. 1525–8. Madrid, Museo Thyssen-Bornemisza. Oil on canvas, 95 × 80 cm

This painting probably represents either the artist's fictitious ideal of female beauty or an actual or generic courtesan of high standing, since a respectable girl or married woman would not have been shown incompletely attired. The opulence of the accessories (the container full of jewels) and the dress (the filmy chemise and two sets of detachable sleeves, elaborately worked or requiring quantities of expensive silk fabric) suggest the material world of Julia Lombardo, Calmo's 'Orsolina' or Fortini's courtesan (14.11, 12, 14). These carefully arranged and crumpled fabrics, however, serve mainly as a frame for the smooth, regular, classically influenced beauty of the body in gentle motion. Palma finds no need to suggest that his sitter possesses the literary, musical or conversational skills admired in the most famous courtesans, but like many praised in words, such as those of Parabosco (14.13) and Fortini, the woman seems to expect to be admired for her dignified mien and canonically beautiful features: pale, shining flesh, arched brows, lustrous eyes, graceful hands, rosy lips and golden tresses. Unlike in other paintings of female beauties by Palma, the gaze of the woman seems to expect homage rather than erotic approach.

2. **Andrea del Sarto,** *Portrait of a Lady with a Petrarchino,*
c. 1528. **Florence, Galleria degli Uffizi. Oil on wood,**
87 × 69 cm

Ut pictura poesis. Perhaps few portraits illustrate more clearly than
this the well-known *paragone* between painting and poetry, which
is at the core of so many sixteenth-century portraits. The painter
is able not only to represent the exterior appearance of the sitter,
but, like a poet, to describe or hint at thoughts and feelings,
conveying to the viewer the impression of an interior life. The
sitter turns her head towards the viewer and engages his attention (the portrait predicates the presence of a male viewer) with
her eyes, while pointing at the book she holds. This is a fashionable *Petrarchino*, a volume of Petrarch's poems, open at sonnets
CLIII (*Ite, caldi sospiri, al freddo core*) and CLIV (*Le stelle, il cielo et
gli elementi a prova*). In the first sonnet, the poet hopes that his 'hot
sighs' will reach Laura's 'cold heart', while the second celebrates
her eyes, 'beautiful beyond measure', fashioned by the stars and
the sky. Both her gaze and her gesture are highlighted by the play
of colours and by light and shade, with her face and her hand
emphasised by the collar of the chemise, the opening of her gown,
and by her sleeve. The ambiguity of her gaze and of her smile –
coy? inviting? – is intensified by the ambiguity of her gesture: is
she keeping the book open so that the viewer can read the poems
on the page, or is she indicating another poem, invisible to him?
In fact, this hidden sonnet, CLII (*Questa humil fera, un cor di tigre
o d'orsa*), fittingly describes the ambiguity of love: fear and hope,
laughter and tears, fire and ice.

3. **Antoniazzo Romano,** *Annunciation with Cardinal Torquemada and Poor Girls,* **signed and dated March 1500. Rome, Chapel of the Annunciation, Church of S. Maria sopra Minerva. Tempera on panel, 130 × 185 cm**

The altarpiece was commissioned by the Confraternity of the *Annunziata* for the Jubilee year of 1500. This charitable institution was founded in 1460 by the Spanish Dominican Cardinal Juan de Torquemada (d. 1468) in order to provide poor girls with dowries, which were given out every year on 25 March, during the ceremonies for the feast of the Annunciation. The emblem of the confraternity (a representation of the Annunciation with two kneeling girls receiving their dowries) was the source for the unusual iconography of this altarpiece: Cardinal Torquemada introduces three girls, dressed in white for the ceremony, to the Virgin who, while accepting the message from the archangel Gabriel, hands a bag of money to one of them. More dowry bags are placed on the base of the Virgin's lectern. The importance of the confraternity's charitable task is indicated by the presence of God and the Virgin. The gold background and the difference in scale between divine and human figures turns the ritual event of the distribution of dowries into a symbolic representation of the confraternity as an instrument of God's mercy.

4. Vittore Carpaccio, St Ursula debating with her father, detail from *The Arrival of the Ambassadors, c.* 1496–8. Venice, Gallerie dell'Accademia. Oil on canvas, 147 × 94 cm approx

This detail comes from the opening scene in the cycle on the life of St Ursula for the hall of the *Scuola* (confraternity) of the saint in Venice. Ursula, a Breton princess of the Dark Ages, received through the ambassadors shown in the main part of the canvas a marriage proposal from the British prince, and here sets her conditions, that she and ten ladies-in-waiting, each with 1,000 virgin attendants, should visit pilgrim sites in a Europe threatened by barbarian invasions. Having obtained the consent of both father and prince, the party departs, Ursula and the virgins being eventually martyred by Huns. Ursula's legend attracted different groups for different reasons: in the Carpaccio cycle the emphasis on sea travel and ceremonial processions suited the interests of affluent male confraternity members in a maritime and mercantile city. Yet the cult of the saint and her companions appealed to females as individuals and in groups (see 4.10, 11.7, 11.38–39), and other details within the cycle, such as the old woman, apparently a servant, sitting below Ursula and her father, or the kneeling tertiary in the *Funeral of Ursula*, connect with this. Ursula herself is here presented as a beautiful yet determined and demanding girl, her inspiration seemingly derived from the painting of the Madonna hanging beside her canopy bed, similar to many images in Renaissance bedrooms felt both to protect and to guide their owners.

5. Anon., Frontispiece showing Colomba da Rieti fed by an angel, from Leandro Alberti, *La Vita della Beata Colomba da Rieto* (Bologna, 1521). Woodcut, 17.5 × 11.1 cm

As the only illustration to Alberti's book (see 4.13), this visually encapsulates the notions of a female mystic cherished by the Dominican order to which both he and Colomba belonged, although the book, which was translated and abbreviated from earlier Latin lives, must have been intended for an at least partially lay audience. Colomba appears to have been praying alone close to a small altar within her convent, suggesting her long vigils and devotion to the Eucharist. She is rewarded by the appearance of the angel who feeds her communion bread from paradise, as suggested by the palm-tree behind the wall. Colomba crosses her arms in humble acceptance. Emphasis is thus placed on her private devotions and visionary experience, rather than on her prophetic or protective powers or her role within the politics of Perugia, which were suggested in other images of the saint.

B· COLOMBA·

6. **Domenico Beccafumi, *Tanaquil*, c. 1519–25. London, National Gallery. Oil on panel, 92.1 × 53.3 cm**

Together with Marcia (National Gallery, London) and Cornelia (Galleria Doria Pamphili, Rome), this famous woman from antiquity was painted for the bedroom of Francesco Petrucci, *de facto* Lord of Siena from 1521 to 1523, and of his wife Caterina Piccolomini del Mandolo. The three panels would have been linked together by a frame, and hung as a *spalliera* behind a chest or a *lettuccio*. They were part of an ensemble which also included a *lettiera* with a headboard painted with a Venus (Barber Institute, Birmingham), a chest, two *spalliere* representing *The Cult of Vesta* and *The Lupercalia* (Collezione Martelli, Florence), and a *lettuccio*. The ideals conveyed by these three exemplary women, who are identified by inscriptions, refer to their virtues as wives and mothers. Marcia, praised for her fertility, was Cato's perfect spouse. Cornelia was the exemplary mother of the Gracchi. The Etruscan Tanaquil, wife of Tarquinius Priscus, was skilled in the art of prediction, and was also an example of a virtuous matron: she is represented with a spindle, symbol of domestic industriousness. Their virtues also had consequences for the public lives of their husbands and sons and, in Tanaquil's case, they were decisive in Tarquinius's bid for the throne. In the struggle for power among the most important families in Siena, the bedroom furniture would have brought fame to a couple who showed their humanistic learning in the choice of subject matter, as well as their taste in their patronage of the most successful artist in contemporary Siena.

7. Giovanni Antonio Amadeo, *Tomb of Medea Colleoni,* **after 1475. Bergamo, Colleoni Chapel (originally in the Dominican convent of S. Maria della Basella, Malpaga, moved in 1842). Marble, 2 m high**

This funerary monument, one of the very few erected for a young unmarried girl, was commissioned by the *condottiere* Bartolomeo Colleoni to commemorate Medea, his favourite among his eight daughters, who died in 1470. Colleoni, born into the minor aristocracy of Bergamo, made a considerable fortune as a captain fighting for Milan and Venice. At his luxurious castle at Malpaga he held a court which, according to Antonio Cornazzano, was like a prince's. Plans for prestigious and politically advantageous marriages had been made for the adolescent Medea, but her father's aspirations for her and his well-documented affection could only be embodied in a funerary monument, commissioned from one of the most important Lombard sculptors, and erected in the convent he had founded. The Virgin Mary and the Man of Sorrows, traditional funerary imagery, indicate hope of eternal life. Unusually, two female saints, Catherine of Alexandria and Catherine of Siena, the latter in a nun's habit and holding Christ's heart, act as intercessors. The effigy's features, shown in the detail, with the fashionable high forehead and long neck, together with detailed representation of the elegantly arranged hair and rich gown, convey an idealised image of Medea as the member of an important family. The coat of arms on the sarcophagus and on the bodice of Medea's gown signal the Colleoni name. As well as indicating the name of her famous father and his allegiance to Venice, the inscription identifies Medea as '*virgo*' and, as customary, gives the date of her death.

8. **Attributed to Ambrogio de' Predis,** *Portrait of Bianca Maria Sforza*, **probably 1493. Washington, National Gallery of Art. Oil on panel, 51 × 32.5 cm**

This portrait was almost certainly painted on the occasion of the marriage of the niece of Ludovico il Moro to the Holy Roman Emperor Maximilian, from whom Ludovico gained the imperial investiture which legalised his bid for power. As part of the bargain, the bride's dowry was set at 400,000 ducats, while her jewels were assessed at 31,373 ducats (see 7.14). This portrait is the visual evidence of her value as a bride. Bianca Maria, considered not to be any longer in the first flush of youth at the age of twenty-one, is represented in the profile pose conventionally used for female portraits during most of the fifteenth century. Ambrogio de' Predis, the Sforza court painter, who also worked as a goldsmith and a lace designer, focuses the viewer's attention on the detailed rendering of her gown and jewels, which signal Milanese wealth and elegance, and Sforza ambition. In fact the bodice and sleeves of her brocade gown are decorated with the heraldic device of the houseleek (*sempervivum tectorum*) which links the Sforza to the Visconti, while the large jewel pinned to her headdress represents one of Ludovico's own devices, the *scopetta* – the brush which sweeps away corruption. Around it is a gold ribbon engraved with the Sforza motto *Merito et Tempore* (With Merit and Time). Bianca Maria's jewels also have bridal connotations: the belt, a symbol of virginity, was an essential item for Milanese brides; the 'handle' of the *scopetta* is surmounted by a heart-shaped emerald, a symbol of chastity, and the 'bristles' are decorated with five pearls, also symbols of chastity traditionally worn by brides. She wears large pearls around her throat, and still more are wrapped around the *coazzone*, the long plait fashionable at the Milanese court.

9. Marco del Buono Giamberti and Apollonio di Giovanni, *The Story of Esther*, *c.* 1460–70. New York, Metropolitan Museum of Art. Tempera and gold on panel, 44.5 × 140.7 cm

This panel, once the front of a *cassone*, was produced in one of the most important Florentine workshops specialising in the painted and gilded chests which were commissioned for weddings. It would have had a companion, probably illustrating the first part of the story, while the sides of both chests would have also been painted with either allegorical figures or the coat of arms of the families of the bride and groom. The architectural setting creates a strong sense of three-dimensional space and helps organise the story in a continuous narrative. On the left, Ahasuerus rides with his courtiers towards the wedding ceremony. At the centre of the panel, under the loggia, he places a ring on Esther's finger in front of a priest. Finally, on the right, Esther, together with other ladies, is shown sitting at a table, taking part in the wedding banquet. Decoration and refinement, rather than drama and emotional content, were clearly a priority. The story of Esther does not lack dramatic episodes (see 5.6), but here the painter has been at pains to stress the beauty of the architectural setting and the elegance of the elongated figures, and to display his virtuoso technique in the representation of their fashionable clothes. The palace on the left and the loggia on the right set the story in contemporary Florence (see 7.19), while the church in the centre is an interesting hybrid of fourteenth-century Gothic elements and an *all'antica* dome.

10. Paolo Caliari (Veronese), *Happy Union, c.* 1570–80. London, National Gallery. Oil on canvas, 187.4 × 186.7 cm

Veronese's so-called *Happy Union*, one of four canvases on the theme of man and woman for unknown patrons, places the strongest emphasis on a female as heroine. The foreground figure, while not a portrait, suggests a contemporary bride, with her loosened blonde locks, fine jewels (rings can be seen on her left hand) and resplendent pink and gold brocade dress. Holding an olive branch with her less prominent male partner, she reverently approaches the seated female figure, to be crowned with myrtle. A putto appears to be about to chain man and woman together, accompanied by a dog, symbol of marital fidelity. These emblems of peace, union and fidelity are supplemented by the white sphere, topped with the cornucopia issuing gold and pearls, on which the nude female sits, suggesting harmony, unity and prosperity. Wearing a marriage girdle, she is likely to be Venus herself, in her aspect of protectress of marriage (see 7.21). The painting would have been hung either on a ceiling or high up on a wall, and shows the later sixteenth-century Venetian taste for large-scale paintings to adorn important rooms. With its companion pieces, which deal with the deceits and temptations of love and their chastisement, it connects with the Renaissance interest in distinguishing between higher and lower forms of love or lust (see 2.16). *Happy Union* itself connects also with later marriage treatises which laud not only the social utility but the harmony, peace and fruitfulness to be gained from marriage. Here this is advocated not by reference to exemplars, but by linking elements from real life to an ideal world of myth and allegory.

11. Domenico Ghirlandaio, Daughters of Francesco Sassetti, detail from *The Miracle of the Roman Notary's Son*, 1482–85. Florence, Sassetti Chapel, Church of S. Trinita. Fresco

The funerary chapel of the Florentine banker Francesco Sassetti and his wife is decorated with a fresco cycle with episodes from the life of Sassetti's patron saint, St Francis. The Sassetti and their relatives and business associates are represented as taking part in the sacred narratives, thus stating their place in Florentine society and their political allegiances, as well as their piety. The significance of their clothes, demeanour and physical appearance would have been instantly recognised by their contemporaries. Directly above the altarpiece two groups of men and women in contemporary clothes, standing in the square in front of the church of S. Trinita, just outside the door of the Sassetti palace, witness the miraculous intervention of St Francis resuscitating a little boy. A number of beautifully characterised female portraits in the group on the left have been tentatively identified as some of Francesco Sassetti's five daughters. Two of them, an elegant young woman dressed in a brocade gown and a younger girl in blue staring out towards the viewer, attract attention. Their fashionable clothes, the way their hair is dressed and the prominent place they occupy in the composition, signal that these two girls are still unmarried. They are probably Lisabetta (b. 1468) and either Vaggia (b. 1471) or Maddalena (b. *c.* 1474), while the plump young woman in black and her neighbour, their heads covered with a veil, could be Violante (b. 1462) and Sibilla (b. 1466), already married at the time of the commission. Behind the group of wealthy Florentines the head of a black slave can be seen peeping past the pilaster on the far left.

12. Illustration from Scipione (Fra Girolamo) Mercurio, *La commare o riccoglitrice* (Venice, 1601 and 1621), chapter 2. Woodcut, 11 × 8.5 cm

As Mercurio himself writes, this print from the 1601 and later editions of his book (see 1.8, 9.11) is a necessary aid for the midwife. It shows 'with greater clarity' what he explains in great detail in the text: how a woman who has difficulty in giving birth should be placed on the bed in a sloping position, supported by pillows, and how the midwife should kneel between her legs, placing her hands into the vagina in order to help the expulsion of the baby. Therefore, as with all the other illustrations in this manual for midwives, the aim of the image is didactic and not decorative, even if the action takes place in an elegant bedroom with a richly carved bed surmounted by a fashionable canopy. The midwife is the true protagonist of this treatise, as shown by the dedicatory poem written in her praise by Camillo Zuccati:

> Wise midwife,
> Daughter of a wise and honoured father,
> Because of your many and graceful actions
> Go happy into the world,
> While every poet sings your praise.
> Learned and gentle mistress,
> Wise and gentle,
> Everyone praises and honours you,
> And is in love with your beauty.
> Thanks to you, women will give birth happily,
> And we shall always praise you.

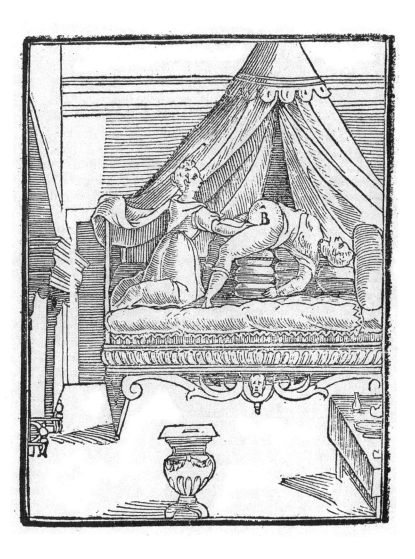

13. **Lavinia Fontana,** *Portrait of a Widow with a Girl,* **late 1590s. Bologna, Pinacoteca Nazionale. Oil on canvas, 116 × 98 cm**

The unknown woman, dressed entirely in widow's black, is presumably from the Bolognese patriciate which formed Fontana's clientele, judging by the expensive textiles, lace and jewellery she shares with her daughter, who also wears the colour of mourning in her overdress. This restrained opulence testifies to her desire to pay respect to her deceased husband's memory in ways felt to be suited to his wealth and status, and to her own personal and family honour: they may have conveyed additional meanings, now lost to us, for viewers aware of whether such garb had been provided in the husband's bequests, or was paid for by the widow's own dowry-based wealth. The painting seeks to project neither the widow's intense grief, nor her enjoyment of a less restricted life, nor any hope for remarriage. Rather, her facial expression and body language suggest a settled determination to live by the ideals of rectitude approved in her society, taking on both male and female roles as head of household and guide and model for her daughter (see 10.16). The gestures imply both protection for the little girl and, through the book of devotion, instruction in Christian belief and morality.

14. Interior of nuns' choir, S. Maurizio (Monastero Maggiore), Milan, architecture *c.* 1503 onwards, paintings 1522–24 and 1556–58

The Benedictine nunnery of S. Maurizio is perhaps the best example of a rich female monastic house surviving in Italy today. Dating back to very early times and accommodating women from the leading families of Milan, it attracted ample endowments, allowing major rebuilding after 1503 in a Bramantesque style. As well as the usual cloisters, cells, refectories, infirmaries and smaller oratories, the monastery also included spacious kitchen gardens, orchards and vineyards. Following the introduction of a strict *clausura* in 1444, a clear architectural separation was established between a public church, reached from a main city thoroughfare, and the nuns' choir, from where public masses could be viewed through a central opening. This was blocked up after 1569 at the behest of the strict reformer, Archbishop Carlo Borromeo. Both churches contain altarpieces and frescoed surrounds by the leading early sixteenth-century Milanese artists, Bernardino Luini, Vincenzo Foppa and Giovanni Boltraffio, mainly eucharistic images, passion scenes and representations of female saints, in line with nuns' usual devotional interests. Donor portraits of important benefactors and certain of their nun-relatives are also present in the public part. In the nuns' sector, spacious landscapes may have been meant to promote a meditative calm, or to help the sisters imagine the sacred sites of the Holy Land.

15. Lorenzo Costa, *Virgin and Child with the Bentivoglio Family*, signed and dated August 1488. Bologna, Bentivoglio Chapel, S. Giacomo Maggiore. Tempera on canvas, 368 × 342 cm

The Bentivoglio Chapel, where masses were celebrated in the presence of important guests and of the citizens of Bologna, was a backdrop for the display of familial power. This painting, on the right-hand wall of the chapel, is part of the decoration commissioned from Lorenzo Costa by Giovanni II Bentivoglio. Giovanni and his wife, Ginevra Sforza, are represented kneeling at the sides of the Virgin, larger in size than their sons and daughters who are grouped in front of the throne. Together with large amounts of gold, the Bentivoglio heraldic colours, red and blue, dominate the composition. Giovanni struggled long to attain the *signoria* of Bologna, and this painting shows some of the means through which, during this significant year of 1488, he finally achieved his goal: artistic and architectural patronage, display of magnificence and the help of his clever and ambitious wife Ginevra, who bore him numerous children. Ginevra, a very able political partner, was extremely influential in her second husband's bid for power. Celebrated by Sabadino degli Arienti in his *Gynevera delle clare donne* (1490), in this devotional painting she is shown modestly dressed in accordance with Giovanni's simple citizen dress, though she was the owner of magnificent palaces and villas and of a famous collection of jewels. The couple was able to establish a network of kinship with the most important families in the area through shrewd marriage choices for their sons and daughters.

16. Bonifazio de' Pitati (Bonifazio Veronese), *The Finding of Moses*, c. 1535–45. Milan, Pinacoteca di Brera. Oil on canvas, 175 × 345 cm

This painting, very probably commissioned for the upper hall of a Venetian palace, is based nominally on the Old Testament story of the infant Moses, hidden in the bullrushes, then discovered and presented to Pharaoh's daughter by her handmaiden, as shown towards the centre. However, this seems to serve only as a pretext for displaying a group of sumptuously dressed men and women who, accompanied by a page, a dwarf, a jester, servants and various animals, disport themselves in a variety of pleasant pursuits against a luscious landscape background. A strong erotic tension underlies the scene, from the couple on the left, absorbed in each other, to the couple in the left middle-ground, discussing poetry as they walk, and finally to the group on the right, listening to music with music-books in hand, but lost in reverie. The richness of the colour range, and the attention given by the painter to the representation of texture – different types of cloth, women's hair, skin and jewellery – highlight the sensuous delights of looking, inviting the viewer to share in the pleasure of young men and women looking at each other. What we see here is an evocation of an idealised court of love, created around a woman (see 12.1), where youth and beauty reign. Here, the special qualities possessed by women are imagined as necessary to the very existence of courtly life (see 12.2). In reality, women played a central role in the numerous courts of Renaissance Italy, and themes of love and devotion to the lady served not only as the subjects of learned conversations steeped in Neoplatonic philosophy, but were also expressed through music and poetry, indispensable accomplishments of the court lady.

17. Vincenzo Campi, *The Kitchen, c.* 1580. Milan, Pinacoteca di Brera. Oil on canvas, 145 × 220 cm

This is from a series of four paintings, seemingly hung in a refectory or dining room and all dominated by women at work – in the case of the others, women selling fish, poultry or fruit, sometimes accompanied by husbands, babies and children. The pictures are not simple 'slices of life', as the densely packed compositions follow conventions popularised by such early painters of genre scenes as Aertsen and Bassano. Yet many features relate to the actualities of the sixteenth century, such as the type of *credenza* for displaying dishes in tiers, and the greater number of female as compared to male servants in this large establishment, perhaps an inn rather than a private household. Young, seemingly unmarried women dominate, though an old woman is allotted the less demanding task of grinding spices. While the men do the heavier butchery or place fowls on a spit, women prepare poultry, make dough or put the finishing touches to pastries. In other comparable paintings by Campi, sexual *double entendres* in male gestures may suggest the common perception of market-girls and female servants as sexually available (see 13.1, 13, 14).

18. Benedetto Caliari, *Virgin and Child with Mary Magdalene and the Inmates of the Soccorso*, 1597. Venice, Gallerie dell'Accademia. Oil on canvas, 246 × 265 cm

This painting, one of many later sixteenth-century works presenting biblical exemplars for women's institutions, was executed for the *Ospedale del Soccorso*, set up as a refuge for penitent prostitutes in Venice in 1580 (14.24). At the right centre, the matron, dressed in a sober dark dress, introduces to the heavenly figures three newly arrived penitents, one of whom is casting off her rich jewels, symbols of her former attraction to such worldly vanities, in an action recalling that of Magdalenes depicted in contemporary devotional literature and art (4.4). In the sky, the saint herself and the Madonna and Child sympathetically acknowledge the women's repentance, suggesting the future heavenly rewards promised them by contemporary preachers and moralists. To the left, six other women evoke the everyday life of the institution, where women were professed nuns cut off from families and associates, but wore secular dress and supported themselves by work. At the centre, two women hold the pillow used in making lace; to the right another holds a basket and another carries vessels suspended from a yoke. On the left, two more gaze reverently upwards to the heavenly figures, expressing their desire to emulate the contemplative Magdalene above, rather than their industrious, Martha-like companions.

19. Jacopo Tintoretto, perhaps with Domenico Tintoretto, *Danae, c.* 1580–90. Lyon, Musée des Beaux-Arts. Oil on canvas, 143 × 197 cm

Tintoretto's canvas for an unknown patron depicts the young Danae, who, according to classical myth, was locked away by her father lest she fulfil a prophesy that her son would be the cause of his destruction. Danae is surprised by the advances of the lustful Jupiter, who has disguised himself as a shower of gold and penetrated her bedroom. The erotic theme had become popular by the mid-sixteenth century, allowing the painter both to present a voluptuous female nude and to provide titillating suggestions of venal love. The latter allusion is explicit here, for many elements relate to features associated with contemporary courtesans. The opulently canopied bed, the rich fabrics and the lute were all part of such women's surroundings (see 14.10, 11, 14), and Danae's maidservant enthusiastically collects the shower of gold coins, as might an avaricious procuress. Tintoretto was acquainted with literary figures such as Parabosco, who in 14.13 had claimed his mistress' beauty surpassed that of Danae. However, his task was also to create an ideal of feminine beauty in specifically pictorial terms, one drawing on classical standards in its sense of regularity, measure and graceful mobility, yet giving a sense of soft and yielding flesh, accentuated by the dark yet lustrous draperies, indicated with his usual painterly vivacity.

20. Anon., frontispieces for the *Rime* of Vittoria Colonna (Venice, 1540) and of Laura Terracina (Venice, 1548). Woodcuts, 9.2 × 6.9 and 8.7 × 5.8 cm

Both of these woodcut portraits, with whatever level of intervention from the writers, show attempts to construct visually the personas of creative women in different and suitable ways. The edition of Colonna's poetry shows the authoress dressed as the Franciscan tertiary she became in life, in intense meditation before a crucifix, appropriately in that the volume presents firstly her religious verse, and only lastly the secular sonnets and *canzoni*. Vittoria does not here physically resemble other possible portraits of her from a similar time, seeming considerably older than her actual fifty years, and having a hooked nose. Rather than presenting a physical likeness, or a scion of a famous Roman house, the woodcut shows Vittoria as an ideal type, the devout widow and tertiary.

Laura Terracina, by contrast, aged twenty-nine in 1548, is shown as youthful and classicised in features and in the presentation in profile, resembling images on ancient coins and medals, although her costume is contemporary and decorous, revealing no flesh. A few tresses of hair swirl loosely, injecting movement into an otherwise static composition, suggesting both a standard feature of female beauty and the tantalising untied locks of Terracina's namesake, Petrarch's Laura. A poem to Terracina in this collection by her associate, Luigi Tansillo, praises her beauty as well as her *'ingegno'*, in a comparable way:

> Beautiful girl, whose holy locks
> the tree beloved of Apollo [the laurel] should well crown,
> just as it gives its name ...

Index

'n.' after a page reference indicates the number of a note on that page.
Numbers in *italics* refer to illustration captions